CW00923901

# Fairey Swordfish and Albacore

## Other titles in the Crowood Aviation Series

|  |  |
|---|---|
| Aichi D3A1/2 Val | Peter C. Smith |
| Airco – The Aircraft Manufacturing Company | Mick Davis |
| Avro Lancaster | Ken Delve |
| Avro Shackleton | Barry Jones |
| BAC One-Eleven | Malcolm L. Hill |
| Bell P-39 Airacobra | Robert F. Dorr with Jerry C. Scutts |
| Boeing 737 | Malcolm L. Hill |
| Boeing 747 | Martin W. Bowman |
| Boeing 757 and 767 | Thomas Becher |
| Boeing B-17 Flying Fortress | Martin W. Bowman |
| Bristol Britannia | Charles Woodley |
| Consolidated B-24 Liberator | Martin W. Bowman |
| Douglas A-26 and B-26 Invader | Scott Thompson |
| Douglas AD Skyraider | Peter C. Smith |
| Douglas Twinjets | Thomas Becher |
| English Electric Canberra | Barry Jones |
| English Electric Lightning | Martin W. Bowman |
| Fairchild Republic A-10 Thunderbolt II | Peter C. Smith |
| Fokker Aircraft of World War One | Paul Leaman |
| Hawker Hunter | Barry Jones |
| Hawker Hurricane | Peter Jacobs |
| Junkers Ju 87 Stuka | Peter C. Smith |
| Junkers Ju 88 | Ron Mackay |
| Lockheed C-130 Hercules | Martin W. Bowman |
| Lockheed F-104 Starfighter | Martin W. Bowman |
| Luftwaffe – A Pictorial History | Eric Mombeek |
| McDonnell Douglas A-4 Skyhawk | Brad Elward |
| McDonnell Douglas F-15 Eagle | Peter E. Davies and Tony Thornborough |
| Messerschmitt Bf 110 | Ron Mackay |
| Messerschmitt Me 262 | David Baker |
| Nieuport Aircraft of World War One | Ray Sanger |
| North American B-25 Mitchell | Jerry Scutts |
| North American F-86 Sabre | Duncan Curtis |
| North American T-6 | Peter C. Smith |
| Panavia Tornado | Andy Evans |
| Short Sunderland | Ken Delve |
| The Turret Fighters | Alec Brew |
| V-Bombers | Barry Jones |
| Vickers VC10 | Lance Cole |
| Vought F4U Corsair | Martin W. Bowman |

# FAIREY SWORDFISH AND ALBACORE

*W. A. Harrison*

The Crowood Press

First published in 2002 by
The Crowood Press Ltd
Ramsbury, Marlborough
Wiltshire SN8 2HR

**www.crowood.com**



**British Library Cataloguing-in-Publication Data**
A catalogue record for this book is available from the British Library.

ISBN 1 86126 513 3

Photographs not credited in the text are from the author's own collection.

Typefaces used: Goudy (*text*),
Cheltenham (*headings*).

Typeset and designed by
D & N Publishing
Lambourn Woodlands, Hungerford, Berkshire.

Printed and bound in Great Britain by Bookcraft,
Midsomer Norton.

# Acknowledgements

Many thanks to the following for their help in the preparation of this book: Ian Huntley, Ray Sturtivant, Steve Gillard, BAe Heritage Centre, Brough, Andy Thomas, Ing. N. Geldof , Instituut Maritieme Historie (RNNAS), Richard Riding, Lt Cdr E. W. Whitley, Eric Tyler, Cdr J. H. Stenning RN (Retd), J. K. Cannon, C. R. Jeffs, Lt Cdr M. B. W. Howell, Lt Cdr R. E. F. Kerrison, Tom Mogford, A. B. Singleton, Lt Cdr F. C. Rice DSM RN (Retd), Cdr S. H. Suthers DSC RN (Retd), Capt Eric Bown OBE DSC AFC RN (Retd), J. K. G. Taylor, Capt L. E. D. Walthall DSC RN (Retd), Capt K. Williamson, Lt Cdr C. Wines DCM, Capt F. M. A. Torrens-Spence DSO DSC AFC RN (Retd), J. T. Canham, Alan Ryman, I. G. Templer, John Dickson, George Mitchell, Lord Kilbracken (formerly Lt Cdr John Godley DSC RNVR), RAF Museum, FAA Museum and The Society of Friends of the FAA Museum, and Imperial War Museum.

# Contents

# Preface

> I must tell you that during the last Home Fleet exercise in the Atlantic, in normal Atlantic weather, we found it quite impossible to operate Fireflies and Sea Furies without breaking them, and our Admiral stated at the post-exercise discussion that he didn't think the GR.17 [Gannet] was the complete answer. We needed something slow and robust, even more, approaching the Swordfish type, if we were to conduct continuous anti-submarine operations from light fleet carriers in the Atlantic.

The above was sent as a letter by Derek Empson, CO of No. 814 Squadron, operating Fireflies, to Fairey on 16 November 1949, just over ten years after the Swordfish went to war as an already obsolescent biplane. What a tribute to a biplane in the monoplane era! But the remarks of Mike Lithgow in his 1954 autobiography *Mach One* fairly well summed up what they, as naval pilots at the time, thought of it:

> The Swordfish, or 'Stringbag' as it was affectionately called, was the standard torpedo bomber of the day – and for that matter, of many a day thereafter. It carried a prodigious load of bombs, mines, torpedoes, depth charges or anything else that could be thought up for it – and a great deal was – without, to any marked degree, prejudice to its handling qualities other than to knock a few more knots off the speed, if such a term can be applied.

Of the Albacore he remarked:

> We took to the Albacore with mixed feelings; it was certainly faster – it could be persuaded to fly at 130kt (just) and it was capable of carrying a heavier load. The cockpits were enclosed, and there was a large fuel tank between the pilot and observer. It thus lacked the personal touch which had so endeared us to the Swordfish. The engine, a Taurus, took some time to settle down, and we had several failures in early days. Luckily, the trouble was sorted out by the time we went to sea, when it was phenomenally dependable.

John Kilbracken's view was, 'The Albacore was never popular. Despite its more modern appearance, it never had the guts and manoeuvrability of the Swordfish and its Bristol Taurus II engine wasn't a patch on its stablemate, the much loved Peggy (Pegasus).' It must have been about this time that someone wrote a new song, to be sung to the tune of 'Bring Back My Bonny'. It soon became an FAA favourite and has been bawled out around wardroom pianos ever since:

> The Swordfish relies on her Peggy,
> The modified Taurus ain't sound,
> So the Swordfish flies out on her missions,
> And the Albacore stays on the ground
> *(Chorus)*
> Bring back, bring back,
> Oh bring back my Stringbag to me – to me!
> Bring back, bring back,
> Oh bring back my Stringbag to me!

The comments of Capt Eric Brown, a most experienced naval test pilot, perhaps best sum up the characteristics of both machines:

> Late in 1940 I was posted to a Martlet [i.e. Grumman Wildcat] squadron, No. 802 at Donibristle. This station was also a naval repair yard and received Swordfish straight from the manufacturer for minor modification before issue to squadrons. Since no regular ferry pilots were available, I found myself on the station roster for this duty and, from time to time, despatched to the new production plant at Sherburn-in-Elmet, between Leeds and Selby, where Blackburn Aircraft had begun to assemble Swordfish, to ferry new aircraft back to Donibristle. I immediately discovered that claims for the Swordfish's handling qualities had, if anything, been understated: it was unbelievably easy to fly, there being virtually only a 20kt speed range to cover climb, cruise and landing. A pair of hamfists were no serious disadvantage in flying the Swordfish, for no aircraft could have been more tractable or forgiving, but its pilot did need two qualities: patience and the physical attributes of a brass monkey! The Swordfish ambled along lazily at about 85kt if the wind was favourable and staggered along valiantly at barely more than 70kt if it was not – it could be somewhat disconcerting at times to be travelling in the same direction as an express train. The cockpit was just as comfortable as an exposed hilltop in a Force 10 gale – the elongated aft cockpit was even worse as it provided a perfect wind scoop – with its occupants freezing in consequence. In September 1941, as squadron armaments officer, I was assigned the task of assessing the ability of the Swordfish to evade fighter attack. I was already familiar with the amiability and tractability of the Swordfish, and I soon discovered that it possessed quite remarkable manoeuvring qualities that completely belied its appearance of unwieldliness. It could be stood on its wing-tips and almost turned round in its own length! I even braved the gale-force winds in the rear cockpit to assess the field of fire of the observer's single rifle-calibre Lewis gun and found that, puny as defensive armament though this machine gun undoubtedly was, it possessed an excellent field of fire upward and to the rear and, with one in three bullets a tracer, was likely to prove decidedly off-putting to any fighter pilot successful in coaxing his mount down to the speeds at which the Swordfish trundled along.
>
> For starting, the fuel cock was set to MAIN ONLY, the throttle was opened a half-inch and the oil cooler bypass control set to IN. A couple of matelots then energized the inertia starter by cranking the starting handle, one standing on the port wheel facing aft and the other on the port wing facing forward. They cranked away until peak speed was attained and then one of the red-faced and perspiring ground crew would signal the pilot to engage the clutch. As soon as the ground crew called 'contact', the pilot switched on the ignition and the hand starter magneto. If he was lucky, the immense propeller began flailing and as soon as the hideously noisy Pegasus was running smoothly he switched off the hand starter magneto. The throttle was opened slowly to 1,000rpm and the engine allowed to warm up until the oil temperature reached 15°C. Power checks were then performed with one of the matelots lying across the tailplane. The rpm and oil pressure were checked at cruising boost but with the mixture control at ALTITUDE, and then, with mixture

control in override position, the throttle was opened fully and take-off boost, static rpm and oil pressure checked.

Taxiing was the essence of simplicity, although the Swordfish had a tendency to weathercock in high winds and in such conditions it was advisable to have a couple of matelots on the wingtips. For take-off, the elevator was trimmed 3 degrees nose up, half full port bias was applied to the rudder, the mixture control was set RICH (Override), the flaps were raised fully and the oil bypass control was set IN. The throttle was opened slowly to full power of +2lb boost and 2,200rpm, the take-off was short, any swinging tendency being easily counteracted by the rudder, and climb could be initiated at 70kt. When stabilized in the climb boost was reduced to +½lb. The climb was a long drawn-out affair in which, theoretically, you could reach a cruise altitude of 5,000ft in about 10 minutes with a take-off weight of the order of 6,750lb. In flight the Swordfish was very stable about all axes and was very easy to fly on instruments, but harmony of control was somewhat spoiled by over-sensitivity of rudder, although this cancelled itself out in aiding the slightly heavy ailerons in endowing this ungainly-looking aircraft with agility totally out of keeping with its appearance, and its rate of turn was phenomenal. There was no warning of a stall other than a gentle sink which occurred at about 52kt and the Swordfish regained flying speed almost immediately without the least tendency to spin. A normal landing was ridiculously easy. With mixture set at RICH, carburettor air intake set COLD and brakes checked OFF, the Swordfish would virtually land itself. This was normally effected without flap at 70kt on an airfield and at 60kt on a carrier. The ideal method of dive-bombing was to fly almost immediately above the target and then turn the Swordfish over to the near vertical, diving until the target could be seen above the upper wing. With a forward CG no real muscle had to be applied in recovery, gentle pressure pulling the Swordfish positively and reasonably rapidly out of the dive, but with the CG aft the elevator called for some muscle and response was sluggish.

In September 1942 I joined the Service Trials Unit at Arbroath, where the test programme listed for the Swordfish reflected the fact that, having been replaced by the Albacore and Avenger in the classic torpedo-bombing role, it had taken on a new lease of life in the anti-submarine warfare role. Most of the consequent work involved performance and handling trials with a clutter of external stores and was related to the decision to operate the Swordfish from the new escort carriers that were being commissioned and MAC-ships. Incredibly, it did not seem to matter what one slung under a Swordfish, for external loads made little or no difference to handling or performance. The heaviest load I ever lifted beneath a Swordfish comprised a Leigh Light and its battery pack, an 18in torpedo and eight 100lb anti-submarine bombs!

In May 1942, when I was to make my first acquaintance with the Albacore at the Deck Landing Training Unit in which I was serving at Arbroath, Fairey's Hayes factory was full of Albacores when it should have been full of Fireflies, and this last British operational biplane had barely more than 18 months of operational service left to it. My first impression of the Albacore was one of size. Of course, its beautifully cowled Taurus offered a lot more power than the Pegasus but I wondered how much of this was absorbed in compensating for the built-in drag! After clambering in the Albacore's cockpit, which was a long way off the ground, I found no major departure from the essentially simple theme that characterized the entire aircraft, the layout being very neat and clinical. Both the pilot's cockpit forward of the mainplanes and the crew's cockpit aft of the mainplanes – the two being divided by a very substantial 193 imperial gallon fuel tank – were enclosed by a wealth of transparent panelling, and the view from the lofty pilot's perch was most impressive, being very good forward, above and below. The Albacore had been designed with an eye to ease of deck landing, and I could certainly understand the Swordfish boys' initial delight at exchanging their draughty cockpits for all this luxury.

The starting procedure for the Taurus sleeve-valve engine was quite straightforward, as, indeed, was everything about the Albacore. The propeller was turned slowly a couple of times by hand as a safeguard against oil causing an hydraulic lock of the pistons or sleeves, the induction system primed and the ignition switched on. The Coffman starter charger knob on the lower right-hand side of the panel was pulled out slowly, the starter was switched on and the priming pump handle pulled. One stroke of the pump was given as the starter button was pushed, and the engine usually fired readily, being warmed up at a fast tick-over until cylinder temperature reached about 100°C and oil temperature 15°C. After a few minutes warm-up, the Taurus was opened up to maximum boost for weak-mixture cruise, propeller operation checked, the magnetoes tested for drop with rich mixture and then full throttle (3,000–3,100rpm), and boost and oil pressure checks. The Albacore revealed no vices during the take-off run and at 11,185lb was pulled off at about 60kt IAS with 3,100 rpm and 4¾lb of boost, the climb out starting at about 85kt IAS and the recommended climbing speed being some 96kt IAS at 2,800rpm with 3½lb of boost up to 6,000ft. This altitude was reached in about eight minutes but above 6,000ft it was recommended that the climbing speed be reduced by 1kt per 1,000ft. The Albacore was certainly a well-behaved and likeable aircraft. It was somewhat unstable longitudinally and a degree of concentration had to be exercised when climbing through cloud, the ailerons proved to be on the heavy side, while the elevator was fairly sensitive. The Albacore was designed for diving at speeds up to 215kt IAS with flaps either up or down, and it was certainly steady in a dive, recovery being easy and smooth, but some care had to be taken not to use the elevator too sharply. The Albacore could not, of course, be spun and aerobatics were definitely not permitted. The stall was a fairly innocuous affair, taking place at about 68kt with flaps up and at 66kt with flaps down. The final approach was made at 75kt and throughout this gentle beast behaved impeccably, leaving one with an impression of quiet reliability and efficiency but the inescapable conclusion that here was a truly unspectacular aeroplane.

I have two very distinct recollections of the Albacore. One was during my time with the Service Trials Unit at Crail when carrying out anti-fighter attack tactics. The theory was that straight and level flight at nought feet over the sea would effectively counter any fighter attack, which, in fact it did, but in my enthusiasm to get really low I misjudged the distance beneath my feet that the damned big undercarriage extended – until the Albacore made skimming contact with the water! Comments from the rear cockpit were voluble in telling me that the wheels were wet and spinning! The second incident took place in 1942 when still with the same unit, and resulted from a crazy wager that I could fly every aircraft type that we had under the Tay Bridge! This was easy enough under the centre spans, but when the wager progressed to the much smaller spans nearer the bank …! The Albacore proved to be the tightest fit!

CHAPTER ONE

# The Fairey Aviation Company

## Early Years

Like many of the aviation industry's pioneers, Charles Richard Fairey (later Sir Richard) started out in electrical engineering, although his father was a timber importer. Richard was born on 5 May 1887 and left school at the age of fifteen to join the Janus Electric Co. of Holloway, north London. He was later employed at Finchley Power Station, where he quickly became assistant to the manager. To supplement his income he gave evening lectures at Finchley Technical College and Tottenham Polytechnic; he had studied at Finsbury Technical College five nights a week after work.

His hobby was making model aeroplanes, including models of his own design. He won many prizes including the Challenge Cup and gold medals at the Kite and Model Aeroplane Association competition of June 1910, and a silver cup for best model at the Aero Models Association meeting of August 1910. One of his designs was accepted by Gamages, a famous London store, who eventually sold more than 200. Unbeknown to him, however, he had infringed patents held by Captain John William Dunne, who had formed the Blair Atholl Syndicate at Eastchurch, Isle of Sheppey. Fairey offered to pay a licence fee for each model sold, but Dunne asked that 'Licensed under J. W. Dunne's Patents' be printed in the instruction booklet for 'The Fairey High Flying Model Aeroplane'. Impressed by the 24-year-old and his background, Dunne offered him an engineering job with the Syndicate. It was here, overseeing the building of Dunne aeroplanes, that Fairey learnt the tools of his trade: stress calculations, weight reduction, power-to-weight ratios and much more. At Eastchurch he met many of the people setting out in the new and exciting world of aviation, including the three Short brothers. They offered him a job as Chief Stressman, but he rapidly moved up to become works manager and chief engineer.

## The Birth of the Fairey Aviation Company

When war was declared in 1914 he was sent call-up papers in error and tried to join the Royal Flying Corps (RFC). However, his work had brought him into contact with Cdre Murray F. Sueter, Director of the Air Department at the Admiralty, who suggested he might better serve his country by building aeroplanes rather than flying them. Fairey said he would be pleased to do so if he could form his own company to make them. Sueter, recognizing the need for the new aeroplane industry to expand, agreed, and in 1915 the Fairey Aviation Company Limited was formed. Sueter kept his word and a contract was received to build twelve Short 827 seaplanes and later 100 Sopwith 1½ Strutters. To meet delivery dates and demonstrate efficiency, Fairey leased part of the premises of the Army Motor Lorries Co. in Clayton Road, Hayes, and also took on some of their employees, who were Belgian refugees. A hangar was built in a field at Harlington to assemble the Short 827s and this site gradually became the famous factory at North Hyde Road, remaining until the demise of the company many years later. Assembly shops were built and the Admiralty offered the use of a site at the mouth of the Hamble river as a seaplane testing base. Fairey employed Sydney Pickles to flight-test the machines prior to their delivery.

With things settled, Fairey started work on his own designs, the F.2 fighter and Campania seaplane, receiving orders for sixty-two of the latter. Orders for 180 Sopwith Babys followed but Fairey only built fifty, the others being subcontracted to Parnall Aircraft. Fairey used the Baby to test his new camber gear, an early form of flap, to provide

**(Opposite)** **Sir Richard Fairey with his eldest son, also named Richard, in a 1945 publicity shot in front of a Firefly. The younger Richard had lost part of his legs due to frostbite when the ship he was travelling in across the Atlantic, the Norwegian tanker *Ringstadt*, was torpedoed. He managed to get into a life-raft, but it was five days before they were rescued by a US Navy destroyer. He was General Manager of Fairey Aviation from 1946 until 1960 when he retired, but he died shortly afterwards.**

**(Right)** **Some sixty-two Fairey Campanias were built in three versions, the first appearing in 1917. The first two were powered by Rolls-Royce Eagle engines but the rest had Sunbeam Maori engines. Fifty were built by Fairey and twelve by Barclay Curle and Co. of Clydeside, the latter having fifty cancelled at the end of the war.** J. M. Bruce/S. Leslie

extra lift. With various other changes the aircraft was built as the Hamble Baby, with the new flap system being used on most Fairey aircraft until the early 1930s.

Admiralty Specification N.2(a) was issued in April 1917 for a two-seat seaplane to be launched from catapults aboard ships. This led to the Fairey N.9, the forerunner of a long series of aircraft in the Fairey III range. The Air Ministry ordered fifty IIIAs and sixty IIIBs, of which some were converted to IIICs. All were too late to see action during World War One, but some IIICs entered the civil market and odd machines found their way to Canada and Sweden. A number of IIICs were used by the North Russia Expeditionary Force in 1919.

One IIIC, G-EBDI (ex-N9253), was included in a plan to fly round the world in 1922, using four aeroplanes at suitable locations, not unlike the 'Pony Express' idea! Sponsored by the *Daily News*, the flight was organized by Major W. T. Blake, with Fairey test pilot Norman Macmillan as pilot and Geoffrey H. Malins as a cinematographer. The IIIC was located at Calcutta and the crew combined an acceptance flight with setting off for Burma. Amid many adventures, the IIIC and the rest of the flight were cancelled when engine failure forced them down in the sea and the aircraft subsequently sank.

At the same time as the N.9, Fairey produced the N.10. Registered G-EALQ, the N.10 went through a number of changes and, with a reduced wing span and a Napier Lion engine, took part in the 1919 Schneider Cup Race at Bournemouth. An Air Ministry competition for a commercial aircraft the following year saw G-EALQ entered in trials for the amphibious section and flew as such at Felixstowe and Martlesham Heath. The Fairey aircraft came third in the competition being beaten by the Vickers and Supermarine designs.

## Post-War Designs

During World War One Fairey had answered an Admiralty specification for a very large flying boat and received orders to build three: N118 and N119, named the Fairey Atalanta, and N129, the Fairey Titania, the largest flying boats in the world at that time. Such was the development and build time that it was 1923 before the Atalanta flew, with the others two years behind. Plans for further versions were later abandoned, and in the event only N119 and N129 were built, N118 being scrapped before full assembly. The Pintail, a fighter-reconnaissance seaplane, was the first post-war Fairey design but only six were produced, three different prototypes and three for the Japanese Navy.

The first really successful design, from a commercial point of view, was the Fairey IIID, of which 207 were built for the RAF and FAA, with twenty sold overseas. One IIID was ordered by the Portuguese Government in 1921 for a flight across the South Atlantic to Brazil. This aircraft foundered in high seas after reaching St Paul's Rocks and a standard IIID was acquired to complete the flight. This, too, foundered after the engine cut out and a third IIID managed to complete the flight in five stages, arriving in Rio de Janeiro on 17 June 1922 after 4,367 miles (7,027km) at an average speed of 72kt (133km/h). There were many other notable flights by IIIDs, such as the Australian Navy IIID which, in 1924, flew right round Australia, 8,568 miles (13,786km) in forty-four days. Between 1 March and 27 May 1926, four Napier Lion-engined IIIDs made one of the RAF's first long-range formation flights when they flew from Cairo, Egypt to Cape Town, South Africa and back led by Wg Cdr C. W. H. Pulford. When they arrived back at Cairo, they were fitted with floats and flew to Lee-on-Solent after covering 14,000 miles (22,530km) in 180 flying hours, which, apart from the odd sandstorm, went without incident.

One of the most successful aircraft built by Fairey was the Flycatcher. It was designed to Specification 6/22, which called for a deck-landing single-seat fighter that could also be operated as an amphibian. Three prototypes were built, of which the first, N163, made its maiden flight on 28 November 1922 in the hands of Vincent Nicholl. All three prototypes were powered by Armstrong Siddeley Jaguar II engines but the 192 production aircraft had the Jaguar IV. Although never considered an attractive aeroplane, with its 'kink' just aft of the pilot's cockpit, it was loved by all the pilots who flew it. It had almost ideal handling characteristics, which came out well when operating from carrier decks. The Flycatcher entered service in 1923 and eventually equipped all eight fleet fighter flights until superseded by the Hawker Nimrod, which had replaced them all by 1934. When operated as an amphibian it was not so successful. The flat-bottomed floats tended to 'stick' in the water when calm and pilots could be seen frantically taxying around in an effort to get off.

Plans for a Flycatcher II to meet Specification N.21/26, a new deck-landing single-seat fighter for the Fleet Air Arm, only reached the prototype stage. This was powered by an Armstrong Siddeley Jaguar and taken on its first flight by Norman Macmillan on 4 October 1926. Although using the same name as its predecessor it was a much better design, without the 'kink' behind the cockpit and with a more useful fin and

**Fairey Flycatchers on the packed deck of HMS *Courageous*. It was one of Fairey's few single-seat fighter designs that went into production, 195 being built, and was very popular with its pilots. Flycatchers entered service in 1923 and stayed in use until 1934.** J. M. Bruce/S. Leslie

rudder area. It was re-engined with a 540hp supercharged Jaguar VIII and conducted trials aboard HMS *Furious* in July 1927. The following month it started trials fitted with floats. In 1928 it was fitted with a 480hp two-speed supercharged Bristol Mercury IIA and with all-metal wings, first flying in its new form on 31 May. Performance was considerably improved, but the Flycatcher II was lost on 8 May 1929 when the engine cut on take-off.

The Fairey Fawn was designed to Air Ministry Specification 5/21 for an army co-operation type, but entered service with the RAF as an light bomber, with seventy built in three versions, all powered by the Napier Lion engine.

Specification 44/22 was issued for an aeroplane capable of a round-the-world flight. Named the Fremantle and powered by a 650hp Rolls-Royce Condor, this large biplane was fitted with five floats, the two main ones being of mahogany planking to give greater strength. The pilot's cockpit was just behind the engine bay with an enclosed cabin aft of this for at least two crew plus equipment and food for a long trip. Norman Macmillan made the first test flight on 28 November 1924, stating that it was pleasant to handle both in the air and on water. The pilot for the round-the-world flight was to have been Capt R. H. McIntosh of Handley Page Transport, with Capt F. Tymms as navigator. It seems that Capt Tymms was employed in the Civil Aviation Department of the Air Ministry – who had issued the specification! In the event the Americans completed a round-the-world flight in September 1924 using three Douglas Cruisers, and the flight was cancelled. The aircraft ended its days doing radio navigation research.

It has always been said that the Fairey Ferret was the missing IIIE series between the Fairey IIIA and IIIF, although there appears to be no evidence to support this claim. In fact, the Ferret was more pleasant to the eye and was not unlike the Flycatcher II in layout. Three prototypes were built, Mk I, Mk II and Mk III, each differing slightly in wingspan, engine type and fin/rudder area. The first two Ferrets were three-seaters and the third a two-seater. Two were offered to meet Specification 37/22, an Air Ministry requirement to replace the Avro Bison, Blackburn Blackburn and Parnall Panther. The two-seater was offered to the Air Ministry as a general-purpose machine for the RAF but, despite service trials, no orders were placed for any of them.

**The Fairey Fawn (this is Fawn Mk II J7187) was built to Specification 5/21 to replace the DH.9A, providing the RAF with a light bomber. Powered by the Napier Lion, seventy were built for the RAF, serving with Nos 11, 12, 100, 503 and 602 Squadrons.** IWM

## The Fox

One of the most significant, and controversial, aircraft in British aviation history was to come from the design office of Fairey Aviation – the Fox. In September 1923 the Schneider Trophy Race came to Britain, and watching practice flights from the Downs behind Portsmouth was Richard Fairey and his half-brother, Geoffrey W. Hall. Impressed by the Curtiss R-3 racer entered by the US Navy, they went over to Cowes on the Isle of Wight to have a look at it. The course that year was an elongated triangle taking in Cowes, Selsey, Southsea and back to Cowes. On the day the Curtiss, flown by Lt David Rittenhouse USN, won at an average speed of 177mph (285km/h). On examining the aircraft Fairey noted that it was powered by a 450hp Curtiss D-12, a twelve-cylinder vee liquid-cooled engine of very low frontal area. (The Air Ministry had for years been supporting the air-cooled radial engines that powered many aircraft of the inter-war period.) Fairey went home and on his drawing board drafted out his own ideas for what was then a revolutionary two-seat day bomber with a low frontal area. He went to the Air Ministry and asked for their support in developing such an aircraft, but without success. He realized that the answer lay in America and raised all the money he could for a visit, almost mortgaging his company in the process. He came back with a Curtiss D-12 engine and a licence to manufacture it, the licence also covering the Curtiss-Reed metal airscrew, wing-surface radiators and high-efficiency aerofoil sections. Although some fifty D-12 engines, named Felix, were imported by Fairey, he never produced any under licence.

Work on the new design began immediately with Fairey's chief designer, Marcel J. O. Lobelle, and head of the technical and aerodynamics department, P. A. Ralli, formalizing his layout. Norman Macmillan took the first Fox, unmarked except for its construction number, F.573, on its first flight from Northolt on 10 December 1925.

It was the desire to reduce all parasitic drag on the Fox that led Fairey to design their 'high-speed gun-mounting', which, unlike the standard RAF Scarff ring-mounting, was installed in a recess below the upper fuselage level, allowing the gunner to stow the Lewis machine-gun out of the airflow when not in use. These mountings became a standard fitting on most Fairey open-cockpit aircraft up to the Swordfish.

The Fox exceeded even Fairey's expectations: thanks to its low frontal area and extensive streamlining, the machine approached nearly 160mph (260km/h) at 10,000ft (3,000m). This was not only faster than the current bombers in service, but faster than all the fighters too, including just about every fighter in service around the world!

Fairey invited dignitaries from the Air Ministry to Northolt to inspect the new

Fox and see it perform. Among those present was Air Chief Marshal Sir Hugh Trenchard, at that time Chief of the Air Staff, Air Vice-Marshal Sir Geoffrey Salmond, the Air Council member for Supply and Research, Air Vice-Marshal T. I. Webb-Bowen, Air Cdre F. V. Holt, Sdn Ldrs Sholto Douglas and Alex Gray, and various civilian officers. After the demonstration flight Trenchard took Macmillan aside and asked him if he thought young RAF pilots would be safe flying the Fox. Receiving Macmillan's reassurance, Trenchard boomed out 'Mr Fairey, I have decided to order a squadron of Foxes.' This unprecedented order was in fact an act of bravado stemming from embarrassment, and eventual orders amounted to only twenty-eight machines. This was not the re-equipment of the RAF with a bomber force superior to anything flying at that time, as envisaged by Fairey. He had, in fact, upset the Air Ministry with his unorthodox ways and had to have a lesson in protocol. Only one squadron, No. 12, received the Fox – forever perpetrated by the fox's head on their squadron badge.

## The Fairey IIIF

The most widely used aircraft in FAA service during the inter-war years was the Fairey IIIF, a two-bay equal-span biplane powered by the Napier Lion engine. The FAA operated 379 IIIFs in four versions (Mk I, Mk II, Mk IIIM and Mk IIIB) and the RAF used 243 in five versions (Mk IVC, Mk IVCM, Mk IVM, Mk IVM/A and Mk IVB). The aircraft was never given a name and was known by its designation, which also specified its type of construction, C indicating a composite structure, CM a composite and metal structure, and so on. With slight variations the basic structure was a metal fuselage and wooden wings. Some were converted into dual control machines, others received strengthening for catapult work and all were capable of operating with floats. At least twenty-five were sold to Argentine, Chile, Egypt, Greece, Ireland, New Zealand and Russia. A few appeared on the civil register, including one that found its way to the goldfields of New Guinea.

The IIIF line continued with the Mk V for the RAF and Mk VI for the FAA, named the Gordon and Seal respectively. They were powered by the uncowled 525hp Armstrong Siddeley Panther IIA engine. Some seventy-nine RAF IIIFs were converted into Gordons, including the last few IIIFs on the production line. The RAF received 157 new-build Gordons with a further twenty going to Brazil and one to China. Ninety-one Seals were built for the FAA, with thirteen being exported to Peru, Argentine, Latvia and Chile.

## The Belgian Connection

The Air Ministry, wishing to benefit from the experience of the Fairey Fox, issued a new specification, No.12/26, in May 1926, calling for a light day bomber to enter service around 1931 or 1932. It had to have a top speed in excess of 160mph (260km/h) which, with other high performance requirements, most firms said would be hard to achieve. A. V. Roe and Hawker were invited to tender, Fairey being snubbed. Richard Fairey personally protested to the Chief of Air Staff and later received an

**Fairey had fallen foul of the Air Ministry with his earlier private-venture Fox and Firefly designs, but received orders for later models of both from the Belgian Air Force. The first twelve Fox IIs were built by Fairey at Hayes, after which production was moved to the new Fairey factory in Belgium where about 185 were built, alongside sixty-three Fireflies.**

invitation to tender. Despite the loss of design and production time, Fairey offered an improved all-metal Fox Mk II powered by a Rolls-Royce F.XIB 12-cylinder in-line liquid-cooled engine, later called the Kestrel IB. In the event Fairey were way behind their competitors and their machine, J9834, did not fly until 25 October 1929. This was about a year behind the other two contenders, and the winner, the Hawker Hart, had already been announced.

Desperately disappointed, Fairey consoled himself with the thought that he had at least broken the Air Ministry's hold on design layout – and then set off to promote his aircraft abroad. His biggest success was with the Belgian Government, who not only ordered twelve of the new Fox, but came to an agreement that any other orders would be assembled in Belgium, using Belgian labour. Consequently, in 1931 a subsidiary factory was built at Gosselies, near Charleroi, Brussels, named Avions Fairey (later Fairey SA). Initially a further twenty-six Foxes were assembled there using components manufactured at Hayes. Eventually around 160 more were produced in a range of models, including versions with enclosed cockpits and different engines. Two of these were sold to Switzerland for trials, but no orders were forthcoming. Fairey UK built six Sea Fox floatplanes for Peru in 1933 and that was about the end of it. Many Foxes were still in service with the Belgian Air Force in 1940 when the Germans overran the Low Countries, but were hopelessly outclassed by then and suffered heavy losses.

Along with the Fox bomber Fairey offered the Firefly fighter. Designed by the same team slightly later on, the Firefly I looked very similar to the Fox I and was powered by the same Curtiss D-12 engine. The Air Ministry were not interested in the new fighter, for the same reasons that they had not been interested in the Fox. Later marks were also ignored but twenty-five were built at Hayes and sixty-three at Gosselies for the Belgian Air Force. A Firefly III was tested with wheel and float undercarriages, and later offered as a naval fighter, but that competition was won by the Hawker Nimrod. In floatplane form it was used as a trainer by the 1931 RAF Schneider Trophy team. Also used by the team was a Fairey Fleetwing, which owed its genesis to the Fox/Firefly design. It was built to meet Specification O.22/26, for a FAA two-seat spotter/reconnaissance fighter. Like the Fox II it was of all-metal construction and first flew in May 1929, but did not get any orders.

## The Fairey Long Range Monoplane

In late 1927 the Air Ministry issued Specification 33/27 for an aircraft which was to use all possible means to achieve significant increases in range and endurance, but was not said to be intended for any specific record. Various elements were specified, such as a Napier Lion engine and a range of 5,000 miles (8,000km), but the general design was left to the manufacturer. A number of different mono- and biplane designs were considered at Fairey's, under the leadership of D. L. Hollis-Williams, and Fairey were asked to build one machine, J9479. Although a Rolls-Royce F.XIIB (later Kestrel IIB) engine had been considered for the aircraft, undergoing consumption and endurance tests in a DH.9A, it was the 570hp Napier Lion XIA that was actually used. The aircraft was known for a time as the 'Postal Aircraft' and then, because no-one thought to give it a name, the Fairey Long Range Monoplane. However, the eventual aircraft was painted in RAF colours and Fairey were told that any long-distance flights would be conducted by an RAF crew, Sqn Ldr Jack Noakes and Flt Lt N. H. Jenkins.

The world's absolute distance record in a straight line had been set in July 1928 at 4,466 miles (7,188km), by Capt Arturo Ferrarin and Major del Prete flying a Savoia S-64 from Rome to Touros, near Port Natal in Brazil. By then development of the Fairey aircraft was well under way and it was no secret that there would be some long-range flying, although no-one actually mentioned attempts on the world record.

The airfield with the longest run for take-off at that time, which would be necessary for a single-engined aircraft carrying more than 1,000 gallons of fuel, was RAF Cranwell in Lincolnshire. The crew had been changed and was now Sqn Ldr A. G. Jones-Williams MC with Flt Lt F. V. Major as navigator. After preliminary trials it was planned to fly non-stop from Cranwell to Cape Town in South Africa. Jones-Williams made the first flight on 14 November 1928 with very few problems, and the aircraft left for Cranwell later that month. During flight tests a number of problems arose that delayed the planned flight. These were overcome, but it was April 1929 before the aircraft was ready

**A fine study of the second Fairey Long Range Monoplane, K1991. The first aircraft, J9479, was known as the 'Postal Monoplane' but was lost in an accident. K1991 went on to make a number of significant long-range flights, the one to Walvis Bay in February 1933 creating a world record after flying 5,410 miles (8,705km).**

and more crew changes had occurred. Flt Lt Jenkins was reinstated as navigator when, during the trials, Flt Lt Major was found unsuited to long-range flying.

Jones-Williams and Jenkins took off from Cranwell on 24 April 1929 and landed at Karachi 50 hours and 37 minutes later, having covered 4,130 miles (6,650km). The aircraft was flown back between 13 May and 15 June, and prepared for another flight. While this was going on, two Frenchmen, D. Costes and M. Bellonte, flying the Breguet XIX A.2, known as 'Question Mark' from the ? sign painted on its fuselage, flew from Paris to Manchuria, a distance of 4,912 miles (7,905km), which had to be beaten by 100km (60 miles) for a new record. On 16 December 1929, J9479 took off from Cranwell for Walvis Bay in South West Africa, although Cape Town was the ultimate destination if conditions were suitable. Unfortunately they ran into poor weather with turbulence, strong winds and snow, and in steadily deteriorating conditions flew into high ground 30 miles south of Tunis: Jones-Williams and Jenkins were killed and the aircraft destroyed.

Having shown much promise with the first machine, Fairey were offered a new specification, 14/30, for another. The basic structure was to remain the same, apart from small detail changes and better equipment. Chris Staniland took K1991 on its first flight on 30 June 1930 and it was delivered to the RAF at the end of the following month. The new crew was Sqn Ldr O. R. Gayford DFC and Flt Lt G. E. Nicholetts AFC. During 27/8 October 1931 a proving flight was made from Cranwell to Abu Sueir, the home of No. 4 FTS in Egypt. Taking 31 hours, they covered a distance of 2,857 miles (4,597km). The previous planned flight to Walvis Bay was then resurrected, but the record had again been exceeded: two Americans, Boardman and Polando, flew 5,012 miles (8,064km) from New York to Istanbul in Turkey, in a Bellanca. Leaving Cranwell on 6 February 1933, the Long Range Monoplane landed at Walvis Bay 57 hours and 25 minutes later, having travelled more than 5,410 miles, a great circle distance of 5,341 miles (8,597km). The aircraft did not make any further attempts on long-range flying and, though the Air Ministry considered fitting K1991 with diesel engines, nothing came of it.

## Monoplane Bombers

In 1930, P. A. Ralli died at the early age of 41 and Hollis-Williams became head of Fairey's technical department – a position he held until 1934 when R. T. Youngman took over. Also during 1930 Fairey bought 150 acres of land near Harmondsworth in Middlesex and, after clearing, levelling and draining the site, established his own aerodrome there. Adjacent to the main road, it became known as the Great West Aerodrome and was one of the best in the land (it has since disappeared under London's Heathrow Airport). A large hangar was built with office blocks at each end and a small control tower. The name FAIREY was painted in large letters on the hangar roof and became a famous landmark, appearing in many publicity photographs. Prior to this, all of Fairey's flight-testing since 1917 had been conducted from Northolt aerodrome.

The RAF's first monoplane bomber, the Fairey Hendon, became the first new Fairey type to be flown from the new airfield, making its first flight there on 25 November 1930. It was initially powered by two 525hp Bristol Jupiter XF radial engines, but after an accident on 15 March 1931 it was fitted with two 480hp Rolls-Royce Kestrel IIISs. Following service trials fourteen were ordered in 1934, followed by two further orders bringing the total to seventy-six aircraft – but the Hendon, with a crew of five, internal bomb bay, enclosed cockpits, metal construction and low-mounted cantilever monoplane wings was just too innovative for the Air Ministry. All but the first fourteen, which went to No. 38 Squadron at Mildenhall, were cancelled. The bomber force was made up with additional Handley Page Heyford biplanes!

In August 1932 the Air Ministry issued Specification P.27/32 for a light bomber, which Fairey answered with the Battle, a low-wing three-seater monoplane powered by the new Rolls-Royce Merlin engine. The prototype, K4303 was first flown by Staniland on 10 March 1936 and the first Battles

**Fairey Air Surveys**

In 1923 R. C. Kemp, an ex-Short Brothers test pilot, set up the Air Survey Co. to provide aerial photography. The following year it was taken over by Col C. H. D. Ryder, but with Kemp staying on as managing director. Operating from Burma and covering the Far East, the new company attracted other shareholders and in September 1929 Fairey bought a controlling interest and installed Norman Macmillan, M. E. A. Wright and A. G. Hazell on the board. To cover other areas a succession of overseas subsidiaries were formed, many lasting for more than fifty years. Initial equipment consisted of DH.9 floatplanes, supplemented by two Jaguar-engined Fairey IIIFs fitted with Williamson Eagle cameras for oblique and vertical overlaps. In later years a number of Douglas DC-3s joined the fleet, as did a Bristol Freighter.

**Surely one of the most attractive fighters ever designed, the Fairey Fantôme, which first flew in 1935. Powered by an Hispano Suiza engine, it did not find favour and only four were built. Two of these went to Spain during the Spanish Civil War, where one gave a good account of itself.** *Flight*

**Another bomber that did not see favour because it was too far ahead of its time for the traditionalists, was the Fairey Hendon night bomber. It should have equipped many bomber squadrons, but orders were slashed and it was only used by No. 38 Squadron based at Mildenhall.** Crown Copyright

entered service with No. 63 (Bomber) Squadron at RAF Upwood in May 1937. The Battle's poor reputation, gained when it suffered heavy losses during the Battle of France in 1940, was not really deserved: it should be remembered that it was built to a specification for a light day bomber that was intended to be used only with a fighter escort, which was often not actually present.

In the autumn of 1935, with orders for the Hendon and Battle to fulfill, Fairey needed more production capacity. They bought the old Willys-Overland Crossley motor works at Heaton Chapel, Stockport, where aircraft could be ferried by road to Barton aerodrome for assembly and test flights. All the production Hendons and the first five Battles followed this route, but with the opening of Manchester Municipal Airport at Ringway in 1939, Fairey transferred their assembly and flight test departments to a new hangar on the edge of that airport. When war was declared the Battle was in full production at Heaton Chapel and with Austin Motors at Longbridge. Fairey built 1,172 and Austin 1,029 with some of these going to Australia (364), Belgium (16), Canada (739), Poland (1), South Africa (129) and Turkey (29).

## Fairey Aero Engines

As recounted on page 11, Richard Fairey shook the British aircraft industry with his Fox and Firefly aeroplanes, which were powered by the Curtiss D-12 engine. He believed that there was room in the industry for more powerful in-line liquid-cooled engines such as this, and in 1931 he set up his own aero-engine department.

In charge was Capt A. Graham Forsyth, who had worked for Wolseley Motors before serving as a pilot in World War One. After working on racing car engine design for the Sage company he joined the Air Ministry, being responsible for liquid-cooled aero-engine development. He designed the world's first hydraulically operated constant-speed propeller in 1926. His work involved him with the projects at Napier and Rolls-Royce, and in 1931 Richard Fairey enticed him away to become Chief Engine Designer and form a new branch responsible for the development of a range of aero-engines and propellers.

By the end of 1934 Forsyth had designed, tested and was offering the Fairey P.12 Prince (650–710hp) and Super Prince (720–835hp) engines. Test bed results confirmed his design layout and the Prince was flight-tested in a borrowed Belgian-built Fox II. Based on these results he planned the P.16, a 16-cylinder vee engine, in January 1935. He offered a 'guaranteed' 900hp at 2,500rpm at 12,000ft. This was now in direct competition to Rolls-Royce's private venture vee 12-cylinder engine, which was to become the famous Merlin. Both companies had worked together for years with Rolls-Royce engines powering Fairey aircraft, and both must have known what was happening in each other's camp.

Forsyth was now forging ahead with plans for a whole range of powerplants including a helicopter engine. His next venture, way ahead of current thinking at that time, was the P.24, which consisted of two P.12s coupled together through a common crankcase driving contra-rotating three-blade propellers. It was proposed that one half of the engine could be shut down for economy on long flights. The P.24 had the potential to go to at least 3,000hp and by early October 1938 had proved the concept with two-hour runs on the test bed. One was installed in Battle K9370 for flight testing, first flying on 30 June 1939. Some eighty-seven hours were logged test-flying the combination, which proved beyond all doubt that the P.24 was a winner. It was found that the Battle/P.24 combination, with little or no torque from the engine, could out-fly many contemporary aircraft, including fighters.

When General 'Hap' Arnold, in the UK on a fact-finding mission, saw the engine he asked for an evaluation in the USA. There was a proposal that it could be an ideal engine for the new Republic Thunderbolt, with the engine being manufactured in the USA by Ford. The P.24 Battle was shipped to Wright Field where 250 hours were flown before the Japanese attack on Pearl Harbor on 7 December 1941 ended the plan. The American authorities decreed that they were pushing through only their own engines, and those already under development. The P.24 was offered for a number of British fighter designs, including the Hawker Tornado/Typhoon, but the Air Ministry refused to support the setting up of another aero-engine company, saying that they had more than sufficient to cover their needs and Fairey was to stop wasting time, especially as the Ministry was openly supporting the Rolls-Royce Merlin.

Forsyth had been developing propellers alongside his engines, hoping that the two would be offered as a package. He worked on two- and three-bladed constant-speed and variable-pitch propellers, some of which were flight tested on an Armstrong Siddeley Cheetah engine. During the war Fairey produced 33,234 new two- and three-blade propellers with a further 57,544 repaired, this figure including propellers from de Havilland, Rotol and Curtiss. Many Fairey-produced propellers are still in use all over the world today.

**The Fairey Battle light bomber was intended to be used only with fighter escort, and did not deserve the poor reputation it acquired when obliged to operate without such protection. This picture shows the first Battle off Austin Motors' production line at Longbridge, under the Shadow factory scheme. This was the first of 1,029 built by Austin Motors, who were turning out thirty each month in 1939.**

## World War Two

Apart from the Battle and, of course, the Swordfish and Albacore, whose story is related in the subsequent chapters of this book, Fairey produced three other important warplanes during World War Two. The Fulmar was a two-seat monoplane naval fighter, powered by the Merlin and armed with eight 0.303in Browning machine-guns. Six hundred Fulmars were built at Heaton Chapel; fifty-three FAA squadrons used the type between 1940 and 1946.

The Fulmar's successor was another Fairey Firefly. Intended as a naval reconnaissance fighter and superficially similar to the Fulmar in appearance, it was a much more capable aircraft, powered by the Rolls-Royce Griffon (the more powerful successor to the Merlin) and armed with four 20mm Hispano cannon. 1,702 were built, mostly at Hayes, consisting of 739 Mk 1s, 591 Mk 4/5/6s, 151 Mk 7s (110 at Hayes, 41 at Heaton Chapel), 34 Mk 8s at Heaton Chapel, 54 Mk 4s and NF.5s for the Royal Netherlands Naval Air Service, and 132 Mk 1s built under licence by General Aircraft Limited at Hanworth. There were numerous conversions to dual control and target tugs with many ex-FAA Fireflies sold overseas to Australia, Canada, Denmark, Ethiopia, India, Thailand and Sweden. Forty Mk 5s were converted to target drones. The Firefly gave sterling service in the last two years of the war, and went on to serve in such roles as ground attack and even anti-submarine warfare. The Firefly later distinguished itself as a ground-attack fighter during the Korean War.

The Barracuda was designed to Specification S.24/37 as a replacement for the Albacore. A high-wing three-seat monoplane powered by the Merlin and, in later versions, the Griffon, the Barracuda was intended as a carrier-borne torpedo bomber and dive bomber, primarily serving in the latter role in a career lasting from late 1942 to 1953. Fairey built 1,192 Barracudas, Blackburn 700, Boulton Paul 692 and Westland eighteen.

Fairey also undertook production of other manufacturers' aircraft after extending their production facilities. These included 325 Bristol Beaufighter ICs, 175 Beaufighter VICs, 246 Handley Page Halifax Vs, 104 Halifax IIIs, 222 Halifax B.IIIs and ninety Halifax A.VIIs/B.VIIs. At the end of the war many orders, which would have considerably increased these figures, were cancelled. In addition, repairs and refurbishment were conducted on most Fairey types, including some of those built by the likes of Blackburn.

Once Barracuda production had started, at Heaton Chapel, work started on the Spearfish. This was an enormous single-engined aeroplane designed to replace the Barracuda, but suffered protracted development as the war progressed and operational requirements changed. Its principal difference from its predecessors was that the torpedo and other weapons were to be carried in a large bomb-bay. External weapons consisted of two forward-firing 0.5in Browning machine-guns mounted in the wings and

*(Top)* F. H. Dixon and J. C. Evans, two Fairey test pilots, pose in front of an early Firefly Mk IV. Evans was to lose his life test-flying Firefly I PP463 on 27 November 1945, and Dixon in the Gyrodyne G-AKIF on 17 April 1949.

*(Above)* Start to another day! Aircraft rolled out at Fairey's Heston aerodrome before the move to White Waltham. Lined up is Firefly Z1835, which started life as the prototype Firefly III but was developed into a prototype Mk IV. Next is a Firefly FR.I for the Royal Netherlands Navy and Spearfish RN241.

A model of the Fairey Naval Strike Fighter which was to have been powered by two Merlins driving contra-rotating propellers via a common gearbox. Wing cannon were mounted in pods. Its performance would have been around or better than that of the de Havilland Hornet. This design, to Specification 0.5/43, was later developed into the Spearfish.

In 1938 Fairey tried to enter the airliner market with the FC.1 airliner, but World War Two terminated the project. In 1944 they started to design a number of airliners to meet various requirements for the post-war era. This is a model of the FC.6, which was intended for 'Empire' and transatlantic routes.

two more in a remotely-controlled Fraser-Nash 95 gun turret just aft of the cockpit glasshouse. Sixteen rockets could be mounted under the outer wings. An Air-to-Surface Vessel (ASV) radar scanner was to be mounted in a retractable radome just aft of the bomb-bay. Designed to Specification 0.5/43 the first machine, built at Hayes, was powered by a Bristol Centaurus 18-cylinder two-row radial engine delivering 2,600hp. The first Spearfish, RA356,

### Tipsy Aircraft

One of the characters involved with Fairey was Ernest Oscar Tips, who had joined Fairey in 1915 after escaping from Belgium and stayed until the end of the war. Following the decision by the Belgians to order the Fairey Fox and Firefly, a factory was built at Gosselies in 1931 with Tips as manager. Once production was under way Tips found time to design his own idea of what a light aeroplane should be capable of. In 1934 the Tipsy S appeared, an advanced single-seat low-wing cantilever monoplane that was a joy to fly. Registered OO-TIP, it was the forerunner of a number of similar two-seat designs, the S.2, B and Belfair, which were built in small numbers both in Belgium and Britain. World War Two stopped any further development, but Tips still believed in the simple-design aeroplane that could be built at home.

After the war he designed the advanced Tipsy Nipper, a single-seat shoulder-wing aircraft with a tricycle undercarriage and powered by a modified Volkswagen car engine. This could be bought factory-made or as a kit, both versions finding favour all over the world. Many local modifications were made, such as more powerful Volkswagen engines modified for aerobatics.

Three other designs should be mentioned here: the Tipsy M, the Fairey Primary Trainer and the Fairey Junior. Tips designed the M as a logical step from his single- and two-seat side-by-side aircraft to meet a Belgian Air Force requirement for a new trainer. His design appeared as a low-wing tandem-seat machine with the cockpit hooding faired to a raised rear fuselage decking. It was registered OO-POM and flew just before the war. In 1940, with the German advance across the Low Countries, it was dismantled and moved to the UK where it was assembled and flown by the Fairey company until 1941 when it was dismantled and stored.

After the war the M was shipped back to Belgium and restored. It re-emerged as the Fairey Primary Trainer, later called the Primer, and was offered as a competitor to the de Havilland Chipmunk for an Air Ministry requirement for a new basic trainer to replace the Tiger Moth. Interest was shown from overseas and an initial production run of ten started against the possibility of such orders materializing. In the event only two were completed and these were dismantled in 1951.

The Fairey Junior was another attempt to provide a simple, single-seat, low-wing, wooden aeroplane kit for the home-builder. The only one built, G-AMVP, is still extant.

was flown by F. H. Dixon on 5 July 1945. Orders were placed for three prototypes from Hayes and two from Heaton Chapel, and 150 production machines to be built at Heaton Chapel. Only the first four machines flew, the rest being cancelled.

During 1944 the Government took over the Great West Aerodrome, which would later become absorbed into London's Heathrow Airport. Fairey initially moved to Heston, but flying from there soon infringed Heathrow's airspace, so in 1947 the company moved to White Waltham in Berkshire. The airfield is still in extensive use by various aviation concerns, but all traces of Fairey's operations are long gone.

**The last production aircraft built by Fairey was the Gannet, a successful design with 349 built in various marks. This is AEW.3 XL472 '760/BY' of No. 849 Squadron when based at Brawdy in South Wales.** Crown Copyright

## The Gannet

Work was proceeding on a two-seat anti-submarine and strike aircraft to Specification GR.17/45, which was to become the Gannet. The Gannet was originally to have been powered by a Rolls-Royce Tweed turboprop engine, but this was discontinued and the Armstrong Siddeley Double Mamba was chosen instead. This was in fact two modified Mamba engines coupled together driving contra-rotating propellers through a common gearbox. Either engine could be shut down and its propeller feathered. The Double Mamba developed 3,600shp plus 730lb residual jet thrust, giving a total 'equivalent horsepower' of 3,880ehp.

Two prototypes were ordered, VR546 and VR557, with first flight dates of 19 September 1949 and 6 July 1950 respectively. A third prototype, WE488, joined the programme after the Admiralty said they wanted a three-seater instead. The first production Gannet, WN339, was flown from Northolt, Fairey's original flight test airfield, on 9 June 1953 in the hands of Peter Twiss. Hayes built 271 Gannets and Heaton Chapel 78. Equipped with ASV radar and able to carry a substantial load of depth charges, bombs, rockets or torpedoes, the Gannet served in the carrier-borne anti-submarine role until helicopters took over in the late 1960s.

There were a number of variants produced, including dual-control trainers. The best known, perhaps, was the airborne early warning version, the Gannet AEW.3. This housed the two radar operators within the fuselage, and the bomb-bay and ASV housing were replaced by an enormous AEW radar. Other changes were made to improve its deck operating capabilities, including a more powerful 3,875ehp Double Mamba. The first prototype, XJ440, took to the air on 20 August 1958, followed by forty-three others, the last of which were not retired until 1978.

## H. E. Chaplin

Herbert Eugene Chaplin MBE MIMechE FRAeS MSAE was born on 10 March 1896 at Easter Compton, a small village in Gloucestershire. He was educated at St George Secondary School, Bristol, and while serving an apprenticeship as a draughtsman with George Adlan & Sons Ltd, Brewers and General Engineers, in Bristol, completed a part-time course in the Faculty of Engineering at Bristol University. In 1916 he joined The Royal Gloucester Hussars, but after transferring to the Royal Flying Corps (RFC), was discharged as medically unfit in November 1917.

He then joined the newly-formed Aircraft Design Staff department of George Parnall & Sons Ltd, Bristol, as a draughtsman under the leadership of Harold Bolas. This team produced the Parnall Panther two-seat wooden biplane, designed to operate from aircraft carriers on fighter-reconnaissance duties. This aircraft was probably the first machine designed specifically for carrier operations. It was a successful design with 300 being ordered, but almost as soon as the first production batch was started, World War One ended. Soon after this Parnall decided to give up making aeroplanes. However, a licence to produce the Panther was granted to the Bristol Aeroplane Co., and they produced the 300 Panthers that were ultimately sold to the Japanese Government for their air force.

Chaplin moved on and became Chief Draughtsman of the Engineering Division of Wellman Smith Owen Engineering Corporation at Darlaston, Staffordshire, until November 1919, when he returned to Parnall, who had reformed their aviation interests. He remained with Parnall's as a Senior Designer Draughtsman until November 1929. During the ten years he was there the design staff never exceeded twenty people, even though they designed a large number of aircraft, of great variety. These included the Parnall Puffin, an amphibian with a retractable undercarriage; the Parnall Possum, an unorthodox type built to explore possibility of shaft drive; the Parnall Perch naval trainer; the Parnall Pike three-seat naval bomber; the Parnall Peto twin-float two-seat naval spotter-reconnaissance aircraft, designed from the start to be catapult-launched from a small hangar on the deck of a submarine; the Parnall Pixie I and II, built to take part in the first and second Light Aeroplane Trials at Lympne; the Parnall Plover single-seat naval fighter; the Parnall Imp two-seat private biplane, which had the upper wing heavily swept back and the lower wing without any sweepback, giving the pilot an excellent view; the Parnall Pipit single-seat fighter; and the Parnall Elf, a small two-seat aircraft for the private owner. The company also designed the first autogyro using the ideas of autogyro pioneer Juan de la Cierva.

By 1929 the outlook for the British aircraft industry was by no means rosy. Harold Bolas accepted a post as Chief Engineer to an American company that had obtained a licence to build the Blackburn Bluebird in the USA. He invited Chaplin to join him, but the venture proved unfortunate as it coincided with the Wall Street Crash, so Chaplin returned to England and in April 1930 secured a position with the Fairey Aviation Company as Senior Draughtsman under their Chief Designer, D. L. Hollis Williams.

Chaplin's early tasks with Fairey's included working on the (biplane) Firefly which was being produced by Avions Fairey for the Belgian Air Force. He also did some work on the Hendon bomber, but his first design starting from scratch was the S.9/30. He worked with F. Ordidge on the G.4/31 and P.27/32 projects, the latter becoming the Battle light bomber. Although he worked on Swordfish drawings, he was tasked with designing a 'Swordfish replacement' under his new boss, domiciled Belgian Marcel Lobelle. This ultimately became the Albacore. Chaplin, now Chief Designer, and known throughout the Company as 'Charlie', also prepared the basic project design of the exciting thirty-seat FC.1 airliner, unfortunately cancelled at the outbreak of World War Two.

Lobelle moved on to form his own company, ML Aviation, and Chaplin was made Head of the Fairey Design Department in September 1939. His first task was the design of a new naval fighter to Specifications N.8/39 and N.9/39, which in their revised form of N.5/40 became the successful Firefly. In January 1943, after Firefly production was under way, he was given the job of running a 'Fairey future thinking project design team'. From this came the Fairey full-span flaps, and investigating and constructing laminar flow wings, which initiated the Fairey envelope tooling method of construction.

He made a significant and brilliant piece of design history when he designed a twin-Merlin engine installation, the two engines operating in tandem with a common crankshaft driving contra-rotating propellers, as part of Fairey's answer to Specification O.5/43, later known as the Spearfish.

Linked with this, Chaplin was given a free hand to investigate the possible use of gas turbine engines in new designs, and whether they would be suitable for carrier-type aircraft. He envisaged aircraft operating in the anti-submarine role shutting down one engine, which would give greater 'loiter' time on station. He designed a naval strike aircraft powered by a 5,000shp engine, of which Rolls-Royce undertook the design, becoming the Tweed, which never went into production. About this time a new specification was issued, N.17/45, which Chaplin wanted to compete for. Rolls-Royce had abandoned the Tweed engine by now, so Chaplin went to Armstrong-Siddeley, and asked them to produce a coupled Mamba gas turbine for his new design for a two-seat shipborne anti-submarine aircraft, which of course eventually became the Fairey Gannet. Fairey's experience with coupled engines was also passed to Saunders-Roe, who adopted it for their Princess flying boat.

Another innovative design he was involved with was to have a twin Rolls-Royce Avon-powered vertically launched strike fighter. These were planned to be launched from ramps on the sides of aircraft carriers, leaving the flight deck free for other types of aircraft. The Air Ministry were impressed enough to fund three research aircraft, to fly in the normal mode initially, but to investigate different modes, including delta wing planforms. The first was built as the Fairey Delta I, but the Air Ministry got cold feet and the other two were cancelled. However, small delta models were ramp-launched successfully.

The Air Ministry were interested in new advanced jet fighters and approached industry for supersonic designs. Chaplin and his small team designed the advanced Fairey Delta 2, including a future fighter version; and having flown two Delta 2a supersonically was disappointed when the contract went to English Electric for their P.1, which was later developed into the Lightning.

After completing work on the Gannet AEW.3, Chaplin became a Design Consultant for Fairey, based at White Waltham airfield, until he retired.

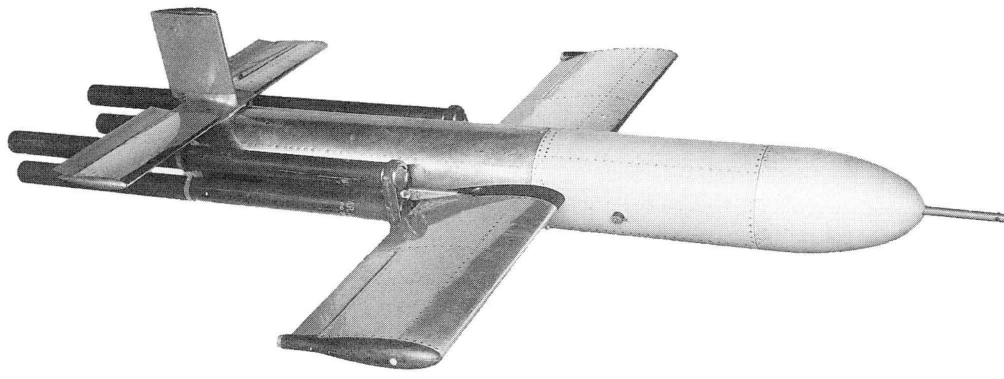

***(Right)*** **Fairey were approached by the Air I to develop a flying bomb to be used in the v Far East. The result was the successful Fai Stooge, shown here in early development form. The end of the war meant that there was no requirement for such a missile, but gave Fairey the opportunity to enter the missile market, designing the Fairey Fireflash.**

***(Below)*** **Test pilots of the later era, Gp Capt Slade and Lt Cdr Peter Twiss DSC OBE, in f the FD.2 WD774. Both served as Chief Test I Fairey's.**

## Advanced Research

During the 1950s four separate, but equally exciting and innovative, branches of design were being developed at Hayes. One concerned the helicopter, starting with the complexity of combining the autogiro and the helicopter, which resulted in two test vehicles, Gyrodyne G-AIKF and Jet Gyrodyne G-AJJP, and the Rotodyne airliner. G-AIKF had first flown in 1947 and in June 1948 set a new international speed record for helicopters of 124.3mph (200km/h). The Rotodyne, XE521, was unfortunately ahead of its time. Despite promises of orders and interest from overseas, the machine was being built for use by British European Airways (BEA) and they kept changing their requirements and wanting more capacity. In the end the Ministry of Supply withdrew its support and the project was cancelled. A well-thought-out series of Ultra-Light helicopters to meet Specification H.144T was built and proved successful, but again orders dried up.

Another branch, later moving to Heston, investigated ground- and air-launched missiles, leading to the Stooge flying bomb and the beam-riding Fireflash AAM. Later, the MoS asked Fairey to assemble Australian-built Jindivik jet target drones, implement modifications where required and carry out flight-testing at Llanbedr.

Investigations into vertical take-off interceptor fighters were initiated, resulting in trials with 10ft span models and the E.10/47 Fairey Delta 1, which should have ended up as a swept-wing tailless fighter. However, the Delta 1 proved to be directionally unstable and the project was abandoned.

Finally, design studies for the Air Ministry for a piloted supersonic research aircraft led to the superb Fairey Delta 2, the last conventional aircraft built by Fairey. Despite being offered as a fighter to the Air Ministry, no orders were placed.

***(Above)*** **Fairey Delta 2 WG774 in the purple colour scheme applied after taking the world air speed record in 1956 at 1,132mph (1,821km/h). It was later modified into the BAC.221 research aircraft and, with WG777, the second FD.2, survives in museums. Offers to the Air Ministry for a fighter version fell on stony ground.** Charles E. Brown

***(Below)*** **A model of a 60-degree supersonic pilotless aircraft that was designed as part of Delta 2 and supersonic airliner research.**

## The Final Years

In the 1950s Fairey, like other aircraft manufacturers, were encouraged by the Ministry of Supply to join the new British Aerospace company. Under this scheme, new projects would be undertaken on a shared basis within the industry, and companies under the British Aerospace umbrella would get subcontracted work from the controlling authority to keep their factories going. Anyone not joining could expect few orders for aircraft: Fairey – like Handley Page, another long-established aircraft manufacturer – tried to go it alone but found it increasingly difficult to get contracts.

By the late 1950s Fairey found themselves with very little production work, none of their projects had reached fruition, and the accountants started to draw in the purse-strings. On 31 March 1959 the Fairey Aviation Co. Ltd became the The Fairey Co. Ltd, as a holding company for their subsidiary companies, and on the same day formed Fairey Aviation Ltd to look after UK aircraft, design and manufacturing interests.

A complete restructure of the British helicopter industry in 1960 resulted in Westland Aircraft taking over Fairey Aircraft and Bristol Aircraft's helicopter division, and Fairey's other factories branched out into areas other than aviation. Hamble built high-speed launches with old Fairey aircraft names such as Swordfish and Fantôme. (The Fantôme was a single-seat fighter developed in the 1930s, of which just four were built.) Heaton Chapel became Fairey Engineering Ltd and moved into the nuclear energy and other business. The hangars at Heston now built hydraulic components and filters for modern aircraft such as the Harrier, Jaguar and Tornado.

The company moved back into the aviation business in August 1972 when they acquired the entire share capital of Britten-Norman (Bembridge) Ltd. Fairey by now did not have facilities in the UK, so Fairey SA in Belgium took over production of the Islander and its derivatives, the Trislander and the military Defender, with Britten-Norman (Bembridge) Ltd looking after design and marketing.

CHAPTER TWO

# A Brief History of British Torpedo-Carrying Aircraft

The first torpedo-carrying trials with an aeroplane, it is claimed, were carried out by an Italian, Capt Guidoni. In 1912, a lawyer named Pateras Pescara proposed to the Italian Ministry of Marine that dropping torpedoes from aircraft was now reaching the stage of becoming a practical proposition. By that he meant that the development of aircraft power and airframe suitability had reached a stage where a torpedo could be carried; hereto the machines had been under-powered or too frail. Also, as the Italian Navy operated chiefly in the relative calm of the Mediterranean, such attacks would be easier to carry out than in more turbulent waters.

Lieutenant Allessandro Guidoni was ordered by the Italian Navy to assist Pescara in the design and testing of torpedo dropping from aeroplanes. Guidoni used a Farman biplane on floats, fitted with Forlinini vanes, to carry out initial flying from Venice harbour. Guidoni, realizing the limitations of the Farman, designed his own aircraft specifically to carry out the torpedo role. Naming it 'Pateras Pescara' after his mentor, the machine had a wingspan of 71ft 6in and was a monoplane, powered by a 160hp Gnome rotary engine, and operated off two floats. It was completed in 1914, with Guidoni making the first flight. In August 1914, World War One started and with Italy a neutral country development of some of their weapons was curtailed. Guidoni continued with his flying, however, using the Italian hydroplane-carrying ship, *Elba*, moored in Venice harbour. When Italy entered the war, the *Elba* was required at their Taranto base and the flying experiments ceased, the aeroplane gradually rotting away in a corner of the Italian navy arsenal at Venice. Any further plans for the development of torpedo-launching aircraft were abandoned for the time.

Rear Admiral Bradley A. Fiske of the United States Navy (USN) had advocated the use of aeroplanes for dropping torpedoes in combat in 1912, but as no aeroplane was capable of flying with a torpedo at that time, nothing further was done.

British interest in the use of torpedo-carrying aircraft started around 1911, principally among naval officers such as Cdre Murray Sueter, Cdr N. F. Usborne, Lt Hyde-Thomson and Lt L'Estrange Malone. It should be pointed out that at this time aeroplanes were in their infancy and could hardly carry passengers, let alone a warload, but these men had a vision and were prepared to stand by their beliefs. Cdre Sueter frequently discussed the idea of torpedo-carrying aircraft with his fellow officers while he was involved with the building of the rigid airship *Mayfly* at Barrow. Lt Hyde-Thomson prepared a paper, complete with rough sketches, about the possibility of aircraft being used by the Royal Navy for torpedo attacks. This prompted Cdre Sueter to seek his attachment to the Naval Air Department to further develop this work.

Prior to World War One, the initial title was Air Department of the Navy and on 13 April 1912 it became the Naval Wing of the RFC. On 1 July 1914 this became the RNAS and stayed as such until 1 April 1918 when the RFC and RNAS merged to form the RAF. In the post-war era the naval element of the RAF was run down and by 1919 there was only one spotter-reconnaissance squadron, half a torpedo squadron, a fighter flight, a seaplane flight and a flying boat flight.

The RAF had responsibility for naval air development and with expansion plans for new aircraft carriers they looked at suitable aircraft. On 1 April 1923 all naval squadrons were disbanded and a series of aircraft flights were formed, each having six aircraft. On 1 April 1924 the Fleet Air Arm of the RAF was formed and became known as the FAA to all – a term used to this day. However, during the period 1939–53 it was known also as Air Branch of the Royal Navy and/or Naval Aviation.

The timing was fortuitous, for Lt Hyde-Thomson had just completed a torpedo course at HMS *Vernon*. Under the watchful eye of Cdre Sueter these officers came up with a suitable design in 1913, set out professionally by a draughtsman, Mr Bowden. Now they needed help with building such a machine and T. O. M. Sopwith was invited to comment and offer advice on their proposal. He constructed two machines: a fast skimmer hydrofoil for preliminary experiments, but not intended to get off the water; and an aeroplane, based on or at

**A Short 184 carrying a torpedo.** J. M. Bruce/S. Leslie

the limit of aviation technology of the day, that would just be capable of lifting a torpedo. With details of the trials in hand, a special Sopwith Canton-Unné seaplane was ordered in September 1913, powered by a 200hp engine. Later that year this machine made its first flight, from Calshot, carrying a 14in torpedo. The Rubicon had been crossed: it was possible to carry a torpedo by aeroplane, and presumably therefore to drop it against enemy shipping.

Due to the limited output and unreliability of early aero-engines it was thought a twin-engined machine would be more suitable. At this time all the effort was being directed towards shore-based machines with floats; the aircraft carrier idea would swell from these initial efforts. The twin-engined machine was killed off with the Naval Review of 1914. The authorities could see more use for carrier-borne torpedo aircraft than those operating from a shore base. Three Short seaplanes, powered by 160hp engines, flew from Portsmouth to attend the Review and afterwards Lt Hyde-Thomson temporarily lashed up an installation for a 14in torpedo, weighing 810lb (370kg) which was test-flown successfully. Full of enthusiasm, further experiments were carried out during July and August 1914 using a 160hp Gnome-powered Short seaplane.

Arriving in 1915, the Short 184 was one of if not the most important aircraft developed for British naval aviation. It became to World War One what the Swordfish became during World War Two. Both made history by carrying out torpedo attacks and earned respect and reputations for reliability when operating in many theatres of war. The Short 184, of which 650 were ordered, served at practically all coastal air stations around the UK, the French coast, Mediterranean, Mesopotamia, Red Sea and the Aegean. The Short 184 was the first aircraft in the world to sink an enemy ship at sea by using a torpedo.

Short Bros. had also developed one of their aircraft to take a 225hp Sunbeam engine specifically to carry the 14in torpedo. All torpedo aircraft development work had by now been concentrated at Felixstowe and a new Mark IX 18in torpedo weighing 1,000lb (450kg), including 170lb (77kg) of TNT, was specially produced to be carried by aircraft. Also, thought was given to the carriage and delivery of torpedoes over long distances: two Short seaplanes with 310hp engines were ordered to meet these needs.

Developed in parallel with torpedo-carrying seaplanes and ships to carry them was the operation of aircraft from ships' actual structures. Pioneering this technique was Lt C. R. Samson, who had made the first flight from HMS *Africa* on 10 January 1912, piloting a Short-modified S-27 Box-Kite, aircraft No. 38. The naval dockyard at Chatham had installed a long wooden ramp sloping towards the prow on HMS *Africa*, a King Edward VII class battleship of 15,700 tons. Further trials were carried out with a similar sloping structure aboard HMS *Hibernia*. The first take-off from a ship under way occurred on 2 May 1912 when Lt Samson took the S-27 off the ramp on *Hibernia*.

When World War One broke out in August 1914, it was planned to use torpedo-carrying aircraft over the North Sea. To do this two converted channel packet steamers, HMS *Engadine* and *Riviera*, were fitted out and both embarked three or four 160hp Short seaplanes, with specific Admiralty instructions that they carry torpedoes. The ships, however, were given other work and operational difficulties arose. A planned torpedo attack against a German cruiser had to be cancelled after the aircraft were withdrawn to be used on the 'Cuxhaven raid', against Zeppelin airship sheds at Cuxhaven on 25 December 1914.

## Operations in the Dardanelles

The trials with the Sunbeam-powered Short seaplane carrying the 14in torpedo were successful and the first two production machines were embarked aboard HMS *Ben-my-Chree*, which sailed for the Dardanelles on 21 May 1915. There was an unofficial plan to torpedo the German ships *Breslau* and *Goeben*, but when they arrived in the Dardanelles the aircraft were subject to operational difficulties and only used for reconnaissance.

Eventually the aircraft were used for their intended role, the first torpedo attack in history being against a merchant ship off Injeh Burnu on 13 August 1915. During a spotting flight in the Gulf of Xeros on 11 August a ship was observed off Injeh Burnu, on the north shore of the Sea of Marmara, some 12 miles east of Isthmus of Bulair. Just before dawn the next day *Ben-my-Chree* (Sqn Cdr C. L. Malone) arrived at the eastern end of the Gulf of Xeros. A Short 184, carrying a 14in torpedo and 45 minutes-worth of fuel, was hoisted out and took off, piloted by Flt Cdr C. H. Edmonds. He climbed to 800ft (250m), which appears to have been about the aircraft's ceiling with such a load, and, crossing the Isthmus of Bulair, arrived at Injeh Burnu. He dropped the torpedo at a range of 350yd (320m) and on doing so hit a steamer of about 5,000 tons amidships, with debris and spray flying as high as the masthead. There was no opposition to his flight other than some desultory rifle fire whilst crossing the Bulair.

Further attacks followed, against a Turkish ammunition ship off Ak Bashi Liman and a tug off Nagara. Seaplane reconnaissance had revealed that Ak Bashi Liman, on the Gallipoli Peninsula, just above the narrows, was being used as a base where the enemy unloaded supplies delivered by ship. It was planned to attack the supply vessels with torpedoes. Just before dawn on 17 August *Ben-my-Chree* arrived in the same position it had used on the 12th. Two Short 184s were hoisted out and flown off with 14in torpedoes, one piloted by Flt Cdr Edmonds, the other by Flt Cdr G. B. Dacre DSO. The plan was to climb to about 1,000ft (300m), cross the Isthmus of Bulair and fly over the enemy aerodrome at Galata, hoping to get past it unopposed before daybreak, then to fly down the Straits at low altitude to Ak Bashi Liman, hoping anyone who saw them would mistake them for Germans. Also, the machines would be approaching from the direction of the aerodrome at Galata and would be difficult to recognize, flying low against a background of hills and with the rising sun behind. Flt Cdr Edmonds carried out a perfect attack based on this plan. At Ak Bashi Liman he released his torpedo at the centre ship of three in the harbour, and hit it. The ship was gutted by the ensuing fire, though the hull was saved and moved to Constantinople (now Istanbul). Again, very little opposition was noted, just some rifle fire. Flt Cdr Dacre had to descend into the Straits with engine trouble, so did not reach Ak Bashi Liman. However, he saw a steam tug close to the shore, taxied in and released his torpedo at it under rifle fire, and then taxied away towards Bulair! Playing with the controls, he enticed a few more revolutions out of the engine and managed to get airborne and climb to 200ft to cross the Isthmus and reach his ship.

In this hot climate, it would require a new machine to lift a 14in torpedo and as there were no new machines there could be no follow up or further attacks. One may conjecture that had the Allies had the chance to mount further attacks on Turkish shipping, the outcome of the campaign might have been changed.

**Short 184 single-seat torpedo aircraft no. 8349. Trials were conducted at Felixstowe on 12 March 1917; here the aircraft has just dropped its torpedo.** J. M. Bruce/S. Leslie

**The torpedo from 8349 bouncing across the surface of the water.** J. M. Bruce/S. Leslie

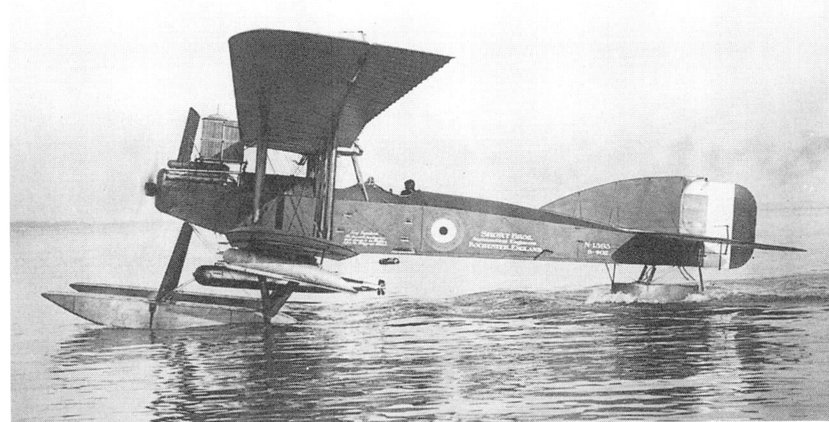

**Short 310-A4 N1393/S402 taxying out with a torpedo. The stencilling aft of the roundel says 'Short Bros, Aeronautical Engineers, Rochester England'. The italics under the cockpit reads '*Very Important. The removeable rear cross bar must always be in position before the wings are folded*'.** J. M. Bruce/S. Leslie

**A close-up view of a torpedo loaded on Short 310-A4 N1481 during trials at the Isle of Grain on 20 August 1917.** J. M. Bruce/S. Leslie

***(Above)* The torpedo launching device fitted to the cockpit of Short N1481 during the trials.** J. M. Bruce/S. Leslie

***(Right)* The torpedo is held up in a cradle with a supporting wire. The cross-wires of the undercarriage struts do not allow much room for error.** J. M. Bruce/S. Leslie

## Development Continues

In 1915 the idea of using a twin-engined aircraft returned. J. Samuel White of Cowes, Isle of Wight, built a 'Wight' seaplane fitted with two 200hp Canton-Unné engines. During trials this machine failed to fly with a Mk IX torpedo and a full load of fuel. It continued to be tested, first at Calshot and later at Felixstowe. The engines were replaced with 225hp Sunbeams, but these did little to improve the performance and work on it was eventually stopped. There was still some support for using a larger machine, and in April 1916 a Porte flying boat carried two 14in torpedoes, one on each side of the lower wing.

A number of papers were written to convince the authorities that torpedo aircraft, as yet in their infancy, were here to stay. One, in September 1915, was by Lt Hyde-Thomson, who had been advocating the cause since 1911. Somewhat later, in June 1917, Flt Cdr Edmonds, who made the torpedo attacks in the Dardanelles, wrote a paper about the employment of torpedo aircraft, obviously using his experiences to good cause.

In October 1916, Lt Cdr Hardy demonstrated to the naval authorities several simulated torpedo attacks, by aircraft from Felixstowe armed with 14in and 18in torpedoes, against HMS *Dreadnought* and *Hindustan*. It was quickly realized that lots of young men would have to be trained, not only to fly, but to specialize in the delivery of a torpedo. Consequently, at the end of 1916 a torpedo school was set up at Felixstowe and in January 1917 plans were laid to form a Torpedo School at Houton Bay, Scapa Flow, in the Orkney Isles.

Events really started to move in August 1917 when the Commander-in-Chief of the (Royal Navy's) Grand Fleet expounded the value of the new form of attack and asked for 200 Sopwith Cuckoo torpedo aircraft as soon as possible! The first 100 were to be built by the Fairfield Engineering Company of Glasgow, fifty by Pegler and fifty by Blackburn in October 1918; neither of the former firms had built aeroplanes before.

Around this time a flight of Short 310 machines was set up at Otranto with 18in Mk IX torpedoes. The Short 310 was powered by a 310hp Sunbeam Cossack engine and made its first flight in 1916; an order for twenty-five followed in January 1917. The plan was to use the new machines to make attacks on the Austrian fleet in Pola, hopefully with the slightly more powerful Short 320 model. In September 1917, six Short 320s loaded with 18in torpedoes were towed by launches to a point 50 miles (80km) south of Traste Bay, to put them in range of submarines lying off Cattaro. Unfortunately the weather changed and the raid had to be cancelled due to heavy seas and gales.

Strangely, no other attacks were planned and the war ended without any further torpedo attacks. One reason may have been that around the middle of 1917 there were two cases of structural failures to Short 310s in the Mediterranean theatre. In one case the fuselage collapsed after the aircraft had released its torpedo and pulled up to 1,000ft: at first it was thought due to the splash of the torpedo hitting and entering the water, but eventually the cause was discovered to be an unsatisfactory method of securing the fuselage bracing wires.

In October 1916 Cdre Sueter and T. O. M. Sopwith had come up with the idea of operating torpedo-carrying aircraft from the deck of a ship. An order was placed with Sopwith for one machine, which was later called the Sopwith Cuckoo. This machine was delivered in June 1917 and went for service trials at the Isle of Grain. The story goes that Sopwith's design was placed with Blackburn Aircraft to be manufactured, and

**Sopwith Cuckoo N6954 at the point of releasing its torpedo.** J. M. Bruce/S. Leslie

**German Torpedo-Carrying Aircraft**

During the early part of 1917 the German Air Service set up a *T Staffel* (torpedo flight) at Zeebrugge equipped with thirty Friedrichshafens, five to seven Brandenburgs, five or six Albatros Scouts and two or three Rumplers. These made several torpedo attacks on British merchant ships off Margate, sinking three. Other raids were made against shipping off Lowestoft and one pilot set off to attack London, but failed to return.

For some strange reason, following the success of these torpedo attacks, the Germans withdrew their machines and sent them to the Adriatic for use by the Austrians. After the war a German officer under interrogation revealed that they had found torpedo aircraft too easy a target for hostile gunfire when they flattened out close to the water prior to releasing the torpedo. It should be pointed out that the Germans used a large twin-engined seaplane which was dropping a torpedo at about 1,000yd (900m), but the message was clear – the requirement was for a fast, manoeuvrable aircraft that could deliver its load and get out quickly.

so the design was hatched in Blackburn's nest – like a cuckoo! The Sopwith T.1 Cuckoo prototype, N-74, appeared in mid-1917, powered by a 200hp Hispano Suiza engine.

Towards the end of 1917 the authorities decided that the Mk IX 18in torpedo would not be powerful enough for use against German battleships. It was proposed to increase the warhead of the Mk IX by 80lb (36kg) to a total of 250lb (113kg), which increased the total weight to 1,086lb (493kg); and to order a machine capable of carrying the Mk VIII torpedo, which had a 320lb (145kg) warhead. Specifications were issued to two companies for a new aircraft, resulting in the Short Shirl and the Blackburn Blackbird. Both these machines had a duration of six hours but were found to be slower than the Sopwith Cuckoo, and lacked the manoeuvrability necessary for close-range attacks. The Cuckoo fitted the bill, and became something of a landmark when it was found it would also be suitable to operate from the flat deck of the new aircraft carriers.

Following successful trials at the Isle of Grain an order for 100 was placed with Fairfields. By the Armistice 350 were on order – though a lot of these were later cancelled – with ninety delivered by several companies, including Blackburn. The Cuckoo, which arrived too late to be used in action, served both in shore establishments and aboard carriers until 1923.

A Torpedo Aeroplane School was established at East Fortune. During April and May 1918 torpedo ratings and stores arrived at East Fortune and torpedo trials began in July, the flying being done from long stretches of sand at Bellhaven, near Dunbar. Some seven squadrons were to be established with torpedo attack as their prime role and spotting for the fleet a secondary one. A second Torpedo Aeroplane School and an Experimental Squadron were formed at Fort Rowner, Gosport. Torpedo development work was carried out at the Royal Naval Torpedo Factory at Greenock.

A series of experiments were set up at Calshot in September 1918 to obtain some firm data of what really happened when torpedoes were dropped at various speeds and heights. Four Short 310s carried out forty torpedo runs at Calshot, while at East Fortune some 230 drops were made.

## The Inter-War Years

However, the expansion of the torpedo-aeroplane force was not to last. With the signing of the Armistice on 11 November 1918 the armed forces were sharply cut back, and by mid-1919 there was only one half-squadron of torpedo-carrying aircraft in the Royal Navy. There was a slow build-up again in the 1920s, but it was the arrival of the fleet aircraft carrier that really opened the door for the development of aircraft specific to navy needs. The first deck landing aboard a flat-top was on HMS *Argus* in October 1918.

The provision of aircraft and air personnel to fly and operate them in the navy had changed dramatically on 1 April 1918 when all responsibility for their development and training was transferred to the Air Ministry. Inter-war rivalry between the RAF and the Fleet Air Arm resulted in the latter often receiving aircraft unsuited to its needs and navalized versions of RAF aircraft that lacked performance. This was reflected in the 1933 review that found the FAA with only 159 aircraft; this had only increased to 230 by the outbreak of World War Two. This retarded development meant that torpedo-carrying aircraft progressed slowly through a whole series of biplanes while the air arms of America and Japan were already testing monoplanes of fairly advanced design in this role.

Naval requirements for the period 1934–40 were focused on only two types: the torpedo-spotter-reconnaissance (TSR); and the fighter-dive bomber or fighter-reconnaissance. Naval aircraft had to fulfil several functions because the number of

**(Above right) One of the dangers during early trials, as shown here by a Sopwith Cuckoo, was the chance that if you got the delivery wrong it could bring you down.** J. M. Bruce/S. Leslie

**(Right) Blackburn Ripon II S1467 '60' releasing from a higher launch point.** BAe Systems Brough Heritage Centre

carriers available for attachment to any particular fleet or part of the world was very small. Also, there were the basic requirements for naval aircraft. Their wings had to fold in order to accommodate as many as possible in carrier hangars. They were subject to limitations of wing loading (and therefore speed) to give the best take-off and landing performance on a ship that could be rising, falling and corkscrewing when in adverse weather. Arrestor gear and catapults to allow accelerated take-offs added to the weight, as did radio requirements. These were all complications for the designer, and adversely affected almost every new naval aircraft project.

## Expansion 'Schemes'

The schemes started as a sort of military deterrent against Germany, which was re-arming its forces, but Hitler was not impressed. The British Government decided that they would at least achieve parity. Eventually eight pre-war schemes emerged. Scheme A of July 1934 aimed for a force of 138 squadrons, of which forty-one would be bombers and twenty-eight fighters, with a total of 1,544 aircraft. Hitler then upset the applecart by saying that he already (March 1935) had 1,888 aircraft. Scheme B was overtaken by events and the Cabinet approved Scheme C in May 1935. Basically the plan was to have the same number of aircraft as Germany by April 1937.

On 6 March 1936, Hitler remilitarized the Rhineland, the Italians were in Abyssinia and the Japanese moved into Manchuria, China. In the light of this, which affected British interests in those areas, it was decided to go for Scheme F (for some reason the missing letters in the sequence of schemes were plans not put forward, due no doubt to the rapidly changing world situation). The Cabinet approved Scheme F, the aim being yet again parity with Germany by March 1939. However, this aim to deter the German rearmament plan failed and it was vital to embark on a plan that would produce enough front-line aircraft to wage war. Therefore, production orders placed for Scheme C were allowed to continue even though the aircraft would in the most part be unsuitable for modern war, for example biplane bombers, but this would keep the aircraft/engine factories running until newer aircraft were ordered. Specifications issued in 1935–36 were to result in aircraft such as the Halifax, Stirling and Manchester/Lancaster. Also Scheme F allowed for reserves of aircraft which was to be 225 per cent of the current front-line strength. Schemes came and went (H, L and M) as Germany rapidly expanded its air force and other military units. The last scheme, M, was still being implemented when World War Two broke out and many of its plans reached fruition as the war progressed.

## World War Two and After

It was at this stage that the Air Ministry decided to support the development of yet another torpedo-carrying biplane, one that was to achieve everlasting fame: the Fairey Swordfish. This aircraft was already in production in 1936 when the Air Ministry raised Scheme F of the expansion plan. That year the Air Ministry issued requirements for its replacement in 1938, by which time the Swordfish would be obsolescent. This replacement eventually became the Albacore, but in 1937 the Admiralty realized that it, too, would be out-of-date in a modern war and ordered a new specification, that led to the Barracuda. Both types suffered from delays outside the Admiralty's control and were late entering service. Both carried out torpedo attacks during the war, although the latter only made a few strikes in its designated role and was mainly used as a dive-bomber.

Notwithstanding this, a replacement for the Barracuda was in due course ordered, still with a torpedo-attack role, the eventual outcome being the Spearfish. The only thing to be said in its favour was that the torpedo could be carried internally in the forward fuselage. Only a few were built, production being cancelled as the role disappeared in the post-war era, although the Gannet was designed with the capability to deliver a torpedo, as were many of the helicopters that later served at sea.

***(Above left)*** **Swordfish L2817 'T4F' of No. 767 Squadron flown by Pat Chambers makes a dummy torpedo drop – very low!** via Ray Sturtivant

***(Left)*** **An Albacore goes out to practise dummy torpedo dropping.**

CHAPTER THREE

# Design, Development and Production of the Swordfish

The origins of the Swordfish design can be traced back through three previous attempts to design a three-seat aircraft capable of meeting a number of naval needs. These were a design for the Greek Naval Air Service and Specifications M.1/30 and S.9/30. All were to play a part in what was to become the Swordfish.

## The TSR.I

The Greek Naval Air Service had been operating ten Fairey IIIF Mk IIIB aircraft and it seemed natural to ask Fairey to design a replacement machine specific to their needs. A design was agreed and the aircraft was built in 1932–33. It was initially powered by a 625hp Armstrong Siddeley Panther VI 14-cylinder radial engine driving a two-blade metal airscrew. Chris Staniland, Fairey's chief test pilot at the time, took it on its first flight from the Great West Aerodrome on 21 March 1933. Apart from having a more pointed fin and rudder, this machine looked very similar to the Swordfish. In June the Panther was replaced by a 635hp Bristol Pegasus IIM 9-cylinder radial fitted with a Townend ring cowling, with Staniland taking it for its first flight with the new engine on 10 July. Other changes included a Watts two-blade wooden propeller, undercarriage spats and an arrestor hook.

Knowing that the Air Ministry were looking to the requirements of the Admiralty for new TSR-type aircraft, Fairey informed them of what they were doing for the Greek Navy, as well as the work they doing on S.9/30 (*see* below). Although known in the factory as 'the Greek machine' the Greeks' interest cooled as Fairey tried to convince the Air Ministry that it would also suit the Admiralty's requirements for a new three-seat TSR aircraft. Along these lines it started to be known as the TSR.I. Although the TSR.I, F1875, had been painted in British service markings Fairey did not have a contract and were going ahead with it as a private venture, the Greeks having now withdrawn completely.

Staniland continued to test fly the TSR.I throughout the summer of 1933, seemingly with few problems, until 11 September. He was carrying out spinning trials at different loadings at 14,000ft, but even with the aircraft stalled and the leading edge slots unlocked it was reluctant to enter a proper spin. Trying again the aircraft entered a right-hand spin, but without any sort of

**Powered by a 625hp Armstrong Siddeley Panther VI 14-cylinder two-row radial, the TSR.I first flew on 21 March 1933, from the Great West Aerodrome. The capacious rear cockpit is most apparent in this picture.**

**Re-engined with a 635hp Bristol Pegasus IIM nine-cylinder radial, the TSR.I is seen here being run up by Flt Lt Chris Staniland prior to a flight, with an arrestor hook fitted. He was flying this machine when a flat spin developed – electing to bale out, he was flung into the rear cockpit, but he managed to escape on the second try!**

warning it then became very flat with the nose on the horizon and a smooth but fast rotation. Staniland found the controls ineffective and tried opening the throttle, but that caused the aircraft to shake violently. Having descended through twelve turns Staniland decided that the aircraft was unmanageable and elected to bale out. With the aircraft spinning to the right he left the cockpit to the left, only to find that the slipstream and g-forces had flung him into the rear cockpit! With a large open cockpit at the rear he had no difficulty leaving the aircraft a second time, the TSR.I crashing at Longford in Middlesex.

## Specification M.1/30

Specification M.1/30 was sent out on 22 March 1930, requesting tenders for a two-seat torpedo-bomber 'ship-plane' capable of carrying a 1,866lb Type K torpedo or a 2,000lb bomb load, within a maximum all-up weight of 9,300lb. The requirements of the specification were as follows:

### *Performance*

1. The speed at 4,000ft (1,200m) with the engine running at maximum permissible rpm was to be not less than 130kt (240km/h). Landing speed was not to exceed 55kt (100km/h) and the service ceiling to be not less than 16,000ft (5,000m).
2. The tank for the fuel system was to be large enough to hold fuel for half an hour at full throttle at sea level and seven hours' cruising at 100kt (185km/h) at 4,000ft carrying a military load of 2,874lb (1,303kg). Oil and reserve water tanks were to be enough to allow eight hours' cruising at these figures.

### *Stability and Control*

When fully loaded, the aircraft was to:

1. have positive stability about all axes;
2. respond quickly to the controls and be fully controllable at any speed, especially near the stall and during a steep dive, when it should have no tendency to 'hunt';
3. be reasonably easy to manoeuvre;
4. not be tiring to fly;
5. form a steady platform for bombing and firing at any speed within its range; and
6. not experience excessive fluctuations in the speed for which it was trimmed if the throttle control was moved from the correct position for that speed to either of its limiting positions

The design of the ailerons' controls was to be such that their operation would produce minimum adverse yaw. A 'slot' device of an approved type was to be incorporated to ensure adequate lateral control and stability at and below the stalling speed.

### *Engine*

Although the specification asked for any suitable British engine that had passed the 100-hour test, it specifically mentioned the Rolls-Royce H.10 or 825hp Armstrong Siddeley Leopard, fitted with a metal airscrew.

*Construction*

All parts of the aircraft that contributed to its strength in flight were to be made of metal and protected against corrosion.

A crew of two were to be accommodated in such a way that the pilot and bomb-aimer could communicate without difficulty. The maximum dimensions were to be: span 50ft (15.25m), wings folded 23ft (7m), length 44ft (13.4m) and height 14ft (4.3m).

*Weapon Load*

The load was to be one Type K, Mk VIII or Mk X torpedo, one 2,000lb bomb, one 1,000lb bomb, two 520lb bombs, eight 230lb or 250lb bombs, plus four 20lb practice bombs in each case. The torpedo installation was not to interfere with the installation for the 2,000lb bomb. Defensive armament was to consist of one gun firing forward and one in the rear cockpit.

Six companies tendered to this specification: Avro, Blackburn, Fairey, Handley Page, Supermarine and Vickers. Fairey was already thinking, however, of using this in conjunction with the work on the Greek machine to meet another specification, S.9/30.

## Specification S.9/30

Only two firms, Fairey and Gloster, submitted design proposals to this specification, which was drawn up in June 1930 and which called for a TSR aircraft. Following Fairey's submission in October 1930, the Air Ministry placed a contract for one prototype, S1706, on 3 August 1931. The resulting design looked very much like what would become the Swordfish, apart from its nose section. This housed a 525hp Rolls-Royce Kestrel IIMS (Moderately Supercharged) 12-cylinder vee liquid-cooled engine, driving a two-bladed metal Fairey-Reed propeller. The Kestrel used steam cooling, the condensers being mounted on the underside of the upper centre section. This may have seemed a good idea at the time, but it only needed a stray bullet or two for the system to be punctured and without water/steam cooling the in-line engine would fail.

The first flight, as a landplane, was made by Staniland on 22 February 1934, with the floatplane version being flown by Staniland on 15 January 1935. The difference to the twin-float arrangement on the TSR.I was immediately apparent – it consisted of a 30½ft-long (9.3m) single float below the fuselage with a stabilizing float on the outer section of each lower wing. Following land and sea flying tests, S1706 went to the MAEE (Maritime Aircraft Experimental Establishment) at Felixstowe in May 1936 for its service trials. By now, though, events had overtaken the S.9/30, thanks to the promising performance of another type, the TSR.II.

## The TSR.II

The flight trials of the TSR.I having been quite promising with no serious problems, apart from the flat spin hiccup, there were proposals, with strong Air Ministry interest, to build a second private venture TSR. All the departments involved, such as flight test, drawing office, technical office, assembly and others, were called together over

**The Swordfish TSR.II prototype having a ground run at the Great West Aerodrome – even the windsock has 'Fairey' on it! The small tailwheel and full-length rudder do not allow much ground clearance.**

25–26 September 1933 to discuss whether the idea was viable. It was decided to go ahead incorporating any lessons learned from the previous machine, although it would be by modification rather than radical redesign. As an example, the experimental department asked for seventy-eight minor changes to be made to improve maintainability. Staniland had experienced tail buffeting at low speeds with some fore-and-aft instability. He recommended a number of changes to get rid of the spin problem, which included fitting a three-blade metal propeller.

On 30 November 1933 the Air Ministry received a design study for the new TSR.II from Fairey and thought it worthy of trials. They issued a contract for one prototype on 11 January 1934, to be used for service trials and issued the serial number K4190. The agreed changes from the TSR.I were included in the new machine as it was built. The fuselage was lengthened by adding an

**THIS PAGE:**
***(Above)*** **The nose section of Swordfish prototype K4190 showing forward detail: the Pegasus engine with a Townend ring, oil cooler and tank, fuel tank and pilot's forward-firing Browning machine-gun.**

***(Left)*** **The area around the pilot's cockpit showing the instrument panel and Browning machine-gun.**

***(Below left)*** **The port side, showing rear of engine with inertia starter hand-gear and engine controls.**

***(Below)*** **Petrol and oil tanks.**

**OPPOSITE PAGE:**
***(Top left)*** **The rear cockpit, showing the observer's position with mountings for the compasses, and the recessed Fairey High Speed Gun Mounting for the TAG.**

***(Top right)*** **The tailplane of K4190 with anti-spin strakes and low-set tailwheel.**

***(Bottom)*** **The completed machine: Swordfish prototype K4190, still with the low-set tailwheel and full-length rudder.**

K
4190

K
4190
K 4190

extra bay but the upper wings had to be raked back 4 degrees to compensate for it. The opportunity was taken to fit the latest 690hp Pegasus IIIM3 in a wide-chord Townend ring. The fin and rudder were of a broader chord than had been fitted to TSR.I, and anti-spin strakes were fitted on the rear fuselage just forward of the tailplane. With other minor changes Staniland took the TSR.II, as it had become known, on its first flight on 17 April 1934.

Early flight trials of the TSR.II showed that although some of the shortcomings of the TSR.I had been eliminated, it was still prone to some fore-and-aft instability when the centre of gravity was aft. In June 1934 K4190 went to the Aeroplane & Armament Experimental Establishment (A&AEE) at Martlesham Heath for its initial trials, which found spins to be acceptable but a bit slow in recovery. The machine then went to the Royal Aircraft Establishment (RAE) Farnborough for catapult launching tests, followed by deck landing trials aboard HMS *Courageous*. As the Air Ministry requirement asked for the aircraft to be operable on either land or sea, K4190 went to the Fairey factory at Hamble where Fairey-designed twin floats were fitted. Staniland conducted tests on Hamble Water and was catapult-launched from the battlecruiser HMS *Repulse*. Trials continued at the Marine Aircraft Experimental Establishment (MAEE) at Felixstowe before moving to the Torpedo Trials Unit (TTU) at Gosport where, in February 1935, it suffered an engine failure and crashed into a hedge between two barrack blocks. No-one was injured and the aircraft was returned to Fairey at Hayes.

K4190 was rebuilt and emerged in January 1936, being used for a time by Fairey to evaluate various improvements to the Swordfish, such as modified ailerons, oleo legs, a larger-diameter tailwheel and conversion sets for the fitment of dual controls. On 6 September 1937 K4190 joined the FAA at Gosport.

In April 1935 Martlesham Heath released its test report on the trials it had undertaken with the TSR.II. Generally, the testers were quite happy with the aircraft's performance, apart from some criticism of its stalling, recovery from spins and longitudinal instability in dives with an aft centre of gravity. The ailerons were light and effective, although there was some 'snatch' at the stall and in spins. The elevators and rudder were also light and effective, but with the slots out the rudder struggled to control a tendency to roll. Spinning trials were conducted at a ballasted weight of 7,500lb (3,400kg), the equivalent load of a torpedo. Inducing spins from the right was difficult, but once achieved was acceptable, and recovery was swift once the controls were centralized. Dives were made up to 240mph (390km/h) without any real problems. Most of problems were reduced or cured by changes in the range of elevator movement. In normal flying longitudinal stability at all speeds was light and positive, lateral control being heavier, but still positive.

In general, the results of the flying satisfied the Air Ministry, who placed orders on

**The prototype being flown by Flt Lt Chris Staniland near Staines reservoir in May 1934. A blister has been fitted over the Browning gun.** *Flight*

## The Swordfish Appears

The TSR.II having been built, tested and placed into production, the Air Ministry cancelled both M.1/30 and S.9/30, and issued an amended specification, S.15/33, which called for a three-seat general purpose spotter-reconnaissance and torpedo aircraft. Three companies that responded to the revised specification, Blackburn, Fairey and Gloster, were each awarded a contract to provide one aircraft. The Blackburn aircraft eventually became the Shark and entered service with the FAA. It proved a disappointment and was mainly relegated to training duties. The Gloster TSR.38 was not unlike the Fairey TSR.II but had an inline Kestrel engine, which gave it a sharper look. During further trials the Kestrel was replaced by a Goshawk engine, but the project was later abandoned.

**(Above)** **Still in its original form, K4190 undergoes float trials in the Solent.** Real Photographs

**(Below)** **K4190 after being rebuilt as a dual-control machine with a three-blade Fairey-Reed metal propeller. The rudder has been cut away to give more ground clearance.**

11 July 1935 for three pre-production aircraft, K5660–K5662, and eighty-six production machines, K5926–K6011; the aircraft was given the name 'Swordfish'.

Although the TSR.II had performed acceptably on its water trials there had been some problems with the floats. Swordfish K5662 was subjected to similar trials at Felixstowe, and when the report was issued in September 1936 there was some criticism about its performance on the water. The two Dural floats had a track width of 9¾ft (3m), were 26ft 9¾in (8.18m) long, 3ft 6¾in (1.09m) across the beam and 3ft 1⅛in (0.95m) deep. At an all-up weight of 8,900lb (4,000kg) the floats only required 1ft 9½in (0.55m) of water to operate. Generally, it was taking too long to get 'on the step' (the first stage of a floatplane lifting off from the water) and the propeller was picking up large amounts of water, especially if it was choppy. Choppy conditions also induced a premature take-off, when coarse use of the rudder was required to hold the aircraft down. The water rudders had a pivoting blade raised and lowered by a 'tricing line' (a wire cable), each rudder being pneumatically controlled by a servo tab hinged to the air rudder's trailing edge and operated by a small servo motor. The water rudders were considered inadequate in that they exercised little control at low manoeuvring speeds and failed to meet the required standard, which was to circle on water in a 20mph wind at a taxiing speed not greater than 5kt. The water-rudder problem was never overcome; trials of a Swordfish at the MAEE two years later still had the same problem.

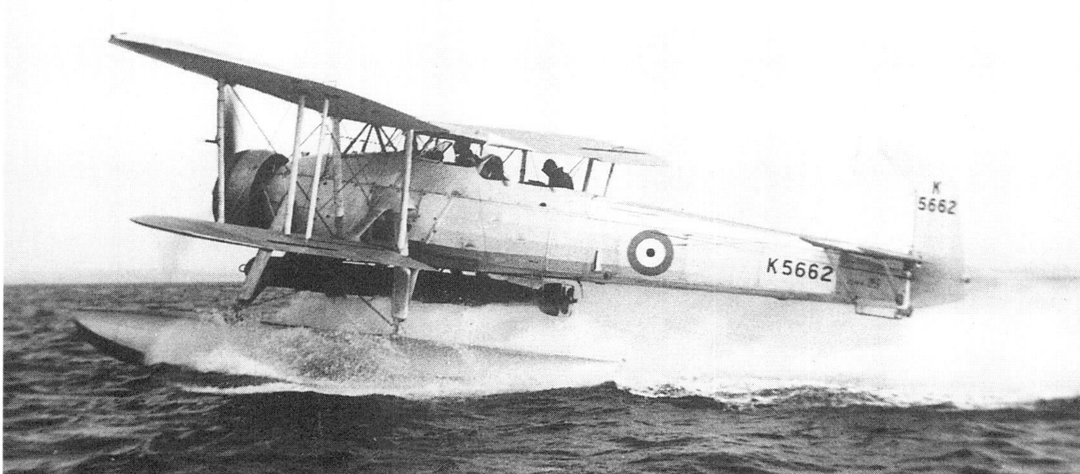


**(Top)** The clean profile of the prototype K4190 before they hung everything on its sisters.

**(Above)** A similar view, but with a three-blade prop and floats.

**(Left)** Pre-production Swordfish K5662 undergoing float trials with a dummy torpedo. Water trials showed the floats to be 'dirty'.

**Roy Fedden and Leonard Butler**

The genesis of the Pegasus aero-engine can be traced back to just after World War One when Roy Fedden, with his friend Leonard Butler, designed the Jupiter nine-cylinder, air-cooled engine. Between 1914–18 the aeroplane and aero-engine had advanced beyond all recognition and in the immediate post-war period manufacturers realized that aviation was the future, both in military and civil applications. There were two accepted types of engine at the time, the water-cooled in-line and the air-cooled radial. Both had advantages and disadvantages in terms of weight, rigidity/stiffness, coolant leaks, thermal expansion, and so on, with manufacturers tending to stick with one or the other, based on their experiences in the recent conflict.

The main rivals in the field of air-cooled aero-engines in the United Kingdom were Siddeley-Deasy at Coventry (later Armstrong Siddeley) and the Cosmos Engineering Company, which failed in 1919 but whose Bristol works formed the basis of the Engine Department of the Bristol Aeroplane Company. The post-war market for air-cooled engines was in the 400–450hp class, and for the next twenty years or so Bristol and Armstrong Siddeley remained arch rivals as they both developed aero-engines ranging from the 400hp units of 1920 to much more powerful engines by the end of World War Two, such as the 18-cylinder Bristol Centaurus, giving over 2,600hp.

Roy Fedden, who was to become Chief Engineer at the Bristol company, had been born on 6 June 1885. After attending Clifton College he rejected an Army commission, saying he wanted to be an engineer. His premier apprenticeship with the Bristol Motor Company was paid for by his father, and by the time he finished in 1906 he had designed his own car. He joined J. P. Brazil Straker, who recognized his skills and successfully produced his car design as the Shamrock.

In 1915 Fedden negotiated a contract for Brazil Straker to re-build and re-engineer Curtiss and, later, Renault aero-engines for the war effort. Henry Royce was so impressed with the work done by Brazil Straker that he allowed them to manufacture and test some of his engines, and although he offered Fedden a job at Rolls-Royce, Fedden declined, staying with Brazil Straker and air-cooled engines. It was in late 1915 that Fedden and his chief designer, Leonard 'Bunny' Butler, designed the 14-cylinder Mercury radial engine. Butler had joined Fedden in 1914 as Chief Draughtsman and the two were to stay together over the next twenty years, forming a formidable team. A reflection of their standing resulted in the Bristol company deciding that all engine component parts would be stamped with their initials, 'FB'.

Born on 29 March, 1888, Leonard Butler went to Sexey's School in Somerset before joining Brazil Straker as an apprentice, staying with them from 1904–09. He left to work at the Derby drawing office of Rolls-Royce on their 40/50 cars, but this was not to his liking and in 1910 he moved to David Brown and Son, then to the Crossley Brothers, before returning to Brazil Straker in December 1911. Based at the Fishponds site, he designed car engines until he joined Fedden in 1914. Following the collapse of Cosmos Engineering Company in 1920, which had in the meantime taken over the aero-engine interests of Brazil Straker, the Bristol Aeroplane Company acquired their assets and set up an engine department at Filton, Bristol. Fedden, Butler and about thirty other staff members moved to Filton as part of the new department, retaining their original jobs.

Fedden and Butler worked together on every major engine project at Filton, including the Pegasus, which powered the Swordfish, and the Taurus, which powered the Albacore. The Pegasus engine ran to twenty-seven basic marks in the single-speed, single-stage, supercharged model and three in the two-speed, single-stage, supercharged model. There were many variables of these, with numbers and letters denoting the principal characteristics. Of those, the Pegasus IIM powered the TSR.I, and the Pegasus IIIM2, IIIM3 and Mk XXX were used on production Swordfish. The Taurus engine only ran to five basic marks and of these only the Taurus II and XII were used on the Albacore.

Butler stayed as Chief Designer until 1941 when serious illness kept him away from work for over a year. Still not a well man, Butler returned to the company in late 1942 as Technical Advisor. On 3 September, 1943 while on company business, 'Bunny' Butler collapsed and died at Paddington Station.

In 1942 Fedden was knighted, but he had been in conflict with Bristol's Board of Directors for some time and decided to leave. He accepted a number of influential positions with the Government, contributing further to the war effort. When the war was over he formed his own company, Roy Fedden Ltd, and designed cars, light aircraft engines and a turboprop. However, in the post-war era finance became a problem, and he rolled his company up and joined George Dowty as a consultant. Following his retirement he supported one of his pet subjects, the education and training of engineers, and as part of this was involved with the College of Aeronautics at Cranfield. Sir Roy Fedden died on 21 November 1973 at his home in Bwlch, Wales.

## Swordfish Production

In the meantime, a request had been issued on 2 November 1934 for a specification to cover the development order for the new aircraft and on 11 December technical officers from the Air Ministry and Fairey met to discuss and set up what was to be Specification 38/34. The production aircraft were to be built to the same standard as K4190, but this was later changed to K6011, which was more representative of the production machine. There were sixty-nine small changes to be incorporated, including the later Pegasus IIIM3 engine. Basically, building the Swordfish did not present any problems – there was just a lot of it!

On 22 March 1935 a Requisition for Purchase was raised with a request that sixty-nine Swordfish be produced by the end of the year. Approval of the request came in May, though it was 11 July 1935 before the first order was placed and that left little time to produce the order. On 29 November 1935 the Air Ministry said they wanted 104 Swordfish delivered between March–May 1936.

The aircraft were initially built at the Fairey factory at Hayes in Middlesex, production eventually being one Swordfish delivered in 1935, 147 in 1936, 201 in 1937, 143 in 1938, 197 in 1939 and three in 1940, after which production of all Swordfish was transferred to the factories of Blackburn Aircraft Ltd. By then the Hayes factory was producing the Albacore, working on the Barracuda prototypes and designing the Firefly. Their northern factories at Stockport were full, producing the Battle and Fulmar, and it was Captain M. S. (later Rear-Admiral Sir Matthew) Slattery, the Admiralty Director of Materiel, who suggested that Swordfish production should be moved to Blackburn, whose factories would have spare capacity as production of the Blackburn Botha reconnaissance/torpedo bomber tailed off.

All the necessary jigs and equipment were ferried to Blackburn, although Fairey retained design rights and supplied some components. Parts and sub-assemblies were produced by 'cottage industries' to prevent disruption by enemy bombing. In the Leeds area companies such as Tate's made centre sections, Thomas Green provided stub-planes and undercarriage parts, and Appleyards produced wings. Many of their staffs were wartime women workers. The parts all arrived at Sherburn-in-Elmet, where a new assembly plant had been built in 1940. Fairey test pilot Flt Lt F. H. Dixon, assisting Chris Staniland with production test-flying, flew up to Sherburn and took the first Blackburn-produced Swordfish, V4288, on its first flight on 1 December 1940. Blackburn production over the next four years amounted to 415 Swordfish in 1941, 271 in 1942, 592 in 1943 and 420 in 1944, when production ceased. By then Fairey had produced 692 and Blackburn 1,699; there were more Swordfish on order, but these were cancelled as Barracudas and other types took over its roles.

**OPPOSITE PAGE:**

***(Top)* Mass production of Swordfish wing ribs by cottage industry workers near Leeds. Many of the workers are women, which released younger men to the forces and others to more technical roles.** BAe Systems Brough Heritage Centre

***(Bottom)* The ribs being fitted in the Swordfish wing shop – don't forget there were four wings to each machine.** BAe Systems Brough Heritage Centre

**THIS PAGE:**

***(Top right)* Fitting the engines, oil tank and oil cooler on part of the final assembly line. These are Swordfish IIIs, with the larger oil cooler and extended exhaust from the collector ring.** BAe Systems Brough Heritage Centre

***(Right)* This picture shows the engine fitting area as aircraft move along a production line. Each aircraft has its own mobile stand on which the tailwheel rests to keep the fuselage horizontal. Those in the second row include NF345, NF346 and NF343.** BAe Systems Brough Heritage Centre

***(Below)* The complete assembly line in the purpose-built factory at Sherburn-in-Elmet, near Brough. Those fuselages nearest the camera are just being set up, while those in the background right await their final paint finish before joining those at the rear for final bits to be added.** BAe Systems Brough Heritage Centre

**Two very early Blackburn production Swordfish Is, V4319 and V4320, in the earlier naval colour schemes. The rear aircraft is undergoing an engine ground-run test.** BAe Systems Brough Heritage Centre

**Specification – Swordfish**

| | |
|---|---|
| Engine: | Bristol Pegasus 7-cylinder air-cooled supercharged radial engine with Fairey-Reed fixed-pitch three-bladed propeller. Mk IIIM3 rated at 775bhp at 2,200rpm at sea level; 690bhp at 2,200rpm at 3,500ft (1,100m). Pegasus 30 rated at 750bhp at 4,750ft (1,450m). |
| Fuel capacity: | Fuselage tank 155gal (705ltr), gravity tank 12.5gal (57ltr); a long-range tank holding 60gal (373ltr) could be fitted in rear cockpit and a 69gal (314ltr) tank could be slung on the torpedo crutch. |
| Weights: | Empty 4,700lb (2,130kg); empty-equipment 5,200lb (2,360kg); with floats 5,300lb (2,400); loaded 8,700lb (3,800kg); max overload 9,250lb (4,200kg). |
| Dimensions: | Span, upper wing 45ft 6in (13.88m); span, lower wing 43ft 9in (13.34m); width folded 17ft 3in (5.26m); length 36ft 1in (11.01m); height, tail down 12ft 10in (3.91m); height on floats 14ft 7in (4.45m); wing area 607sq ft (56.47sq m). |
| Performance: | (Based on loaded Mk I aircraft) Max speed: 132mph (212km/h) at sea level, 139mph (224km/h) at 4,750ft (1,450m); max cruise 128mph (206km/h) at 5,000ft (1,500m); economical cruise 104mph (167km/h); range empty 770 miles (1,240km); range with 1,500lb (680kg) load 546 miles (879km); range with 69gal tank 1,030 miles (1,657km); rate of climb 1,200ft/min (370m/min); time to 5,000ft (1,500m) 10 minutes; service ceiling 12,400ft (3,780m) at 8,700lb; max ceiling (no load) 19,250ft (5,870m); deck take-off run 180yd (165m) into 20kt (37km/h) wind, 115yd (105m) into 30kt (56km/h) wind, 62yd (57m) into 40kt (74km/h) wind; landing run (normal) 550yd (500m). |
| Armament: | One fixed Vickers 0.303in machine-gun (600 rounds) mounted on starboard front fuselage and operated by pilot; one Lewis 0.303in machine-gun (6 magazines) attached to Fairey High Speed Gun Mounting in rear cockpit; one 1,610lb 18in torpedo, or 1,500lb aerial sea mine, or 1,500lb (680kg) bomb load/depth charges; Mk II and Mk III Swordfish could carry 8 × 60lb R/Ps under wings. |

## The Swordfish Described

The actual process of changing production from Hayes to Sherburn was not a problem as the aircraft was conventional in construction. The rectangular steel-tube structure of the forward fuselage consisted of easily detached panels, while the oval rear section was fabric-covered; inspection panels were let into the fabric covering at appropriate points. A cowled Bristol Pegasus air-cooled, poppet-valve, nine-cylinder moderately-supercharged radial engine drove a three-blade Fairey-Reed fixed-pitch metal propeller. The only unusual feature was the protruding U-type 20-element oil cooler on the starboard forward fuselage. A small knob located in the left-hand front corner of the pilot's cockpit allowed him to bypass the filter on start-up or cold mornings, until the oil had warmed up. Surprisingly for a naval aircraft designed for deck operations, there was no engine fire extinguisher, although there were two hand extinguishers, one in the pilot's cockpit and one in the observer's.

There were two self-sealing fuel tanks fitted behind the firewall, a 155gal (705ltr) main tank with a 12½gal (57ltr) gravity tank fitted behind it. Should the engine fail, there was a hand-pump to the right of the pilot's seat, which could be operated by the pilot or observer and which pumped fuel from the gravity tank to the main tank. A single 15gal (68ltr) oil tank was mounted between the firewall and the main fuel tank.

An engine-driven generator charged a 12V battery that supplied electrical services. An arrestor hook, let into the rear fuselage, was lowered by a lever on the right-hand side of the pilot's seat; this was not spring-loaded, and had to be returned to its position by hand. The rear fuselage also contained a large flotation bag of rubberized fabric to give buoyancy to the tail of the aircraft in the event of a ditching. An M-Type Mk IA dinghy was installed in the root of the port upper mainplane, and could be released by hand, although provision was made for automatic release by means of an immersion switch on the forward face of the firewall. The manual release consisted of two cables, one terminating in a handle on the centre section of the upper mainplane, the other leading aft along the starboard side of the fuselage. It was possible to activate the release

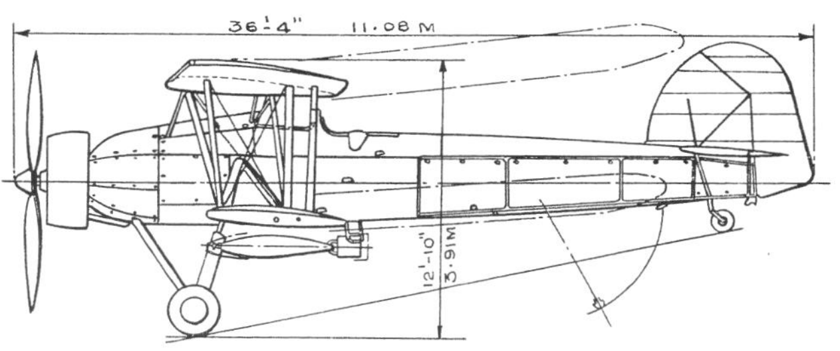


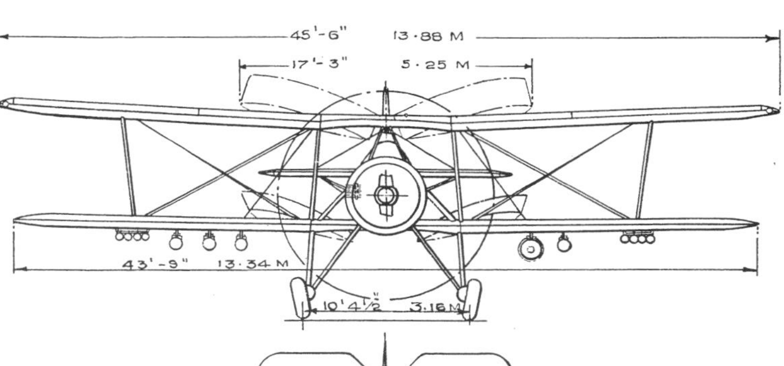


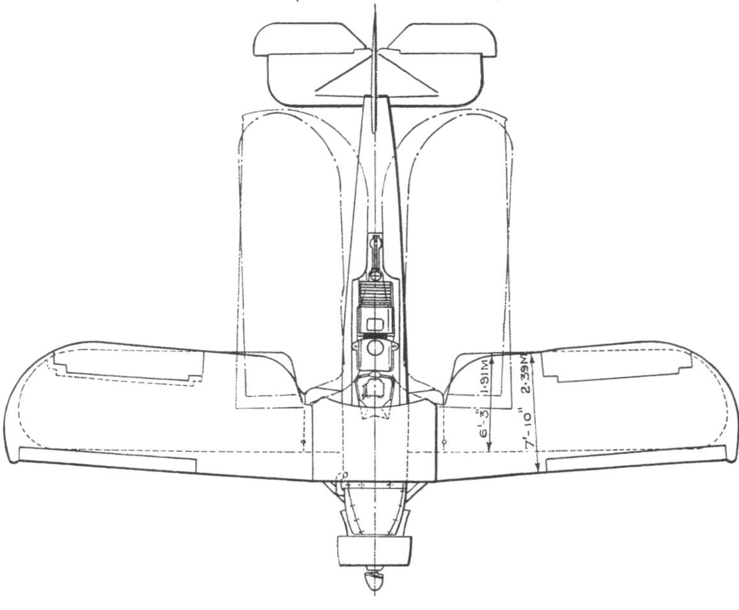


These original Fairey GA (General Arrangement) drawings give dimensions for major parts of the Swordfish (Landplane above and Seaplane below) in both the tail up and tail down configurations, and include wingfold positions and float layout.

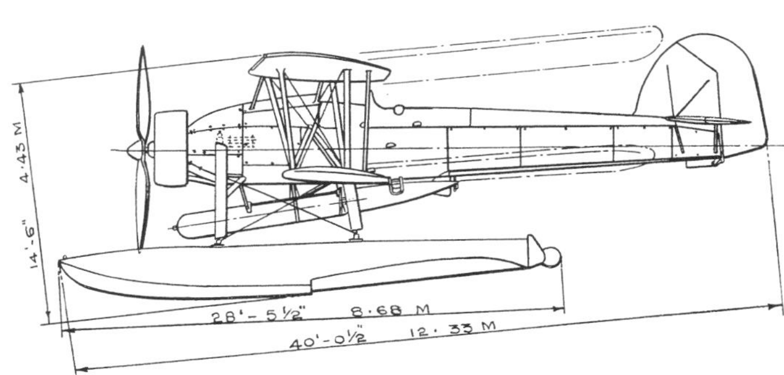


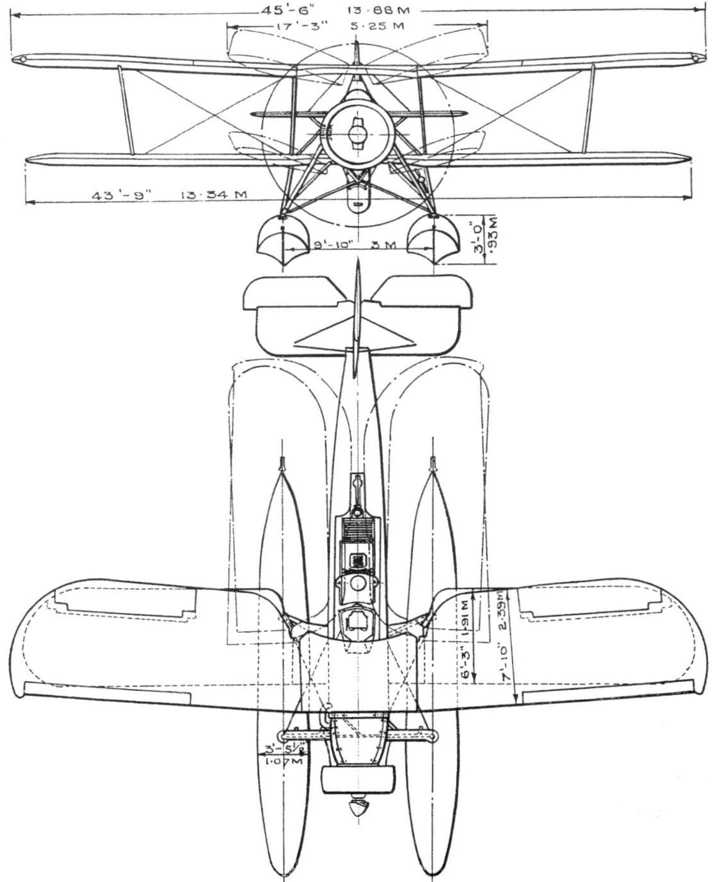

***(Above)*** **Early production Swordfish K6009 in pristine condition. The engine is now fully cowled. This machine was delivered on 18 September 1936 and flew with No. 822 Squadron between November 1937 and March 1939. It then served with Nos 825 and 785 squadrons before being withdrawn from use in 1940.**

***(Left)*** **Swordfish K8869 in pre-war markings of overall silver finish. It was delivered on 23 April 1937 and after gun tests at the RAE joined No. 825 Squadron until late 1938. In March 1941 it went to No. 775 Squadron, to be struck off charge on 1 November 1943.** A. J. Jackson

**Another early production machine, K8878, roped off at a pre-war air day. Delivered on 4 May 1937, it spent 1938 at Lee-on-Solent in the Floatplane Training Squadron. It flew with No. 764 squadron during 1940 but was struck off charge in March 1941.** A. J. Jackson

anywhere along the cables. An ex-rigger, Tom Fagg, recalls that all was not easy:

> The large dinghy which was stowed in the wing needed to be treated with due care when being installed. A vacuum pump had to be used to evacuate all the air from it otherwise any air left could expand the dinghy with increasing height and it was possible for it to be ejected from its stowage – dangerous to say the least! The $CO_2$ bottle to inflate the dinghy was operated by water immersion switches, one low down on the undercarriage and one in the engine bay. If either of these were misaligned the slipstream could cause them to inflate.

**L7686, which was delivered to Gosport Pool on 23 April 1938. It flew with No. 767 Squadron and then joined No. 816 during July 1940.**

There were a number of instances of such mishaps – Lt John Stenning of No. 821 Squadron was out flying Swordfish P4143 on 4 May 1940 when, at 1,000ft, the dinghy inflated and only some deft flying got the aircraft back onto the ground safely. There were other instances of such inflations, including the dinghy wrapping itself round the tailplane!

The wings consisted of two steel strip spars, Duralumin ribs and steel drag struts; all were covered in fabric, as were the Duralumin-frame ailerons. The wings folded back from the inner set of struts but required a small team to achieve this without damaging the wing. The correct procedure was to have one rating holding the wing by a handgrip on the lower wing tip, another pulling forward on a short rope spliced to a ring under the lower mainplane, beneath the front outer interplane strut, to take the weight of the wing once the locking pins were withdrawn. A third rating was positioned at the root end, standing on the wheel tyre to confirm that the weight was being held. He then released the safety catch securing the handle that operated the wing locking pins in the front inner interplane strut, and moved the handle forward and upwards to withdraw the pins from the cone-shaped stub plane fittings. With a small team holding the wing from its natural tendency to swing rapidly inboard, it was slowly folded back until the wing tip was level with the tailplane leading edge. A V-strut locked beneath the tailplane was released and the spring-loaded hook at the end of the strut was attached to a shackle on the wing tip handgrip bracket, thus securing and locking the wing in the folded position. A pyramid structure supported the upper centre-section with the lower centre-section stubs braced to upper fuselage longerons by inverted V-struts. The tailplane horizontal surfaces, fin and rudder were all made from Duralumin and covered in fabric.

The undercarriage consisted of an oleo shock-absorber leg, the upper end being anchored to the front spar of the lower centre-section and the lower end being hinged to the fuselage by an axle forwardly inclined radius rod. The wheels could be removed and twin floats substituted.

A pilot-operated forward-firing Vickers machine-gun was mounted in the forward fuselage on the starboard side, firing through the airscrew. Although pilots fired it as part of their pre-war training, it was hardly ever re-fitted after maintenance, there being little call for its use. A hand-operated Lewis machine-gun was provided on a Fairey High Speed Gun Mounting in the rear cockpit for the TAG (Telegraphist Air Gunner).

## Rockets

Changes to the basic structure of the Swordfish during its years in production were few. The Swordfish Mk II had rocket projectile (R/P) carriers fitted to the underside of the lower mainplanes. The origins of the R/P go back to May/June 1941 when the U-boats were creating havoc with the Atlantic convoys and elsewhere. A special committee, under Professor P. M. S. Blackett, had been formed within the Admiralty to look at all possible methods of attacking enemy submarines. On the committee was Lt Cdr Nevil Shute Norway, who was pressing for the use of some form of rocket. Norway was an engineer, having been involved in the building of the successful R.100 airship and served as managing director of Airspeed Aircraft Ltd. Under the pseudonym Nevil Shute, he wrote quite a few novels as well, most with aviation connections, and he later penned his autobiography, *Slide Rule*. At the time that the committee was formed Norway was working with Sir Dennistoun Burney on the design of a gliding torpedo for the Fleet Air Arm.

Several months earlier Norway had discussed with Charles Goodeve, a Royal Navy technical research officer, the possibility of mounting 2in rockets under the wings of a Swordfish. His aim was to use them to attack oil and fuel storage tanks, and other industrial targets. Nothing came of this idea because others felt there would be trouble firing the rockets accurately enough to do the job. The new committee, however, allowed him to resurrect his ideas. His objective was a rocket-propelled spear with a cast-iron, fluted head, which would rip a large hole in the pressure hull of a U-boat. Successful trials of the so-called 'Rocket Spear' at Birnbeck did little to convince the sceptics and no-one showed any interest – that is, until the Army asked for anti-tank missiles! A Hurricane was allocated for the Army's trials at Boscombe Down and it was decided to see at the same

FIRE
EXT.

**OPPOSITE PAGE:**
***(Top)* A crashed Swordfish, W5911, in the Fairey factory at Hamble for repair.**

***(Bottom)* W5911 after some repairs at Hamble. It had been delivered on 18 November 1941 and joined No. 810 Squadron early in 1942. It was involved in a collision on HMS *Illustrious* on 11 March 1942 and then went to No. 766 Squadron at Donibristle. It was written off on 13 August 1942 when Sub-Lt H. Stapleton made a force-landing in poor weather.**

***(Right)* An ATA pilot collected this Swordfish from the Fairey factory at Ringway but flew into a balloon cable, with the resulting damage seen here. The cable cut right through to the rear spar and damaged the tailplane, but the pilot got back to Ringway.**

time what effect the Rocket Spear would have on submarine plating.

The Commander-in-Chief, Western Approaches, directing the Battle of the Atlantic from Liverpool, was Admiral Sir Max Horton. Impressed with the idea of the Rocket Spear, he sent Cdr Phillimore to Boscombe Down to see whether it would be of use to the Navy in the battle against the U-boats. Acting on his enthusiastic report, Horton urged the Admiralty to adopt it for use. Phillimore later wrote:

> It seems incredible but it is true that only eight weeks elapsed to introduce the new weapon, get aircraft fitted with it, crews trained in its use, and get a kill with it in mid-Atlantic.

Swordfish with rocket modifications were first issued to No. 819 Squadron, under Lt Cdr O. A. G. Oxley, which embarked on HMS *Archer* in May 1943 and were also the first squadron to take the new weapon to sea. Each Swordfish had strengthened lower mainplanes and four rocket rails under each wing. According to the scientists, a Swordfish loosing off all eight Rocket Spears was about equivalent in firepower to a cruiser loosing off a broadside with 8in guns.

The first aircraft to score with the new weapon was Swordfish 'B' of No. 819, flown by Sub-Lts H. Horrocks, W. W. Noel Balkwill and LNA J. W. Wicks, who sank U-752 on 23 May. Neville Norway was out of London when the news broke, but Goodeve sent him a cable:

> You will be pleased to hear, if you haven't done so already, that the Anti-Submarine Rocket Projectiles from aircraft scored a success the first time they were used. I am particularly pleased as it fully substantiates the foresight you showed in pushing this in its early stages. My congratulations.

**Swordfish pushed outside for any final touches and test flying prior to delivery to the FAA. Identifiable are NF301, NF302 and NF305. The ones with engine covers have the ASV scanner cover in place, while others have bomb racks and/or rocket rails fitted. Despite not being used in the torpedo role, the sights were still fitted.** BAe Systems Brough Heritage Centre

**Once complete the aircraft were subject to a test flight by production test pilot H. P. Wilson before being released for collection. Test flights were usually of short duration and once any minor snags were cleared the aircraft would be cleared for collection by FAA or ATA pilots, depending on circumstances.**
BAe Systems Brough Heritage Centre

It falls to a survivor from an Italian submarine sunk by a Rocket Spear to describe what it was like on the receiving end:

> In this case the weapon was fired at such close range that the rocket was still burning when the spear smashed its way into the engine room. Once inside the hull of the submarine it ricocheted off the engines and thrashed wildly about before tearing a way out on the opposite side of the boat. On its passage back into the sea it ripped a second hole 3ft wide.

Later the Rocket Spear's name was changed to rocket projectile (R/P), and it became one of the most successful weapons used in the war.

## Other Modifications

The Mk III Swordfish was fitted with ASV radar. The scanner was housed in a plastic radome under the fuselage, between the undercarriage legs, with the rest of the equipment mounted in the forward rear cockpit, and by a built-up fairing. The Mk III also had the R/P carriers.

Some Mk II Swordfish were retrospectively fitted with the ASV equipment, and those aircraft fitted with the later Pegasus 30 engine had a larger oil cooler and longer exhaust muffler.

The so-called Mk IV was introduced with 'Mod. 408', which allowed the fixing of an enclosed cockpit to protect crews from the Canadian winter. The top panels of both the pilot's and observer's hoods were jettisonable. It seems illogical that Swordfish crews, operating on the Russian convoys and subjected to much harsher weather conditions, were not allowed this luxury or, indeed, the use of Albacores with their heated enclosed cockpit.

Some Swordfish had 'Mod. 465' fitted, which allowed the use of rocket-assisted take-off (RATO), essential sometimes when trying to get a heavily loaded Swordfish off a short deck. As early as 1928 a Mr Salmon at RAE Farnborough had investigated the problem and come up with a workable plan. Unfortunately, at that time, no-one was interested and it was 1941 before anyone else came up with the same idea. An initial experiment on a Blackburn Shark proved successful, using a standard 3in R/P motor, which gave 1,800lb (800kg) thrust for 1.2 seconds. This was refined, enlarging the diameter of the motor to 5in, and was introduced for Swordfish use in 1943. Modified aircraft had three new controls in the cockpit: a master electrical switch mounted below the throttle quadrant, just forward of the trimming wheel; a firing button, of the gun-firing type, on the control column; and a jettison lever mounted below the instrument panel on the port side, forward of the throttle quadrant – this had to be pulled firmly back to release the rocket motors after use. The number of RATO motors carried could vary according to aircraft weight, flight-deck length and wind speed.

**Nine Swordfish of the Torpedo Training Unit from Gosport in mid-1937. The patch area at the base of the port upper wing held the dinghy. Formation flying was a part of a pilot's training, and these are in quite tight.** IWM

## Introduction into Service

Swordfish replaced Fairey Seals in No. 825 Squadron during July 1936, and it was this squadron that would operate the Swordfish throughout the war until April 1945 after emulating the squadron motto many times: *Nihil Obstat*, 'Nothing stops us'. There was no problem introducing the big biplane; if anything it was even simpler to fly than the Seals it replaced. Only the role had taken on a more sinister note: the squadron had been formed as a spotter-reconnaissance unit; with the introduction of the Swordfish it became a torpedo-spotter-reconnaissance squadron. The squadron embarked in HMS *Glorious* and proceeded to work up with its new aircraft as part of the Mediterranean Fleet. One of the first tasks was night flying trials to test new deck landing aids (pillar and sector lights) which had been designed onboard.

**The same formation in line abreast over the south coast. In order they are L2727 '7', L2728 '8', K5965 '4', K8875 'K', K8873 '3', L7651 'B', K6007 'L', L7650 'I' and K8424 'D'. The fourth machine in is K8875, a dual control conversion that was still in use with No. 785 squadron at Crail in 1943.** IWM

***(Above)*** **These four Swordfish from Gosport broke away from the other five and presented a pleasing study of good formation flying over a sunlit sea.** IWM

***(Below)*** **Swordfish L2824 being brought up to the flight deck of HMS *Argus* for service trials before the war. L2824 was with the Fleet Requirements Unit, normally based at Lee-on-Solent, during 1938 and served with No. 810 Squadron before being struck off charge on 15 November 1940.** Fox Photos

***(Right)*** **A pre-war picture of Swordfish K8350 when it was serving with the Seaplane Training Squadron at Calshot during 1937. The cowling and wheels were painted the same colour.**

***(Below right)*** **Swordfish formation of No. 814 Squadron when operating from *Ark Royal* in 1938. Identified are L9779 '702', L9777 '701', L2733 '703', L2764 '710', L9774 '708', L9773. The squadron colours around the fuselage were blue–red–blue.**

Next to re-equip was No. 811 Squadron, which exchanged its Blackburn Baffins for Swordfish in October 1936. In December No. 812 also relinquished its Baffins for Swordfish, followed by No. 823 who had been using Seals. Each year there was a Royal Review of the Fleet and S. M. Russell, a Fitter, Aero-engines, remembers taking part in one from HMS *Courageous*:

> For the Fleet Review, I was one of two in the rear open cockpit of a Swordfish. We had nine aircraft in the formation and when over the Royal Yacht we dived almost vertically. The formation was very tight and the aircraft behind us hit our elevator with his wingtip. Had it been a foot further forward it would have been the tailplane and a number of aircraft could have been involved. As it was the naval wireless operator, who had not fastened his harness chain to the floor, shot out and was killed when he hit the sea. I had done up my chain and had a burning desire to jump out, but the 'G' forces were such that I couldn't. The aircraft was shaking badly but we were by now clear of the other aircraft so I shouted to the pilot up the Gosport tube that all was well. On landing at Lee-on-Solent the pilot was shocked to learn about the wireless operator but agreed that there was nothing he could have done had he known.

The Swordfish became the only torpedo-bomber in FAA service in 1938 when Nos 810, 820 and 821 all converted from Blackburn Sharks. By the time war broke out in September 1939 some thirteen front-line squadrons were flying Swordfish. Of these, twelve were at sea, embarked in carriers: HMS *Ark Royal* had Nos 810, 814, 820 and 821, HMS *Courageous* Nos 811 and 822, HMS *Eagle* Nos 813 and 824, HMS *Glorious* Nos 823 and 825 and with HMS *Furious*

**A Swordfish 'A5F' of No. 821 Squadron embarked in *Ark Royal* is brought up on the lift with the engine already running. Mixed deck crews of naval and RAF fitters/riggers were common before 1940.**

**Testing the engine before flying is Swordfish P3992 'G5K' of No. 825 Squadron when embarked in HMS *Glorious* during 1939. The squadron band and fin were in yellow with the squadron badge on the fin.** RAF Museum

***(Below)*** **Swordfish K8369 of No. 3 AACU (Anti-Aircraft Co-operation Unit) being lowered into the water, its engine already running. The target-towing winch is in position, mounted across the rear cockpit. This unit was based at Kalafrana, Malta, until 1940 when it was absorbed into No. 830 Squadron.** Charles E. Brown

***(Right)*** **Swordfish floatplanes of No. 701 Squadron were embarked on the battleship HMS *Malaya* in September 1937 for operations around Mudros. Hangars were not available for all the aircraft. Three served aboard *Malaya*: K5950 '63', K5957 '72' and K5959 '73'.**

***(Below right)*** **Preparing to launch Swordfish K5957 with the winch already fastened to the hoist hook in the centre section of the wings. The squadron badge was put on the fin.**

were Nos 816 and 818. In addition, the type served with numerous training and second-line units, such as catapult flights operating from cruisers and battleships. The last front-line squadron to receive Swordfish was No. 860, on 15 June 1943 at Donibristle. This was actually a Royal Netherlands Naval Air Service (RNNAS)-manned squadron, formed to operate from MAC-ships. It was the latter, with No. 836 Squadron, that at one time provided eighty-three Swordfish as a pool for nineteen MAC-ships. No. 836 finally disbanded on 29 July 1945. Over forty-five second-line units operated Swordfish from 1936 to 1945.

The RAF also used Swordfish. Before the war the Torpedo Development Squadron at Gosport trained RAF pilots in the art of dropping torpedoes. No. 202 Squadron operated Swordfish floatplanes from Gibraltar between October 1940 and January 1942. A number of RAF Anti-Aircraft Co-operation Units (AACU) used Swordfish for drogue-towing at places such as Malta and Seletar. No. 8 Squadron in Aden operated a flight of Swordfish for anti-submarine patrols during 1940–41. An unusual operator was No. 9 (Pilots) Advanced Flying Unit (AFU) based at Errol where naval pilots were given advanced training between August 1942 and early 1945. Operating from forward bases in Belgium, No. 119 Squadron, previously operating Wellingtons, was equipped with Albacores taken over from No. 421 (RCAF) squadron in July 1944 to carry out anti-submarine patrols in the Channel. By early 1945 the squadron was based at Bircham Newton and included Swordfish on its strength, but was eventually disbanded during May 1945.

**One squadron from *Eagle* was No. 813, also using black markings as on K8396 '587'. On 12 June 1939 this aircraft swung into the netting when landing on *Eagle* and went over the side into the sea.** H. Liddle

**THIS PAGE:**

***(Left)*** **Swordfish K8390 '946' of No. 824 Squadron aboard *Eagle*. Conversion to floats was a regular thing before the war.** H. Liddle

***(Below)*** **Two RAF fitters winding the inertia starter handle of a Swordfish aboard *Eagle*. It sometimes required two men to spin the starter enough to get the magneto to produce a strong spark. Quite a few RAF ground tradesmen transferred to the FAA in 1940.**

**OPPOSITE PAGE:**

***(Top)*** **It wasn't only male fitters who worked on Swordfish: here we see WRNS (Women's Royal Naval Service) helping with a major overhaul, with the aircraft pulled over an inspection pit.** IWM

***(Bottom)*** **These WRNS are testing and checking the radio equipment in a Swordfish on a nice, sunny day.** IWM

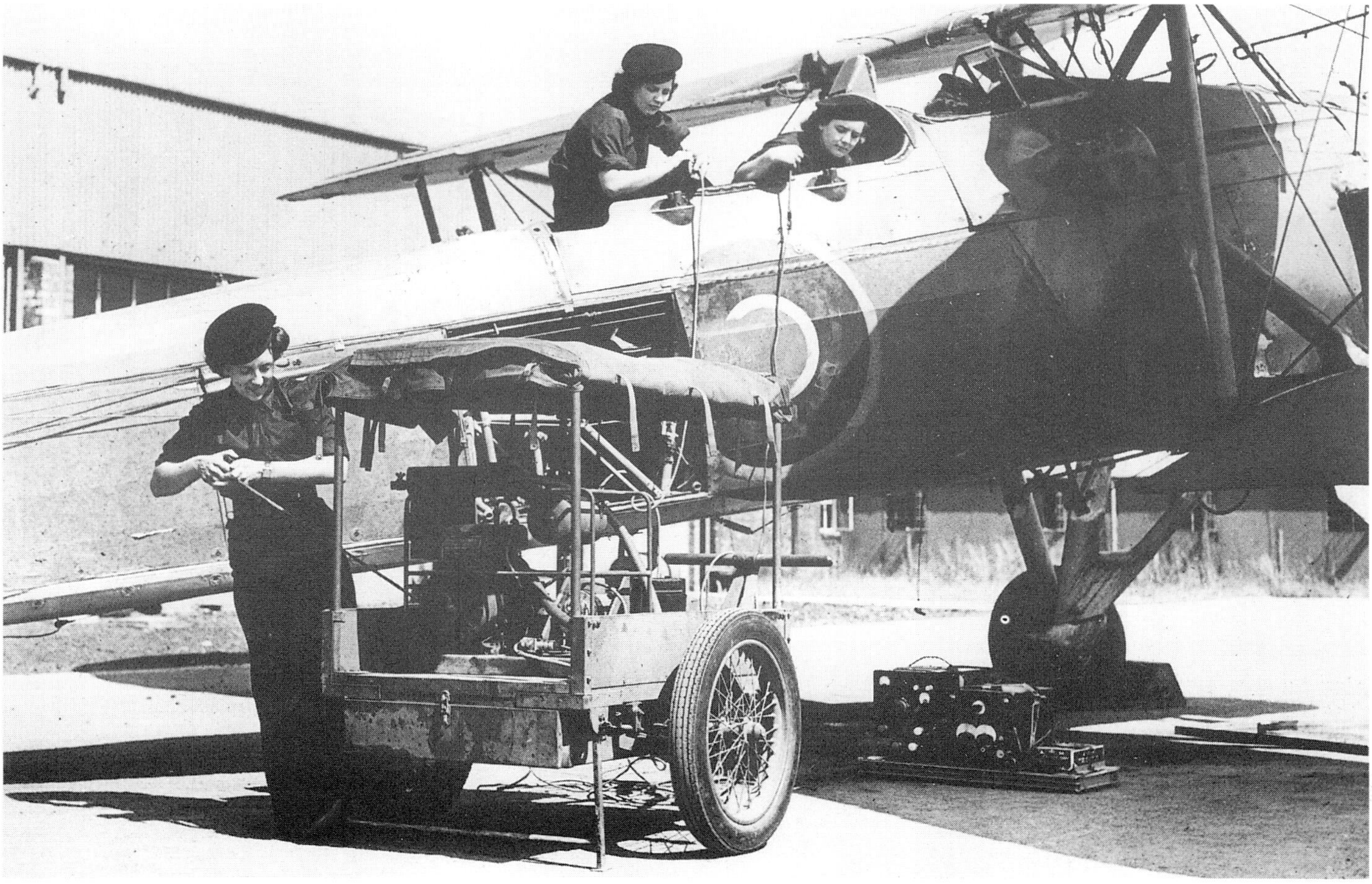

**Like other aircraft, the Swordfish had its share of problems. Here locals wonder at the skill of pilots while RAF and naval ratings examine what can be saved. K5942 of No. 823 Squadron shows the fuselage chrome yellow band from *Glorious* in 1937.**

***(Right)*** **Swordfish L2761 '610' of No. 811 Squadron, wearing the red band of *Furious*, after overshooting on landing at Turnhouse on 16 January 1939. The aircraft became a training airframe numbered 1356M.** A. G. Griffin

***(Below)*** **Not many pictures were taken of Swordfish being launched by catapult, but this one has just been catapulted from *Ark Royal* in the south Atlantic during the hunt for *Graf Spee* in 1939.**

CHAPTER FOUR

# FAA Flying Training

Upon the creation of the RAF on 1 April 1918, some 2,500 naval aircraft were transferred to the new Service, along with all the equipment and what would remain of 55,000 men after demobilization following the end of World War One on 11 November that year. All aviation matters, including those of the former RNAS, were now handled by the Air Ministry. As such, the RAF controlled most of the flying including the provision of aircraft, flying training, aircrew and maintenance groundcrew. This extended to 'sharing' air- and groundcrews, whereby an RAF pilot could be posted to a naval squadron for four years, and vice versa. Similarly, groundcrews could find themselves doing carrier duty. The Air Ministry controlled all aviation policy and the ordering of suitable aircraft types to fill different roles. Between 1919 and 1937 the Royal Navy was kept in a backwater as regards receiving modern aircraft, the RAF always demanding the best for themselves. When war was declared on 3 September 1939 the Navy still relied on the RAF for its air- and groundcrew training. In fairness, it is also true to state that many admirals had little time for naval aviation, and were not convinced otherwise until the value to the fleet of aircraft for air defence and attack was demonstrated during World War Two.

The RAF were also able to call upon a well-trained reserve of air- and groundcrew in the form of the Royal Auxiliary Air Force (RAuxAF), made up of a number of squadrons each associated with a particular town or city, for example No. 504 (City of Nottingham) Squadron. The Royal Navy did not have this luxury but could make of use the Royal Naval Reserve (RNR), an organization of people who had served in the Merchant Navy and brought with them lots of experience. The Royal Naval Volunteer Reserve (RNVR) were the 'hostilities only' branch, which provided many of the aircrew required for the FAA during World War Two, as well as officers and ratings serving in all branches of the RN. The RNVR air branch was recognized by appending (A) after the rank, for example Lt (A) O. N. E. Pegleg RNVR. The RNVR's origins go back to 1903, and during World War One many fought as part of the RNAS before being absorbed into the new RAF on 1 April 1918.

In 1924 the Fleet Air Arm was formed within the RAF, with 70 per cent of the pilots and all the observers being naval officers. In 1931 the Air Ministry, under pressure from the Admiralty, appointed Rear Admiral R. G. Henderson as Rear Admiral, Aircraft Carriers. After a long, hard fight within the corridors of power, the FAA became a branch of the Royal Navy in 1938 with its headquarters at Lee-on-Solent airfield which became HMS *Daedalus*. Thereafter all FAA bases were given names prefixed by RNAS (for Royal Naval Air Station), for example RNAS Lee-on-Solent.

With war looming, the new branch started recruiting; in the meantime the RAF loaned them 1,500 mechanics, of whom over 800 later transferred to the FAA. By the outbreak of war the Naval Air Branch had 300 pilots and observers, 232 first-line aircraft – over half of these being Swordfish – eight aircraft carriers and four naval air stations. With the influx of wartime RNVR aircrew the numbers swelled: in mid-1942 there were 1,514 pilots and 392 observers, increasing to over 4,000 pilots and 800 observers by the end of 1943. By 1945 the four air stations had become forty-five scattered worldwide, and the eight carriers had swelled to fifty-two.

## Pilots

Selection for naval aircrew during the early days of the war usually started with a visit to Gosport, or HMS *St Vincent* as it was known. After a medical the candidate appeared before an interview board and, if successful, was offered a position as a pilot or observer.

The recruits, who started as Naval Airman 2nd Class, spent seven weeks at *St Vincent* learning how to march, salute and clean their kit, and the rudiments of navigation, meteorology, Morse code, navigation and semaphoring. On passing out they joined one of the Elementary Flying Training Schools such as No. 14 EFTS at Elmdon, now Birmingham Airport, or at Luton. The first few RNVR pilots were given their elementary flying training by civilian pilots under contract, but later some naval pilots received their basic flying instruction from RAF instructors in RAF aircraft, such as the de Havilland Tiger Moth or Miles Magister, at RAF stations. These trainees then moved to No. 1 Service Flying Training School (SFTS) at Netheravon to be selected for fighter pilot training or TSR pilot. In the early days the flying training at SFTS would have started on Fairey Battles as a starter to join Skua or Fulmar squadrons, but later it moved on to Sea Hurricanes, Seafires, Wildcats or Hellcats, and eventually the formidable Corsair. TSR pilots would move on to Swordfish or Albacore squadrons, but later probably Fairey Fireflies or Grumman Avengers. Once they had been awarded their 'wings' they moved to operational training units, with all naval pilots and observers receiving commissions.

At this time there was some concern about German aircraft roaming the UK skies and the authorities decided that a percentage of the trainee pilots would go to Canada or America to receive their training without the worry of being shot down in the process. Therefore, some trainees were sent to America under the Towers Scheme. This was originally set up by Admiral Towers of the USN to train thirty FAA pilots a month and 100 for the RAF, operating from the USN base at Pensacola. Those aircrew sent to Pensacola found themselves in another world, seemingly remote from the struggle going on in Europe. The base Commanding Officer was Captain A. C. Read, who in 1919 had led the famous flight of flying boats across the Atlantic via the Azores. Their training was pure flying and classroom work with no base duties. The flying training, however, was streamed as fighter pilot or TSR pilot, the instructors being very strict: students could be 'washed out' for things such as air sickness or poor height judgement. Flying was in different aircraft to those used in the UK, basic flying being in the Naval Aircraft Factory N3N-3 or Vought OS2U-3 Kingfisher. Those selected for fighters moved to Opa Locka, about 14 miles (22km) north of Miami, to fly the North American SNJ-3 (known in the UK as the Harvard). Early trainee pilots then moved on to Brewster Buffalos (supplied to the UK under Lend-Lease but hopelessly outclassed by enemy fighters) and later in the war moved on to Grumman Wildcats, Hellcats and Chance Vought Corsairs. TSR pilots moved on to the SNJ in the USA, but then returned to the UK for training on the Swordfish or Albacore.

Deck-landing training started with Aerodrome Dummy Deck Landings (ADDLs) and then using USS *Challenger*, an escort carrier originally intended for the Royal Navy but instead retained for training purposes. Two paddle-steamers were converted into 'flat-tops' as USS *Sable* and *Wolverine* to provide deck-landing training without the USN having to use an operational carrier. Once a pilot had completed his flying training, there was still much training to do before becoming a useful member of an operational squadron, so he returned to the UK for operational training before joining a squadron.

In the case of TSR pilots this meant Crail. On 4 November 1940 No. 785 Squadron had been formed at Crail to provide torpedo-bomber-reconnaissance (TBR) training. Initial equipment consisted of five Swordfish and thirteen Sharks, although as more Swordfish arrived the Sharks were dispensed with. By August 1941 the squadron consisted of Swordfish and Albacores, as did No. 786 Squadron, formed on 21 November alongside No. 785 at Crail to provide similar training. Operational training consisted of seven weeks at Crail learning to drop torpedoes, followed by three weeks' deck-landing training to RN standards at Arbroath. Additionally they did formation flying, night flying, depth-charge dropping and dive-bombing.

**Aspiring naval pilots undergoing basic flying training in Tiger Moths at No. 14 EFTS (Elementary Flying Training School) at Elmdon, now Birmingham Airport. This was good training for the pilots sent to TSR squadrons, as the Tiger Moth also had open cockpits and the Sidcot suit worn by these trainee pilots afforded some protection from the elements!**

The TBR/TSR pilot usually began his training with low flying over the sea, taking off with a dummy torpedo, aiming and making different types of attack without dropping it, and then landing with it. A visit to a target ship allowed them the luxury of seeing how an attack should be made, in the first case by instructors. The next stage was to drop dummy torpedoes as part of a sub-flight and led by an instructor. Then it was on to the 'runners', as live torpedo practice was called. Night attacks were also part of the course, the target being lit by flares. The flare-carrier was fitted under the aircraft on the torpedo rack and contained twelve parachute flares. In action the leader would carry the flares, and after reaching the target would make his way round to the far side while the attacking force circled. When in position, a curtain of flares was dropped at 3,000–4,000ft, silhouetting the target for the strike aircraft. Towards the end of the course the trainee would make an attack as part of a squadron where each sub-flight would attack from different directions. The sensation of such an attack was recorded by Terence Horsley in *Find, Fix and Strike*:

> ... But the torpedo attack is probably unique, in that the dive, at the steepest possible angle consistent with maintaining control, is quite sensational. The airspeed indicator does two complete revolutions of the clock, the bracing wires of the 'Stringbag' [i.e. Swordfish] shriek in wild chorus [Another pilot said 'In this dive it was by no means unusual to register speeds of 200kt, though the old hands will tell you a far more reliable guide was a certain musical note, corresponding approximately to middle C, caused by the many wires and struts humming in the breeze!'], the whine of the supercharger as the engine revs mount to a peak sounding unearthly, and added to all this is the small voice of the pilot who either shouts or sings – a trick which helps to equalize the changing air pressures between his lungs, ears and the outside world.
>
> Seven or eight thousand feet below, the enemy's ships look like toy boats on a smooth pond. They can only be seen by peering closely over the side, for the dive is so vertical that the target seems to be immediately below.
>
> The aircraft are at first in line-astern. The leader throttles back, lifts the nose of his machine a trifle, pushes the stick hard over to one side, and as she falls away, presses the control column forward for a steeper and ever steeper dive. The speed mounts. The enemy comes into view over the top wing. The pilot opens the throttle a trifle to ease the strain on the motor. The needle of the ASI creeps round and the throttle is opened further to one-third. The speed mounts still more. The pressure of the stick against the pilot's right hand is now very heavy. The aircraft is trying to come out of the dive, but the pilot is holding her in, holding her so that the ship, which is growing bigger by leaps and bounds, remains steady in his vision.
>
> Now comes the vital part of the attack – the pull-out to within a few feet of the water. An error of judgement now would be disastrous. It begins at about 500ft – a gentle relaxation of the pressure of the right hand, developing quickly into the need for a definite pull on the stick. The force of the wind on the control surfaces is tremendous. A greater and greater pull is needed as the path of the aircraft flattens out. The nose must be pulled up – up and up as the shape of the ripples on the water begin to define themselves like a developing film. Fifty feet is such a little distance at such a speed ... The judgement of distance, born of long practice, is not made easier by upward rain of coloured tracer from the enemy. The pilot sees it all the time, coming up slowly at first, and then accelerating into little bars of light which flick past with the speed of shooting stars.
>
> He is down near the water now. The needle of the ASI is dropping back. One complete revolution of the clock has been made in the reverse direction, and the throttle has been closed again to help the aircraft to lose her speed. The torpedo has to be coaxed into the water. Its belly, full of easily upset gyroscopes, must not be banged down into the water. Yet the sooner it is over the better. The sea ahead is a smother of white flecks as the enemy's pom-poms tear up the surface, and the heavier shells ricochet off again. The greatest restraint is needed to get the speed off, to hold the course of the aircraft rock steady, not merely lining up the deflection sights, but holding her straight and level, as though this was a flying test at an elementary training school.
>
> The target is now a grey bulk lying across the sights – a bulk split down its sides by innumerable spurts of flame. The range is point-blank.
>
> The end of the suspense comes within a matter of seconds. The pilot's thumb, already on the push-button on top of the throttle, jabs hard against the stop. Almost simultaneously the palm of the same hand pushes the throttle lever forward until it too comes to rest against its stop at the far end of the slide. The boost over-ride is slid back, and then full stick and top rudder come on for a sensationally steep turn just above the water.
>
> Evasive action! Horizontal aerobatics on full throttle with a fading view of the target for the observer over the stern. The next 30 seconds will decide whether they have 'got away with it'. It is the observer's party now. He's standing up, swinging from side to side to keep the thin white track which is the torpedo in view. For him, the only thing which matters is the meeting of that track with the target. He may see out of the corner of his eye the other aircraft of his squadron as the centre of little maelstroms of anti-aircraft

**Most TSR pilots would get a chance to fly the dual Swordfish at training units, and some squadrons had them for continuation and refresher flying, such as K5934 seen here at Gosport in 1936.** RAF Museum

> fire. But the bright flash against the enemy's side is what he has been waiting for. 'Please, God, let it be a hit' is the prayer which has been repeated in these tense moments many a time. Maybe it is not very Christian, but the justification of his existence as a naval airman is at stake.
>
> It is all over. The rain of fire sags and drops short. The observer flops back into his seat. The pilot relaxes, pushes forward the over-ride which has given him extra power for his getaway, and throttles back to cruising revs. They climb. Astern of the enemy, at several thousand feet, they wait in slow circles for the approach of the other aircraft from the inferno of smoke and orange flame. They come one by one, almost incredibly, like insects which have flown through a bonfire.
>
> They are a squadron again. A laconic voice from the rear cockpit of the leader booms down the intercom. 'Home James: 035 magnetic at 90kt – we ought to sight the carrier in 78 minutes'.

During the early war years a Swordfish could be induced to flog along at 110kt, but later when every conceivable device the Admiralty needed to conduct the air war at sea was hung on it, 90kt was usual. However, even later in the war the propeller pitch was fined off a bit to give a better take-off performance on the smaller escort carriers or MAC-ships, after which 85kt was more likely.

Not all torpedo strikes were like this copybook attack, some were made at night in appalling weather conditions. The sound basic training and constant practice would only be judged in a real-life situation attack. Alan Ryman recalls:

> All pilots were required to keep a graph [Form S.424] showing the results of each practice [torpedo] attack made. This was to show our ability and especially how, or perhaps if, we improved with training. Of twenty-one practice attacks in which the 'Result of Shot' could be assessed I scored sixteen hits and five misses. This was considered to be quite a good result and I earned a 'Good Average' endorsement in my logbook at the end of the course at Crail.

Before World War Two, deck-landing training was the responsibility of No. 811 Squadron which, although carrying a front-line number, operated as a training unit, but provided an idea of how a front-line squadron functioned. In those days a batch of twelve new pilots were taken on by the squadron every six weeks. All the ground training and personnel were based at Donibristle, and when sufficient numbers of pupils were ready for their first deck-landings, four Swordfish and two de Havilland Gipsy Moths were taken out to HMS *Courageous* with the relevant operating staff. Upon joining *Courageous* each trainee pilot made three landings in a Gipsy Moth: the first was flown by an instructor to demonstrate the technique, with the trainee making the second and third landings. Once the instructor was satisfied with the trainee's performance, the trainee was transferred to a Swordfish and made three dummy approaches before landing on the fourth. During a week at sea pilots carried out about thirty landings, including one with a passenger, one with a torpedo and one without using the arrestor wires. This training brought the pilots into contact with deck arrestor gear, flag signals aboard ship, deck parties and the 'batsman'. When a pilot had demonstrated he was competent and the course was over, the party returned to Donibristle and he would be posted to a flying unit. Deck-landing training moved to Arbroath during the war.

**The pilot's cockpit of the Swordfish, showing the control column and instrumentation. The white-collared lever is the fuel control cock.** BAe Systems Brough Heritage Centre

***(Right)* The port side of the pilot's cockpit. The ring at bottom left was pulled out once the engine speed – via the two-man handle outside – reached 80rpm. Once the engine fired, the starting magneto on the far left was switched on and the external starting handle could be disengaged.** BAe Systems Brough Heritage Centre

## Observer Training

The position of observer was not one sought by aspiring aircrew: pilot was more acceptable than observer, the glamour of the fighter pilot eclipsing all other roles. Observers had to be expert in many other roles: navigation, operating wireless and radar equipment, photography, air gunnery, aircraft and ship recognition and, in the case of the latter, estimating their type, course and speed for an attack.

This all started, after selection, at observer school, flying in aircraft and trying to navigate without the use of landmarks and in the face of the vagaries of wind, fog and cloud. The role of the observer in naval aviation created something of an enigma, inasmuch as the higher echelons of the Royal Navy believed that even a fighter pilot needed an observer (navigator) if he was to do his job properly and return to the carrier safely. Consequently, and especially in the early part of the war all naval aircraft, even fighters, carried an observer to get the pilot back to the ship. Although he could, and did, provide a useful role, the weight of the observer and his equipment seriously affected an aircraft's performance. However, in the essential role of torpedo attack, a well-trained crew of pilot, observer and TAG could be a formidable team.

The specialist Observer branch was formed within the RN in 1920. Thereafter only naval-trained Observers could fly as such in naval aircraft. After two months of basic training the Observer passed out as a Acting Leading Naval Airman. He would then go to HMS *Excellent* (a shore unit) to carry out gunnery training, followed by two months going through navigation, signalling, wireless-telegraphy and other subjects. He then moved to either No. 1 Observers School in the West Indies or No. 2 Observers School at Arbroath, to start air exercises in Swordfish, Albacores or Walrus aircraft. Here he would learn to find his way about in the air without using landmarks, relying on his skill as a navigator. Most carriers later had a beacon on board and the Observer could pick this up to check his position. Eventually he would become a qualified Observer capable of bringing his pilot into contact with the enemy, despite wind, fog and cloud, and then find his way back to the carrier, if need be, in the dark.

No. 1 Observer School was initially set up at Ford in 1939, out of the RN Observers School, but when Ford was bombed it moved to Yeovilton. However, in the fear that such training units might be bombed at some future date it was decided to carry out observer training overseas. Consequently it moved to Piarco in Trinidad, West Indies. Here, Nos 749, 750 and 752 Squadrons provided training in a wide range of aircraft: Albacores, Barracudas, Percival Proctors, Supermarine Walrus

**Each pilot was required to undertake a catapult launch take-off in preparation for such launches when serving on a carrier. Here a pilot has just left the catapult at Gosport in March 1939.** Fox Photos

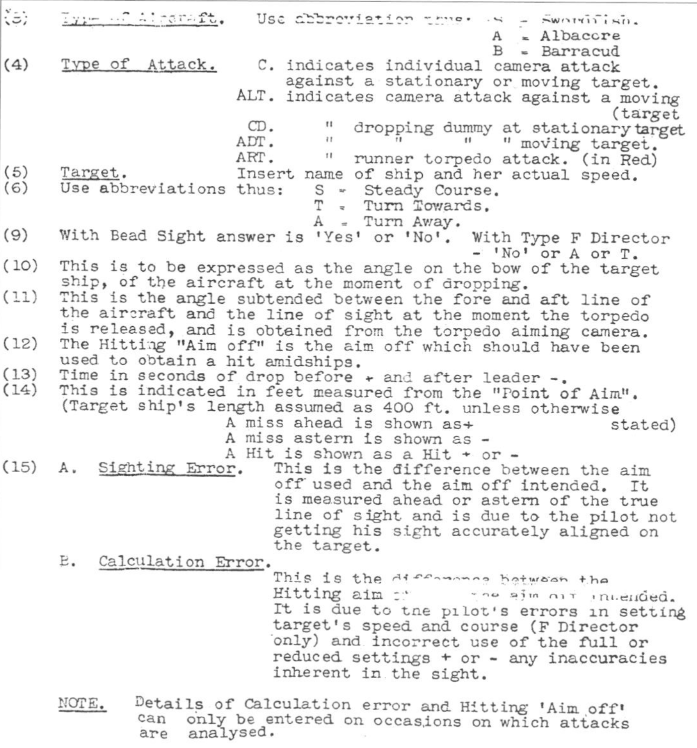

(3) Type of Aircraft. Use abbreviation thus: S - Swordfish.
A - Albacore
B - Barracud

(4) Type of Attack. C. indicates individual camera attack against a stationary or moving target.
ALT. indicates camera attack against a moving (target
CD. " dropping dummy at stationary target
ADT. " " " " moving target.
ART. " runner torpedo attack. (in Red)

(5) Target. Insert name of ship and her actual speed.

(6) Use abbreviations thus: S - Steady Course.
T - Turn Towards.
A - Turn Away.

(9) With Bead Sight answer is 'Yes' or 'No'. With Type F Director - 'No' or A or T.

(10) This is to be expressed as the angle on the bow of the target ship, of the aircraft at the moment of dropping.

(11) This is the angle subtended between the fore and aft line of the aircraft and the line of sight at the moment the torpedo is released, and is obtained from the torpedo aiming camera.

(12) The Hitting "Aim off" is the aim off which should have been used to obtain a hit amidships.

(13) Time in seconds of drop before + and after leader -.

(14) This is indicated in feet measured from the "Point of Aim". (Target ship's length assumed as 400 ft. unless otherwise stated)
A miss ahead is shown as +
A miss astern is shown as -
A Hit is shown as a Hit + or -

(15) A. Sighting Error. This is the difference between the aim off used and the aim off intended. It is measured ahead or astern of the true line of sight and is due to the pilot not getting his sight accurately aligned on the target.

B. Calculation Error.
This is the difference between the Hitting aim [illegible] aim off intended. It is due to the pilot's errors in setting target's speed and course (F Director only) and incorrect use of the full or reduced settings + or - any inaccuracies inherent in the sight.

NOTE. Details of Calculation error and Hitting 'Aim off' can only be entered on occasions on which attacks are analysed.

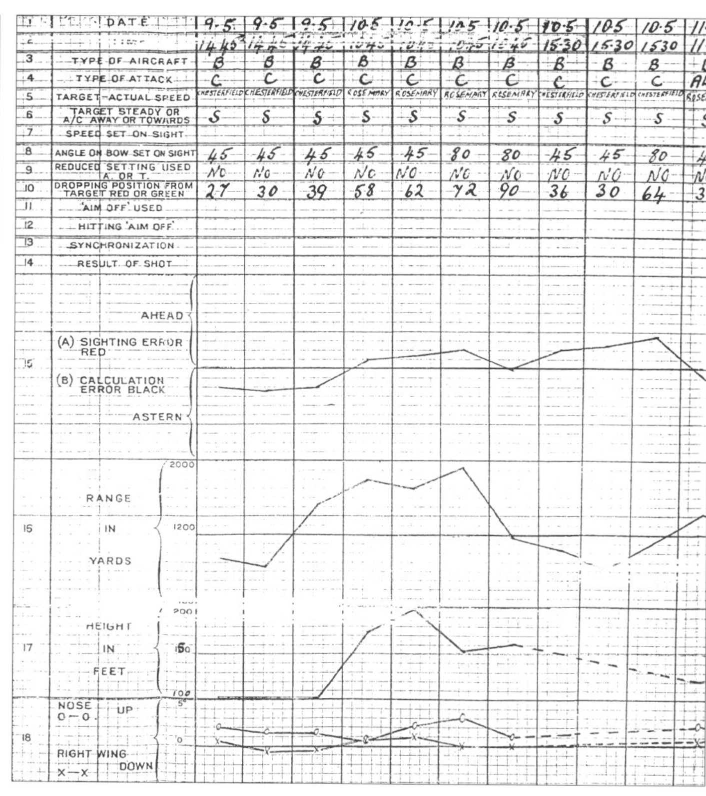

| | | | | | | | | | | | | |
|---|---|---|---|---|---|---|---|---|---|---|---|---|
| 1 | DATE | 9·5 | 9·5 | 9·5 | 10·5 | 10·5 | 10·5 | 10·5 | 10·5 | 10·5 | 10·5 | 11· |
| 2 | [illegible] | 1445 | 1445 | [illegible] | [illegible] | [illegible] | [illegible] | [illegible] | 15·30 | 15·30 | 1530 | 11· |
| 3 | TYPE OF AIRCRAFT | B | B | B | B | B | B | B | B | B | B | B |
| 4 | TYPE OF ATTACK | C | C | C | C | C | C | C | C | C | C | AL |
| 5 | TARGET – ACTUAL SPEED | CHESTERFIELD | CHESTERFIELD | CHESTERFIELD | ROSEMARY | ROSEMARY | ROSEMARY | ROSEMARY | CHESTERFIELD | CHESTERFIELD | CHESTERFIELD | ROSE |
| 6 | TARGET STEADY OR A/C AWAY OR TOWARDS | S | S | S | S | S | S | S | S | S | S | S |
| 7 | SPEED SET ON SIGHT | | | | | | | | | | | |
| 8 | ANGLE ON BOW SET ON SIGHT | 45 | 45 | 45 | 45 | 45 | 80 | 80 | 45 | 45 | 80 | 4 |
| 9 | REDUCED SETTING USED A. OR T. | NO | NO | NO | NO | NO | NO | NO | NO | NO | NO | N |
| 10 | DROPPING POSITION FROM TARGET RED OR GREEN | 27 | 30 | 39 | 58 | 62 | 72 | 90 | 36 | 30 | 64 | 3 |
| 11 | 'AIM OFF' USED | | | | | | | | | | | |
| 12 | HITTING 'AIM OFF' | | | | | | | | | | | |
| 13 | SYNCHRONIZATION | | | | | | | | | | | |
| 14 | RESULT OF SHOT | | | | | | | | | | | |

15 AHEAD
(A) SIGHTING ERROR RED
(B) CALCULATION ERROR BLACK
ASTERN

16 RANGE IN YARDS 2000 1200

17 HEIGHT IN FEET 200 150 100

18 NOSE O—O UP DOWN RIGHT WING X—X

An example of the torpedo attack training record kept by all pilots.

One important aspect of pilot training was formation flying, firstly as a flight, and later at squadron strength. Here three 'vics' of three from No. 1 NAGS demonstrate a typical squadron formation. J. Bryant

and Grumman Goose. It had been intended to use Swordfish but in 1940 they were all needed, and Albacores were substituted. No. 2 Observer School was based at Arbroath and was made up of Nos 740, 741, 753 and 754 Squadrons, again operating a variety of aircraft the observers would fly once posted to a squadron. Like most military organizations the observers had their own parody, in this case of Kipling, to reflect their lot in life:

If you can keep your track when all about you
Are losing theirs and setting 'mag' for 'true',
If you can trust yourself when pilots doubt you
And get back to the ship out of the blue;
If you can keep control of your dividers
And Bigsworth board and Gosport tube and pad,
Or listen to the wireless and the pilot
Talking in unison – and not go mad ...
If you can fill the unforgiving minute
With sixty seconds' worth of ground-speed run,
Yours is the Air – and everything that's in it,
And – what is more – you'll be an 'O', my son!

## TAG Training

The first TAGs (telegraphist air gunner) appeared around 1922 when a number of ratings trained in wireless telegraphy volunteered for aircrew duties. They were expected to operate any guns in the rear cockpit in addition to their normal job of operating the wireless. Although they drew flying pay their status remained as ratings: TAGs were not offered commissions although they undertook the same risks as pilot or observer. During World War Two volunteers for TAG (Aircrew) duties were drawn from the telegraphist and seaman branches, from the Royal Marines and Royal Navy 'Y' entry scheme for ex-ATC or Sea Cadets.

Once accepted, they attended the RN Signals School at Portsmouth, HMS *Vincent* or HMS *Royal Arthur* before going to No. 1 Air Gunners School at RNAS Worthy Down, near Winchester. TAG training was provided by Nos 755, 756, 757 and 758 Squadrons. The syllabus of instruction at these schools included wireless telegraphy (W/T), Morse, wireless procedure, theory, radio telegraphy (R/T), fleet and spotting procedure, flags, semaphore, coding and decoding signals, visual signalling by Aldis lamp, air radar procedures, camera guns, aircraft recognition and target-towing. This was usually a mix of classroom work and airborne experience.

On successfully completing around sixty hours of flying training they attended the Air Armament Training Station at St Merryn, Cornwall. Here they mastered the intricacies of the Lewis, Browning and Vickers machine-guns and cine-camera guns, and then put it all to the test in air-to-air firing, air-to-ground and aerial attack exercises.

On passing out they became Acting Leading Air Gunner 3rd Class and, hopefully, were posted to a squadron to begin training as part of a team. This included non-flying activities such as manning the ship's radar and anti-aircraft guns, being part of the deck-handlers and a number of other duties. However, it was 1942 before the Admiralty recognised TAGs as aircrew and allowed them to sew TAG 'wings' on the left cuff of their uniform. As the war progressed some became Petty Officers and Chief Petty Officer Airmen. Later types of attack aircraft still required air gunners and TAGs operated until the end of the war.

In 1942 the Admiralty approached the Canadian Government about setting up a school in Canada for TAG training. As a result of this a document dated 11 December 1942 was raised with the title 'Secret Organisational Order Number 104'. This agreed that No. 1 Naval Air Gunners School would be established under the British Commonwealth Air Training Plan at the Canadian base at Yarmouth, Nova Scotia. All administration was to be handled by the RCAF with aircraft supplied by both countries. As such, three second-line units were set up: No. 745 with forty-three Swordfish supplied by the Admiralty, No. 743 with twenty-three Ansons provided by the RCAF and No. 744 with forty Stinson Reliants, which would come directly from the USA.

**Another formation training exercise photographed in 1940.** IWM

The first Commanding Officer was Wing Commander D. D. Finlay RCAF, who assumed command on 11 January 1943. The first four Swordfish IIs were taken on strength on 6 February 1943 but the Reliant order was changed to Curtiss Seamews on 1 March 1943 with first deliveries from Roosevelt Field, New York, starting a few days later. The Seamew proved to be a disappointment – all were grounded for lack of starter cartridges for the air-cooled Ranger engine, and the tailwheel needed strengthening. There had been many cases of tailwheels collapsing, some wag saying that it was the fault of the FAA pilots not used to American toe-brakes! Technicians from Curtiss-Wright arrived and modified three Seamews with pneumatic tailwheels and stiffened the rear fuselage to handle the stresses. At one time the school wanted to change the Seamews for more Ansons but they got more Swordfish instead! By 31 May the school strength consisted of twenty-seven Swordfish, twenty-three Ansons, sixty Seamews (all grounded) and one Walrus for air-sea rescue. Wing Commander Finlay was replaced on 5 June 1943 by Commander I. M. N. Mudie.

Normal training procedure for the trainee TAGs was to do their radio training in the Swordfish, then to move on to Ansons which could train two at a time. Final gunnery training was to be done on the Seamews, where they would practice live firing with a camera gun, but the withdrawal of the Seamews meant Swordfish were used.

A large number of aircraft used for training duties would, inevitably, have a number

**Some training of TAGs was moved to Canada and Swordfish were provided, along with a modification that gave the TAG protection from the cold: an enclosed cockpit. Some 105 Swordfish and five Albacores found their way to Canada, some later being modified as target towers.** R. A. Goss

***(Below)*** **The modification fitted to Swordfish in Canada. HS553 was the test aircraft for the new canopy, but why on earth could they not be fitted for use on cold runs such as Arctic convoys?**

of accidents. The first was when Swordfish HS322 had to force-land, damaging its port mainplane and propeller, on 8 April. Another Swordfish force-landed on 24 June 1943 when HS486 landed on a beach at Cotton Bay, Lockeport, Nova Scotia, but was flown off successfully four days later. Robert A. Joss suffered an engine failure in HS487 on 16 October, a result of excessive boost in a steep turn. Joss was involved in another mishap on 28 January 1944 when he wrote off HS486, the Swordfish in the force-landing incident the previous June. The aircraft crashed near New France, Southville, about 20 miles (32km) inland from Weymouth, Nova Scotia. He stated:

> [The] cause was an incorrectly assembled fuel-cock. The Swordfish had a rather peculiar arrangement of fuel tanks, consisting of a main tank and a gravity tank which was kept full by the engine-driven fuel pump with an overflow into the main tank. The correct procedure was to take off with the fuel cock selecting 'main only' and, once airborne and cruising, to switch to 'normal', in which case the gravity tank was kept topped up by some of the fuel from the fuel pump, so that there was always an emergency supply in the gravity tank should the fuel pump itself pack up. In this particular instance the aircraft had just come back from servicing and the indicator on the fuel-cock was assembled rotated 90 degrees on its shaft. When I selected 'normal' I was actually running on 'gravity' and in due course drained the gravity tank. We were fairly low over trees at the time and I had no choice but to pancake into the forest. We landed on top of a tall, dead tree which I couldn't see, and the aircraft rolled up into a ball! I received a broken left ankle and a broken right thigh, the joyrider behind me a cracked hip, but the poor student, who didn't even know we were crashing, wasn't injured, perhaps due to his rearward-facing seat. Some loggers from a nearby camp got us out of the aircraft, minutes after the crash.

The Swordfish Mk IV appeared on strength during February 1944. These were locally modified Mk IIs with a totally enclosed top, the rear gunner having a clamshell-type door which, when opened, enabled him to have a clear field of fire to the rear with his Vickers K gun. Modification No. 408 had been raised by Fairey in the UK after requests for protection from the Canadian winters. Swordfish HS554 did all the approval flying in the UK. All the open-cockpit Swordfish IIs at the Britannia Royal Naval College at Dartmouth were flown to Yarmouth for their updates.

On 19 July 1943 a Swordfish modified to carry target-towing gear had made its first test flight. This was not new, Swordfish having been capable of being quickly converted for target-towing duties by a kit. Later on, eight of the Swordfish IVs were modified to carry out target towing and had their undersides painted with the usual black and yellow stripes. Although never given an approved designation, these eight were referred to at Yarmouth as Swordfish Mk IVAs.

Eight days after Joss's crash, flying training at No. 1 NAGS ceased and all the pilots were posted overseas, except of course for Joss, as he was in hospital! All training at the school ended on 19 March 1945 and the station closed on 30 March 1945. Fourteen months after this the Royal Canadian Navy withdrew the Swordfish from service use in Canada, although they initially kept six at Dartmouth for communications duties, operating as part of No. 743 Squadron. By November 1948 the

**An interesting picture of torpedoes on their trolleys with hydraulic jacks to push the torpedo up to the crutches under the fuselage. These are intended for the Albacores of this training squadron.** R. E. F. Kerrison

**Albacores out on a training exercise. N4294 '13' and X9114 '6' display a 1940 colour scheme, some still with serials under the wings. The numerals have been painted crudely on by brush.** R. E. F. Kerrison

***(Below)*** **Apprehensive trainee pilots watch one of their colleagues attempting a deck landing prior to having a go themselves. This was on *Courageous* in 1939, the nearest pilot being PO Fred Rice, who went on to fly a Swordfish floatplane from HMS *Warspite* during the Norwegian Campaign and won a DSC.** *Flight*

**The flight deck of *Argus*, the ship on which many FAA pilots made their first deck landings.** Fitzsimmonds

***(Below)* The view seen by the TAG as a Swordfish leaves the deck, in this case of MAC-ship *Amastra*. The short take-off run is quite apparent in this interesting picture.**

Swordfish was considered a bit 'long in the tooth' for a modern navy and they finally left the Service.

Of the rest, eleven were flown to naval reserve units across Canada for use as ground instructional airframes. Many ended up as scrap, but Ernest Simmonds, an eccentric collector of military hardware, bought seven for £15 each and put them in his collection. During his lifetime he constantly refused to sell anything on his farm at Courtland, Ontario, but he finally agreed to one Swordfish being sold to the National Air Museum at Ottawa. This was eventually rebuilt to static condition by the joint efforts of the RCN and The Fairey Aviation Co. Ltd of Canada. It was difficult to find any true identification on any of the Swordfish at Simmonds' Farm so their choice eventually became NS122 TH-M, one of the post-war aircraft. After his death the best of the remaining Swordfish were put to auction and bought by various people with plans to restore them to flying condition. Nick Pocock, an Englishman living in Texas, bought two, selling one on to fund work on the other. Bob Spense managed to get his in the air again after a long rebuild. It flies to air displays as HS554. Other projects continue.

**Getting off the deck was one thing, getting back onto it was quite another. Here a Swordfish pilot lines up to join his carrier.** IWM

## Flight Deck Party

Each flight deck party was composed of an officer and twenty ratings, each party working in four-hour watches. They handled all aircraft and associated equipment to conduct an efficient operation when flying took place. Skilled tradesmen were known as Artificers, while less-skilled ratings were known as naval air mechanics, and could be a Air Mechanic (A), known in the RAF as a rigger, or Air Mechanic (E) who worked on aircraft engines. The former usually spent six months at RAF Henlow and four months at RAF Locking, near Western-Super-Mare, with Air Mechanics (E) receiving instruction at Speckington. Once aboard a carrier the flight deck parties worked in all weathers to keep the aircraft flying, and no one has put it better than Ern Crimp, one of the flight deck party on HMS *Victorious* 1941–45:

*The Aircraft Handler*

They said, here's a job to keep you
hale and hearty
I found myself as one of the flight deck party –
Pushing aircraft around on a carrier's deck
And in general sticking out my ruddy neck,
Lying flat on the deck holding on to the chocks
Above me, in slipstream, the aircraft
trembles and rocks,
With your wits all about you,
you need to look out
For with all the noise, lost, is any warning shout
You're so very aware of that flashing airscrew
And all the damage that it could do,
'Away chocks' comes the signal,
you then wrench them clear
As in all directions your eyes frantically peer,
To the edge of the deck you then run so fast
The aircraft takes off with a strong engine blast –

For a while there's a calm just meant to deceive
As the pipe then is made, 'Stand by to
receive' …
Just when you thought that all
the danger had gone
Your job's now unhooking as they
now land on!
Standing there on the deck as the
aircraft swoop in
Is calculated to make your blood run thin …
To catch that steel hook on arrestor wires
They slam to the deck with a scream
from the tyres.

It's true that this job keeps you so hale
and hearty
Though I have my doubts if this is a 'party'?
I was told it was all part of the charm
Of being a sailor in the Fleet Air Arm –
We now push them on to the lift, strike
them down
I believe we are slow … by our Petty Officer's
heavy frown,
Then more aircraft come up and we all spread
the wings
In fact, we are doing remarkable things!
We run out of patience … we're getting
'two blocks'
As we find we are lying back down
with our chocks,
Then just to see if we can stand the strain
We fly off our aircraft all over again!

It seems as well as being hale and hearty
A sense of humour is needed in the
flight deck party …
Lying there at the wheel a-nursing my chocks
I think of gentle sea that is wet on the rocks
Of gentle surf breaking so fine on the sand,
Peacetime seaside visits that really were grand
Of Reginald Dixon's organ at Blackpool Tower …
Or that Welsh rocky coast that they call
The Gower,
Of Dartmoor, china clay pits of white …
Of cosily sleeping in a real bed at night
But on this flight deck a rolling away on the
sea
All this is just but a dream now for me.

**Just coming in over the round down ...** IWM

**... waiting for 'cut' from the batsman ...** IWM

**... caught the wire, thank God!** IWM

**THIS PAGE:**

***(Left)*** **The result of a landing gone wrong on *Argus*. Apart from shock-loading the engine and bending the propeller, both lower wings are damaged. The low-visibility roundels on the upper wings work!** Fitzsimmonds

***(Below)*** **Once trained, the different crew members were posted to training or operational units. Here two TAGs aboard *Ark Royal* don Sidcot flying suits before going flying in open cockpits.** via Ray Sturtivant

**OPPOSITE PAGE:**

***(Top)*** **Once in a squadron each crew-member became part of a team, the pilot and observer flying together as much as possible. TAGs tended to be moved around a bit more, but sometimes the same crew could stick together.** IWM

***(Bottom)*** **The open cockpit was fine in sunny climes, but in the winter more protective clothing would be required. The operation of the Fairey High Speed Gun Mounting is most apparent in this posed picture.** IWM

## Lt Cdr E. W. Whitley recalls his time as a member of deck parties, and other tasks:

I was an RAF apprentice at Halton, starting in January 1937, transferring to the FAA in mid-1939. On passing out in December 1939 I went to a clearance camp at Duckpool on the Isle of Wight.

In January 1940 I was sent to join No. 819 Squadron at Ford with three other young air fitters. I was most disappointed to be on a Swordfish squadron as I had been trained on Blenheims, Spitfires etc. On No. 819 we had twelve RN pilots, twelve observers, twelve TAGs, twelve AM(E), twelve AM(A) plus a few electricians, armourers, store bashers, a regulating CPO and team of RAF NCOs. When the aircraft arrived we fuelled them up, painted squadron letters on the fuselage and did a number of other jobs, such as smearing the wires with lanolin. The squadron, under Lt Cdr 'Daddy' Hale, worked up at Ford and then moved to West Freugh at Easter 1940. I remember the aircraft dinghies arriving and spending the Easter weekend packing all twelve, the first, not knowing how to do it, taking five hours, the last fifty-five minutes. In May two Swordfish flown by Lts Garton-Stone and Shelton flew to Speke to conduct flying trials aboard the new carrier, *Illustrious*. The Swordfish were towed to Gladstone Dock and lifted on board by a dockside crane: Swordfish had a built-in sling hook on the centre section.

Out in the Irish Sea I joined the pilot of Swordfish L5L to make the first deck landing on the ship's armoured deck. On the way to Greenock some engine-less Swordfish were fired off the catapult to test it, much to the consternation of some local fishing boats! After the trials we flew to Roborough before embarking for the ship's shakedown cruise to Bermuda. This was a welcome break, then back to the Clyde for some repairs, and for some a spot of leave, before departing for the Med in August 1940.

We had time in Gibraltar to meet some chums in *Ark Royal*, and then through to join the Eastern Mediterranean Fleet on the first anniversary of the outbreak of war. The squadron flew anti-submarine patrols from dawn to dusk, which gave us a long day, especially when we had a role change and bombed up for raids on the Greek islands and North Africa. The squadron laid magnetic mines and for the raids on desert targets the bombs had long extensions on the nose to achieve an explosion before they buried themselves in the sand.

In heavy weather the Swordfish took a fearful bashing at sea: being at readiness on deck meant being ranged with wings folded, even with bombs on. We had problems with the tailwheel tyres and oleos when consistently left loaded. We made up tyres from discs of old main wheel tyres when the constant use and damage from landing on and crossing wires and barriers used up all our stocks of spare tyres. Sea blast also caused damage to the fabric-covered wings and fuselage, and if not careful we lost bits overboard.

The Swordfish had Minor inspections at thirty hours, which at that time meant every week, and a Major inspection at 120 hours, every four or five weeks. During all this work we changed the fuel tanks for a self-sealing version. I reconnected the pipes finger tight and my fitter chum, Wilf Jones, thought I had fitted them properly and wire-locked them up. The result on testing was a shower of fuel in the CO's face! On return to harbour we inevitably had to fit the heavy target-towing winch to one aircraft for gunnery practice. The Fleet was based at Alexandria and when in harbour our aircraft flew ashore to Dekheila.

**A crew in sensible flying kit about to go flying.**

**A young Sub-Lt M. B. W. Howell, wearing suitable flying kit, finds his way into the Swordfish cockpit.**
M. B. W. Howell

CHAPTER FIVE

# Torpedo Delivery and Tactics

**A pair of Swordfish belonging to the Torpedo Training Unit at Crail in 1940 being loaded with practice torpedoes.** IWM

The *Air Crew Torpedo Manual*, AP.2459A, states that 'Dropping a torpedo from aircraft is a highly skilled job.' It certainly was, and only time and constant practice improved the proficiency of the crew delivering such a weapon. One of their difficulties was that no matter how often you trained, nothing could simulate the conditions during an actual attack under fire and in bad weather. The *Manual* further states that,

> To get the best out of the torpedo, one of the first things you have to do in dropping it from an aircraft is to give it a 'good entry' into the water. After that, providing you have sighted correctly and set a proper depth setting, the torpedo should do the rest.

Simple, isn't it! It was this 'good entry' that had been the subject of much research, including what happens during the torpedo's flight through the air – the period between releasing it from the aircraft and its entry into water. In the 'good old days' torpedoes were dropped at very low heights and very slow speeds so that the time of flight in air was short and any external forces acting on the torpedo negligible. This did mean, however, that the torpedo could only be dropped from certain types of slow aircraft and that the type of attack was very limited.

## The Torpedo in the Air

As aircraft developed, the speed and height of dropping also increased, and this started to have an effect on the flight of the torpedo through the air. Generally speaking, an 18in torpedo had to be dropped so that the trajectory angle was between 14 and 24 degrees, the trajectory being the actual path of the centre of gravity of the torpedo in the air after its release. An angle below 14 degrees usually resulted in a bellyflop, while above 24 degrees the torpedo would enter a steep dive. Another way to achieve a bellyflop was to drop too fast and too low, giving a very low trajectory angle.

No fixed dropping height and speed were laid down, these depending on the type of aircraft. The parameters for delivery by the Swordfish and Albacore were known and practised constantly at torpedo training units and later on operational squadrons. As an example, at a dropping height of 100ft (30m) and a speed of 120kt (220km/h), the time of flight in the air would be 2.5 seconds, covering 170yd (155m). But let John Kilbracken take you through:

> Dropping a torpedo is an extremely tricky business. It weighs getting on for a ton and should be

THIS PAGE:

*(Above)* **Loading the torpedo under a Swordfish. It would be offered up to the two curved crutches, a wire passed around and fastened to a quick-release mechanism.** Fox Photos

*(Left)* **A torpedo after being loaded under a Swordfish. The wire can be seen near the front of the torpedo. The rear was fastened to a spring-loaded device that let go a few moments after the wire.** R. E. F. Kerrison

OPPOSITE PAGE:

**(A) Statistics of the 18in torpedo.**

**(B) The standard configuration of the 18in Mk IX torpedo.**

**(C) The air tail of a torpedo, to give greater stability whilst travelling through the air.**

**(D) The bar sight of the Swordfish's torpedo sight. The 'black' light is the moment of release in this case.**

(A)

NOTE:- WOODEN DUMMY SHEATHED IN STEEL.

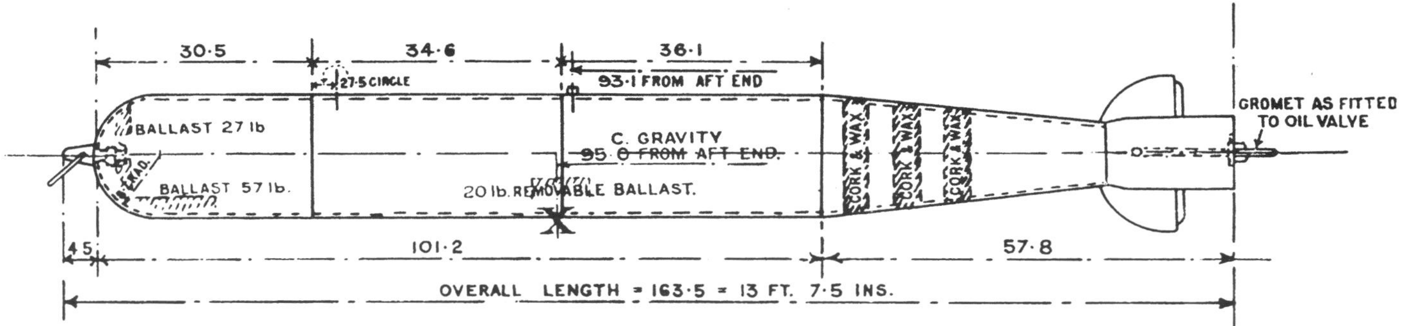


TOTAL WEIGHT IN AIR = 1076 lb. (SAME AS TORPEDO WITH WARHEAD)

BOUYANCY = +44 lb. AS SHOWN: ADDITIONAL 20 lb. CAN BE TAKEN OUT BELOW C of G. AT X.

CENTRE OF GRAVITY 95·0 FROM AFT END.

AIR LEVER.

REDUCING VALVE.

43·85

(B)

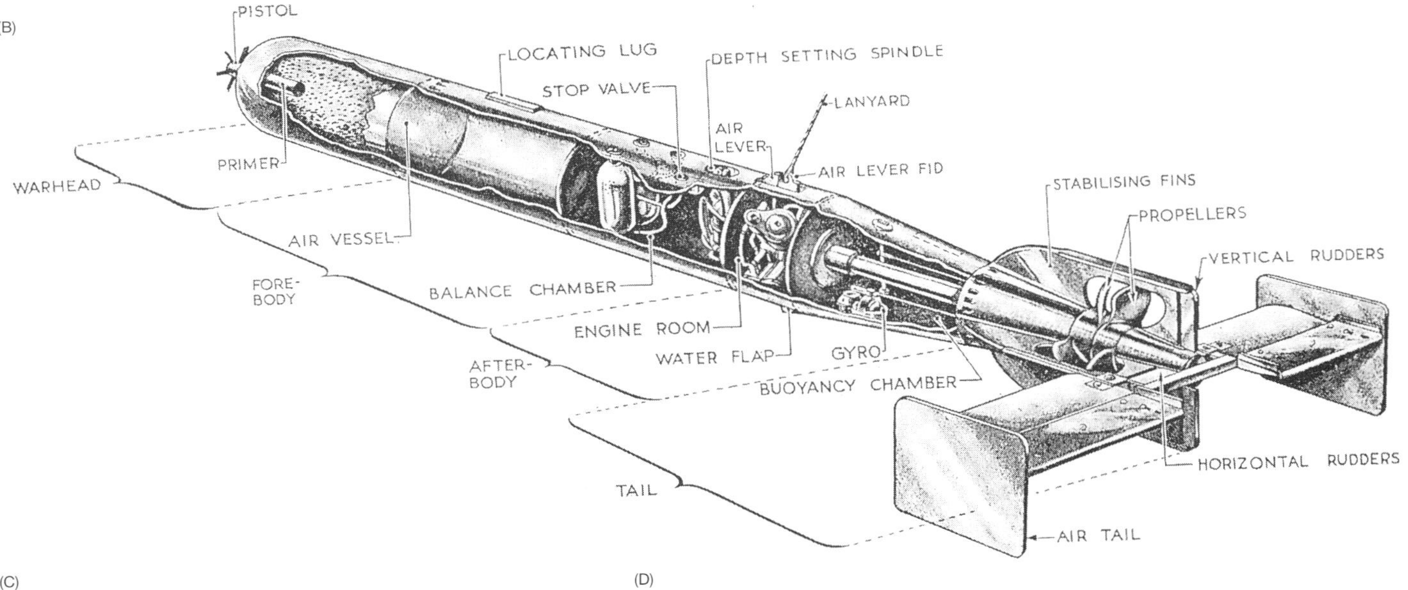


(C)

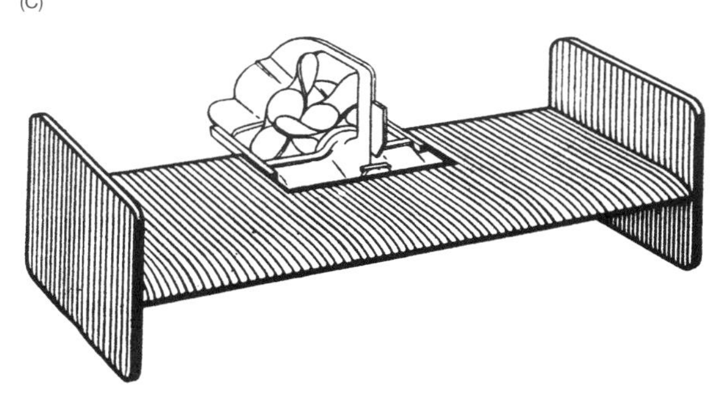

(D)

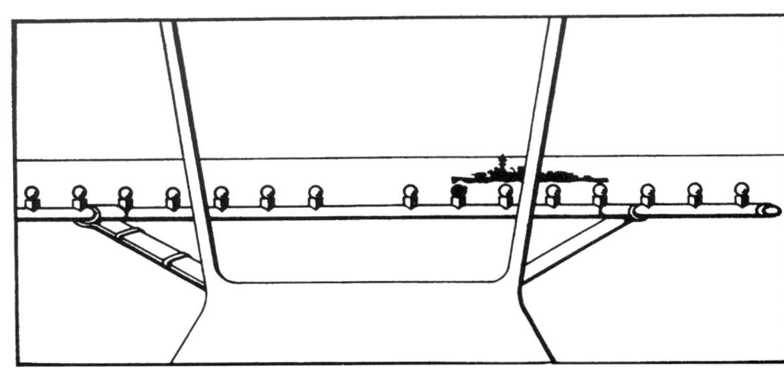

**Most torpedo attacks were started at height, with the Swordfish diving in an attempt to get into the best position. Here the pilot of L7701 'K' of the TTU starts his dive.**

dropped into the sea from a height of 50–70ft. After entering the water, it runs on its own power at 25kt a few feet below the surface for over 2,000yd unless anything gets in its way, in which case it goes off bang with devastating effect. A single torpedo (also known as a tin-fish) can sink a merchantman. The trickiness lies in the fact that you have to be flying at the correct low speed, and as straight and level as possible, and at the right altitude, at the moment you release it and for several subsequent seconds, if it's going to run accurately or indeed run at all. This is none too simple if your target is the friendly *Brigadier*, our usual target vessel in the Firth of Forth. It's quite a different matter if the tracer is coming at you from a heavily defended enemy fleet or convoy. Another little matter is that over a minute will elapse, if you drop from 1,000yd, before the tin-fish reaches its target, which will meantime have travelled 800yd if steaming at 20kt. You must judge her speed, aim the right distance ahead and guess what avoiding action she may take. Our attacks would start from several thousand feet, whence we would dive seaward, spend not more than ten seconds at sea level if possible, then climb steeply away for home. Our first efforts were made light, then we'd fly with a dummy torpedo weighing 1,600lb. In both cases a camera automatically took a picture at the moment you pressed the tit (button), from which could be computed your altitude, attitude, range and, given the speed of the target vessel, whether you would have hit her. Later, we dropped 'runners', which were the same as real torpedoes but without the explosive charge, set to run deep so that they would pass under the target vessel and then rise to the surface for recovery. Otherwise the tin-fish, worth several thousand pounds, would be badly damaged on impact and very probably lost. They were so scarce and valuable that we were rationed to three drops each! In twenty-three attacks I scored nineteen hits and all four misses were less than 30yd.

Assuming the vertical aspects are ignored at this stage the aiming and delivery of the torpedo is exactly like trying to hit a rabbit on the run; that is, you have to lay off for the distance the rabbit will have covered by the time your missile gets there. It all stems back to the triangle of velocities, but in this case it had to be reproduced and solved to give an aim-off angle before the torpedo was actually dropped. Basically, the three factors are the target's speed, angle on the bow and the average torpedo speed. The target's speed had to be guesstimated, especially under combat conditions, although the speeds of enemy ships were usually known; the angle on the bow was set ideally at 60 degrees; and the average torpedo speed was 27kt or 40kt. All the pilot had to do was to put his head against the rest provided to eliminate parallax error, sight his lamps and press the plunger to release the torpedo. The sight fitted to Swordfish and Albacore aircraft was known as a bar torpedo sight and consisted of a row of lamps mounted on a bar outside the cockpit in front of the windscreen. The lamps were spaced so that the angle subtended at the pilot's eye by two successive lamps was 4 degrees, so they represented 4-degree steps. The lamps were operated by a selector switch calibrated in knots to represent a ship's speed.

As mentioned previously, once it leaves the aircraft the torpedo is unstable: unless it is controlled in some way it may oscillate about its trajectory and could enter the water in any attitude, or even somersault. Ideally the torpedo should enter the water with its nose approximately along the correct trajectory. Like a dart, which has feathers to stabilize its flight, the most obvious way to stabilize the flight of a torpedo was to add an air tail. Early trials made with simple fixed tails were not very successful, but later they had an air tail control gear. This was mounted on or inside the torpedo and moved the tail in such a way it damped out any oscillation in the trajectory once dropped. Once the torpedo entered the water the air tail would break away so that it would not interfere with the run. Once again, all is not simple. Theoretically, the air tail should be of a size that allowed control of the torpedo under any dropping conditions. However, the layout of many torpedo-carrying aircraft was unsuitable for the fitting of a large air tail, so different tails would be required for each type of aircraft carrying them. Also, the slipstream of the aircraft influenced the airflow around the tail and upset any control.

To overcome these problems a device known as a drum control gear was fitted, which served two purposes. The first was to keep the torpedo steady until it was clear of the aircraft's slipstream and the second was to help the air tail by inclining the nose of the torpedo at the right trajectory when released. The drum control gear consisted of two pulleys fixed to a shaft, which in turn was attached to a flywheel that could be loaded with weights. Two wires of equal length were wound round each of the two pulleys, with the end of each wire attached to the tail of the torpedo. Once the torpedo was released the pull on the wires caused the flywheel and pulleys to revolve; the inertia of the flywheel opposed this and in doing so caused tension in the wires, which pulled up on the tail. As an example, if the torpedo rolled to the left the right wire became slack and the pull on the drum control system was thrown on the left side, correcting the roll. Simultaneously the

***(Above)*** **Levelling off, the pilot selects his target, adjusts the angle and launches his torpedo. Swordfish L7651 'B' in a 1938 demonstration.** IWM

***(Right)*** **Swordfish P3993 '22' of No. 785 Squadron at Crail tries his hand in 1941.** FAAM

wires pulled the nose of the torpedo down, imparting an angular velocity that hopefully set up the correct trajectory. During the first few seconds after release the torpedo was still attached to the aircraft by these wires and the pilot had to fly straight and level until it was clear. This is aptly described by Lt Cdr E. W. Whitley:

> I was an Air Fitter and Leading Air Fitter in No. 819 Squadron in *Illustrious* during 1940–41 when one of my jobs was to wind the 21½ feet of cable on the two spools of the Drum Control Gear, located just behind the TAG's cockpit. These were attached to the air tail of the 'fish', and as they wound off the weighted shaft the tail was delayed to get the right drop angle. I did all the ones for the Taranto raid [*see* page 129]. The ship ran out of rubber bands that held the wire on the spools and I was sent ashore at Alexandria to buy some. I got lost and at 18 years of age found myself without a single white face or a policeman in sight! I was getting a bit worried until one of the ladies, only eyes being visible, said 'Good Morning!'.

The main reason for having the drum control gear was that the air tail operated on a horizontal axis, and although it had vertical stabilizers, any slight deviation in roll and/or yaw would result in the torpedo running erratically once in the water. In fact, if there was considerable roll, the horizontal action of the air tail then acted as a rudder again, resulting in erratic running, in this case, vertically up or down! Therefore a considerable amount of piloting skill was required to deliver a torpedo accurately, and only constant practice would provide those skills. The aircraft had to be flown into the attacking position with much verve and held there until the right distance for release was reached, followed by the wait for those vital couple of seconds after the torpedo had been released before being able to pull away.

## The Torpedo in the Water

Once the torpedo entered the water it plunged to its best operating depth for the attack, an average plunge for a good delivery being around 40ft (12m). On the initial plunge, as it descended below its set depth to run, the depth gear inside the torpedo activated and turned the horizontal rudders in the torpedo tail upwards, ending its dive and gradually stabilizing its path. The initial dive, known as the plunge, took up about 30yd (27m) of the torpedo's run in the water, during which it decelerated from its airspeed to its set water speed.

Other factors had to be taken into consideration for the torpedo attack to be successful. These were the Recovery Range, the Arming or Safety Range, and the Minimum and Maximum Running Range. The Recovery Range is the distance the torpedo travelled in water, measured from the point of entry to the point that it commenced its run at the correct depth; that is, after all the variables dampen down so that it runs at its pre-determined depth, usually after around 250–300yd (230–270m). The Arming Range is the distance in water the torpedo runs to arm the firing pistol, and that depended on the type of pistol fitted. If the length of flight in the air is added to the Arming Range, this is the Minimum Dropping Range, the minimum distance from the target that the torpedo could be dropped so that the pistol was armed when it reached its target. The Maximum Running Range was from the point of entry to where the torpedo crossed the target's track and then, if no hit was made, the distance the torpedo travelled before running out of steam and sinking. If the torpedo was set to run at 40kt, the Maximum Running Range was in the region of 2,000yd (1,800m). If set to run at 27kt the Maximum Running Range was 3,000–4,000yd (2,700–3,700m).

The aim of the torpedo attack was to strike the enemy ship at a depth where it would do most damage. Naval ships would have some protection below the waterline such as armour, bulges and side compartments, which, if hit, would hopefully only flood, rather than cause the ship to sink. Other factors were the shape of the hull and draught depth when loaded and empty: too shallow a setting might mean the torpedo running below the keel.

**A fine study of an Albacore from Crail launching a practice torpedo. The freed wire can be seen between the undercarriage legs.** Central Press via Ian Templer

# CHAPTER SIX

# For Swordfish Replacement – Read Albacore

The Albacore was designed to Specification 41/36 as a replacement for the Swordfish from 1938 onwards. From the very first the Air Ministry intended to bring the type into production as quickly as possible by omitting both competitive tenders to other companies (issued to a selective list but recalled shortly afterwards) and going through protracted prototype stages. In fact, it was at the special request of the Admiralty, who had emphasized that they wanted Fairey to build the new machine, that the order be placed 'straight off the drawing board'. It was these attempts to shorten the development time and entry into service that had the opposite effect and delayed it by six months, as they hadn't allowed for the development of the new engine.

The Albacore had already had a protracted design history via Specifications M.7/36 and O.8/36. The Air Staff issued Specification M.7/36 on 8 September 1936, requiring a TSR aircraft for the FAA. It could be a single- or twin-engine aircraft, to operate from a carrier and be capable of low-level bombing, dive-bombing, torpedo attacks, fleet spotting and general reconnaissance. Conversion to a twin-float arrangement was asked for, following the pattern of the Swordfish. A crew of three was called for, pilot, observer and air gunner, the latter to operate a twin-gun power-operated turret amidships. A fixed forward-firing gun was to be provided for the pilot. Heating in the enclosed cockpit was called for, although not of the hot air jacket over the exhaust pipe type. A wingspan of not more than 50ft/15.25m (18ft/5.5m folded), length no more than 37ft/11.3m (44ft/13.4m with floats) and a height of no more than 14ft 9in/4.5m were specified, along with an AUW not to exceed 10,000lb (4,500kg) in either ship or float form. A cruising speed at two-thirds maximum engine power at maximum cruising rpm was to give not less than 183kt at 6,000ft (340km/h at 1,800m). Stalling speed was to be not less than 58kt (107km/h). Endurance was to be six hours at 2,500ft (750m), cruising at 120kt (220km/h). Enough fuel was to be allowed to give a range of 600nm (1,100km) at 7,000ft (2,100m) at the cruising speed of 120kt, allowances being made for maximum power at sea level when taking off carrying a torpedo or bomb load. Service ceiling should be not less than 20,000ft (6,000m) at normal loadings. Take-off distance should be 200ft (60m) against a 20kt (37km/h) wind at normal loads.

There were seventeen design considerations by Fairey to meet M.7/36. Five were large biplanes powered by a single Bristol Hercules at around an AUW of 10,000lb. There was a large monoplane powered by either a Hercules, Alvis Alcides or Armstrong Siddeley Deerhound and a small monoplane using either a Pegasus XX or Alvis Pelides. Five small biplane designs were considered, powered by a Pelides, Hercules, Pegasus XX and two by Bristol Taurus, one design having a modified wing area. Early in 1937 there was a design conference with Fairey looking at a Taurus-powered monoplane with various wing and flap schemes, a Taurus-engined biplane, a Bristol Mercury-engined monoplane and a Taurus-powered large biplane. This specification was cancelled in favour of O.8/36, which was very similar to M.7/36 but deleted the use of a torpedo role. Fairey considered five further designs before that specification, too, was cancelled by the Air Ministry.

On 22 January 1937 the Admiralty confirmed their preference for a biplane layout. Some of the designs were tested as models in the wind tunnel at the RAE at Farnborough, which did much to improve Fairey's knowledge about biplane lift, drag and pitch across a wide range of different conditions. Wind tunnel tests showed that the Hercules-engined biplane did not fare well on performance. Fairey thought a biplane with a Taurus engine would be better, if the wings had a better aspect ratio. The man from the Air Ministry suggested a monoplane design for better performance, but Fairey design staff were not keen. However, there was still a requirement to meet Operational Requirement OR.45, which called for a torpedo, spotter and dive-bomber reconnaissance machine for the FAA. The Air Ministry combined the two previous specifications, and on 11 February 1937 approved the revised Specification 41/36 with Fairey.

The revised specification called for very few changes from those already issued and cancelled, except that the turret was dropped and the normal crew would consist of two, or three for reconnaissance. The engine was to be the Taurus TE-IM, giving 1,075bhp at 4,500ft (1,400m) and driving a three-blade constant rpm propeller. When Fairey had submitted their memorandum to the specifications on 18 December 1936, they stated:

> This aircraft is designed primarily as a torpedo-spotter-reconnaissance (TSR) machine to Specification M.7/36, but can be used as a dive-bomber to cover the requirements of Specification O.8/36. After having examined various wing arrangements, the conclusion has been reached that, having regard to the present stage of development, the requirements of these specifications are best met by a biplane of orthodox design. This decision is dictated principally by the requirements of take-off, the limitation of dimensions and the mechanical difficulties of wing folding.

Final agreement was reached in the New Year and on 6 May 1937 a contract was placed by the Air Ministry for 100 Albacores. There was nothing complicated about producing the Albacore, as seen from a description in a Fairey brochure to the Air Ministry at the time:

> The aircraft was an orthodox biplane of all-metal construction with fabric covered surfaces.

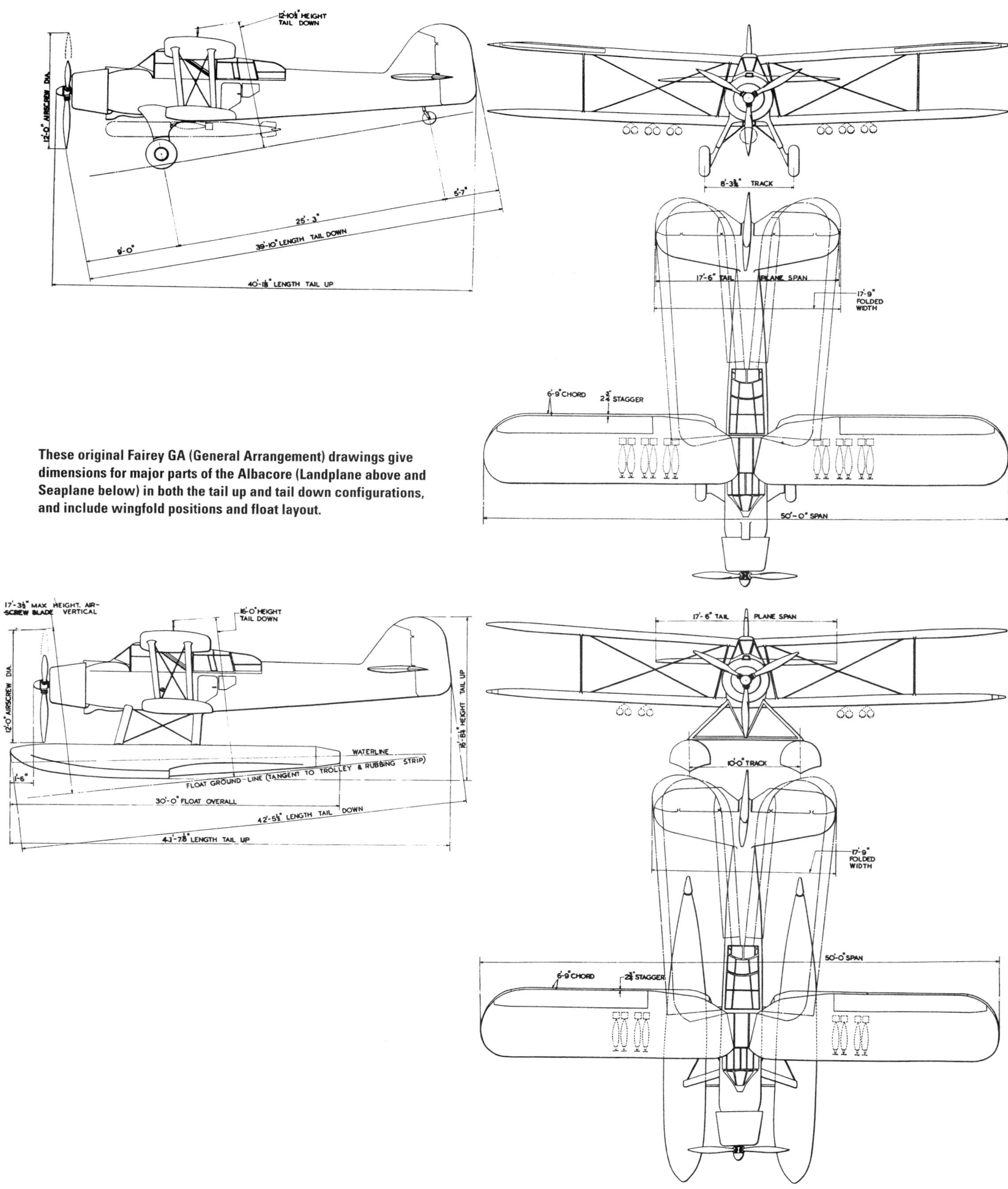


**These original Fairey GA (General Arrangement) drawings give dimensions for major parts of the Albacore (Landplane above and Seaplane below) in both the tail up and tail down configurations, and include wingfold positions and float layout.**

The top and bottom wings were of the same dimensions made up of I-section spars and Warren girder ribs. The wing cell was a single box braced with struts and wires, the upper wing joining the fuselage at the top of the cockpit hooding. The lower surface of the bottom wing was metal covered to take dragloads and provide wells in which the bomb carriers were mounted. Frise-type ailerons were fitted to both wings, which had wing-tip slots, and specially designed quick operation trailing edge hydraulically controlled flaps were fitted to the top wing only. The forward fuselage was of braced tubular steel and provided a mount for the Taurus engine and its ancillaries. Aft of the cockpit was monocoque construction, innovative at that time for biplanes, providing inherent buoyancy, so essential for carrier aircraft when ditching. The crew were completely enclosed under a transparent Perspex hooding which was arranged to fold quickly to allow emergency exits. The tailplane and fin were metal skin covered, trimming was via servo tabs. Rudder and elevators were metal tubular frames covered in fabric. The undercarriage consisted of a pair of cantilever oleo legs carrying a single transverse spar arranged in front of the front spar of the lower wing, but entirely separate from it. This arrangement allowed the wings to be folded without affecting the position of the undercarriage. One Vickers forward firing gun was mounted on the starboard lower wing, outside the airscrew disc and operated from the cockpit. One rear manually-operated Vickers 'K' gun was provided on a Fairey Battle-type arrangement. Weapon loads could include eight 20lb, six 250lb or three 500lb bombs below the wings, or a single 18in 1,650lb torpedo under the forward fuselage.

## Engine Problems

At a design conference on 22 March 1937 Fairey's expressed concern that the Bristol Taurus engine was going to be late. Bristol informed them that a mock-up of the engine for the prototype Albacore would be available by June 1937 and a prototype engine by January 1938, but that the first production engines would not be available until at least August 1938. This was six months after Fairey anticipated Swordfish production would cease at the Hayes factory, when they had planned to go straight on with the making of Albacores. The thought of the production line at Hayes being empty for five or six months horrified everyone. On 15 May 1937 the Air Ministry and Admiralty representatives examined a mock-up of the

**Fitting the final connections to the Albacore's Bristol Taurus engine in the Hayes factory.**

proposed production biplane, as a result of which a request was placed for another 300 Albacores.

The problem now was how to bring production forward once the engines started arriving. One plan was to build another factory at Hayes, another was to expand production to the Blackburn factories. On 8 November 1938 it was decided that, as a result of Botha orders being cancelled, Blackburn could build Albacores. LNER at York would build the wings, and Brough would build the fuselage and set up an assembly line in a new purpose-built shop. Initially it was planned that 100 Albacores would be built there. However, the Admiralty were seeking Treasury approval for a further 400 Albacores and 480 Taurus engines. They wanted ninety Albacores a month, fifty from Fairey at Hayes and forty from Blackburn – but now they wanted them built at the Blackburn Dumbarton factory!

As the Swordfish would be obsolescent after 1940 the Admiralty wanted another stop-gap order of 100 Albacores, but due to the setbacks further Swordfish were ordered – another 300 being provisionally allocated on 5 October 1939. Two weeks later the Admiralty decided that the 400 Albacores to be built by Blackburn would be replaced by Swordfish, taking the latter's production well into the early 1940s. All Albacore production would now be centred at Hayes, which would eventually build 800. Semi-complete aircraft were taken by road from Hayes to the Great West Aerodrome for final assembly and flight testing.

**Cockpit layout of the pilot's 'office' in an Albacore.**

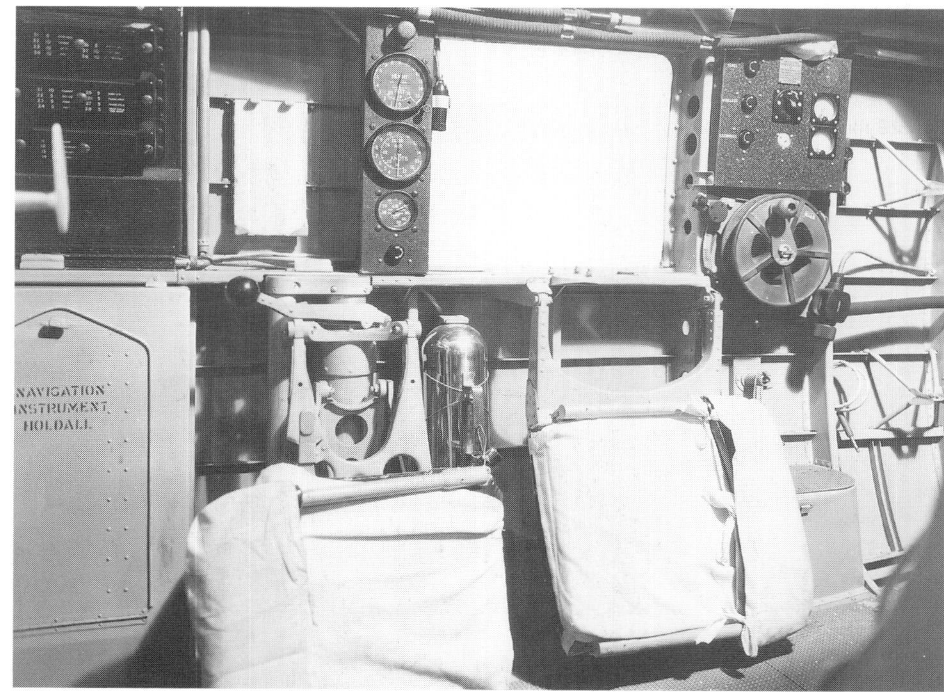


**One side of the observer's position in the rear cockpit of the Albacore, which includes an altimeter, airspeed indicator and air temperature gauge.**

## Flight Testing

Thanks to various problems such as engine sleeve valve distortion, requiring a change in the sleeve material, it was 12 December 1938 before the first aircraft, L7074, was flown from the Great West Aerodrome by test pilot Flt Lt F. H. Dixon, not Staniland as is sometimes stated. The second aircraft, L7075, followed shortly afterwards and then both of them went to the A&AEE at Boscombe Down for trials. In an effort to push the Albacore through its trials and get it into squadron service as soon as possible, L7075 was used for preliminary handling and type suitability for deck landing. Boscombe pilots flew this machine at the GWA on 5–6 May 1939 and it then moved to Martlesham Heath over 16–25 May before flying out to do deck landings on *Ark Royal* on 23–24 May. All agreed that the Albacore, apart from a slight heaviness of rudder and some directional instability, was pleasant to fly and good for the purpose for which it was designed. The first two aircraft featured spats over the wheels, but these were really an unrealistic addition that would prove difficult to maintain in

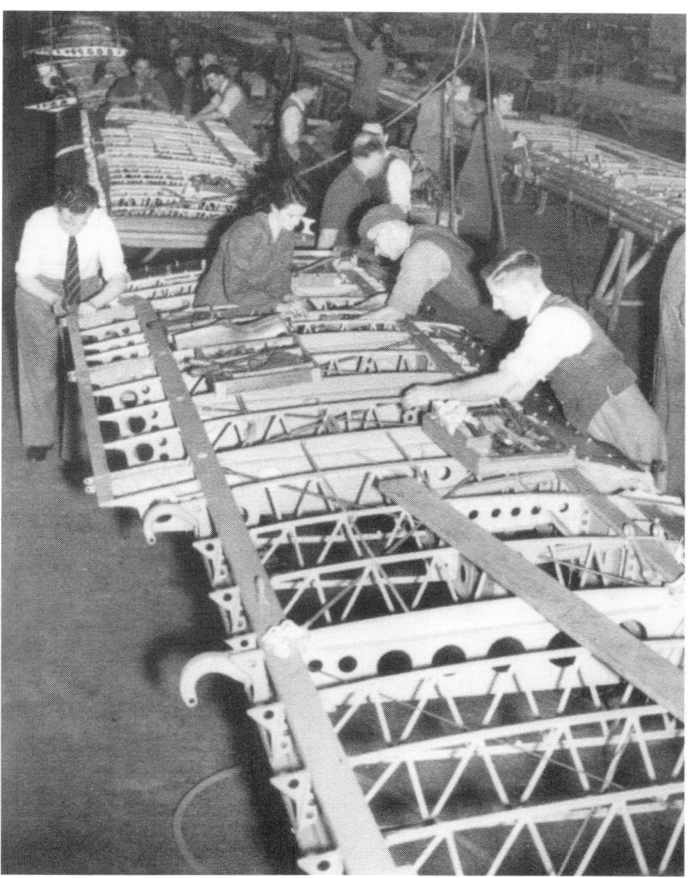

***(Above)*** **Production of Albacores in the Hayes factory, with X9013 in the foreground.** Fox Photos via Ian Huntley

***(Right)*** **Building wings for Albacores at Hayes.** Fox Photos via Ian Huntley

**When complete the Albacore had a more pleasing look about it, as this picture of the front end shows.**

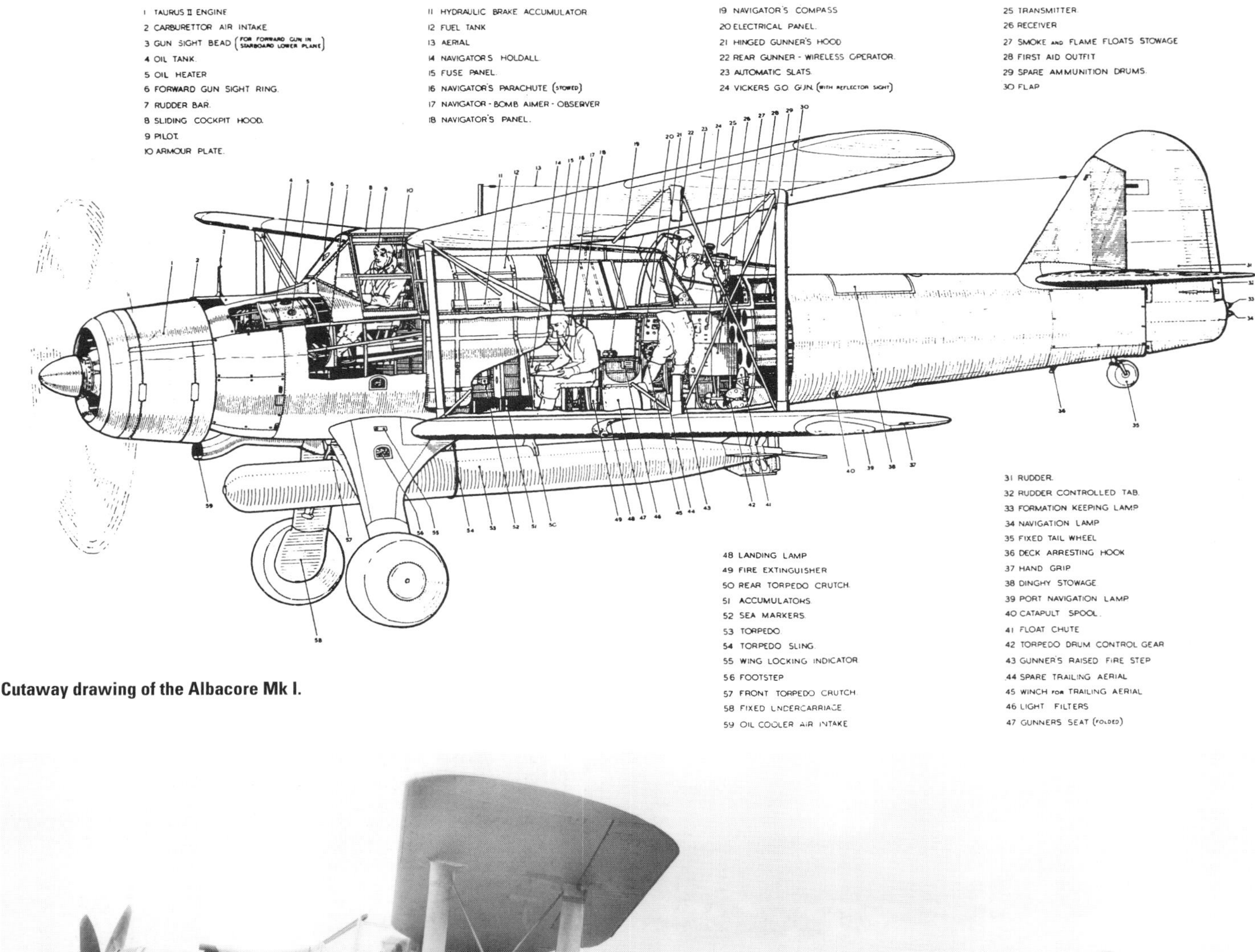


**Cutaway drawing of the Albacore Mk I.**

**L7074 after roll-out at Fairey's Great West Aerodrome. The fin and rudder have been revised. The blanked-out area behind the pilot is a fuel tank**

operational use, and were discarded on subsequent aircraft. Both these aircraft were also fitted with untapered cowlings for the Taurus engine, but subsequent machines had tapered ones.

The third machine, L7076, went to MAEE at Felixstowe for trials with twin floats and operation from a catapult. Trials at Felixstowe/Helensburgh and on the Solent near Fairey's Hamble factory during March 1940 showed the Albacore to be unsuited to floatplane operations. Even in relatively calm conditions it had a tendency to 'porpoise', and water was thrown up into the propeller/engine area. The floats were removed and L7076 joined the other two at Boscombe Down. Trials here revealed a number of problems. The size of the aircraft meant that the pilot had quite a climb to get into the front cockpit, but, once in, it was comfortable, he had an excellent view and

*(Above)* **The second prototype Albacore L7075 with, for some reason, wheel spats, which would have been impracticable for service use. The wire from the rear cockpit to the fitments on the rear fuselage was for a spin recovery parachute.**

*(Below)* **The second prototype Albacore, L7075, undergoing spin recovery trials. Safety attachments at the top of the fin would stop the parachute cords going between the fin and rudder, and fouling the controls.**

**A formation of Albacores, the nearest X9185, carrying a torpedo and bombs under the port wing.**

in general it was easy to fly. Not so in the dive, though, according to Boscombe Down pilots – although it would enter a dive, and settle into a stable velocity, the controls became so heavy that it was difficult to pull out. Carrying a torpedo created all sorts of problems – when the slots on the wing leading edge were in the free position the stall became vicious and unpredictable. Either wing could drop in the stall with some aileron snatch, and if the stick was held fully back a swing developed that could continue into a flat turn but not develop into a spin. If the flaps were down the wing drop was less of a problem, but locking the slots showed that the aircraft could not be fully stalled, remaining stable with a high sink

***(Left)*** **Waiting to be delivered, Albacore X9151 sits on Fairey's aerodrome prior to joining the FAA.** Richard Riding

***(Below)*** **The weathered look of an Albacore in service. The curved torpedo sight ahead of the windscreen was not unlike the one on the Swordfish, but the latter was straighter.** Charles E. Brown

**Albacore BF604 at the Great West Aerodrome, awaiting collection after acceptance flying.** Richard Riding

rate. However, these problems were quickly overcome and production got under way.

There were very few changes to the Albacore during its production life. An early problem was the unreliability of the Taurus engine – force-landings were commonplace. L7078 went to Bristol and was used for flight testing the Taurus during 1939–40, with L7125 joining the test programme the following year; this was in conjunction with changing the 1,065hp Taurus II for the slightly more powerful 1,130hp Taurus XII.

## Alternative Engines

The Admiralty looked at possible alternative engines, in case of further delays. The Wright Cyclone was considered: though like most American engines it used 87 octane fuel, even with this reduced performance they suggested its use. Another consideration was to use the new Rolls-Royce Boreas engine, later to be known as the Exe. Engine D.10 was allocated to the programme at the Rolls-Royce flight test establishment at Hucknall airfield. Originally the plan was for Rolls to deliver the engine to Fairey by 11 November 1939, to be flight tested by their test pilots. Albacore L7074 was allocated for the trials, but due to it being used elsewhere the programme slipped and Rolls installed D.10 in Fairey Battle K9222 instead. Engine D.6 was allocated to replace D.10 but needed to be brought up to D.10 standard. By May 1940 D.6 was ready to be submitted for a 50-hour Type Test at an FAA performance rating prior to flight testing in an Albacore. By now it had been decided that any flight testing would be done at Hucknall, so L7074 was delivered that July to allow detailed drawings to be made to modify the engine bay to accommodate the Exe. The problems of mounting the engine would necessitate complete re-design of the nose section, including the cowlings. The engine mountings were made and fitted, but events now overtook the rate of progress. The

**The sheer size of the Albacore is apparent in this picture of the pilot's cockpit.** M. B. W. Howell

**The later, 1941, colour scheme, applied to Albacore L7083.**

***(Below)* An Albacore formation from No. 817 Squadron, including BF632 '5M', which started to receive them after March 1941.** Real Photographs

***(Bottom)* Three Albacores line up to land as two others join on the right. The Albacore proved to be just as easy to land on a carrier deck as the Swordfish.** IWM

Admiralty wanted Albacores in service as soon as possible and therefore was prepared to accept Taurus-engined aircraft. After much discussion the Exe-engined version of the Albacore was abandoned – fortuitously as it turned out, as the Exe was later abandoned by Rolls-Royce. L7074 languished outside one of the hangars at Hucknall for a time and was then quietly scrapped.

## The Albacore Joins Up

No. 826 became the first squadron to receive Albacores when it formed up at Ford, Sussex, on 15 March 1940 under the command of Lt Frank H. E. Hopkins. He became Senior Observer in the squadron after Lt Cdr C. J. T. Stephens took over command on 7 April. The designated task for the squadron was anti-submarine patrols from RNAS Hatston in the Orkneys. To this end, they carried out more than 400 training sorties on the ranges at Littlehampton, Sussex during April and May. The squadron then flew to Jersey in the Channel Islands for a week of dive-bombing, night flying and some formation practice. After this working up on their new aircraft, No. 826 flew to RAF Bircham Newton on 29 May to provide support for RAF Coastal Command. The squadron made their first operational sorties on 31 May 1940 when they attacked E-boats off Zeebrugge and bombed road and rail targets at Westende. (Full details of their experiences will be found in Chapter 7.)

Albacores were now coming off the production line in useful numbers. Most of these were delivered to various Maintenance Units where they were prepared for

***(Above)*** **As one Albacore taxies forward another lands. The large flap area provided stability during the final stages of the approach.** Andy Wright

***(Right)*** **Albacore X9109 'E2A' of No. 767 Squadron, based at East Haven, in 1943.** FAA Museum

squadron service. By the end of 1940 three more squadrons had received Albacores: in June No. 829 (Lt Cdr O. S. Stevison) formed up at Lee-on-Solent; No. 828 (Lt E. A. Greenwood) received their Albacores at Ford during September; and the following month No. 827 (Lt Cdr W. G. C. Stokes) worked up at Yeovilton, before flying to Stornoway in the Hebrides to provide anti-submarine patrols. Briefly operating under Coastal Command direction at St Eval and St Merryn, No. 829 made nightly attacks on the docks and shipping at Brest. Lt Cdr Stevinson was lost on one such raid during the night of 9 October. His replacement, Lt Cdr J. Dalyell-Stead, took over on 12 October. No. 828 moved to Scotland, and after working up carried out anti-submarine patrols and operations under Coastal Command. During 1940 shore-based operations were the norm for Albacore squadrons and it was well into 1941 before they joined carriers.

Six further Albacore squadrons formed up during 1941: No. 817 (Lt Cdr D. Sanderson DSC) in March; Nos 831 (Lt Cdr P. L. Mortimer) and 832 (Lt Cdr A. J. P. Plugge) during April; No. 820 (Lt Cdr W. Elliott) in June; No. 815 (Lt Cdr F. M. A. Torrens-Spence) during August; and No. 818 (Lt Cdr D. G. Goodwin DSC) in November 1941. Four more front-line squadrons equipped with the Albacore in 1942: Nos 821 (Major A. C. Newsom RM) and 822 (Major A. R. Burch DSC RM) in March; No. 823 (Lt Cdr A. J. D. Harding DSC) during April; and No. 841 (Lt R. L. Williamson DSC) in July. These were the only front-line squadrons to operate the Albacore, except for No. 119 Squadron of the RAF and No. 415 Squadron of the Royal Canadian Air Force.

**Specification – Albacore**

| | |
|---|---|
| Engine: | Bristol Taurus II 14-cylinder two-row sleeve-valve air-cooled supercharged radial engine driving an 11ft 9in (3.58m) de Havilland constant-speed airscrew. Take-off power 1,090hp at 3,300rpm; rated power: Taurus II 925/965hp at 2,800rpm at 5,000ft (1,500m), Taurus XII 1,130hp at 3,500ft (1,100m); fuel capacity – one 193gal (878ltr) tank in fuselage. |
| Weights: | Empty 7,250lb (3,290kg); disposable load 3,210lb (1,460kg); loaded 10,460lb (4,740kg); all-up weight (reconnaissance) 9,910lb (4,490kg), (torpedo) 11,020lb (5,000kg), (bomber) 11,300lb (5,120kg). |
| Dimensions: | Span (both wings) 50ft (15.24m); width folded 17ft 9in (5.41m); length, tail down 39ft 10in (12.14m); height, tail down 12ft 10½in (3.92m); height on floats 16ft (4.88m); wing area 623sq ft (57.95sq m). |
| Performance: | Max speed (sea level) reconnaissance 160mph (257km/h), torpedo 152mph (244km/h), bomber 149mph (240km/h); max speed at 6,000ft (1,800m) reconnaissance 173mph (278km/h), torpedo 167mph (269km/h), bomber 163mph (262km/h); max speed at 10,000ft (3,000m) (reconnaissance) 171mph (275km/h), (torpedo) 166mph (267km/h), (bomber) 161mph (259km/h); range (reconnaissance) 795 miles (1,280km) at 114mph (183km/h), (torpedo/bomber) 670 miles (1,078km) at 114mph; endurance (reconnaissance) 6.96 hours, (torpedo/bomber) 5.8 hours; time to 5,000ft (1,500m) 5 minutes; service ceiling (reconnaissance) 20,300ft (6,200m), (torpedo) 15,200ft (4,640m), (bomber) 17,700ft (5,400m); take-off run (reconnaissance) 240yd (220m), (torpedo) 320yd (293m), (bomber) 345yd (316m). |
| Armament: | One 0.303in Browning machine-gun in starboard wing; two 0.303in Vickers K-type gas-operated machine-guns in rear cockpit mounted on Fairey High Speed Gun Mounting; one 1,610lb 18in torpedo, or 1,500lb aerial sea mine, or 4 × 500lb or 6 × 250lb bomb load. |

***(Above)*** **A fine and unusual study of Albacore X9058 flying along the coast.**

***(Below)*** **A wet murky day on the flight deck of *Indomitable* as No. 817 Squadron prepare to fly. The squadron codes are repeated on the wing fold, identifying '5A' with wings being unfolded; left to right rearwards, the first four are '5B', '5C', '5F' and '5H'.** Charles E. Brown via Ray Sturtivant

CHAPTER SEVEN

# Shore-Based Operations with Coastal Command, 1940–45

When I joined No. 812 Squadron in November 1940 the excitements of the summer were over – the daylight raids on Rotterdam, invasion barges and other strangely assorted patrols over the Channel. Our principal business henceforth was to be minelaying. It consisted of some hundreds of pounds of high explosive slung beneath a Swordfish, and sallying forth by night from some darkened aerodrome to place it with great care in one of the enemy's harbours. The exact point where it was laid mattered a great deal, for the shipping followed a dredged channel, and if it was laid anywhere else it was a waste of taxpayers' money. It wasn't a spectacular job. The mine never went off until hours and probably days later. It might even be picked up by a minesweeper and never go off. On the whole, the weather was a greater menace than the enemy for this type of operations. It never seemed to be fine on both sides of the Channel at the same time. There were of course several places on the 'other' side which were sufficiently well defended to add spice to a night's enjoyment of stooging around in poor conditions trying to find your target. The freezing level was seldom above 2,000ft, and the pilot was usually forced to fly blind with his head down in the cockpit. The limiting factor was the visibility over the enemy coast: if it was bad we 'scrubbed' and came home. Average trip time was five hours but some did more than that – I once did one lasting 6¾ hours.

Unfortunately, a Swordfish doesn't fly very fast, and an extra tank had to be fitted in the rear cockpit to give it the endurance for these trips. It had two disadvantages – it was highly explosive when half empty, and prevented the observer from straightening his back. This meant leaving the TAG at home so we did not have a gunner. This was good, for I never saw any night fighters on our trips, and by flying low our approach to the enemy coast was devoid of much risk from them or serious flak.

There were exceptions, such as Brest. It necessitated a long glide approach with the engine throttled right back, while a simultaneous diversion was provided by an RAF Beaufort squadron. The operation would begin with a long, laborious climb to 8,000ft, timed to arrive over the coast with the diversion already alerting the enemy gunners. An incredible amount of flak would be streaking upwards at the Beauforts, some 5,000ft above. We would throttle back and glide through the curtain of orange, green, violet and gentian lead towards the inner harbour, mentally calculating that the chances of getting hit must be small. Once the mine had gone it was every man for himself. At 200ft one had to make a decision whether to creep round at this height, almost at stalling speed, and hope to creep away mistaken for a motorboat – or slam the throttle open and 'streak' along the harbour wall before guns could be elevated to get their sights on you. Oh, some would get through, some would come back looking like net curtains, and some did not come back at all!

These are the comments of an observer serving with No. 812 Squadron, but fairly typical of shore-based/Coastal Command operational flying throughout the war.

This started when the Air Ministry and Admiralty agreed that certain shore-based naval air units in the UK would be seconded to Coastal Command and made responsible for 'looking after' enemy light naval forces operating in and around the Channel. Also, FAA carrier squadrons based ashore for various reasons could be used in a similar manner to keep up pressure on the enemy. Generically known as E-boats for 'enemy boats', these German light naval forces included the motor torpedo boat, known to the Germans as the *Schnellboot* or S-boat, and minesweepers known as M-boat (*Minensuchboot*) and R-boat (*Raumboot*). In between such operations, these squadrons could attack enemy positions in Channel ports, either by minelaying or by bombing, and carry out reconnaissance/photography. For bombing operations, the Admiralty asked to be consulted as they felt Swordfish and Albacores operating against targets along the coast were vulnerable to flak or fighters. This was a justified concern – such flights resulted in the loss of twelve Swordfish during April–June 1940. However, the deteriorating situation in the Low Countries meant that Swordfish were often used for all sorts of roles in that theatre, including daylight attacks against advancing German columns.

## No. 815 Squadron

No. 815 Squadron moved to Bircham Newton on 8 April 1940 for minelaying and anti-E-boat patrols. The first minelaying operation was on 25 April, when six Swordfish went out to different targets, all returning safely after sorties of over five hours. All operational targets were given code-names, and minelaying was known as 'gardening' and the mines as 'cucumbers'! When the operations were extended later, many other code-names came into use, a lot of them being of a nautical flavour – oysters, jellyfish, limpets, and so on, although there were some horticultural ones.

When the Germans started their offensive on 10 May 1940, however, No. 815 became the first to be diverted for the ground-attack role. The speed of the blitzkreig resulted in a general withdrawal towards the Dunkirk area, and on 12 May seven of the squadron's Swordfish bombed Waalhaven aerodrome, near Rotterdam. There was only light flak but L9784, piloted by Lt A. S. Downes, with Lt R. W. Little, had to land on a beach on the appropriately named Overflakkee Island. Unable to take off again, the crew set fire to the aircraft and got back to the squadron two days later. For a while the squadron operated from Ford and Detling, the last raid being on 31 May 1940. Nine Swordfish attacked Texel, six attacking the harbour defences and shipping with bombs, while three quietly laid mines in the harbour approaches. All aircraft returned safely and shortly afterwards No. 815 Squadron left to embark on *Illustrious*.

## No. 818 Squadron

No. 818 Squadron was involved for a short period. They arrived at RAF Thorney Island on 30 May and undertook a number of operations, including anti-submarine, anti-E-boat and reconnaissance patrols, until 14 June. No. 819 Squadron moved up from Ford to Detling on 21 May for three days of anti-U-boat patrols off the Belgian coast. On 23 May Swordfish '3M' of No. 819 Squadron bombed and machine-gunned two enemy motor boats.

## No. 825 Squadron

No. 825 Squadron moved to Detling on 18 May 1940 to provide support to Coastal Command. However, the unit's first sortie was a fiasco. Eleven Swordfish were flown to Bircham Newton on 20 May, to carry out a strike on German naval vessels reported in the North Sea. Torpedoes were being loaded when it was realized that these particular Swordfish did not have long-range tanks and would therefore not have the range to get to the ships and back to Detling. Three nights later five aircraft, each armed with four 250lb bombs, left at hourly intervals to carry out a night reconnaissance of the area around the Hook of Holland. Sub-Lt C. S. G. Hogg bombed two MTBs, but he missed both so then engaged them with gunfire until dawn, when low fuel forced him to return to base. On 24 May six Swordfish, again each armed with four 250lb bombs, were briefed to attack an enemy gun position in a wood south-west of Calais. Even with a fighter escort they were unable to locate the gun battery, and so attacked targets of opportunity along the coast road. Flying K8351, Sub-Lt J. K. Cannon, a pre-war RAFVR pilot, and his gunner, PO Parker, dive-bombed enemy tanks on the Calais–Gravelines road, being hit in both port wings. Not so lucky were Lt North and LAC C. A. Chichester, who were both killed when their Swordfish was shot down 5 miles (8km) south-west of Calais. Three tanks were destroyed, other motorized traffic damaged and the road bombed to delay traffic. The following day it was back to attacking enemy vehicles still jammed on the Gravelines–St Folquin road. Escorted by fighters from Manston, No. 825 sent eleven Swordfish armed with bombs, and attacked anything looking like the enemy. On the 26 May, with no fighter escort available, two aircraft spotted for the bombardment of a gun battery by the cruisers *Arethusa* and *Galatea*. Swordfish '5H', flown by Sub-Lt J. B. Kiddell, was attacked by two Bf 109s, and in taking violent avoiding action his observer, Lt G. N. Beaumont, was thrown out some 3 miles (5km) north-west of Songatte and killed.

No. 825 Squadron were in action again the following day when nine Swordfish acted as a diversionary force. British troops were under attack in the fort at Calais and getting desperate for supplies. With twenty-four fighters providing top cover, Westland Lysanders dropped supplies while Swordfish operated to the west of the fort, bombing gun positions, while Hawker Hectors of an army-cooperation squadron operated to the east. Once the supplies had been dropped, the Swordfish attacked tanks on the jetty at Calais and machine-gunned troops on the coastal roads. Later that day six Swordfish went out again to bomb the enemy gun batteries that were pounding Dunkirk.

That evening the evacuation of Dunkirk began, which lasted until 4 June. At 16.40 hours on 28 May some MTBs were reported off Texel, and No. 825 Squadron sent eight Swordfish out to find them. In poor visibility the squadron became separated, and the MTBs that were found proved to be British. Some aircraft attacked enemy positions on the coast, Sub-Lt J. K. Cannon and Sub-Lt Shaw in K5955 receiving shrapnel hits in the starboard wings and only just avoiding flying through a balloon barrage on their return in the poor visibility. Swordfish '5B', piloted by Capt W. G. S. Aston RM, crashed on the Goodwin Sands and although Aston was saved, his observer, Sub-Lt P. H. L. Rylands, was not seen again. One aircraft landed at Manston and another force-landed at Ramsgate.

On 29 May the squadron lost five Swordfish in action over France. They flew to Hawkinge, arriving at 17.00, and from there attacked an enemy gun battery shelling the mole at Dunkirk. The battery was some 7 or 8 miles (11–13km) inland, some 4 miles (6km) south-west of Bergues. Arriving over the area at 18.55, they circled but could not locate the site. Some aircraft now looked for other targets and it was during this time that the aircraft were shot down, including the CO, Lt Cdr J. B. Buckley DSC, who became a prisoner of war. The new CO, who arrived at the end of the month, was Lt Cdr E. Esmonde, whose later exploits are related in Chapter Eight.

No. 825 squadron was withdrawn to Worthy Down to re-equip and take on replacement aircrews. During the first part of June the squadron trained extensively, with an emphasis on dive-bombing. During 16–18 June the squadron flew to Thorney Island each morning and then carried out anti-submarine patrols between Poole and Cherbourg, from where the last of the British and Allied forces were being evacuated. The squadron returned to Detling on the morning of 1 July and that night attacked invasion barges at Rotterdam. An account of one such raid was recorded by one of the pilots:

> One day, soon after the fall of France, my squadron of twelve Swordfish was ordered to an aerodrome in Kent. We were told to put ourselves at the disposal of Coastal Command. Well, we arrived at Detling at lunch-time, and were told that minelaying somewhere off the Dutch coast was to be our night's work, so we spent the whole afternoon getting the mines on, and just as we finished orders came through cancelling the mining and telling us to get bombed-up for a visit to Rotterdam to try and sink the invasion barges, which a reconnaissance aircraft had reported were accumulating in the river just west of the town.
>
> The squadron was divided into two waves, the first wave taking off 20 minutes before the second wave. It was a cloudy, dark night when we set out, but over the sea the weather cleared and we climbed to our operational height. As we crossed the enemy coast a thin layer of cloud was encountered about 2,000ft thick, stretching from 2,000ft to 4,000ft above the ground, so the last part of the journey had to be done by dead reckoning. As my observer told me that we ought to be just about there the first searchlights began showing and one or two balls of fire were shot up which lit up the whole sky above the clouds. More and more searchlights came on but, naturally, could not pierce the clouds.
>
> We then went into line astern and I thought I would go down through the cloud and see if I could see the barges. However, when I got through the cloud to about 2,000ft all was pitch black below, but I thought I saw a reflection of a light on some water so I realized I was over the river, so, marking the spot by a group of searchlights, I climbed up again, intending to do a decent bombing attack. Just as I had come out of the cloud again the Hun opened fire and stuff came up all round. I cursed myself for not letting the bombs go when I'd been down the first time. However, all went well and down we went and away went the bombs. My observer reported a large flash but otherwise could see no result due to the darkness. Personally I was too busy trying

to shake off the searchlights as a Swordfish climbing is a pretty easy target to keep on, but after what seemed an interminable age we got into the cloud again, and stayed in them till well out over the sea.

Breathing a sigh of relief we headed for home only to find, when we got there, England covered in a very low ground fog making it all look like the Thames estuary at low tide with mud banks showing. My observer first of all thought we were over Harwich and told me to look out for balloons. Then he thought we were over Deal where there were more balloons. I was so intent on looking for balloons in the dark that when suddenly there was a terrific jar through the aircraft I thought we had hit a cable and it was time to get out. However, glancing at my altimeter, I saw it reading zero feet, and realised we had only hit the sea and bounced off it, so I am glad we didn't have to jump as it would only have been a 6ft fall and we would have looked rather stupid. By this time petrol was getting very short and it looked like being a rather uncomfortable end to an otherwise reasonably pleasant trip, but just after I had switched over to my reserve gravity tank, which gave us another 20 minutes in the air, Margate pier was sighted and at last we knew where we were and home we went.

We were the fourth and last of twelve aircraft to get back actually to the aerodrome. The other members of the squadron had come down all over the place, one upside down in the Thames mud, the crew of which smelled horrible for a long time afterwards; another in a wood; a third knocked up a farmer, having landed in his field. He thought they were Germans and rang for the police. A fourth crew also landed in a field, got held up by Royal Marines who took some convincing that they really were British. The last crew to ring in, very late, was a young crew who landed in a field. Upon knocking at the nearby house the door was answered by two very pretty girls – and, as I say, they took a very long time to report their whereabouts! Although we dropped 12,000lb of bombs we lost two aircraft over the target area.

The squadron laid mines in the Scheldt estuary over the next three nights and then flew north to join *Furious* on 14 July.

## No. 819 Squadron

Meanwhile, on 15 January 1940, No. 819 Squadron had formed up at Ford with twelve Swordfish Is. Although intended for duty aboard *Illustrious*, the squadron was used for a short time to lay minefields and also to bomb the German fleet at Wilhelmshaven and Kiel from around 10,000ft. In March the squadron moved to West Freugh to practise high-level bombing, and in June joined *Illustrious* en route to Bermuda.

## No. 812 Squadron

Also operating within Coastal Command and carrying out similar types of raids, sometimes against the same targets, was No. 812 Squadron. They moved to North Coates on the Lincolnshire coast on 11 May 1940. Long-range tanks were fitted for extended operations such as minelaying and bombing enemy coastal targets along Holland, Belgium and France. Six Swordfish went out laying mines on 21 May but lost P4166 'G3C' with its crew, Lt R. C. Dundas and Sub-Lt J. A. Allen, when it crashed in the sea. On 28 May the squadron took five Swordfish to bomb enemy vehicles at Gravelines but 'G3R' was shot down in flames, killing its crew, Lt K. P. Gurr and Lt R. Carpmael. Bad weather hampered six Swordfish crews when they were briefed to carry out minelaying on 1 June, and 'G3G' crashed into the sea off Spurn Point, though the crew were rescued. Five days later six Swordfish carried out a similar operation, with 'G3B' crashing on a dummy airfield at Ouston, the crew again being saved. Not so lucky on the night of 29–30 June were Sub-Lt J. M. P. Davies and Sub-Lt C. A. Conn in Swordfish L7633 'G3Q', who were out minelaying with five other aircraft when they were shot down and made POW. The following night six aircraft bombed barges – being accumulated for the intended invasion of England – near Rotterdam. During a similar raid on the night of 2 July Sub-Lt B. P. Grigson, the pilot of L7646, and his observer, Sub-Lt F. L. Lees, were presumed killed when they did not return. Another aircraft, L2829, was shot down over Schiphol: the TAG, LAC H. W. V. Burt was killed and the pilot, Sub-Lt Kiddell, survived to be taken prisoner, and later shot trying to escape. Another aircraft, '5M', had engine failure when almost home and crashed whilst attempting a force-landing on Harrock Island, both crew escaping unhurt.

Casualties were not always due to enemy action. Eight Swordfish carried out a simulated dive-bombing attack on 30 July, during which P4161 and L2759 collided, killing both crews. During the night of 3–4 August, six Swordfish bombed oil tanks at Vlaardingen, near Rotterdam, losing two aircraft. Sub-Lt R. C. Eborn and Lt T. A. Johnston RM were killed when P4007 'G3Q' crashed at sea and 'G3B' ditched on the way home after running out of fuel, the crew being picked up by the destroyer *Jupiter*. The Dutch naval base at Den Helder was bombed by six aircraft on 12 August, all the crews returning safely. Six aircraft went out minelaying on the night of 21–22 August, with L2819 being shot down and its crew, Lt N. M. Hearle

**No. 812 Squadron was seconded to RAF Coastal Command in November 1940 and based at North Coates. The carriers under the wings were for flares, bomb racks being re-positioned under the centre fuselage. Swordfish were used to strike at targets just across the Channel.** Fox Photos

and Sub-Lt R. L. G. Davies, being taken prisoner. Vlaardingen oil tanks were bombed again on 31 August by six Swordfish, with L9716 'G3P' being shot down and Lt G. Villers-Tothill killed.

Night targets were mainly E-boats, either at sea or moored up in Boulogne harbour. During September No. 812 went back to bombing barges, and on 9 September carried out daylight bombing attacks on barges, tugs and other shipping near Flushing. Low cloud foiled a planned raid the following night, but on 11 September the squadron moved to Thorney Island to be nearer enemy shipping in the Channel. Minelaying was again on the agenda as the squadron continued its almost nightly attacks on docks containing barges and light shipping. They went back to Rotterdam on 31 October: the Swordfish climbed to 10,000ft, throttled back to 65kt as they crossed the coast, and 40 minutes later each aircraft attacked individually, dropping six 250lb bombs. Six Swordfish of No. 812 Squadron were detached to St Eval in Cornwall on 1 November to provide anti-shipping patrols. Over the next few days aircraft looked for an enemy convoy, unsuccessfully, and attacked dry docks and a power station at Lorient in the face of both searchlights and flak. Returning to North Coates on 10 November, they carried on minelaying and bombing enemy coastal targets. Three Swordfish provided a diversion for Beauforts of No. 22 Squadron, also based at North Coates, when they bombed an enemy airfield, losing one aircraft to flak; another Swordfish couldn't find the target and bombed Boulogne instead, receiving flak damage to the tail area but managing to land at Detling. Boulogne was the target again on the night of 23 November, when five Swordfish approached from three different direction to confuse the enemy gunners and dropped six 250lb bombs each. On the night of 11 December Swordfish L2748, manned by Sub-Lt E. M. Hamilton and Mid P. N. Lofts, was lost on a lone minelaying operation to Brest. No. 812 Squadron continued to operate on its nightly raids until March 1941, when it left for carrier duty.

## No. 816 Squadron

No. 816 Squadron moved to North Coates and continued the night raids on enemy shipping and minelaying to close off Dutch ports. An inconclusive torpedo strike was laid on against shipping in Brest harbour on 15 April, one aircraft crashing in the sea. No. 816 Squadron moved north on 4 June to prepare for carrier duty aboard *Furious*. Three Swordfish had been detached to Detling during April and operated as No. 816X Squadron, carrying out raids against enemy shipping along the French coast and minelaying. Dunkirk and Ostend harbours were bombed with some success during the night of 16–17 June. Three further Swordfish arrived on 1 July and No. 816X became No. 821 Squadron. After a number of raids, such as one on Ostend on the night of 7–8 July when three aircraft bombed the quay and warehouses, the squadron moved north and carried out anti-submarine patrols until embarking for Egypt and action in the Western Desert.

## The Albacore and Coastal Command

The Swordfish wasn't the only type to be seconded to Coastal Command, although it was the most widely used. Its sister, the Albacore, flew similar missions from 1940 onwards. No. 826 Squadron, the first front-line unit to receive Albacores, formed up at Ford on 15 March 1940. After working up, the squadron moved to Bircham Newton and on 21 May flew to Jersey for night-flying training, formation flying and dive-bombing. The squadron returned to Bircham Newton on 29 May, with their first operation taking place from Detling two days later. Nine Albacores, each carrying six 250lb bombs, dive-bombed German forces at a cross-roads behind Nieuport harbour in West Flanders, Belgium. Though this was a daylight attack there was no fighter escort – but little flak and no sign of the Luftwaffe either. That night Albacores patrolled the Channel looking for E-boats, one Albacore bombing three, but to no avail. Another found itself on the tail of a Heinkel He 111, but the front gun failed to fire.

The squadron returned to Bircham Newton, where convoy escort duty was carried out during early June. Some of these could be long and boring if there was no action. Lt L. E. D. Walthall with his crew in Albacore L7081 said 'We flew a daylight convoy escort for five hours five minutes and did not see a dicky bird, except for our own ships.'

On the night of 12 June six Albacores bombed E-boats in Boulogne harbour. Their first minelaying operation was on 15 June, the first of many by No. 826. They went out again on 17 and 18 June – this time Lt Walthall in L7093 was airborne for nearly six hours, laying mines at Flushing. On 21 June the squadron went out looking for an enemy convoy among the Frisian Islands. The squadron became separated in thickening cloud and, unable to locate the convoy, attacked the airfields at Willemsoord and De Kooy. Bf 109s had been alerted and two Albacores were shot down and a third, L7111 '4L', damaged. However, the TAG in '4L', NA C. J. H. Homer shot down one of the attacking fighters, for which he was awarded a DSM. Convoy patrols and night attacks followed, then minelaying in the River Maas on 26 June, Ostend-Bruges canal on 29 June, and River Maas again on 1 July.

The Albacores were grounded on 3 July by the Admiralty because of a spate of engine malfunctions causing forced landings. No. 826 Squadron then took delivery of ten Swordfish, including L2732, L2861, L7643 and K8883, to allow them to remain operational. The Albacores stayed at Bircham Newton, receiving new engines, self-sealing fuel tanks and armour plating for the pilot's head.

These modified Albacores began operations again on 3 August 1940, attacking enemy harbours by night and remaining on standby during the day in case of invasion. They bombed oil tanks at Vlaardingen, near Rotterdam, on 24 August and those at Flushing on 2 September, when one Albacore was shot down by flak. On 11 September six Albacores of No. 826, escorted by six Bristol Blenheim fighters of No. 235 Squadron, were out looking for an enemy convoy off Calais when they were 'bounced' by Bf 109s, who shot down one Albacore and damaged three others. Once again the TAG proved his worth: NA Bugden in '4P' shot down one Bf109 and another was shared between NA R. E. Mathews in '4M' and a Blenheim. Operations continued on an almost nightly basis until 3 October when the squadron was withdrawn. During their time as part of No. 16 Group, Coastal Command, the new Albacores had escorted more than 100 convoys, dropped over 55 tons of bombs and 7 tons of magnetic mines. Five Albacores had been lost, four damaged and eight aircrew killed or missing, although five were later found to be POWs. The squadron left Bircham Newton on 7 October 1940, moving to St Merryn in Cornwall for armament training.

## Supporting Coastal Command in the Mid-War Years

During 1941 Swordfish squadrons were in demand for carrier duties and operational tasks elsewhere, so there was little scope for supporting Coastal Command. It was mid-1942 before Swordfish could be released to resume such operations, to which Nos 812, 816, 819 with 811 Squadrons contributed.

No. 819 Squadron became the first to come under No. 16 Group, Coastal Command, during July 1942. They moved to Bircham Newton on 6 August, and immediately started minelaying, attacking E-boats and patrolling the Channel and southern areas of the North Sea. They operated from Thorney Island during September/October, moving back to RN control on 28 October and flying north to Hatston.

No. 811 Squadron joined No. 16 Group at Bircham Newton on 6 August, after painting their six Swordfish matt black. Joining them later that day would be six matt black Swordfish of No. 812, who were to work alongside No. 811. The following day they flew to nearby Docking to have long-range tanks fitted. Following an exercise in 1940 when No. 815 Squadron flew with long-range fuel tanks, the Admiralty wanted to extend the range of the Coastal Command Swordfish and put a 69gal (314ltr) tank in the rear cockpit. This effectively did away with the TAG as there was no longer room for him, but extended the aircraft's range by 40 per cent. A number of consequences arose. A full 69gal tank weighed five times that of the average TAG and so, being some way aft of the centre of gravity, gave the aircraft a pronounced tail-down flying attitude until at least half the fuel had been used. Disconcerting to the pilot, to say the least! The ASV screen, fitted in the observers position and not removeable, could no longer be used. The observer picked up the TAG's work as well as reverting to dead-reckoning navigation. He was very aware that apart from 167gal (760ltr) of fuel in the upper mainplane section, he now had 69gal immediately behind him – not a good place to be when the flak and tracer starting flying! The tanks were removed not long afterwards.

**An ASV-equipped all-black Swordfish of No. 119 Squadron, operating out of Bircham Newton.**

No. 811 flew twenty-five operational sorties in the four months they were with Coastal Command. Some raids were not without their humour, despite the seriousness of the business in hand. On the night of 15 September 1942 No. 811 was down to three serviceable Swordfish, but they flew off to Thorney Island and went out to lay mines off Le Havre. One pilot on his return from his mission reported his exact dropping position to the operations room and was surprised when somebody pointed out that the mine was still slung under the fuselage! An enemy convoy consisting of nine merchantmen and eight flak ships was detected going from the Elbe to the Hook of Holland on 25 September and a strike was laid on. No. 811 sent five Swordfish, four with torpedoes and one flare-dropper, and were joined by No. 320, a Dutch squadron flying Hudsons. Surprisingly, the Swordfish could carry a greater load than the Hudsons, who would be taking four 250lb bombs each. Just before dark the aircraft all flew to Ludham which would be nearer to the convoy than Bircham Newton. All attacked the convoy and all missed! But they all returned safely. Eleven operational sorties were flown over the next six weeks or so – minelaying off Cherbourg and Le Havre, patrols against E-boats in the Channel, reconnaissance flights between Le Havre and Boulogne, and convoy escorts. On 18 December No. 811 flew north to Donibristle, where the Swordfish lost their black finish and were re-camouflaged, before continuing north to Hatston in the Orkney Isles. No. 811 became one of the first to take part in the Battle of the Atlantic when they embarked in the escort carrier *Biter*.

On 7 September No. 812 had moved into Docking for a series of operations until 3 November when they too left for Hatston. No. 816 operated out of Thorney Island from September until the end of December, when they left for Machrihanish.

No. 841 Squadron, flying Albacores and a few Swordfish, came under the mantle of Fighter Command on 23 August 1942 and operated out of Manston, with occasional detachments to Coltishall, Tangmere and Exeter. The support in the south coast/ Channel areas consisted of patrols to counter U-boats and E-boats, minelaying and attacks on enemy-held harbours. No. 841 stayed until 1 December 1943 when they handed their Albacores over to No. 415 (RCAF) Squadron. Operational night sorties during this time just fell short of 100.

Earlier, and indeed throughout 1943, Swordfish squadrons continued to be loaned to Coastal Command, some of them only for short periods of special need. These almost continuous night operations kept the enemy on the alert, as they never knew when and where the next attack might come from.

No. 825 Squadron moved into Thorney Island on 14 December 1942 to carry on the role, being joined on 1 January 1943 by No. 836 Squadron. During January No. 825 had four Swordfish based at Exeter, but these returned to Thorney Island a month later when the squadron was replaced by No. 833, who sent a detachment to operate from St Eval in Cornwall. To continue operations off the Devon coast No. 834 moved into Exeter, but were themselves replaced by No. 816 for a month starting on 20 May 1943. Three E-boats were bombed and machine-gunned by one patrolling Swordfish on the night of 30–31 May, but they could not discern any results. A similar experience befell crews on the night of 6–7 June when two Swordfish attacked about eight E-boats near the French coast. No. 816 left on 25 June to prepare for escort carrier duty in the Atlantic.

## Support for D-Day

The planned build-up of Allied forces for the projected invasion of Europe had started in earnest early in 1944. Provision was made for Coastal Command to operate a number of aircraft in specific roles during the run-up to, during, and after D-Day. Some naval aircraft were allocated for these tasks under the control of Nos 155, 156 and 157 Wings, and were to be land-based for an indeterminate period. No. 155 Wing operated Beaufighters, but added to these were No. 819 Squadron with Swordfish and No. 848 Squadron with Grumman Avengers. No. 157 Wing was allocated No. 854 and 855 Avenger squadrons, but these were replaced by Nos 819 and 119 Squadrons with a mixed fleet of Swordfish and Albacores. No. 156 Wing, which included No. 838 Swordfish Squadron, moved to Harrowbeer in Devon while Swordfish of No. 816 and Avengers of Nos 849 and 850 Squadrons used Perranporth.

These squadrons all flew the now familiar offensive sorties: anti-submarine patrols, minelaying the entrances of Dutch, Belgian and French ports, strikes on E- and R-boats, and bombing enemy coastal positions, plus any other duties the authorities came up with. On 20 April No. 838 Squadron, under Lt Cdr J. M. Brown DSC, moved from Machrihanish to Harrowbeer under No. 156 Wing. Their task was anti-submarine patrols using twelve Swordfish Mk II and III aircraft equipped with ASV Mk XI. The Swordfish were also fitted with R/P rails and on the night of 30 April–1 May 1944 they were ordered to attack an enemy destroyer with R/Ps. Twelve Swordfish took part, each taking off at five-minute intervals. However, in poor visibility, cloud overcast and considerable flak, only two aircraft found their target, an Elbing-class destroyer beached at Ile Vierge after an attack by RAF fighters. The Swordfish attacked other targets of opportunity, but three were lost in action. This was to be their one night of action, for the rest of the stay at Harrowbeer was relatively quiet and the squadron moved to Northern Ireland before joining Coastal Command in Scotland.

The Avengers in No. 157 Wing were now replaced by the Swordfish of No. 819 Squadron, moving to Manston on 18 April 1944. These Swordfish were equipped with new ASV Mk X radar, which displayed a much wider area of the coastline. The squadron were quickly in action, discovering and chasing E- and R-boats. On the night of 19–20 May an E-boat was attacked and believed scuttled off Ostend. The following night one crew, acting on the visual sighting of a number of ship's wakes, bombed what appeared to be E-boats, resulting in big explosions. Attacks over the next few nights resulted in the sinking of a 200-ton barge off Dieppe, a 250-ton vessel off Calais and an E-boat.

During D-Day on 6 June 1944, and at later dates, depending on requirements, the squadron provided smoke screens over the invasion fleet. Manston then became the home of two squadrons of Typhoons to combat the attacks by V-1 flying bombs, so in August No. 819 moved to Swingfield, which was basically a steel plank/grass runway near Folkestone. They were joined the following day by No. 119 Squadron, which was equipped with Albacores as part of No. 155 (GR) Wing.

This came about when the Albacores' previous owner, No. 415 Squadron (RCAF), released them to re-equip with the Halifax. No. 415 had formed in July 1941 in the torpedo-bombing role, initially flying Beauforts and Blenheims, then moving on to Hampdens and Wellingtons, and later adding an Albacore/Swordfish Flight. Both types flew with No. 415's codes, such as Swordfish L2739 NH–F and Albacore X9281 NH–K. No. 415 (RCAF) Squadron operated within Coastal Command and

**(Above) Colourful Swordfish of No. 816 Squadron in July 1944 when they were seconded to Coastal Command for operations over and across the Channel. During the D-Day landings in Normandy all Allied aircraft carried black/white invasion markings for easy identification.** IWM

**View from the rear cockpit of an 816 Squadron Swordfish as it lays a smoke screen on D-Day, 6 June 1944.** Ray Sturtivant

was based at Bircham Newton, although a lot of the time the biplanes were based on Thorney Island. They carried out similar duties to the other squadrons attached to Coastal Command.

On 9 April 1944 Albacore X9117 and its crew, pilot Fg Off Mackie and observer Fg Off MacFarland, were tasked to carry out a fighter affiliation exercise. As this was a non-operational flight they agreed to take a Flying Control Officer, Flt Lt L. G. Loft, and AC2 A. L. Thomas along for the ride. Fg Off Mackie took off from Thorney Island in formation with another Albacore X9281 flown by Fg Off William George Brasnett. Once airborne and in position, Mackie made a pass at Brasnett, attacking from above and to starboard. However, he got it wrong and lost control as he went into a steep right turn, and dived into the grounds of Walton Farm Nursery near Bosham, killing all four of them. On 19 July 1944 No. 415 Squadron swapped its Wellingtons, Swordfish and Albacores for the Halifax, and moved to Bomber Command.

Coastal Command wanted to retain the Swordfish/Albacores and formed a new squadron, No. 119, under the command of Sqn Ldr J. I. J. Davies DFC, and based it at RAF Manston. This re-organization took time and it was January 1945 before the first two Swordfish were made available for training. Throughout January they carried out dive-bombing practice, but even though more Swordfish turned up they all had to have the latest modifications fitted before being released for operations. In the meantime the new squadron decided the Albacores were not as suitable as the Swordfish for the type of role expected of it, and by the end of January four Albacores had been 'pensioned off' to the Maintenance Unit (MU) at Wroughton and Swordfish strength had increased to ten. The squadron diarist remarked 'Former Albacore enthusiasts were rapidly becoming expert Swordfish manipulators'!

On 6 February 1945 Fg Off Rabbets, flying Swordfish 'J', carried out the squadron's first operational patrol. The squadron operated day and night: on the night of 24–25 February Fg Off Rabbets released four bombs on a target only identified by radar blips, and later that day six Swordfish flew anti-E-boat patrols. Five more Albacores were retired on 10 March. The following day Sqn Ldr Williamson and Fg Off Gardiner, flying Swordfish 'H', made a depth charge and bomb attack on a 'biber', as midget submarines were known.

**The ASV radar helped to locate any targets at sea during their nocturnal patrols and crews frequently bombed on radar 'blips', sometimes with success. A number of the black Swordfish had cartoon characters; this one, NH-F, has Donald Duck on the forward fuselage.** IWM

**Based at Bircham Newton, the all-black Swordfish of No. 119 Squadron went out at night to locate E-boats and midget submarines.** IWM

**The all-black Swordfish NF343 NH-O of No. 119 Squadron. Codes were in dull red.**

The squadron then moved to airfield B.83 at Knocke in Belgium and operated from there. The next day Plt Off Coles was flying Swordfish 'L' with Flt Sgt Street when, at around 4pm, they encountered a midget submarine a few miles off Overflakee. Coles dropped two depth charges and followed it up with another, the 'biber' disappearing. Also in March, Sqn Ldr Williamson, out in Swordfish 'R' with Flt Lt Matkin, attacked another midget submarine from 50ft with two depth charges about a mile north of Schouwen. On 21 March Flt Sgt Moses flying 'F' bombed and hit an E-boat, as did W/O Scantlebury in 'N' the following night. So for March the squadron had sunk four 'bibers' and damaged four E-boats.

On 12 April Plt Off Goundry flying 'F' attacked two 'bibers' on the surface, blowing one completely out of the water! In May there was a plan to move the squadron to Copenhagen, but this was not required so they continued to fly from B.83. On 4 May Sqn Ldr Williamson, with Flt Lt Matkin in 'P', found a 'biber' on the mudflats and although he dropped his depth charges they seemed to have little effect: the submarine appeared to be either stranded or abandoned. Williamson returned to base, re-armed with bombs this time and carried out a second attack. It was difficult to see what damage had been caused, but oil spread away from the submarine, suggesting some damage. Enemy targets were now getting hard to find, and on 22 May 1945 fourteen Swordfish of No. 119 Squadron flew in formation from Belgium to Bircham Newton.

Meantime, patrols and attacks by No. 819 continued: between 12–31 August 1944 some 108 sorties were made over fifteen nights, with forty-six attacks on enemy vessels. One night the squadron provided flares for Beaufighters to make a night attack on some shipping. No. 819 was then allocated a new patrol area between Gravelines and Flushing. This was a very active area and aircraft suffered from considerable flak. Seven aircraft went out on 1 September with crews attacking various boats and shipping near Ostend, Westkapelle and Zeebrugge, the aircraft flown by Lts Gellatly and Culshaw and LAC Amphlett receiving considerable flak damage to the upper mainplane. Another aircraft attacked fifteen vessels and received flak damage to the tailplane.

No. 819 now moved to Bircham Newton where it was a bit quieter. A detachment flew to St Croix, near Bruge in Belgium and only 6 miles (10km) from the front line, at the end of the month. In November the squadron moved to Maldeghem, about 8 miles (13km) from St Croix, which had a concrete runway, the one at St Croix being earth and puddles. Three motor vessels were detected off The Hague and two Swordfish took off to locate them. Sub-Lt Chambers and Howe lit the enemy ships by flares and then carried out a dive-bombing attack from 1,500ft.

During late November a number of patrols were flown and targets attacked, unusual sights being the launch of a V-2 ballistic rocket and wave-hugging He 111s that launched flying bombs at England. By December, No. 819 were operating out of Knocke-le-Zoute with No. 119, and were subjected to random strafes by Bf 109s and Fw 190s on 1 January 1945. That night six Swordfish and two Albacores went out on patrols, but apart from one attack on minesweepers the night was uneventful.

No. 819 Squadron now changed its Albacores for new Swordfish Mk IIIs with ASV Mk XI radar. Patrols were carried out when weather permitted, but it was 15 January before Sub-Lt Chambers caught sight of five ships and after dropping flares made a bombing attack, but saw no results. Lt Bannerman, flying close by, saw the flares and used the same light to drop his bombs on the same target. Crews were becoming quite adept at using the ASV and one Swordfish bombed its target using radar alone. Therefore, if the ASV set was unserviceable the aircraft returned to base. On the 19 January No. 819 sent out nine aircraft, two returning with ASV failure. The rest of the squadron found five or six E-/R-boats about four miles off the Hook of Holland, but despite repeated attacks between 7.30pm and midnight no ships were sunk.

The squadrons were briefed to look for midget submarines, a 'biber' single-man submarine and a *Seehund* two-seater. Operating from Dutch ports, these would venture out under cover of darkness and try to get back to base before being caught on the surface in daylight. One of the problems trying to bomb moving targets at sea and at night was judging distance. Quite often, although a target could be illuminated by flares, by the time a slow aircraft like the Swordfish or Albacore was in position the target had moved, resulting in under- or over-shoots. Flt Lt F. G. Sutton, with Fg Off R. P. Radford in NH-R, failed to return from a mission on 9 March 1945, the squadron's first loss. A midget submarine was sighted by Fg Off A. O. Corble and Fg Off P. O. Donnell on 11 March, who made four attacks using depth charges. Oil streaks were seen but to make sure another aircraft dropped four 250lb bombs. Two 'bibers' were attacked the following day, both disappearing and leaving oil slicks.

No. 819 Squadron flew to Bircham Newton on 22 May and disbanded three days later.

**No. 819 Squadron operated under Coastal Command in black Swordfish. In 1945 they were flying from Le Loute in Belgium, one of the crews being Sub-Lts Yearsley and Patterson, with TAG LAC Tom Mogford.** Tom Mogford

CHAPTER EIGHT

# Operations – The Atlantic, Arctic and Home Waters, 1939–45

## 1939

Swordfish from *Ark Royal* attacked U-boat U-30 on 14 September as it was manoeuvring to torpedo the SS *Fanad Head*; this ship had earlier been unsuccessfully attacked by U-39, which was later sunk by Blackburn Skua aircraft from *Ark Royal*. On 17 September all twenty-five Swordfish of Nos 811 and 822 squadrons were lost when HMS *Courageous* was sunk after being torpedoed by U-29 in the South-West Approaches.

## Norway

The first large-scale torpedo attacks of the war were carried out by Swordfish of Nos 816 and 818 Squadrons from HMS *Furious* during the Norwegian campaign. *Furious* was on a refit in the Clyde when the Norwegian situation – Germany had invaded on 9 April – demanded her presence and she sailed on 10 April. Such was the urgency that her Skua squadrons, which were still based ashore, were left behind.

The two Swordfish squadrons had nine aircraft each, with which to support the land forces going ashore at Aandalsnes and Namsos. The German cruiser *Admiral Hipper* was reported to be at Trondheim with some escorting destroyers, but in fact she had left before the Home Fleet closed the gap. No. 816 Squadron, led by Lt Cdr H. Gardiner in Swordfish P4169/'U4A', and No. 818, led by Lt Cdr J. Fenton in P4212/'U3A', took off from *Furious* at dawn on 11 April to carry out a torpedo attack. When they got there they found three German destroyers, but all their torpedoes grounded in shallow water.

Two other Swordfish of No. 816, P4167/'U4B' crewed by Sub-Lt Ball, Lt A. S. Marshall and NA R. Pike, and 'U4H' flown by Lt A. J. Read with Sub-Lt K. H. Gibney and NA G. N. Thompson, took off the same day to carry out an armed reconnaissance around Trondheim. Th e weather for once was good, with 20 miles' (32km) visibility and blue skies. After taking some photographs the crew flew to Stornfjord, where they discovered a German destroyer. Sub-Lt Ball dived to 2,000ft and released four 250lb bombs, with Lt Read dropping two 250lb bombs 30 seconds later. No results could be seen and both aircraft returned safely to *Furious*.

**A picture from the rear cockpit of *Warspite*'s Swordfish floatplane, L9767, during the Second Battle of Narvik. Under the flak-damaged tailplane can be seen British destroyer *Hero*, after being hit by a torpedo.** IWM

The following day further strikes were made against German warships in the Narvik area with No. 818 Squadron's CO, Lt Cdr P. G. O. Sydney-Turner in P4212/'U3A', being shot down and 'U3L' ditching in Ofot Fjord. 'U3G' was hit by flak and caught fire, but made it back to the carrier. Fortunately both crews that ditched were rescued by the British destroyer *Grenade*. The weather later turned to snow and sleet with a low cloud base, seriously hampering any further efforts. Despite this, five enemy destroyers were located and bombs dropped on two. Lt S. Keane of No. 818 Squadron, flying 'U3K', was first back and, knowing his undercarriage had been damaged by enemy flak, he decided not to block the flight deck and remained airborne to let all the others land on. Despite the conditions Keane made a perfect landing at night on one wheel! Swordfish K6002/'U4L' of No. 816 went over the side whilst landing on, with the crew, Lt M. D. Donati and LAC Smith, being picked up by the destroyer *Hero* after spending 45 minutes in the sea.

Another major action took place on 13 April in what became known as the Second Battle of Narvik. Knowing that there were German ships in the fjord, Vice-Admiral W. J. Whitworth KCB, DSO took HMS *Warspite* and nine escorting destroyers through Ofot Fjord towards Narvik. To give him air cover *Furious* flew off an anti-submarine patrol and prepared ten Swordfish for a possible attack. To give him an aerial picture of what was going on, the Admiral launched *Warspite*'s Swordfish floatplane, L9767 at 11.52. Flying it was PO F. C. Rice with Lt Cdr W. L. M. Brown as observer and LAC M. G. Pacey as TAG. Despite appalling weather around the fjords the Swordfish strike force arrived and, finding a small gap in the clouds, dive-bombed the enemy destroyers from 2,000ft. They dropped thirty-five 250lb bombs and seventy of 20lb, without hitting anything.

Meanwhile, Fred Rice was flying up the fjord in the floatplane: his observer said it was like flying up a tunnel as clouds stretched across the tops of the mountains each side of the fjord. Despite this, visibility inside Herjangs Fjord was around 6 miles (10km) and they came across U-64 at anchor about 50yd from the jetty at Bjerkvik. Rice immediately attacked: diving to 300ft, he released his 250lb bombs, the first hitting the bows of the submarine and another either hitting it or getting a near miss. As they flew over, Pacey raked the conning tower with his guns, with return fire damaging the tailplane and making the controls sluggish. U-64 sank within half a minute, the first U-boat sunk by an aircraft in World War Two. Manoeuvring carefully in the damaged Swordfish, Rice reported three German destroyers moving behind a smoke screen along Rombaks Fjord. The surface force intercepted them and set the *Giese* and *Roeder* on fire. The Swordfish reported more enemy positions and around 3pm the destroyer *Eskimo* took on two enemy destroyers, losing her bow to a torpedo in the process. The destroyers *Hero* and *Forrester* opened fire, causing a German destroyer to run aground and be finished off by *Warspite*'s guns, and bombs from the Swordfish.

Visibility in the fjord was poor due to low clouds, sleet or snow and smoke from the battle. It was these conditions that led Rice to later say:

> During the Second Battle of Narvik, as the cloud was too low we could not do any spotting so we landed in a small bay down the fjord. A couple of Norwegian fishermen took Brown and myself ashore in a small boat to the local post office. We left poor old Pacey to guard the floatplane with a 0.45 revolver. We then made a 'phone call to an Englishman on the other side of the fjord and I gave some chocolate to the children at the post office because in those days no flying rations were issued. After about an hour the gunfire in the fjord had eased so we decided to take-off and go back to the ship

However, Vice-Admiral Whitworth asked them to spot for further action, and later stated:

> The enemy reports made by *Warspite*'s aircraft were invaluable. I doubt if ever a ship-borne aircraft has been used to such good purpose as it was in this operation.

The result for the day was eight German destroyers sunk with no loss of British surface ships or aircraft. PO Rice and his crew had been airborne for over four hours, and later Rice was awarded a well-earned DSM and Lt Cdr Brown received a DSC but, as was quite often the case during the war, the TAG received nothing.

On 15 April the Home Fleet sailed for Scapa Flow, leaving *Furious* to provide support to any ground forces. Her Swordfish were in constant action after this, attacking enemy positions and shipping in the Narvik area, providing anti-submarine patrols and performing other tasks – one day nine Swordfish went out and bombed Luftwaffe transport aircraft parked on a frozen lake. Apart from enemy fighters, the Swordfish crews found themselves flying through snow and sleet, quite often around cloud-obscured mountains, and using out-of-date maps. The crews, often wet and frozen through, would then return to *Furious* to land on a pitching and slush-covered flight deck in winds gusting to over 50mph (80km/h). Capt T. H. Troubridge, Commanding Officer of *Furious*, later had this to say about the Swordfish crews:

> It is difficult to speak without emotion of the pluck and endurance of the young officers and men, some of them midshipmen, who flew their aircraft to such good effect ... All were firing their first shots in action, whether torpedo, bomb or machine-gun; many made their first night landing on 11 April, and undeterred by the loss of several of their shipmates, their honour and courage remained throughout as dazzling as the snow-covered mountains over which they so triumphantly flew.

On 18 April *Furious* suffered damaged turbines, severely restricting her engine output, in a bomb attack by an He 111. Carrying out a reconnaissance on 19 April, Swordfish 'U3K' ran short of fuel and force-landed on the shore of Lake Skogsfjord, Ringvassoy, the crew being recovered later. During another action on 22 April, Swordfish P4163/'U3G' was shot down by flak, crashing in the fjord north of Narvik. Sub-Lt P. C. Roberts was wounded but rescued by the cruiser *Aurora*, Lt C. R. D. Messenger died of his wounds and the TAG, LAC G. Cutler, was killed. On 24 April *Furious* was withdrawn, her place being taken by *Ark Royal* and *Glorious*. During the last fourteen days the Swordfish from *Furious* had dropped eighteen torpedoes and 409 bombs, flown 23,870 air miles (38,407km) and taken 295 photographs. The cost was nine Swordfish lost in action with twelve aircrew casualties, three fatal; another seventeen Swordfish had been damaged by enemy action.

Acting in support of ground forces, Swordfish of Nos 810 and 820 Squadrons from *Ark Royal* dive-bombed Vaernes aerodrome on 25 April. Two Swordfish from No. 810 Squadron (K8879/'A2R' and L2790/'A2G') and one from No. 820 (P4124/'A4A') were forced to ditch, and L2768/'A2K' of No. 810 ditched due to engine failure just after taking off from *Ark Royal*. Five Swordfish attacked the railway line east of Narvik on 9 May, one aircraft, L2723/'A2B' of No. 810 Squadron, suffering an engine failure and ditching shortly after leaving the carrier. The crew, Lt A. Stewart, Mid G. T. Shaddick and LAC H. W. Burt, were unhurt and picked up by a destroyer. Due to high winds the force took two hours to get to the target area and split up, one section attacking Hunddallen railway station and overturning a train, the other bombing the Nordalshoen viaduct near the Swedish border.

When the decision was made to withdraw from Norway, all surviving RAF Hurricanes were flown aboard *Glorious* even though none of the pilots had made deck landings and the Hurricanes had no tail hooks. Caught at sea with neither air cover nor strong escort by the *Scharnhorst* and *Gneisenau*, *Glorious* was sent to the bottom, along with her two supporting destroyers. However, one of the destroyers, *Acastra*, launched a torpedo which damaged the *Scharnhorst*, before being herself sunk by gunfire. *Scharnhorst* set out for Trondheim to affect repairs, being unsuccessfully dive-bombed on the way by Skuas.

The opportunity to strike at a major German warship was marred by the lack of suitable aircraft in the area to make an attack. Consequently on 21 June, the crews of six Swordfish, three from No. 821 and three from No. 823 Squadrons, ashore at Hatston in the Orkneys, were alerted and briefed for a strike. All were quickly fitted with long-range tanks in their rear cockpits and loaded with a torpedo each. The six took off with the formation led by Sub-Lt J. H. Stenning flying P4144, although the senior officer, and therefore strike leader, was his observer, Lt V. A. T. Smith, RAN (later Vice-Admiral Sir Victor Smith, equivalent to a First Sea Lord in the RAN). Stenning wrote:

The aircraft had a long-range tank in the observer's seat so each aircraft had an observer or a TAG. We took off at 12.45hr and, as usual, my logbook says practically nothing – height 1,500–8,000ft. To Utsire Island and search north – torpedo attack on *Scharnhorst* and seven destroyers – no hits – two aircraft shot down.

We took off and flew to the Norwegian coast climbing in fairly open formation. It was a slow business as the aircraft with torpedo and long-range tank plus crew were a bit heavy for the power of the old Pegasus engine! It took nearly two hours to climb to 8,000ft and reach the Norwegian coast, find our navigation objective and turn north, proceeding up the coast a few miles out to sea. After quite a short time we spotted *Scharnhorst* with a close escort of seven destroyers steaming south at high speed.

I gave the hand signal for attack formation, pointing my thumbs backwards for line astern. Our sub-flight stayed to the east of the enemy while the other moved to the west. When the flak started it wasn't too accurate and once I started my dive I didn't notice it until after I had dropped my 'fish – too many things to think about! The destroyers must have been about 1,000–2,000yd from the battleship. It was quite tricky having to manoeuvre between two destroyers to get inside the screen and have a clear run for the torpedo. It then left very little time to adjust everything and drop the 'fish within the necessary criteria for a good run, namely, height 50–120ft above the water – wings level – nose not down and not much up – aim off for ship's speed at the right dropping range which had to be 800–1,000yd – airspeed 80–100kt.

The torpedo sight on those Stringbags was two horizontal rows of light bulbs either side of the fuselage ahead of the pilot's cockpit. You had to estimate the target speed and set it so that the correct bulb lit up. I estimated 30kt but I had never carried out practice attacks (ALTs) on big ships at that speed: most of ours didn't do more than 20–24kt. Anyway, after dropping I did a violent starboard turn and went like hell at zero feet. I found this was a mistake as all the shots being fired at me ricocheted off the sea all round the aircraft. I was just able to see my torpedo pass through the kick of the wake as *Scharnhorst* altered course – a miss just astern. I got away to the east and circled at about 1,000ft until two other aircraft joined me. Couldn't wait too long because the fuel situation was getting critical. Smith gave me a course to steer and after 4¾ hours we landed at Sumburgh in South Shetlands to refuel. We took off again at 18.25hr and landed at Hatston just over an hour later. Four out of six got back and we never heard anything about the other two Swordfish, both from No. 823 Squadron.

On 23 October 1940, I was still with No. 821 Squadron at Hatston. We took off in Swordfish L9743, with observer Lt C. L. F. Webb and TAG LAC Craig. We left Hatston at 07.15hr for an anti-submarine patrol armed with depth charges and orders to patrol to the south-east of Fair Isle at 1,000ft. Flying along, we noticed another aircraft approaching and assumed it was an RAF kite. It approached from our starboard quarter and when the tracer came whizzing past I alarmingly started avoiding action, weaving, jinking and throwing the old Swordfish about.

We identified it as a Dornier 215 and he subsequently made five attacks from dead astern, firing the front gun/turret on the approach then, when nearly on us, turned away to starboard and letting the rear gunner have a go! Whilst he completed his circle for another attack I flew flat out (all of 120kt!) towards the Orkneys. After the sixth attack he gave up and flew away eastwards and I belted for Hatston. My observer told me afterwards that each time I started avoiding action Craig had a go with our Lewis gun each time he was within range. When I landed I realized that I had not even jettisoned my depth charges, which would have made it easier to fling the Swordfish about. It crossed my mind that had I thought of it I could have dropped down over the sea and as he came up astern, to drop the depth charges and hoped the column of water thrown up might knock him down. Now that would have been something – to have shot down a Dornier bomber with depth charges! Examining the aircraft on the ground we found a bullet in the radio, holes in the wings and an interplane strut shot through.

During September/October 1940, *Furious*, with Nos 816 and 825 squadrons embarked, each with nine Swordfish, plus the nine Skuas of No. 801, carried out a series of strikes on Norwegian targets. One such, planned for 22 September, against enemy shipping at Trondheim, would have been the first wartime night torpedo attack – almost a month before the Taranto raid (*see* page 129). This raid was led by Lt Cdr E. Esmonde, CO of No. 825 Squadron, with his observer, Lt J. G. Cardew, who later said of this raid:

Esmonde was leading the two Swordfish squadrons (Nos 816 and 825) of nine aircraft each. The plan was to cross the coast some 50 miles north of the entrance of the fjord leading to Trondheim, drop right down on to the water of the fjord leading north-east from Trondheim, and attack on a south-westerly course. The moon would be silhouetting the target area.

On reaching the coast we found the cloud base was to below 1,000ft. The maps we had were atrocious, out of date and inaccurate. There was no way we could reach the inner fjord as a co-ordinated strike force even if we could manage to miss the mountains. It would mean blind flying, blind navigation and a blind let-down into the fjord where we had no knowledge of the cloud base height. We could not fly through Trondheim fjord as this was heavily protected with guns, and wires stretched across the fjord. Both ways in would be suicidal. Esmonde wanted to press on over the mountains. We had a flaming row in the aircraft for about five minutes. I could not pull rank on him but had to convince him through experience that should he press on with the attack eighteen valuable aircraft and crews would certainly be lost.

Our secondary target, namely to seek and destroy enemy coastal shipping, had been given to us in case we should encounter exactly these conditions. Seventeen aircraft were following us in sub-flights as we circled a couple of miles off the coast whilst Esmonde and I had the argument – eventually common sense won and I passed the order by light to break formation and to seek and attack shipping. After about 15 minutes we spotted a German sloop or escort vessel at anchor close under the cliffs. We circled to identify it as German. On the run-in we were challenged but no guns opened fire. At about 300yd Esmonde dropped his torpedo. It was perfectly sighted but failed to go off. Maybe the depth setting was too great, although as far as I remember we were using the new magnetic type pistol.

At least three crews of No. 825 Squadron failed to return to *Furious*, mainly I fear through observer error. *Furious* had been at sea for about four days in baddish weather, therefore our take-off position could have been a few miles in error. Possibly the young observers took their return departure from a known position on the coast and so failed to find the carrier, whereas the experienced observers noted the error from the landfall position and corrected accordingly.

**Torpedo-armed Swordfish of No. 810 Squadron ranged on *Ark Royal* just prior to going after *Bismarck* on 26 May 1941. Fourteen Swordfish took part in the attack, in rain and gale-force winds.** Lt Cdr M. B. W Howell

At the end of October 1940 *Furious* was detached from the Home Fleet, and with *Argus*, was used to ferry aircraft from the UK to Takoradi on the Gold Coast of West Africa: from here aircraft destined for use in North Africa were ferried to Egypt, so avoiding a perilous journey through the Mediterranean. This left the Home Fleet without a carrier until the following spring, *Ark Royal* having joined the newly formed Force H to operate in the Western Mediterranean. To provide air cover for the ferry trips to Takoradi, *Argus* had two Swordfish embarked for anti-submarine patrols and *Furious* had six Skuas. The German heavy cruiser *Admiral Hipper* discovered a supply convoy heading for Takoradi on Christmas Day 1940 but shadowing by the Skuas and gunfire from the British cruisers escorting the convoy drove it away. The two Swordfish on *Argus* were actually prepared for a torpedo strike, but in the event were not required.

When it was discovered that *Scharnhorst* and *Gneisenau* were out in the Atlantic during March 1941 *Ark Royal* joined the search and one of her Fairey Fulmars found and shadowed them. However, before a torpedo strike by her Swordfish could be laid on contact was lost in poor visibility. Force H spent much of April in mid-Atlantic, but the German ships had returned to Brest and the breakout for German waters that they were expected to attempt did not occur until February 1942.

## *Bismarck*

The drama of the first and last violent sortie of the German battleship *Bismarck* became a household story during May 1941 as a great battle was fought out in poor weather conditions in the Atlantic.

On 22 May a Martin Maryland of the Fleet Air Arm's No. 771 Squadron, operating in abysmal weather, found the *Bismarck*, which had sailed on 19 May from Gotenhafen and was sailing towards the Atlantic with the heavy cruiser *Prinz Eugen*. It was by pure chance that early in 1941 Swedish intelligence officers had decided it was to their country's advantage to inform the British of German activities in the area. The Norwegian-government-in-exile's military attaché in Stockholm was Colonel Roscher Lund and on the evening of 20 May Lund heard, via Major Tornberg of the Swedish intelligence service, that during that day two large German warships and several other types had passed through the Kattegat into the North Sea under air cover. Lund informed the naval attaché at the British embassy, Captain Henry W. Denham, and Denham cabled the Admiralty in London that at 1500hrs two large warships, escorted by three destroyers and five escort vessels, with ten or twelve covering aircraft, had passed Marstrand going north-west. This information had already set the wheels in motion at the Admiralty by the time the Maryland's sighting was received.

At this crucial time, HMS *Victorious*, a newly commissioned carrier, was loaded with Hurricanes for a run to Malta. On board were nine Swordfish of No. 825 Squadron and six Fulmars of No. 800Z Squadron, totally unsuitable for a strike as they had been embarked only for ship protection during the journey to Malta. In addition, No. 825's Swordfish crews had had very little recent training in torpedo attacks. The Hurricanes were quickly off-loaded and a plea was made to use the fully worked-up No. 828 Squadron with its Albacores, then based in the Orkneys. At that time No. 828 fell under the control of RAF Coastal Command, and by the time approval had been granted the *Victorious* had sailed.

The British cruisers *Suffolk* and *Norfolk* found *Bismarck* in the Denmark Strait on 23 May, with the latter's Supermarine Walrus reconnaissance flying boat shadowing her for 48 hours before contact was lost in deteriorating weather. On 24 May the battlecruiser HMS *Hood* and the battleship HMS *Prince of Wales* opened the battle, but a direct hit on *Hood* from the *Bismarck* shocked both sides when it caused *Hood* to blow up with a heavy loss of life. During the late afternoon of 24 May, the British commander, Admiral

Tovey in HMS *King George V*, moved *Victorious* and four cruisers to a position that would be less than 100 miles (160km) distant from *Bismarck*, if his assumptions were correct. He planned to launch a torpedo attack by the Swordfish of No. 825 Squadron when within range. He realized that *Bismarck*'s heavily armoured belt might be too strong for a hit by an aerial torpedo to sink the battleship, but a hit might nonetheless slow the Germans up enough for the cruisers to finish the job.

After nightfall on the 24 May *Bismarck* and *Prinz Eugen* parted company. A short time later nine Swordfish of No. 825, led by Lt Cdr Esmonde flying Swordfish '5A' with his observer, Colin Ennever and TAG Parker, made a torpedo attack in poor conditions with one aircraft obtaining a hit on the *Bismarck*'s armoured belt. The leader of the second flight was Lt Percy Gick who later reported:

> Only after we sailed were we told of the *Bismarck* panic. My problem was how to get all nine aircraft serviceable, with torpedoes on, and the pilots briefed on how we were to attack. As we steamed at full speed towards the *Bismarck* to intercept, it was becoming abundantly clear that we were going to run out of daylight. I had always been crazy about operating at night – it struck me as the only sensible thing to do because the opposition couldn't see you so well and they were therefore less likely to shoot you down. I'd done my deck landings at night because I had done some of the initial trials in the old *Ark Royal* before the war. The rest of the pilots had done very little night flying and not one of them a night deck landing. When I was asked whether or not we should attempt to attack at such a time that we would arrive back after dark, I gave as my advice that probably half the aircraft would get back on board intact, and if the rest of the air crews couldn't make it, at least they could ditch and get picked up by a destroyer.
>
> In due course we were launched. In the back of my aircraft, '5F,' I had as a TAG a delightful man, PO L. D. Sayer, and my observer was Sub-Lt V. K. Norfolk, who was a genius with the old Mk 2 ASV radar. As we approached the *Bismarck*, Norfolk quietly shouted down the speaking tube, 'She's on the port bow and I've got an idea I can see someone shadowing her'. A little later he confirmed that he had the *Bismarck* as a big blip on the port bow, a slightly smaller one on the starboard bow and, some few minutes later, something even smaller roughly ahead.
>
> We were flying in three sub-flights, each in a Vic of three, and the three flights in a Vic. Looking across at Esmonde's aircraft it was abundantly clear that Colin Ennever's set was not working as well and he had nothing. Of course, we had no radio communication then. I had to bring my sub-flight ahead to attract Esmonde's back cockpit's attention so that Norfolk could make hand signals to indicate to Colin Ennerver that the enemy was on the port bow. To this day I don't know what happened to the set in Esmonde's aircraft but apparently the port aerial wasn't working and the starboard was, and all Colin could see was *Sheffield* on the starboard bow.
>
> In spite of all our efforts Esmonde peeled off and we lost our gorgeous height in attacking the *Sheffield*! Fortunately, everybody recognized the *Sheffield* and no torpedoes were dropped; we tried to reform and climb away. As we did so, on our starboard beam we saw first, the coastguard cutter *Modoc* and, a bit later, the *Bismarck* on our starboard bow. Swordfish with torpedoes on did not climb easily and it was quite clear that if we were going to do a successful attack we had to get a bit of altitude in order to pick up some speed, and, as a squadron, we started to climb away. Our cruising speed at this time was about 75kt.
>
> *Bismarck* sighted us and opened fire, which was astonishingly accurate for range and looked nasty because there were great balls of black where shells exploded ahead of us. Even at this, about 4 miles' range, a shell tore away one of Esmonde's ailerons. Eventually, Esmonde peeled off with his sub-flight and went into the attack.

**Swordfish 'A4K' of No. 820 Squadron starts its take-off run in a howling gale on 26 May 1941 to attack *Bismarck*.** Lt Cdr M. B. W. Howell

Esmonde's observer, Colin Ennerver, later went on record with his version of what happened in '5A':

> The first shells were thrown against us and we had to abandon sub-flight tight formation at a distance of about 4 miles. As we neared *Bismarck*, the equivalent of pom-pom with tracer alarmingly seemed to pass through the mainplanes. Although we didn't know until we landing, our starboard lower mainplane was ripped and holed badly. I called out to Esmonde via voice pipe at ¼- and ½-mile distances until he considered our position and sang out, 'Going down'. I tapped the air gunner on his shoulder and gave him the sign and we buttoned on our breast parachutes – more against splinters than otherwise. Esmonde made a perfect drop at 800yd or so and turned downwind to the left. As we came round Parker was firing his K-gun madly at the *Bismarck* – most cheering! The *Bismarck* seemed to be swinging to starboard or away from us. At a few feet above the waves we seemed to be lower than their fire. Passing the

bow, I saw a column of water jump funnel high on the starboard amidships side and black smoke issue from her funnel – a definite hit – followed by a smaller water column on the port side. I instructed our TAG to wireless 'One definite hit, one probable. Returning'. Gick, from the anti-aircraft mêlée, attacked from starboard, probably unseen, and it may have been his drop.

We joined four other aircraft, the weather now calmer but almost dark. I conferred with Esmonde on obtaining a radio D/F [Direction Finding] bearing, which meant breaking radio silence in the vicinity of the fleet. He agreed, and on receipt we wheeled another 25 degrees left towards the carrier. It was now dark with visibility uncertain. After 25 minutes Esmonde instructed me to send a message asking for a searchlight into the air. The landing after that was almost an anti-climax.

Percy Gick's description of the attack on *Bismarck* continues:

Obviously, if we all went in from the same direction, she would turn in to us, so I carried on still climbing a little and then levelled off. My problem was that Esmonde having started his attack meant that unless I got in reasonably soon she would comb his torpedoes and then mine. By this time 'Speed' Pollard had also peeled off and I lost sight of him because there was a lot of misty cloud around. So I decided I must go in. As we got within a few thousand yards I saw Esmonde drop his torpedoes and pull out. It was clear that *Bismarck* had plenty of time to comb his torpedoes and then turn to mine. So I pulled away and dived straight down to sea level, and then turned back, hoping to get in unobserved. There was hell of a sea running and I got down on the surface and kept losing sight of her behind the waves. On my left, Pat Jackson [Sub-Lt D. P. B. Jackson] was doing the same, but on my right, Bill Garthwaite [Lt W. F. C. Garthwaite] went in steadily and, when we were sighted, drew all the fire. His observer, Sub-Lt W. A. Gillingham, commented afterwards 'He didn't mind the stuff going above him and below him, but it was those beastly little balls of fire that nipped in between the wings that upset him.' I like to think that I got the right range, but she was hell of a big ship and I have a horrible feeling I may have dropped a little too early. Anyhow, I did, and as I dropped Bill and Pat did so also and we pulled and turned away. By this time there was hell of a lot of fireworks going on, but my dear observer had brought with him a very expensive camera and was determined to get some pictures, and insisted that I should turn this way and that whilst he photographed the ship. Frankly, I thought the whole thing terribly unhealthy and stupid, and in fact it very nearly was, when he was satisfied and I got down near the water and flew away. *Bismarck* did what I regarded as one of the most unsporting things of all, which was to lob 15in shells at us. These caused great inconvenience because one of them landed ahead of us and I flew through the splash. The whole aircraft gained about 30ft in altitude, and the only comment that came out of Sayer during the whole 4-hour flight was 'Goddam! Some rotten sod's knocked the bottom out of my house.' The splash had literally ripped the fabric off the bottom part of his cockpit, and he was gazing into fresh air for the rest of the trip back.

**The crew of Swordfish 'A5S' of No. 818 Squadron wave to *Ark Royal* as they return from the third strike against *Bismarck* on 27 May 1941.** IWM

This was an excellent achievement in very poor conditions, against a highly manoeuvrable foe and with no recent training. All the Swordfish returned safely except one. Sub-Lt Jackson became separated from the other attacking aircraft in the general confusion and poor visibility. He made his way back, only to find no carrier. The normal procedure in such cases is to carry out a square search or steer into wind – he continued to do this for close on five hours without sighting the carrier. Down to his last drop of petrol, he informed his crew he was going to ditch – and at that exact moment he saw an empty lifeboat drifting in a deserted sea. He ditched alongside and climbed into the boat with his crew, pulling their own aircraft dinghy over the top. The lifeboat had full provisions and fresh water, which was to the good for they were adrift for nine days before being picked up by a passing Norwegian steamer.

Baron Burkard von Mullenheim-Rechberg who was fourth gunnery officer aboard *Bismarck* recalls the Swordfish attack:

Aircraft alarm! In seconds every anti-aircraft gun on the *Bismarck* was ready for action. One after the other, the planes came towards us, nine Swordfish, torpedoes under their fuselages. Daringly they flew through our fire, nearer to the fire-spitting mountain of the *Bismarck*, always nearer and nearer. Watching through my director, which, having been designed for surface targets, had a high degree of magnification but only a narrow field, I could not see all the action. Our anti-aircraft batteries were firing and now and again one of our 38cm turrets and frequently our 15cm turrets fired into the water ahead of the aircraft, raising massive water-spouts. To fly into one of those spouts would mean the end. And the aircraft: they were moving so slowly that they seemed to be standing still in the air, and they looked so antiquated. Incredible how the pilots pressed their attack with suicidal courage, as if they did not expect ever again to see a carrier.

We had increased speed to 27kt and began to zigzag sharply to avoid the torpedoes that were splashing into the water. This was an almost impossible task because of the close range and low altitude from which the torpedoes were launched. Some of the planes were only 2m above the water and did not release their torpedoes until they had closed to 400m or 500m. The enemy's tactics were such that torpedoes were coming at us from several directions at the same time and, in trying to avoid one we were liable to run into another. Back and forth we zigzagged; all at once the ringing report of an explosion punctuated the roar of the guns and the *Bismarck* gave a slight shudder. A torpedo had hit the armoured belt amidships from a Swordfish [Percy Gick] that had attacked out of the setting sun.

Actual material damage was slight, with one man killed and five with broken bones. However, all was not well. Increasing speed to 27kt, water pressure on the damaged bulkheads increased and water began rushing in again, resulting in the ship being down by the bow more than before. We continued to head for St Nazaire.

Contact was again lost with *Bismarck* in the ever-changing weather conditions, and not regained for 30 hours. During this time searches were made to the north-west of *Bismarck*'s last position and Force H sailed to join and assist the Home Fleet.

**Reputed to be the aircraft that hit and damaged *Bismarck*, Swordfish K8376 'A2Q' 'Queenie' is seen here serving with No. 833 Squadron in Jamaica, October 1941.**
Lt Cdr M. B. W. Howell

Unbeknown to the attackers, *Bismarck* had been damaged more heavily than originally thought in the battle off Iceland and, having taken a hit on her fuel tanks from the guns of the *Prince of Wales*, was now running short of fuel. Also, after the shell damage, *Bismarck* took on nearly 2,000 tons of seawater, which resulted in her being 3 degrees down at the bows and listing 9 degrees to port. Some intentional flooding improved the trim, and 28kt was achievable. However, the fuel leak was leaving an easily followed trail of diesel oil in the water.

Anticipating a run for Brest, the Admiralty moved Force H north to block such an escape. Included in this force was *Ark Royal* which had Nos 810, 818 and 820 Squadrons with thirty Swordfish between them, plus Nos 807 and 808 with twelve Fulmars each. Contact was made again during the forenoon of 26 May by an RAF Consolidated Catalina, but this was damaged by enemy gunfire and had to leave. Ten Swordfish from *Ark Royal*, acting on this information, found and continued to shadow the German battleship. Six others, fitted with auxiliary fuel tanks to increase their loiter time, joined them. During the early afternoon a strike was laid on with *Sheffield* detached to give ASV help. Unfortunately, the crews had not been briefed about this and fifteen Swordfish accidentally attacked the *Sheffield*, eleven of them actually dropping their torpedoes. It was most fortunate that the weather was appalling, with gusty winds, low cloud and poor visibility; as it was, some of the torpedoes blew up on striking the surface and the *Sheffield* avoided all the remainder, and the aircraft returned to the carrier. Lt Mike Lithgow recalls:

> Somewhat crestfallen, we returned to the ship to find a further hazard in store. The rise and fall of the stern was distinctly alarming – it was at this stage that it was measured and found to be 56ft. The only thing was to aim at the middle of the flight deck (the barriers were not in use) and hope to slide in over the stern when it wasn't looking, so to speak. In spite of many voluntary wave-offs if the pitch was thought to be excessive, we smashed the undercarriages of three aircraft in the process of landing on. This was due to no fault of the pilots. The *Ark* was almost stopped to keep the wind speed over the deck as low as possible, but even so it was gusting 30–50kt.

Each Swordfish as it landed had the wings quickly folded and was struck down into the hangar. All were refuelled and loaded with another torpedo. A second strike was laid on after nightfall and this time the *Sheffield* provided ASV radar directions, but due to the bad weather a full squadron attack was impossible and most aircraft attacked individually. The CO of No. 818 Squadron, Lt Cdr Coode, had as his observer Lt Carver who later said:

> The formation of fifteen [Swordfish] arrived over *Sheffield*, and they started to climb to get some height to attack, thus entering dense cloud and, as a result, sub-flights became separated and

**Decorated for their part in the raid on *Bismarck* are, from the left, Lt P. D. Gick, Lt Cdr E. Esmonde (CO of No. 825 Squadron), Sub-Lt V. K. Norfolk (Gick's observer), PO L. D. Sayer (Gick's TAG) and LAC A. L. 'Ginger' Johnson.** IWM

> had to attack individually. Our sub-flight of three was the first to attack and came in on the port beam. We had been fired upon in cloud during the approach, so there was no question of surprise. At about 2½ miles from Bismarck all the AA weapons opened up – very impressive and frightening with a load of glowing billiard balls flashing past.

Coode held his course, despite a gale of 40kt, and released his torpedo at about 1,200yd (1,100m) before turning to port at 'nought feet' – in September 1941 Coode would receive the DSO and Carver the DSC for their part in the attack. Two hits were made by the attacking aircraft, one on the armoured belt and one aft which destroyed the steering gear, jammed both rudders and damaged the propellers. In fact, with the flooding forward, the propellers were partly out of the water. All the Swordfish returned safely although many had suffered hits – one had 180 bullet holes.

Due to the damage she had suffered, *Bismarck* steamed in unpredictable directions, but she still had her main armament and continued to fight a difficult running battle during the night. Harassed by British destroyers during the night, she was finally sunk by the combined gunfire of the Home Fleet and Force H the following morning, just as the third strike of Swordfish arrived to give the *coup de grâce*. For some unknown reason they were not required to attack and watched the death throes of the *Bismarck* before jettisoning their torpedoes and returning to *Ark Royal*.

## Operations in the Arctic

In June 1941 Hitler launched Operation *Barbarossa*, the invasion of the Soviet Union. The Soviets appealed to the Allies for help in any form, direct or indirect, but especially where it would take the pressure off for a short time. As part of this support the Royal Navy agreed to make a strike on German communications in northern Norway. Carrier aircraft would attack Petsamo in Finland and Kirkenes in northern Norway, while a large supply of mines were delivered to Archangel by the minelayer *Adventure*.

The ships involved included *Furious*, with No. 812 Squadron (nine Swordfish), No. 817 (nine Albacores), No. 800 (nine Fulmars) and No. 880A Flight (four Sea Hurricanes). She was joined by *Victorious* who had Nos 827 and 828 Squadrons with twelve and nine Albacores respectively, and No. 809 with twelve Fulmars. They sailed from Scapa Flow during July in company with two cruisers and six destroyers, and proceeded to Seidisfjord, Iceland, to refuel before moving into position.

On the afternoon of 30 July the carriers launched their strike force, even though a

German shadowing aircraft had reported their position. *Furious* launched a strike on Petsamo: nine Swordfish of No. 812 Squadron, six armed with torpedoes and three with bombs; the four Sea Hurricanes of No. 880A Flight for fighter cover; nine Albacores of No. 817, again, six with torpedoes and three with bombs; and six Fulmars of No. 800 Squadron. Flying low over the sea to avoid detection, the formation entered the Gulf of Petsamo where the aircraft with bombs broke away to carry out their attack. Swordfish 'L' dropped its bombs on oil tanks, setting one on fire, while 'G' traded bullets with gunners on a lighthouse at Numeroniemi. There was only one suitable target, a small steamer, which they sank; the other torpedoes were used to attack wooden jetties. One Albacore and two Fulmars were lost.

*Victorious* launched twenty-one Albacores and nine Fulmars against Kirkenes, but the enemy were ready with all defences manned, including air cover by the Luftwaffe. Albacores sank one 2,000-ton freighter, the MV *Rottver*, set another on fire and damaged shore installations, but the loss was terrible: enemy fighters and flak shot down eleven of the Albacores and only one out of the other twenty was undamaged; that one managed to shoot down a Junkers Ju 87 *Stuka* with its front gun. Two Messerschmitt Bf 110s and a Bf 109 were shot down by the Fulmars, who lost two of their number.

During the attack an Albacore flown by Sub-Lt D. Myles, Sub-Lt A. Keep and air gunner H. Griffin force-landed after being shot up by a German fighter, all becoming POWs. Another Albacore, shot down by a Bf 110, was crewed by Lt L. E. R Bellair, Lt D. M. Lubbeck and air gunner L. F. Beer, who was unfortunately killed. The aircraft crash-landed about 25 miles south-east of Kirkenes, the pilot and observer walking 12 miles (19km) to Grense Jakobselv and becoming POWs.

The remaining Albacores on *Furious* were transferred to *Victorious* to make good her losses, and then *Furious* returned to Scapa Flow as she was low on fuel. Although there were plans for further strikes, it was decided that they would wait until more suitable aircraft were available. Consequently in August *Furious* took part in anti-shipping operations in Varanger Fjord, accompanied *Ark Royal* to Malta twice in September, delivering much-needed Hurricanes, and then left for a refit in the USA.

## *Tirpitz*

Convoy PQ12 left Iceland for Murmansk on 1 March 1942 with QP8 leaving Murmansk for the UK at the same time. On 4 March PQ12's escort, consisting of the battleships *King George V* and *Duke of York*, the battlecruiser *Renown*, the cruiser *Berwick*, the carrier *Victorious* and nine destroyers left Scapa Flow to join the convoy. On the 6 March the ships were informed that it was almost certain that Bismarck's sister-ship *Tirpitz* was sailing north, probably to attack the two convoys, which were now being shadowed by enemy aircraft. The weather was kind to the convoys: heavy seas, with snow and sleet in high winds. The two convoys passed each other and *Tirpitz* missed them both, sailing back south for a haven in Norway.

Estimating the German battleship's track, Admiral Tovey decided to fly off a search party of Albacores, all going in different directions for about 150 miles (240km) in the hope that one of them would find *Tirpitz* in the poor weather. In miserably cold weather and poor visibility the six Albacores were launched in the early hours of 9 March. Amazingly, considering the conditions, one Albacore, flown by Lt W. H. G. Brown, discovered *Tirpitz* only 80 miles (130km) from the fleet and heading south at high speed – she was capable of 30kt (almost 60km/h). Another Albacore joined the first and the pair continued to keep track of the enemy ship.

Less than an hour after the six Albacores had taken off, a strike was launched consisting of twelve Albacores from Nos 817 and 832 Squadrons, armed with torpedoes. Leading the formation was Lt Cdr Lucas, an officer who had not made a torpedo drop, even in practice, for four years; he spotted the *Tirpitz* with one escorting destroyer at around 9am and decided to attack immediately. In his inexperience he failed to take advantage of cloud cover and/or a tail wind, so the slow Albacores battled into a strong wind in plain view of *Tirpitz*. Heavy and accurate flak shot down two of them straight away, and the others took on damage as they closed in. Under the circumstances it was no surprise that all the torpedoes missed and *Tirpitz* made the safety of a fjord. Despite this the German commander, Admiral Otto Ciliax, remarked in the log for *Tirpitz* that the attack was 'pressed home with dash and determination'.

*Victorious* returned to Scapa Flow for refuelling and supplies. A new type of torpedo was added to the stores, supposedly two and a half times more powerful than those used previously and only 1cwt (50kg) heavier. The fleet sailed again on 22 March to cover PQ13. On the evening of 23 March Lt Beer was tasked to do an anti-submarine patrol, but as his Albacore approached the carrier's island structure on take-off it veered slightly to the right and caught a wing. The resulting swing pushed the aircraft over the side and into the sea, where the depth charges blew up, killing the crew. The convoy was subjected to a howling gale: 100mph (160km/h) winds, the sea swells rising to over 70ft (20m) and breaking over *Victorious'* flight deck. Albacores, ranged on the flight deck armed with torpedoes, were literally held down by deck crews who had a job not to be blown away themselves. The gale eventually blew itself out but the temperature dropped to –25°C and the carrier was encrusted with tons of ice. The ships returned to Scapa Flow to carry out repairs. *Victorious* continued on the Murmansk run without any further action and then moved south during August 1942, ready for Operation *Pedestal*, the famous convoy that fought its way to Malta with supplies vital to the island's continued resistance.

## Breakout – Channel Fiasco

In January 1942 a special conference was set up between the British joint chiefs of staff to discuss what to do if the three major German warships, *Scharnhorst*, *Gneisenau* and *Prinz Eugen*, all in Brest harbour, attempted to break out into the Atlantic or head north to Norway. In actual fact it was Hitler, in one of his poorer tactical decisions, who precipitated the action that followed. Admiral Raeder, Commander-in-Chief of the German Navy, was called to a conference at Hitler's 'Wolf's Lair' on 17 September 1941 where he was informed that he (Hitler) thought the battleships would be more useful in Norwegian waters to help repel the expected Allied invasion of that country. Raeder managed to convince Hitler that at the moment it would be better to leave the ships at Brest, but at the November meeting Hitler was adamant that the Allies were planning to move on Norway. In December 1941 he informed his naval chiefs that unless they moved the battleships to Norway he would have them dismantled and their heavy guns added to the defence of Norway.

## Eugene Esmonde

There was much controversy about Eugene Esmonde. Some officers thought him rash, even dangerous, as he continually made attacks on the enemy, regardless of odds and self-survival. He believed there was good in all men and stood by this belief during their training as a team and in his determination that his squadron would be the best carrying the fight to the enemy. He rebuilt his squadron and its morale many times, always with the same purpose – to attack the enemy where necessary in the best traditions of the Royal Navy. Those who knew the man said he was a true professional, dedicated to his purpose without thought for personal gain or glory. Some, however, said it was the latter that drove him and there may have been a grain of truth in that, for some of his ancestors had served in the British Army and Thomas Esmonde had been awarded the Victoria Cross for personal bravery at the siege of Sebastopol during June 1855.

Eugene Esmonde was born on 1 March 1909 at Huthwaite House, Thurgoland, a mining village near Sheffield in Yorkshire. He was one of seven children raised by his mother Eily and father John Joseph, who had a medical practice. Esmonde senior also had six children from his first wife. Eugene was twin brother to James. In 1919 the family moved to London and he attended the Jesuit College at Wimbledon. There was a family home in Ireland, and in 1923 the family moved there so that Eugene could become a missionary, starting his ordainment at Clangroves Wood College and then joining the Mill Hill Fathers at St Peter's College in Freshfield, Lancashire, before going on to Burn Hall, County Durham.

At this point he had serious misgivings about his vocation for missionary work, and applied for a five-year Short Service Commission in the RAF, joining up on 28 December 1928. He reported to No. 2 Flying Training School (FTS) at RAF Digby, Lincolnshire, on 13 January 1929. Here he started his flying training on such types as the Avro 504N, Bristol Fighter, de Havilland DH.9A and Vickers Vimy. He was awarded his wings on 13 December 1929 and posted to No. 26 (Army-Co-operation) Squadron at Catterick in Yorkshire, flying Armstrong Whitworth Atlas aircraft. His skills were rewarded with a move to a fighter squadron, and on 3 March 1930 he joined No. 43 Squadron at Tangmere flying the lovely Armstrong Whitworth Siskin IIIA. He took part in numerous air displays, including tied-together aerobatics.

Promoted to Flying Officer, he was posted on 3 May 1931 to RAF Gosport for a sixteen-week course on the handling and flying of aeroplanes from aircraft carriers, including torpedo dropping. On completion of the course he was posted to No. 463 (Fleet Torpedo Bomber) Flight with the Fleet Air Arm, which operated Blackburn Darts from the carrier *Courageous*. There were nine flights aboard, operating Flycatchers, Fairey IIIFs, Blackburn Darts and Avro 504Ns. Over the next year he took part in squadron and carrier activities including 'showing the flag' cruises to such locations as Gibraltar, Portugal and Malta.

By November 1932 he was an instructor at Gosport and one of his former pupils described him as:

> A quiet-spoken man, looking somewhat older than his real age. He knew precisely what he needed from me in terms of flying and was equally precise in his teaching technique. He never once lost his patience with me, despite several howling errors on my part, but simply explained in detail what I had done wrong, then proceeded to demonstrate the correct method or procedure.

On 10 April 1933 Esmonde was posted to No. 7 Squadron at Worthy Down, flying Vickers Virginias. He was officially transferred to Class A Reserve on 28 December 1933, after some 855 flying hours in a wide variety of aircraft and situations. He remained on Reserve until 1 April 1936, when he was promoted to Flight Lieutenant.

By then, with his flying experience and skills, he had taken a position as First Officer with Imperial Airways, the forerunner of British Airways. His first posting, in 1935, was to No. 2 Operating Division at Karachi, India, flying the four-engined Armstrong Whitworth Argosy airliner. He also flew the Short Scylla and Handley Page HP.42, flying all three on the Karachi–Singapore run. He became a Captain in mid-1936 and was detached to the Irrawaddy Flotilla Co., based at Rangoon in Burma, flying Short Scion Senior four-engined floatplanes. After a while he returned to the UK base at Hythe to convert onto the Short S.23 Empire-class flying boats, after which he flew them on the UK–India–Singapore run.

A surprise letter from the Admiralty in January 1939 offered him a commission in the FAA. He would be thirty years old on 1 March and had accumulated 5,500 flying hours; now he had to decide whether to stay with Imperial Airways or return to service life. He chose the latter and re-enlisted on 14 April with the rank of Lt Cdr (A). He went to Lee-on-Solent where Nos 753 and 754 squadrons formed No. 2 Observers School, providing training in Blackburn Sharks and Supermarine Walrus/Fairey Seafox aircraft respectively. Esmonde was appointed CO of No. 825 Squadron on 31 May 1940 and was to stay with this unit for the rest of his time in the FAA.

The squadron operated nine Swordfish and were quickly in action, being seconded to Coastal Command and carrying out daylight raids over France in support of the British withdrawal to Dunkirk. Eight Swordfish were lost in action during this hectic period. No. 825 embarked in *Furious* during September 1940 alongside the Swordfish of No. 816 Squadron and the Blackburn Skuas of 801 Squadron. During the Norwegian Campaign Esmonde was in his element, leading two Swordfish squadrons against designated targets: the raid on 22 September against German shipping at Trondheim is described on page 99.

In February 1941 *Furious* ferried fifty urgently needed Hurricanes to Takoradi on the Gold Coast (*see* page 100); No. 825 provided anti-submarine patrols during this trip. They returned in April and re-formed at Hatston before moving to Campbeltown on the Mull of Kintyre. On 17 May they embarked on the new carrier *Victorious*, and provided anti-submarine patrols while the carrier ferried forty-eight crated Hurricanes to Gibraltar.

Then *Victorious* hurried north to counter the breakout into the Atlantic of the major German ships *Bismarck* and *Prinz Eugen*. On 24 April the latter was damaged by a magnetic mine and returned for repairs. Esmonde led off nine Swordfish of No. 825 at 10pm that evening, although one aircraft turned back with technical problems. They attacked the *Bismarck* with torpedoes, getting one hit under difficult conditions. The following day surface ships closed in for the kill, including the destroyer *Zulu*, whose engineering officer, Lt Cdr Witham Esmonde, was Esmonde's brother. In a convoy less than 20 miles (32km) away was his twin-brother, James, a mining engineer returning from the Gold Coast. The full story of this attack is recounted on page 100. For leading and pressing home the attack on *Bismarck*, Esmonde received the DSO and other members of the squadron were awarded two DSCs and two DSMs.

*Victorious* was then engaged on ferrying Hurricanes to Gibraltar again and joined up with Force H, which included *Ark Royal*, the fleet arriving in Gibraltar on 11 June 1941. Esmonde's No. 825 Squadron was transferred to *Ark Royal*, where they joined Nos 810 and 818 with Swordfish, plus Nos 807 and 808 with Fulmars. Convoys to Malta became the important job, with dive-bombing and torpedo attacks by the enemy air forces a daily occurrence. On 13 November 1941 U-73 torpedoed *Ark Royal*, which subsequently sank with most of its aircraft and Esmonde was one of the last to leave, looking after the safe evacuation of the last of the *Ark Royal*'s crew.

Esmonde returned to Lee-on-Solent and yet again re-formed No. 825 Squadron. During this quiet period he took some leave and visited the family home in Ireland, borrowing a friend's biplane to go round visiting friends and giving them rides. By early 1942 he still had only managed to acquire six replacement Swordfish and six crews. With the anticipated breakout of German capital ships from the Atlantic coast to German home waters (*see* the section on 'Breakout – Channel Fiasco') he took the Swordfish to RAF Manston in a blizzard on 4 February. On 11 February he went to Buckingham Palace to receive his DSO. The following day he was killed leading a daylight torpedo attack against the enemy ships, for which he was awarded the Victoria Cross, announced in the *London Gazette* on 3 March 1942.

Under such threats Raeder had little choice and set the wheels in motion to move the ships quickly from Brest to Germany and then on to Norway. Admiral Otto Ciliax, commander of the Brest Group, was placed in overall charge of plan. Initially he was opposed to Hitler's orders, but planning began on 12 January 1942. The aim was to sail through the English Channel as fast and as far as possible before discovery by the Allies. This meant breaking out from Brest as soon as it was dark and creeping up the French coast as far as possible before discovery. The plan was called Operation *Cerebus* with Operation *Thunderbolt* for the Luftwaffe air cover.

The plan drawn up by Admiral Ciliax was brilliant, and also meticulously detailed so that there could be no ambiguity, or misinterpretation of orders or instructions by his officers, during the journey. In a total security blackout Ciliax only informed those members of staff who would be directly involved: his Chief-of-Staff, Captain H. J. Reinicke; the three battleship captains, Kurt Hoffman (*Scharnhorst*), Otto Fein (*Gneisenau*) and Helmuth Brinkmann (*Prinz Eugen*); Scharnhorst's navigator, Helmuth Giessler, as Ciliax intended to fly his flag and lead in *Scharnhorst*; and the commander of the destroyer screen and certain specific officers involved with the planning. The timing of the voyage was critical: there was no room for mistakes. Ciliax talked to his meteorologists and told them what he was looking for: favourable tidal dates, and a start after dark with low cloud cover and poor visibility. The date was set for 11 February 1942, when most of the conditions could be met; with luck, by the time the British woke up the fleet would have covered two-thirds of its journey, although by daylight they would still only be entering the Straits of Dover.

The surface force giving protection was another well-organized plan. The initial escort out of Brest and up to Cherbourg consisted of seven destroyers, but as they moved north they would be joined by fifteen torpedo boats and some minesweepers to keep the route clear of mines. Ports and harbours along the route, including Cherbourg, Le Havre, Flushing and the Hook of Holland, were prepared as bolt-holes in case things went wrong.

On the air side, Hitler put the famous fighter ace Adolf Galland in complete charge of Operation *Thunderbolt* with strict instructions that Luftwaffe air cover was to be continuous with bad weather not permitted as an excuse. Galland planned an imposing air umbrella for the ships. Le Touquet, roughly halfway along the route, became his command post with Caen and Schiphol as the early and late points, respectively. His plan included 282 aircraft: 252 Messerschmitt Bf 109Fs and Focke Wulf Fw 190As from *Jagdgeschwadern* (Fighter Wings) 1, 2 and 26, and training units at Abbeville, plus some thirty Messerschmitt Bf 110 and Junkers Ju 88 twin-engined night-fighters from *Nachtjagdgeschwadern* (Night-Fighter Wings) 2 and 3. He appointed Colonel Max Ibel as his liaison and control officer, based aboard *Scharnhorst*. Galland planned that at least sixteen fighters would be over the ships at all times. With careful overlapping of incoming and outgoing patrols, he arranged that at the end of each patrol there would be thirty-two fighters over the convoy. As the convoy moved north each air patrol would be refuelled and re-armed progressively along a string of Luftwaffe airfields in France and Holland. Any aircraft attacked by interfering RAF units would be immediately reinforced by combat-ready Luftwaffe fighters within range.

## The British Plan

It seems very naive now, but the RAF thought the Germans would go during daylight hours. Operation *Fuller*, the British plan to attack and/or contain the German battleships at Brest, covered most of the alternatives – at least on paper. The ships at Brest were under surveillance almost continuously during daylight hours with aircraft fitted with ASV covering three designated patrol areas; 'Stopper', off the entrance to Brest; 'Line SE', from Ushant to Île de Brehat; and 'Habo', from Le Havre to Boulogne. 'Jim Crow' flights, usually a couple of Spitfires from 11 Group, were tasked with a general reconnaissance of the Channel area, despatched every two hours from dawn to dusk. Bomber Command laid mines along possible routes and three squadrons of Bristol Beaufort torpedo-bombers from Nos 42, 86 and 217 Squadrons were maintained in a state of constant readiness. With the confidence of the *Bismarck* and Taranto attacks behind them, the senior officers in the RAF and Admiralty thought that at least some Beauforts would get through any shield to carry out a torpedo strike and damage the ships, which would then be finished off by Naval surface forces in conjunction with the RAF.

However, the people planning Operation *Fuller* agreed with Vice-Admiral Ramsey at Dover that the German ships would pass through the Straits at night. Consequently, he requested a Swordfish squadron to be based at RAF Manston so that these relatively slow aircraft could carry out a torpedo attack under the cloak of darkness, when they would not require supporting fighters and the majority of the enemy fighters would be on the ground.

Lt Cdr Eugene Esmonde, the CO of No. 825 Squadron, was working to re-build his squadron after losing most of his aircraft when *Ark Royal* went down after being torpedoed on 13 November 1941. He was based at Lee-on-Solent with six Swordfish, seven pilots, six observers and six TAGs. Of these, two pilots had only recently completed their training, only two observers had operational experience and all the TAGs came from *Victorious*. The aim was to get back to strength – nine Swordfish and a full complement of crews. Esmonde's squadron was earmarked to join one of the new escort carriers being ferried from the USA and was preparing to move when he was called to a high-level conference, along with a number of other squadron commanders. Operation *Fuller* was explained to them, emphasizing that their part in the action would be a combined effort by strong RAF, naval and FAA forces. As the action might be at night, the FAA officers were made aware that any action would have to be on a voluntary basis. Esmonde offered No. 825, believing that, by the time any breakout occurred, his squadron would have their full complement of aircraft and be fully trained.

It was typical British winter weather on 4 February 1942 as Esmonde led his six Swordfish from Lee-on-Solent to Manston through a snow blizzard. Maintenance crews followed in squadron vehicles, and when all assembled the squadron loaded their Swordfish with torpedoes and were put on five-minute readiness. Every effort was made to get the squadron on the top line and trained for the attack, flying day and night. Esmonde apparently thought their best chance was to arrive head-on at the ships, split his squadron into two sub-flights and attack simultaneously from both port and starboard quarters. No one knew the target, but with torpedo practice there could be little doubt that it was to be an attack on enemy shipping of some sort. Esmonde had been awarded the DSO for his part in the attack on *Bismarck* and on 11 February he attended the investiture at Buckingham Palace.

## The Breakout Begins

The following day, 12 February 1942, just after noon Sub-Lt B. W. Rose was returning to the mess with his observer after a practice flight when a lorry tore past with some of the squadron officers aboard. 'The balloon's gone up' one of them shouted. Rose and his observer ran back to the crewroom and put their flying kit back on in time for a briefing. Esmonde said 'The *Scharnhorst*, *Gneisenau* and *Prinz Eugen* have had the cheek to put their noses out into the Channel, and we're going out to deal with them.

Fly at 50ft, close line-astern, individual attacks and find your own way home. We shall have fighter protection.' There was one small problem, however: there were seven pilots for six aircraft. Who was to be left behind? Sub-Lts Peter Bligh and Bennett tossed a coin, and Bligh won.

The crews climbed into their aircraft, took off at 12.30pm and climbed above the aerodrome, where they were joined shortly afterwards by ten Spitfires of No. 72 Squadron. Esmonde led the first sub-flight away, about 50yd apart in line astern. Lt J. C. Thompson led the second sub-flight half a mile behind, but in vic formation, not in line astern as instructed: perhaps Thompson thought that if the three of them could release their torpedoes together there would be more chance of hitting one of the ships. The squadron was still untrained as a unit and it was daylight, going against all they had been told. They were to find also that all other units had been caught off-guard and support from the promised squadrons was not forthcoming, at least not until it was too late to support the Swordfish.

In fact, Operation *Fuller* had specified that No. 825 would be controlled by RAF Swingate, Dover. Also, as it would theoretically have been dark, some Hurricanes from either Nos 607, 615 or 3 Squadrons, all based at Manston, would fly ahead of the Swordfish and drop flares, the others providing fighter cover.

According to German accounts, the three capital ships and escorting destroyers left Brest after an RAF raid the night before at 8.30pm. Hugging the French coast, they were joined at dawn by a large force of minesweepers and E-boats. Luftwaffe fighters provided constant air cover. As they started to pass through the Straits they were attacked by British destroyers and MTBs, and the long-range gun batteries on the Kent coast; constant changes in direction by the German ships confounded all of these attacks.

### *The Attack*

Only twenty minutes after setting out, Esmonde's strike force sighted the enemy – and what a sight. Under a lowering overcast with intermittent rain and deteriorating visibility, which was down to less than 4 miles (6.5km), they could see the escort forming inner and outer screens. Inside these was an even closer destroyer screen virtually hugging the great ships – all swathed in wisps of mist and smoke from the constant firing of the guns from every ship. Whatever Esmonde or his crews thought of this vision of hell was lost as he aimed his aircraft straight at the leading ship, the *Scharnhorst*. Taking his three Swordfish down to 50ft, Esmonde set off across the water.

Around 10 miles (16km) east of Ramsgate, two flights of Bf 109s spotted the Swordfish and managed to slip below the Spitfires. They flew down the Swordfish formation, spewing bullets and cannon shells through the flimsy fabric of the biplanes. The Spitfires quickly chased them off to the north, but another flight of enemy fighters slipped in through the rain and positioned themselves so that they came out between the Swordfish flights. The Spitfires raced in, allowing the Swordfish to re-form and set off again. By now the Biggin Hill and Hornchurch Spitfire Wings had taken off to rendezvous with the Swordfish. The Hornchurch Wing was too far south and missed the convoy: they patrolled for a short time and then returned to base. The Biggin Wing had arrived late, but after looking south, turned north and ran into the Luftwaffe rearguard, which effectively kept them away from the main action.

Slowly the biplanes battled on towards the enemy ships, handicapped by a blustery wind and the fact that the ships were sailing at 30kt away from the Swordfish, which under those conditions could probably only manage a groundspeed of 70kt or so. Despite intense anti-aircraft fire Esmonde led his small formation over the outer screen and thus drew the full fury of all the defending ships and aircraft. The battleships had depressed their main guns and were firing over open sights to create waterspouts, which on their own could have brought an aircraft down. Many of the shells ricocheted off the water to join the maelstrom of fire being directed at the attacking aircraft. The Swordfish, although generally heading towards the enemy ships, had to take avoiding action at times, banking tightly with wingtips almost in the sea, as enemy fighters kept coming in. By now some of the Swordfish were streaming ripped fabric as attack after attack was mounted. More Luftwaffe fighters joined in, including some Focke Wulf Fw 190s, these sometimes queuing with undercarriage and flaps down to make firing passes, but more than one got it wrong and stalled, crashing into the sea. The second Swordfish, flown by Brian Rose, followed Esmonde across the outer screen, followed by Kingsmill, but the latter was dropping further astern as he tried to avoid the enemy fighters.

A veritable swarm of fighters were attacking the rear vic of Swordfish and it is doubtful that they ever managed to cross the outer destroyer screen – none were seen again. These fighters now joined the others to attack the three remaining Swordfish, which were now fighting for their very lives. Esmonde was weaving again to put the fighters off; Rose's TAG, Johnson, was hit and slumped over his guns. Edgar Lee, Rose's observer shouted into the intercom, 'I'll keep watch astern, Brian, and let you know when the bastards are coming.' Rose swerved violently into any attacker, forcing them to break off, and any fighter coming from the rear had to pull up to avoid a collision. Lee stood up in the open rear cockpit shouting warnings as attack after attack came in. Behind and slightly below he caught sight of Kingsmill's Swordfish, still with them and with Kingsmill's crew, Samples and Brunce, shouting and waving at the enemy from their open cockpit. Esmonde battled on, his aircraft afire just behind the rear cockpit. In the midst of this living hell his gunner, Clinton, climbed out onto the fuselage and started to beat out the flames with his gloved hands. Wide holes in the fuselage showed where heavy shells had passed through without doing much damage.

Esmonde passed over the inner screen, still intent on his target. There was now a veritable curtain of water as all the guns that could be brought to bear tried to knock the biplanes out of the sky, if not with a hit, then with waterspouts. In what was earlier thought to be an amusing effort to sink their ships, the Germans now watched worriedly as the three Swordfish battled their way through attack after attack and continued to get closer. Rose was suddenly hit as a cannon shell exploded against the thin steel plating on the pilot's backrest. Shrapnel and steel splinters gouged into Rose's back: the aircraft staggered but, responding to Lee's shouting, Rose regained control and passed over the inner screen. Lee checked for the other aircraft and as he watched he saw Esmonde's complete lower port wing taken off by a shell. Amazingly, Esmonde regained control and flew on, but a few seconds later a burst of tracer tore through the cockpit. Both his crew, Clinton and Williams, were now dead, and Esmonde probably mortally wounded in the head and back. He was seen to pull the nose up slightly and his last action was to release his torpedo. Enemy fighters lashed the aircraft with bullets and it crashed into the sea. Rose was seriously wounded and it was only with Lee continually shouting at him that he kept control. The fuel tank was hit but they managed to switch to the reserve and, lining up on *Prinz Eugen*, Rose dropped his torpedo.

Once the fighters realized that Rose's aircraft no longer posed a threat they left it alone and went after the last one. Kingsmill passed over the destroyer screen, but by now all three crew were wounded. The fighters pounced yet again – the two top cylinders of the Pegasus engine were shot away and it burst into flames, the port wing caught fire and, in a last desperate effort, Kingsmill lined up on *Prinz Eugen* and released his torpedo. Kingsmill's engine died just as he cleared the last E-boat and the aircraft dropped into the sea. Rose headed for the outer screen and once clear ditched in the sea. For the gallant Swordfish and their crews it was all over except for some strafing by E-boats as they passed by, and now, wounded, they had to endure being in the sea until an MTB picked them up. Out of the eighteen brave crewmen only five had survived. Admiral Ciliax in *Scharnhorst* remarked to his staff 'Those Swordfish did well to get their torpedoes away. The English are throwing their mothball navy at us now, apparently.' Admiral Ramsey, in command at Dover, signalled the Admiralty 'In my opinion the gallant sortie of these six Swordfish constitutes one of the finest exhibitions of self-sacrifice and devotion to duty that the war has yet witnessed.'

### *Aftermath*

After the event there was a Court of Inquiry, and there were pundits who said it was foolhardy of Esmonde to put his crews through what was considered a 'suicidal' attack. Others thought that Esmonde was a glory-seeker and that the attack was another chance for him to further these private aims. Be that as it may, in time of war sudden decisions have to be made and there was only going to be the one good opportunity to make a strike in the narrow neck of the Channel. As already mentioned, the attack should have been at night with fighter cover, but circumstances dictate the situation and people must respond to such circumstances as they arise.

In a little known follow-up to the raid by Esmonde, No. 819 Squadron flew north to Hatston in the Orkneys in February 1942. Their Swordfish were fitted with long-range tanks and armed with torpedoes. This was an effort to try to catch the remaining ships of the German 'Channel Dash' convoy as they passed along the Norwegian coast. The crews waited, fully kitted up, for RAF reconnaissance reports, knowing that there was a stretch of about 20 miles (32km) along the Norwegian coast where they could attack and still have enough fuel to get back. Yet again, however, there was a slip-up. The RAF had got their position reports wrong and the German ships were out of range by the time the mistake was sorted out.

## The Battle of the Atlantic

Grand Admiral Dönitz once said 'Aircraft can no more eliminate the U-boat than a crow can fight a mole.' I do not know about the latter, but the experience of World War Two showed that the former is certainly not the case.

The submarine/U-boat was one of the most dangerous weapons in the world, and the weapon that nearly brought Britain to her knees in World War Two. Losses would have been much more grievous than they were, had the convoy system pioneered during World War One not been reintroduced at the very beginning of the war. Some 75,000 merchant ships were escorted in British-controlled convoys during World War Two, losing 574 to enemy action. Using the convoy system there could be as many as 700 merchant ships in the Atlantic at any one time, with 100 escort warships. Crossings invariably took between 20–26 days, depending on the speed of the slowest ship and the weather. RAF Coastal Command and the RCAF flew more than 120,000 sorties while trying to protect these convoys, about 850,000 flying hours in all weathers.

Despite this pressure the U-boat Command never lost its objective, and morale was always good. Germany had fifty-seven operational U-boats at the outbreak of war; but by the end of 1942 this had risen to 485. In 1939 Great Britain had around 200 surface ships fitted with ASDIC sonar sets, but most were not suitable for operations in the open ocean. Between 1939 and 1945 the U-boats sank 2,775 Allied merchant vessels, amounting to 14½ million tons or forty ships each month. Against this the Germans lost thirteen U-boats a month. As late as the last two months of the war, U-boats sank forty-four Allied ships: the night before Germany surrendered, U-boats sank two merchant ships near the entrance to the Firth of Forth, and a minesweeper in Lyme Bay.

The war against the U-boat was a huge struggle lasting five and a half years, in which neither side retained the advantage for long. Despite the dislocation and disruption by Allied bombing, their war potential was by no means exhausted. It was fortunate that the Allies succeeded in attaining the upper hand at crucial stages of the war, helped sometimes by the timely withdrawal of U-boats required elsewhere. It was even more fortunate that the war ended when it did, before the Germans could put into service powerful new types of U-boat that were not constrained by the limitations of the earlier boats. Fortunately for Britain those limitations included having an underwater transit speed of only 2–3kt, which meant travelling mostly on the surface to keep up with a convoy. This they had to do anyway, to ventilate the boat and recharge the batteries used for propulsion underwater. Quite often U-boats travelled to their patrol areas on the surface, and were fair game to RAF Coastal Command, who started to attack them in the Bay of Biscay and northern waters.

The Battle of the Atlantic was fought in three phases. During the defensive period, 1939–41, convoys had little protection and no air cover, and many ships were sunk by U-boats. During 'the turn of the tide', 1942–43, bitter battles were fought as Allied ships and aircraft increased in numbers and went after the U-boats, eventually subduing them. During the offensive phase, 1944–45, convoys were protected by sufficient numbers of escorts, MAC-ships (explained in more detail later in this chapter) and long-range aircraft capable of covering the whole of the Atlantic from shore bases.

The first real breakthrough was the introduction of airborne radar (ASV) in May 1941, which meant that locating U-boats on the surface, even at night, became much easier and so sinkings increased. In May 1942 the RAF introduced the airborne searchlight – the Leigh Light – which came as a nasty surprise to the enemy. Radar would guide the aircraft to the target, which would then be illuminated and depth-charged. The U-boat

## 'Pumpkin'

The Admiralty had watched the trials of the Leigh Light with interest. They could see the advantages of such a device mounted on anti-submarine aircraft at sea, and instigated trials. The Leigh Light, as produced for the RAF, was far too heavy to be mounted on a Swordfish or Albacore. The mine and torpedo unit based at HMS *Vernon*, Portsmouth, was given the task of producing a smaller version of the Leigh Light, codenamed 'Pumpkin'. This they did and Swordfish DK777 was fitted with the new device. A test was made on the evening of 19 December 1942, when the Swordfish was put on the slipway at Lee-on-Solent and illuminated a boat 300yd (275m) off shore (visibility was poor that night!). With the success of the first light, the unit designed and produced two newer types, Pumpkin A and Pumpkin B.

Pumpkin A used a 16in (400mm) reflector in a spherical mounting, power being provided by four 12V batteries in a streamlined bomb-shaped container. Two types of carrier were produced, one to be mounted under the fuselage and one to replace bombracks under the wing. The total weight came to 200lb (90kg). The light was controlled by the observer in the rear cockpit using a small joystick. Pumpkin B was the same, but used a water-cooled mercury arc source to provide higher output. The Director of Air Warfare and Flying Training (DAWFT) attended a demonstration on 18 March 1943 and went away suitably impressed. He suggested the set at Lee-on-Solent be installed in a Swordfish and tested by No. 778 Squadron, the Service Trials Unit (STU). He also suggested HMS *Vernon* build ten further Pumpkin As for operational trials.

DK777 was flown to Machrihanish for the trials after some minor modifications had been carried out. There wasn't a submarine available to act as a target, so buoys and drifters were used instead. The target was picked up on ASV followed by a dive to 1,000ft, the minimum safe height at night without a radio altimeter (although there were plans to fit these to Pumpkin aircraft when they were modified). The light beam was to be switched on at 1,000yd range followed by a dive to 300ft. STU Report No. 237 commented favourably on the preliminary trials, and the C-in-C Western Approaches suggested testing the new equipment on aircraft embarked in the escort carriers, *Archer*, *Attacker* and *Biter*.

DK777 was flown to Fairey's Great West Aerodrome for them to examine the modifications required to convert other Swordfish. However, it was impossible to carry both ASV and the Pumpkin under the fuselage, so it was decided to fit the latter under the wing. The ASV equipment had already seriously degraded the performance of the Swordfish fitted with it, and the thought of additional weight and drag from the Pumpkins worried the scientists. However, Swordfish V4634 was modified to carry the underwing attachment with no problems. A further twelve Pumpkin sets were sub-contracted to George Forrest & Son of Acton, London with HMS *Vernon* providing the fabrications. Forrests said they could produce six sets a week, but this was not enough, or fast enough, for the Admiralty, who wanted 250 Pumpkin sets as soon as possible. GEC said they could produce ten per week, but it would take both companies at least three months to get up to full production.

At a general progress meeting held by the Director of Air Warfare (DAW) on 26 March 1944, the C-in-C Western Approaches was asked for any results from the ships operating the trials aircraft. *Activity* and *Biter*, which in the end carried out the trials, reported that Pumpkin was virtually useless in poor weather, and wind conditions had not been suitable, except on a couple of occasions, to launch a Swordfish loaded with ASV Mk XI, a Pumpkin and two depth charges.

Although the Pumpkin system had not had time to really prove its worth, events again overtook the situation. Convoys at sea were going to be permitted to use flare illumination beyond their 6-mile perimeter. As such, on 26 April 1944 the C-in-C Western Approaches informed the Admiralty that the tactical reason for the use of Pumpkins was no longer valid and suggested their withdrawal. Any existing orders were quickly cancelled and the project dropped. At one point there were schemes to try to fit Pumpkins to Barracudas and/or Avengers, neither of which proved suitable to carry them.

**Swordfish DK777 fitted with the experimental 'Pumpkin A', a navalized version of the RAF's Leigh Light. The light had a 16in reflector with power from the bomb-shaped container between the undercarriage legs, which held four 12V batteries.**

usually had no time to dive, and with only deck armament had little time to engage an aircraft they could not see, being blinded by the bright light. They now started to surface by day to recharge their batteries, and Coastal Command had yet more success. To this were added the first long-range bombers going into service over the Atlantic, simultaneously with tremendously powerful new depth charges.

When America entered the war at the end of 1941, the U-boat packs had moved to the rich merchant ship routes along the American and Caribbean coasts, where convoys were not initially used. The decisive phase in the Battle of the Atlantic began after Dönitz, flushed with the successes of his U-boats off the Americas, but increasingly aware that the improving air and sea defences there would now limit such actions, declared 'The war on shipping has now to be switched back to operations against the convoys to and from Britain in mid-Atlantic where they are beyond the range of land-based aircraft.'

The strategy of the U-boat Command was to start an offensive during the latter part of 1942 with patrol lines on either side of the mid-Atlantic 'air gap', an area some 300 miles (480km) wide beyond the range of Allied land-based aircraft. With nearly 300 U-boats on strength and about thirty coming from the shipyards each month, the situation must have looked good to Dönitz, on paper at least. The new offensive began in July when two patrol groups, consisting of nine U-boats each, left their bases and headed for the Atlantic air gap. During the next two months, despite the existence at that time of eleven Escort Groups (six British, four Canadian and one American) patrolling the North Atlantic routes, the U-boats sank over one million tons of shipping, half of it in convoys.

U-boats were not the only threat. On 6 September 1942 convoy PQ18 sailed from Loch Ewe on the west coast of Scotland for Russia. The close escort provided for forty merchant ships was the largest ever assembled to protect a convoy, consisting of a cruiser, twenty-nine destroyers, the escort carrier *Avenger*, five armed trawlers and three rescue vessels. U-boats accounted for two merchantmen on 13 September, and then the Luftwaffe started their attacks, operating from Norwegian bases. Within six days, out of the forty ships that started out, thirteen had been sunk, ten of them by aircraft. Others were damaged and there were many casualties. The return convoy of fifteen ships came round further to the north, out of range of the aircraft, but ran into a U-boat pack, which sank four merchantmen, the destroyer *Somali* and a trawler. Clearly such losses were too high to sustain, and the Admiralty cancelled all further convoys to Russia until the winter months, when long dark nights would give some protection from air attack. Only a small trickle of supplies got through on fast merchantmen operating alone.

The Allied Casablanca Conference in January 1943 made the defeat of the U-boat its Number One priority. Within five months or so the first escort carriers were in action. Another solution was the freelance hunter/killer Escort Groups, which had freedom of movement to wherever a threat from U-boats was known. Also being introduced were the new MAC-ship conversions. Throughout the following two years, aircraft operating from escort carriers and MAC-ships did so under extremely harsh and hazardous weather conditions. The extreme cold badly affected the Swordfish crews in their open cockpits, exposed to all the elements, who quite often had to be lifted out of their cockpits after returning from a patrol. That was not all. The cold affected the operation of the weapons: depth charge clips sometimes failed to release when frozen up; the acoustic anti-submarine torpedo known as 'Fido' failed to run; and cold caused gun stoppages on the fighters.

However, for the first time successions of complete convoys were beginning to get through to Britain without loss, despite often being surrounded by U-boat packs, which did not dare attack in the face of continuous air cover. The final sinking of a U-boat in World War Two was on 7 May 1945 by a Catalina of No. 210 Squadron. This was after Grand Admiral Dönitz had sent a signal to all U-boats, at 4.14pm on 4 May 1945, ordering them to cease hostilities and return to base. The full German capitulation was signed during the night of 6/7 May, and at noon on 8 May the Admiralty announced that the German High Command had been ordered to give surrender orders to all of their U-boats.

Altogether Germany built 1,175 U-boats, of which 781 were destroyed. 635 were sunk at sea by Allied warships, aircraft or mines (of which 196 – one out of every six built – were sunk by aircraft of RAF Coastal Command), sixty-three were destroyed in bombing raids and eighty-three were lost to collisions and other causes.

## Escort Carriers

It was in the early 1930s that the staff at the Admiralty in London considered the idea of using escort carriers to provide extra air cover at sea without going to the expensive – and slow – trouble of building new fleet carriers. The principal idea was to either convert merchant ship hulls that were under construction, or to adapt new ones. Although nothing was done, events once war had broken out changed that.

In January 1941 twenty-one ships were sunk by U-boats and twenty by German long-range aircraft – a combined loss of 205,299 tons. It was the Focke Wulf Fw 200 Condors of the Luftwaffe's *Kampfgeschwader* (Combat Wing) KG40, operating out of Bordeaux-Merignac, that were causing concern. Between August 1940 and February 1941 they attacked and sank eighty-five ships totalling over 210,000 tons, and damaged another 125, of which some were so badly damaged they were out of action for weeks. To rub salt in the wounds, KG40's strength was increased to thirty-six machines in March 1941, most of these being the improved Fw 200C-2 model with a stronger airframe, the earlier C-1s having been prone to structural failure when under the stresses and strains of operational flying. With the total losses exceeding forty ships per month throughout World War Two, Britain's struggle to survive by shipping supplies was in danger of collapsing; starvation stared the British in the face.

### *The Escort Carriers are Ordered*

The Admiralty now asked the Ministry of War Transport to release merchant ships for conversion into Auxiliary Aircraft Carriers, later called Escort Carriers. In view of the serious losses being suffered, no merchant ships could be spared, but it was agreed that several under construction would be reserved, and that a loan of six similar conversions from the Americans would be accepted. However, only four British-built escort carriers, *Activity*, *Campania*, *Nairana* and *Vindex*, were constructed because the Ministry of War Transport was reluctant to release large, fast merchant ships, which they felt would be better used for cargo work. Built to Admiralty standards, the four had integral hangars and lifts as laid down for fleet carriers. These four had steel, though unarmoured, flight decks and twin-shaft diesel engines that gave around 18kt.

Thereafter all the escort carriers were purpose-built in the USA. Four others ordered at the same time had the American-style wooden flight deck with one lift and a hangar about half the length of the flight deck. All were diesel-powered and became available in 1942. These early escort carriers, though simpler than fleet carriers, did not meet the fire protection and fuel safety standards of the British ships. It took two incidents to drive this fault home – the loss of *Avenger* to a single torpedo and a tragic explosion in *Dasher*. After that, every CVE – as the ships were designated by the Americans – arriving in the UK had to undergo an extensive modification programme. This included the addition of nearly 2,000lb (900kg) of ballast, which gave the ships better stability at sea than their USN counterparts. The bomb stowage and aviation fuel systems were completely revised.

Two of the newly modified CVEs were damaged by U-boats firing torpedoes at them but survived, and *Ameer*, hit by a kamikaze later in the war, was returned to service within a month. Two USN CVEs, hit by torpedoes, sank with a heavy loss of life, and of ten hit by kamikazes two were lost and the rest damaged beyond economical wartime repair. Another problem was that all subsequent CVEs, apart from the first four, were powered by a single-shaft geared turbine, which proved troublesome at sea and not the most suitable for wartime mass-production methods. A catapult was installed in all the ships after the first four, but only limited use could be made of them when operating British types of aircraft, as these were set up to be launched in the tail-up configuration whereas the USN launched tail-down.

Also in the pipeline were fifty catapult ships that would provide, at least until the small carriers were available, fighter cover via a catapult launch. Known as CAM-ships (CAM standing for Catapult-Armed Merchantmen) they would carry one catapult and one Hurricane each, but once the fighter was launched the pilot had to either fly ashore if close enough, or ditch/parachute into the sea alongside a ship to be picked up. Although five eventually were put into service they were not a great success, and many were cancelled as escort carriers were introduced.

### *The Escort Carriers Enter Service*

The first British escort carrier was actually a German banana boat! The *Hannover* had been launched in 1939 but was captured by Royal Navy ships *Assiniboine* and *Dunedin* and re-named *Empire Audacity*, though the *Empire* was later deleted. Her funnel, bridge, superstructure, derricks and masts were all removed, and a 453 × 60ft (139 × 18m) steel flight with two arrestor wires and a barrier fitted. Neither hangar nor superstructure was provided, so all stowage and servicing had to be done on deck.

Grumman Martlets (later renamed Wildcats) of No. 802 Squadron were the first to embark and start operations, during September 1941. There were plans to include a couple of Swordfish for anti-submarine patrols, but space precluded this. During three runs to Gibraltar with convoys, the Martlets shot down five Condors, damaged three and drove off other shadowers.

It was 1942 before the next escort carrier, *Avenger*, one of those supplied by America, entered service, though she did not give trade convoy protection until April 1943. The first escort carrier to provide convoy protection was *Biter* in April 1943. Between April 1943 and August 1944 *Biter* made sixteen transatlantic and Gibraltar convoys, embarking the Swordfish and Wildcats of No. 811 Squadron. Aircraft numbers varied, but up to October 1943 there were nine Swordfish and three Wildcats; there were six of each to January 1944; and eleven and four until August 1944. On 25 April 1943 her Swordfish, in conjunction with the destroyer *Pathfinder*, depth-charged U-203 and sank it, the first time an escort carrier had done so. A further eight attacks against U-boats were made during this period, culminating in the sinking of U-89 on 11 May, shared with *Broadway* and *Lagan*.

On 16 November 1943 a Swordfish armed with a Mk XXIV 'mine' (in fact a homing torpedo) crashed alongside the ship; fortunately the mine did not go off but it broke free and damaged the ship's rudder. Wildcats shot down a Junkers Ju 290 on 16 February 1944 when it tried to carry out a glide-bomb attack. In what was believed to be the only occasion in which an escort carrier controlled a successful interception by a shore-based fighter, on 16 February 1944 the ship guided Beaufighters of No. 235 Squadron on to another Ju 290, which they shot down. *Biter* took part in other convoys but was laid up after a fire when in dock. After repairs she was loaned to the French Navy, and, renamed *Dixmude*, saw action again with her aircraft striking at Viet Minh forces in Indo-China in early 1946.

The first British-built escort carrier, *Archer*, was to the same standard of the American CVE *Long Island* that had entered service just before Pearl Harbor. In March 1942, No. 834 Squadron had four Swordfish embarked to provide anti-submarine patrols while ferrying twelve Martlet fighters across the Atlantic. She joined the cruiser *Devonshire* and two destroyers to act as a support group working off the west coast of Africa, protecting convoys on their way to Sierra Leone. May 1943 found No. 819 Squadron embarked with nine aircraft. Swordfish 'B' sank U-752 on 23 May with R/Ps, the first occasion on which they were used in anger. The ship then suffered from major engine problems and ended the war as a stores hulk.

The next to enter service was *Unicorn*, which had been designed to provide aircraft repair and support facilities for air groups. In July 1943 *Unicorn* embarked an air group for Operation *Governor*, intended to divert Axis interest from operations in the Mediterranean. This comprised Nos 818 and 824 Squadrons with nine Swordfish each, and No. 887 with ten Seafires. In August she moved to the Mediterranean to act as an invasion carrier. To take part in Operation *Avalanche*, the invasion of Italy at Salerno, her air group comprised No. 818 Squadron with Swordfish, and Nos 809, 887 and 897 with Seafires. After this she underwent a refit and later sailed for the Far East to join the British Pacific Fleet (BPF) as an aircraft repair and supply ship.

Nine Swordfish and six Seafires of No. 816 Squadron embarked in *Tracker* until the end of 1943, taking part in a number of trans-Atlantic and Gibraltar convoys. During March 1944 *Tracker*'s aircraft were engaged in a number of actions, No. 819 Squadron replacing No. 816 and sharing in the destruction of U-288 with the Avengers of *Chaser*'s No. 846 Squadron. Her air group also damaged three other U-boats, shot down three Fw 200Cs, two Ju 88s and a Blohm & Voss Bv 138C.

*Fencer* embarked No. 842 Squadron with nine Swordfish and six Seafires on 31 July 1943. They took part in Operation *Alacrity*, the occupation of the Azores for use as a maritime base, on 3 October. She then sailed on twelve transatlantic and Gibraltar convoys, increasing the number of Swordfish to eleven and taking on nine Wildcats. They sank U-666 and shot down a Fw 200C. In April they took part in Operation *Tungsten*, the FAA attack on *Tirpitz*, and then joined a convoy to North Russia. Her Swordfish sank U-277 on 1 May 1944, and the following day both U-674 and U-959, the Wildcats shooting down a shadowing Bv 138C. Her Swordfish provided anti-submarine patrols on 20 June when there was a strike in Norwegian waters. Over the next couple of months the Swordfish carried out anti-submarine sweeps off the coasts of Scotland and Norway before sailing to join the BPF.

*Battler*, an assault CVE, embarked No. 835 Squadron, operating nine Swordfish and six Sea Hurricanes, during June 1943 for escort duties during two convoy runs to Gibraltar. The ship also had No. 808A Flight with four Seafires; during these operations her aircraft shot down a Fw 200C.

In January 1944 her Swordfish were providing anti-submarine patrols while escorting convoys off East Africa, plying between India and South Africa. By July the patrols were around Ceylon, after which she returned to the UK.

Using fighters on the small escort carriers worked out very well, although the Seafire was not really suitable. Once the composite squadrons found they could operate Swordfish and fighters, usually Sea Hurricanes, Seafires or Wildcats together, it became a widespread tactic. Swordfish operating alone were subject to return fire if a U-boat decided to stay on the surface and fight it out; only when the Swordfish started using R/Ps did they have the strike power to attack alone. However, this was rarely the case. Once a U-boat was spotted on the surface the ship's fighters would launch and provide cover while the Swordfish dropped depth charges or bombs.

**Coming to grief as it landed on *Fencer* on 1 November 1943, Swordfish LS191 'A' of No. 842 Squadron had stalled and hit the superstructure, becoming a write-off. It had only joined the FAA that June.** A. Rudd

**Airborne over the convoy, Swordfish LS354 'H' of No. 842 Squadron up from *Fencer*. It was damaged when landing on Fencer on 2 May 1944.** Bruce Vibert via Ray Sturtivant

*Hunter*, also an assault CVE, took part in only one Gibraltar convoy, during August 1943, embarking No. 834 Squadron with six Swordfish and six Seafires. *Stalker* provided cover for one Gibraltar convoy during October 1943 when she had No. 833 Squadron embarked with six Swordfish.

No. 824 Squadron, comprising nine Swordfish and six Sea Hurricanes, joined *Striker* in October 1943 for convoy duties to Gibraltar. Her Swordfish provided anti-submarine cover for naval air strikes against Bodo on 21 April 1944, and again on 7 May against Kristiansund, and was part of the force that attacked Rorvik on 11 May. Swordfish of No. 824 flew operations against enemy shipping off Norway on 12 June. During August and September *Striker* escorted two convoys to the Kola Inlet, North Russia, and back again; some forget that the return trips could be just as hazardous. She then left to join the BPF.

In February 1943 *Dasher* had joined a convoy to Russia and became the first to make the round trip. However, it fell to *Chaser* to make the enemy respect the work of the escort carrier. No. 816 Squadron took eleven Swordfish and eleven Wildcats on *Chaser* during February and March 1944 and made a dramatic impact. Her aircraft sank U-366, U-973 and shared U-472 with *Onslaught*. Two escort carriers joined the next convoy: *Activity* had No. 819 Squadron with three Swordfish and seven Wildcats; while *Tracker* had No. 846 Squadron with twelve Avengers and seven Wildcats. The fighters from these shot down six enemy aircraft (three Fw 200Cs, two Ju 88s and a Bv 138C) in two days, depriving the enemy of essential convoy position reports. Combined they destroyed U-288, shared U-355 with *Beagle*, and damaged U-362, U-673 and U-990.

Between February and April 1944 No. 819 Squadron, with nine Swordfish and three Wildcats, stayed with *Activity* for escort duty on convoys going to Gibraltar. In late March 1944 No. 833 Squadron with three Swordfish and seven Wildcats replaced No. 819 and joined a convoy to

***(Above)*** **Swordfish NE991 'M' of No. 816 Squadron airborne from *Chaser* flying to the rear of convoy RA57. On three consecutive days, 4–6 March 1944, Swordfish 'B', 'F' and 'X' sank U-472, U-366 and U-973 respectively, all with R/Ps.** via Ray Sturtivant

***(Left)*** **Arctic convoys suffered extremes of cold weather. Deck hands try to keep the flight deck flyable on *Fencer* with No. 842 Squadron embarked with Swordfish and Wildcats. While escorting convoy RA59 to Russia during April–May 1944, *Fencer*'s aircraft sank U-boats U-277, U-674 and U-959, and shot down a Bv 138C.** E. W. Tyler

**On a return trip from Russia in May 1944, Swordfish of No. 842 Squadron on *Fencer* attacked another U-boat.** A. Rudd

North Russia, before going back on the Gibraltar run. In May 1944 *Activity* re-embarked No. 819 with three Swordfish and seven Wildcats, joining *Fencer* with No. 842 Squadron operating eleven Swordfish and nine Wildcats. This time three U-boats were sunk – U-277, U-674 and U-959 – plus one Bv 138C shot down. *Activity* then became a ferry carrier, taking aircraft to Ceylon.

The next escort carrier to join up was *Nairana* which embarked No. 835 Squadron with nine Swordfish and six Sea Hurricanes. Her small flight deck precluded a deck park and, like her half-sisters *Campania* and *Vindex*, *Nairana* was used on the Russian convoy runs as it was felt that her riveted hull was less susceptible to cracking than the welded hulls of US-built escort carriers. She did some runs to Gibraltar and on 9 March 1944 her fighters shot down two Ju 290Bs. For the rest of the year she did the Russian convoys and on 28 January 1945 joined with *Premier* to cover a strike by the air element of *Campania* on Vaagso, followed by another two days later on Stadtlandet. Cover was provided for one more run to Russia, and a night strike on Trondheim, which was cancelled. Early in 1946 she was loaned to the Royal Netherlands Naval Air Service and renamed *Karel Doorman*. Embarking Fireflies, she carried out operations in the Dutch East Indies until 1948 when she was returned and converted back to a merchant ship.

By March 1944 the Royal Navy had enough escort carriers to join with other ships as part of one of the new hunter/killer packs. *Vindex* embarked No. 825 Squadron with twelve Swordfish and six Sea Hurricanes between March and August 1944 to take part in what was the first major anti-submarine sweep since 1939. The 2nd Support Group worked the South-West Approaches, where *Vindex*'s aircraft flew day and night despite awful weather. On 15 March her aircraft were involved in the destruction of U-653 at night. A Swordfish crashed on deck on 24 March, setting off a depth charge that caused damage and a fire.

On a second sweep as part of the 6th Escort Group her aircraft joined in the destruction of U-765 on 6 May. Operating around the clock took its toll: there were only just enough aircrew to man and fly the eighteen aircraft, and the flight-deck handling crews worked wonders under the circumstances to keep everything flying. After two months *Vindex* required a refit, which gave the exhausted men a brief respite.

In August 1944 *Vindex*, in company with *Striker*, was loaned to the Home Fleet for escort duties on the Kola run. *Vindex* still had her same aircraft complement aboard, and *Striker* had No. 824 Squadron with twelve Swordfish and ten Wildcats. On 20 August her Swordfish sank U-354 and shared in the destruction of U-344, U-394 being sunk on 2 September during the return trip. Three BV 138Cs were shot down. In September *Vindex* and *Striker*, both operating the same numbers of aircraft, took part in another convoy to Russia. Only one kill was made on this run – U-921.

In October/November No. 811 Squadron embarked aboard *Vindex* with Swordfish and Wildcats for another run to North Russia and back. This convoy, JW/RA61, was a milestone. The convoy had three escort carriers, *Vindex* (No. 811 Squadron with twelve Swordfish and four Wildcats), *Tracker* (No. 853 Squadron, ten Avengers and six Wildcats) and *Nairana* (No. 835 Squadron with fourteen Swordfish and six Wildcats). There were no kills, but more importantly, there were no convoy losses!

*Vindex* embarked No. 825 Squadron during December 1944 for one convoy when no ships were lost and no kills of U-boats or aircraft were made. After a refit No. 813 Squadron, also flying Swordfish and Wildcats, embarked aboard *Vindex* in April 1945 for a convoy escort to Kola Inlet. No. 813 Squadron had previously served aboard *Campania* when the twelve Swordfish and four Wildcats took part in six convoy escorts to Gibraltar.

It was during December that *Campania* with No. 813 Squadron' twelve Swordfish and four Wildcats, escorted two liners returning released Russian POWs. *Campania* then joined *Nairana* for the next Russian convoy when U-365 was sunk and two torpedo-carrying Ju 88s and a Bv 138C were shot down.

*Campania* and *Nairana* took on Nos 813 and 835 Squadrons during February 1945 with their same complement of aircraft, although one Fulmar was added to provide night fighter cover. The fighters shot down four torpedo-carrying Ju 88s with five probables.

In March 1945 *Campania*, with No. 813's twelve Swordfish and seven Wildcats, was joined by *Trumpeter* which had the eight Avengers and eight Wildcats of No. 846 Squadron. No kills were made but two ships from the convoy were sunk at the Kola Inlet. *Vindex*, with the eight Swordfish and twelve Wildcats of No. 813 Squadron, joined *Premier* who had twelve Avengers of No. 856 Squadron embarked. One U-boat was destroyed by surface escort vessels. *Vindex*'s role was changed in July 1945 when she was allocated to the BPF as a replenishment carrier, taking the Fireflies of No. 1790 Squadron out to Australia.

It fell to *Queen*, with No. 853 Squadron flying eight Avengers and eight Wildcats, to escort the last convoy, which sailed four days after VE-Day. As the attitude of the various remaining U-boat commanders was unknown the escort remained at full strength and the convoy was not attacked.

## MAC-Ships

MAC-ships – Merchant Aircraft Carriers – escorted 217 convoys across the Atlantic, though when ferry duties are added, they made a total of 323 crossings. Some 4,447 days were spent at sea of which 3,057 were in convoy. The Swordfish crews flew 9,016

**Escort Carrier Swordfish Squadrons**

| Ship | Squadrons | Dates |
|---|---|---|
| *Activity* | 835, 838, 819, 836F, 833 | Nov 1942–Sept 1944 |
| *Archer* | 834, 819 | Mar 1942–Aug 1943 |
| *Avenger* | 816, 819, 825, 833 | May 1942–Nov 1942 |
| *Battler* | 840, 835, 834 | Dec 1942–Dec 1944 |
| *Biter* | 836, 833, 811 | Jun 1942–May 1944 |
| *Campania* | 813, 836, 825 | Apr 1944–Apr 1944 |
| *Chaser* | 835, 816 | Nov 1943–Mar 1944 |
| *Dasher* | 837, 816 | Jul 1942–Mar 1943 |
| *Fencer* | 842 | Aug 1943–Aug 1944 |
| *Nairana* | 838, 835 | Dec 1943–Mar 1945 |
| *Striker* | 824 | Oct 1943–Oct 1944 |
| *Tracker* | 816 | Aug 1943–Dec 1943 |
| *Vindex* | 825, 813 | Feb 1944–May 1945 |

**(Above)** **Four Swordfish of No. 860 Squadron at Maydown, Northern Ireland. This squadron and No. 836 provided all the Swordfish for the MAC-ships, and at one time had ninety-two Swordfish on strength.** RNNAS

**(Left)** **The relatively short flight deck of a MAC-ship, in this case *Amastra*'s 461ft (141m) with two Swordfish of No. 836 Squadron 'Easy' Flight during 1943.**

flying hours on 1,183 of those days, flying 4,177 operational sorties for a loss of 114 Swordfish to all causes. Twelve attacks were made on U-boats but none were sunk. During all that time only six pilots, five observers and eight TAGs were lost in action.

Merchant Aircraft Carriers were just that – either a grain ship or tanker to which had been added a flight deck with two or three arrestor wires and a safety barrier. They were, however, still merchant ships and as such still flew the Merchant Navy's Blue Ensign and carried up to 80 per cent of their normal cargo capacity. Thirteen tankers and six grain ships were finally converted. They were crewed by the Merchant Navy with the Royal Navy providing aircrews, aircraft and technical deck hands. The Swordfish could frequently be seen with 'Merchant Navy' stencilled on the rear fuselage in place of 'Royal Navy'. The grain ship conversions were given a lift and a small hangar, and could carry four Swordfish. The tankers had a slightly longer flight deck but no hangar, due to their complicated fuel piping, and were usually limited to three Swordfish. The supporting and deck handling crew consisted of a Petty Officer in charge of four fitters, four riggers, three electricians (one for radar) and two armourers. To provide some protection on the open flight deck, collapsible wind-breaks were provided.

Unlike the escort carriers only Swordfish were embarked for convoy runs, these were drawn from three pool squadrons, Nos 836, 840 and 860, the latter being formed from Royal Netherlands Navy personnel. By the beginning of 1944 they had ninety-two Swordfish on strength. No. 836 Squadron, based at Maydown, near Londonderry in Northern Ireland, provided most of the aircraft and crews in the form of sub-flights. For example, No. 836 B Flight spent much of its time aboard three ships, the MV *Empire MacAlpine*, *Empire MacMahon* and *Empire MacAndrew*. The Flight aircraft were coded: Swordfish II LS434, for example, was B3.

The MAC-ship's regular position in her convoy was in the middle of the centre column, and to fly off her Swordfish she would drop astern and turn into wind – making herself vulnerable to any marauding U-boats. If more than one MAC-ship was escorting a convoy, as they did later in the war, a duty rota was worked out so that one would provide the patrols while the other carried out maintenance/repairs. During the round trip Swordfish aircrew would log, on average, about forty to fifty flying hours. The average run to Halifax, Nova Scotia took about seventeen days, although bad weather and problems with U-boats could stretch this to six weeks. When about 100 miles (160km) off the Canadian coast the Swordfish would fly ashore to Dartmouth, near Halifax.

The first MAC-ship to enter service, in April 1943, was the MV *Empire MacAlpine*, and on 7 May 1943 Lt Cdr R. S. Slater, CO of No. 836 Squadron, carried out the first landing on a merchant vessel (the *Empire MacAlpine*), flying Swordfish V4570. Later that day he returned with the first elements of the new squadron and successfully completed the deck landing trials.

Many of the Swordfish that flew aboard MAC-ships were adorned with markings. For instance, all four Swordfish of B Flight joined the *MacAlpine* on 14 May carrying individual playing card insignia, the Aces of Spades, Clubs, Hearts and Diamonds. The 'Royal' of 'Royal Navy' was overpainted with 'Merchant' and then each aircraft was named after a former ship of the Ben-line – *Bencruachan*, *Benlawers*, *Benwyvis* and *Benalbanach*. A finishing touch was to make the ship's call-sign 'Bearsden', the Captain's home, and aircraft 'Riddle', the Captain's name. Due to aircraft being damaged and/or lost these initial markings could not be sustained, but there were variations.

On 29 May No. 836's B Flight embarked on the same ship as part of a convoy. This was actually a propaganda trip and it was September 1943 before the squadron joined a convoy operationally. This was a combined convoy of ONS18 and ON202, consisting of sixty-six merchant ships and seventeen escorts. Patrol 1 was made on 23 September 1943 by Sub-Lt R. A. Singleton with his observer, Acting Lt Cdr J. Palmer. The early morning found the convoy in a fog but as it warmed up it became patchy and Singleton took off on his patrol. Within a few minutes the fog enshrouded everything again. By excellent airmanship and a combined effort with radar Singleton landed with visibility down to 50yd – an amazing feat! The first sighting of a U-boat was made the very next day. Sub-Lt B. I. Barlow and his observer, Sub-Lt J Boyd, took off in Swordfish HS381 'B' and detected a U-boat on the surface. Swordfish LS281 'C', flown by Sub-Lt P. T. Gifford RNZVR, and Lt J.

***(Top)*** **'Easy' Flight aboard *Amastra* had three Swordfish. One is seen leaving the flight deck with the other two waiting their turn with engines already running. The narrowness of the deck is shown to good effect in this picture.**

***(Above)*** **A few seconds later, after the Swordfish has left the flight deck. Catapults were not fitted, though there were four arrestor wires.**

**MAC-Ships**

| Ship | FDL | Flight deck (ft) | Converted by | Swordfish | EIS |
|---|---|---|---|---|---|
| *Empire MacAlpine* | MH | (G) 414 × 62 | Denny Bros | 4 | 4.43 |
| *Empire MacAndrew* | MK | (G) 423 × 62 | Denny Bros | 4 | 7.43 |
| *Empire MacRae* | MU | (G) 424 × 62 | Lithgows | 4 | 9.43 |
| *Empire MacKay* | MM | (T) 460 × 62 | Harland/Wolfe | 3 | 10.43 |
| *Empire MacColl* | MB | (T) 461 × 62 | Cammel Laird | 3 | 11.43 |
| *Empire MacCallum* | MN | (G) 424 × 62 | Lithgows | 4 | 12.43 |
| *Empire MacKendrick* | MO | (G) 414 × 62 | Burntisland | 4 | 12.43 |
| *Empire MacMahon* | MJ | (T) 462 × 62 | Swan Hunter | 3 | 12.43 |
| *Empire MacCabe* | ML | (T) 462 × 62 | Swan Hunter | 3 | 12.43 |
| *Empire MacDermott* | MS | (G) 423 × 62 | Denny Bros | 4 | 3.44 |
| *Rapana* | MV | (T) 462 × 62 | Smiths Yard | 3 | 7.43 |
| *Amastra* | MC | (T) 462 × 62 | Smiths Yard | 3 | 8.43 |
| *Acavus* | MA | (T) 462 × 62 | Silley Cox | 3 | 10.43 |
| *Ancylus* | MF | (T) 462 × 62 | Palmers | 3 | 10.43 |
| *Alexia* | MP | (T) 462 × 62 | Greenwell | 3 | 12.43 |
| *Miralda* | MW | (T) 462 × 62 | Palmers | 3 | 1.44 |
| *Adula* | MQ | (T) 462 × 62 | Silley Cox | 3 | 2.44 |
| *Gadila* | (RNNAS) | (T) 462 × 62 | Smiths Yard | 3 | 3.44 |
| *Macoma* | (RNNAS) | (T) 462 × 62 | unknown | 3 | 5.44 |

*Notes: All ships carried 5,000gal (22,730ltr) of aviation fuel and 3,100gal (14,100ltr) diesel fuel for the ship. Crew complement was around 100–120. All had four arrestor wires but only a few had a barrier. There was no catapult launch and only the grain ships had a hangar and lift. Standard gun protection consisted of one single 4in QF Mk IV; two single 40mm Bofors; four single 20mm Oerlikon, although some did not have the Bofors in which case they carried eight single 20mm Oerlikon. For Swordfish, all ships carried stocks of Mk XXIV mines (homing torpedo), Mk XI depth charges, 100lb anti-submarine bombs, 3in rocket projectiles, 0.303in ammunition, flares and pyrotechnics.*

**The first MAC-ship to enter service, *Empire MacAlpine*, showing the space available when four Swordfish were embarked. Lt Cdr R. W. Slater made the first landing on a converted merchant ship in May 1943.** FAA Museum

H. G. Tapscott, was launched to join up with Barlow and they both made separate R/P and depth charge attacks. Heavy flak from the U-boat, which had decided to remain on the surface and fight back, made the attack difficult and they both missed. But it was a start.

Three more MAC-ships had become operational by October 1943 and all nineteen were in service by May 1944. That month a Swordfish operating from *Rapana* detected a U-boat astern of convoy SC143 and damaged it in the ensuing attack. It was usual to have at least two MAC-ships escorting convoys, but as many as four were sometimes used. In most cases the Swordfish flew daily anti-submarine patrols around the convoy, the type of patrol being given a code name; for instance, 'Adder' was a patrol a specified distance ahead of the convoy. (*See* the accompanying box for the full list of 'reptile' patrols.)

**'Reptile' Patrols**

*Adder*
Patrol 15 miles (24km) either side of an imaginary centreline through convoy, up to a distance of between 8–12 miles (13–19km) ahead.

*Alligator*
Patrol to port or starboard, along a line 10 miles (16km) from the convoy direction and moving 10 miles ahead or astern.

*Cobra*
Patrol around the convoy at a specified distance, for example 10 miles.

*Crocodile*
Patrol ahead of the convoy at a specified distance, for example a 10-mile radius, from beam to beam.

*Frog*
Aimed at U-boats tailing the convoy. Patrol astern at a specified distance either side of a centreline.

*Lizard*
Search patrol on a specified compass bearing for a specified distance, for example 10 miles at 090 degrees.

*Mamba*
Search patrol along a specified bearing for 30 miles (48km) and return.

*Viper*
Patrol around the convoy at the limit of visibility.

It was patrols such as these that started to make the captains of U-boats think twice before undertaking an attack. In the nine months prior to the introduction of escort carriers or MAC-ships, U-boats sank 362 merchantmen in the Atlantic for a loss of 89 U-boats. The figures nine months after their introduction were 61 and 174, respectively. The Swordfish, apart from carrying bombs and depth charges, now had the option to attack with steel-tipped R/Ps. Four were fitted on long rails under each wing and could be fired either in pairs or all eight together. The effect of all eight hitting a target was the equivalent of a broadside from a battleship: they were so powerful that a single hit was sometimes enough to sink a U-boat. As one pilot said:

> The technique was to approach the target in a dive of 20 degrees and to aim just below the U-boat's waterline from an optimum altitude of 800ft, implying a range of half a mile. A pair of well-aimed rockets could pass clean through a U-boat, making bloody great holes below the water level. There was only one drawback: we needed at least 1,000ft to make such an attack; anything less and it was back to depth charges, of which we could carry six.

In the build-up to the Allied invasion of Europe, some eleven non-operational (i.e. ferrying) trips were made by MAC-ships, bringing over 200 aircraft from the USA to Britain; escort carriers also ferried aircraft across. The MAC-ship's flight deck would be full of cocooned aircraft, minus

**(*Top*) Once across the Atlantic, MAC-ship Swordfish flew ashore to Dartmouth, Nova Scotia, as seen here with LS434 'B3' from *Empire MacMahon*'s B Flight.**

**(*Above*) Warming up at Dartmouth, Nova Scotia, in January 1945, are B Flight's LS434 'B3' and LS225 'B4' from *Empire MacMahon*. The latter was scrapped at Barton, Lancashire, in June 1945.**

**Flying over an Atlantic convoy is Swordfish 'B2', embarked in *Empire MacAlpine*. The chef's hat had a 'B' on the band, indicating an aircraft from 'B' Flight.**

***(Above)*** **Swordfish LS434 'B3' of *Empire MacAlpine* out on patrol over the Atlantic. All aircraft in this flight had names on the nose, in this case 'Benvorlich'. *Empire McAlpine* was the first of the merchant ship conversions and, after conversion back to a merchant ship, survived in use until 1970 when she was scrapped in Hong Kong.**

***(Right)*** **Evidence of the rumour that some MAC-ship Swordfish carried the legend 'Merchant Navy' in place of 'Royal Navy' on the rear fuselage. This one was LS219 'E3' on *Amastra*.**

**Fully armed with R/Ps and bombs, Swordfish LS276 'E2' from *Amastra* patrols near the convoy. It too carries the 'Merchant Navy' legend.**

their propellers and with all the boxed spares lashed down in the middle. The three Swordfish would be stowed, wings folded behind the weather barriers, until they reached the UK again. The ship would put in at Glasgow docks where the aircraft would be unloaded, pulled to Renfrew Airport, restored to flying condition and ferried to their next base.

By early 1945 some of the MAC-ships were being returned to their original status; *Empire Mackay* was re-named *British Swordfish* in 1946 in recognition of those that operated from her during the war.

John Godley, later a Lt Cdr and then Lord Kilbracken, recorded his impression of what it was like to join a MAC-ship for the first time:

> On 23 October 1943 I was airborne out of Maydown on a grey and misty morning, ten seconds behind Phil Blakey and Johnny Gilbert coming up behind to formate with only 4 feet between our mainplanes. Turning short of Derry for the usual show-off fly-past of the toy-town Maydown control tower at zero feet, all the crews waving. Following the Irish coast we skirted the Mull of Kintyre, climbed over Arran for our Firth of Clyde rendezvous. And there, at once unmistakable, on a straight southerly course with her white wake streaming astern, our seemingly new parent vessel, our mothercraft, the MV *Acavus*, ready to receive us. Jesus, she's like a postcard! But in fact the flight deck is 461ft long by 62ft wide – less than a cricket pitch!
>
> A signal from Phil and we plunge down in a dive, maintaining our tight formation for another little ceremonial fly-past at deck level. Another signal from Phil and we break up into extended line astern as *Acavus* turns into wind. We would normally land three aircraft in less than a minute, but this was not the time for split-arse flying. This was going to be the first-ever aircraft to land on the new (old) ship so I allowed three minutes before following Phil. I see him touch down safely and taxi forward, the barrier being raised behind him. 'Come on ahead' signals the batsman. My airspeed is 65kt, I close the throttle slightly, ease back on the stick and lose 5 knots. 'Bats' changes his signal as I approach 'A wee-bit lower' so I slightly close a bit more throttle, slight forward stick and he signals for me to come on. Throttling back I cross the stern around 15ft and he crosses his bats in the mandatory 'Cut your engine.' I do so and sink gently to a three-pointer catching the

**A Swordfish launching its R/Ps during trials. No. 819 Squadron pioneered their use in service and sank a U-boat a few days after being so equipped.** IWM

***(Right)*** **An ASV-equipped Swordfish III HS187 of No. 860 Squadron starts its take-off run from *Gadila* just a few seconds before the pilot selected RATO. This aircraft was built as a Mk II and still has the Yagi antennae on the outboard struts.** RNNAS

***(Below)*** **On 26 December 1943 the *Empire MacKay* carrying 'D Flight' was subjected to bad weather conditions and during a heavy roll Swordfish 'D1' broke its deck lashing, jumped the chocks and ran into 'D3', whose undercarriage collapsed; 'D2' overturned.** Public Archives of Canada

first wire – perfect! Ground crews race towards me from the safety nets to disengage my hook. I taxi smartly ahead of the barrier and switch off.

MV *Acavus* was one of nine ships belonging to the Anglo-Saxon Petroleum Company and displaced 8,000 tons. She was powered by a 3,500bhp diesel motor driving a single shaft, giving her a maximum speed of 13kt. Her defensive armament consisted of two 40mm Bofors, six 20mm Oerlikons and a 4in gun.

The weather in the Atlantic could be troublesome to the Swordfish crews at the best of times, as John Godley said:

During this first crossing of mine, we flew fewer than the average number of sorties because we ran into a gale, which grew into a storm with winds of 60kt and over. You can't fly when the windspeed is greater than your stalling speed – you'd be taking off backwards – and the carrier was pitching so heavily that the forward end of the flight deck was often under water! But these same conditions, which continued on and off for half the trip, also immobilized the U-boats. All our three Stringbags were damaged in the battering they took and repairing them was extremely difficult – often impossible – without protection from the elements. Through bad weather and unserviceable aircraft, we made only ten sorties in seventeen days at sea.

The great majority of MAC-ship sorties were totally uneventful – but they did keep the U-boats away. Prangs were fairly commonplace, and due to the problems of operating from a restricted space if a Stringbag was too damaged to repair *in situ*, it was pushed over the side as soon as anything useful had been removed. However, from time to time an announcement would be made over the tannoy that Swordfish so and so would be pushed over the side in half an hour and if anyone wanted anything off it now was the time. The whole ship's company descended on it like ants and when the 30 minutes was up there was precious little left to throw overboard!

During six months of convoys the *MacCabe* lost fifteen Swordfish to all causes, but one incident was when there was no flying! Two Swordfish were parked side-by-side, wings folded, with an armourer working on one of the R/Ps. He had disconnected the 'pigtail' plug and, after finishing what he was doing, reconnected it. Unfortunately he hadn't isolated the circuit and the R/P fired, going straight through the senior TAG sitting in his cockpit in the adjacent aircraft. The armourer, sitting just behind the R/P, received the full blast from the motor as it fired and was badly burned. Only the efforts of the Surgeon/Lt and sick-bay attendant saved his life.

The weather could produce other problems. Most of the patrols were made ahead of the convoy or down either side. If there was U-boat activity astern of the convoy it was not unknown for a Swordfish, caught in a freshening wind, to be unable to catch up, and a few disappeared astern never to be seen again! Another problem was whales! Sub-Lt John Taylor recorded in his logbook for 9 August 1944: 'Swordfish NF199 – Viper patrol – sighted and attacked dead whale'!

Some extracts from the logbook of Sub-Lt J. T. Canham RNVR, an observer with B Flight, make interesting reading, and are reproduced (*see* box, right). There are lots of entries in between those included here detailing routine patrols and training sorties ashore, and so on. Despite the many lonely and boring patrols the logbook does show that it did not pay to get complacent. However, some pilots, depending on circumstances, had better luck, or may be skill. One crew on the *Adula* completed over 100 deck landings and 156 flying hours in three months without a scratch!

**(*Left*) A damaged Swordfish is stripped of useful parts . . .**

**. . . and pushed over the side of *Fencer* in 1944.** A. Rudd

**Sub-Lt J. T. Canham's Logbook**

| | | |
|---|---|---|
| 9.11.43 B1 | Sub-Lt Singleton/Self/LAC Palmer | 1st operational patrol, Convoy ON209. Viper A/S patrol ASV u/s |
| 9.11.43 B3 | Sub-Lt Gifford/Self/Palmer | Viper A/S patrol. Flashing practice with Catalina. Beat up convoy |
| 25.12.43 B1 | Sub-Lt Singleton/Self/LAC Palmer | Temp. below zero |
| 10.3.44 B1 | Lt Roberts/Self/LAC Palmer | Convoy HX281 Viper patrol. Warm. Vis patchy. Sighted whale |
| 10.5.44 B1 | as above | 2nd patrol ahead of convoy ON253. Hit bridge on landing. |
| 13.5.44 B1 | as above | Adder patrol. Shape at sea turned out to be iceberg. |
| 26.5.44 B3 | as above | Search starb. side of convoy. Pranged u/c on landing. . |
| 29.5.44 B1 | as above | Crocodile A/S patrol. Sighted empty raft and whale. Cylinder missing – landed on *MacCabe*. |
| 14.6.44 NF149 B1 | as above | A/S patrol. Water in petrol engine cut over convoy. Pranged both U/C legs. |
| 15.6.44 NF149 B1 | as above | Search astern convoy. Both oleos wiped off landing. Balanced on deck edge. Ditched over side. |
| 17.6.44 LS316 B2 | as above | A/S search ahead of convoy. Port oleo sheared on landing. Aircraft stripped and ditched. |
| 18.6.44 NE941 B2 | as above | (new B2) A/S search ahead of convoy. Caught 4th wire landing and hit bridge. |
| 17.9.44 NE941 B2 | Sub-Lt Sheepbridge/Self/PO Lane | Testing new wings on B2. |
| 22.9.44 LS164 B1 | Sub-Lt Gifford/Self/Palmer | Search astern convoy HXS309 for lost MVs. Found 4 MVs and Corvette. Gave position to convoy. |
| 29.9.44 LS164 B1 | as above | Morning search. Bounced on landing and went into barrier, wrote everything off but fuselage! |
| 30.9.44 | as above | Search alone for sub 45 miles from convoy. Ran into filthy weather. Hit hook on round-down landing. |
| 14.11.44 NF193 B1 | as above | Convoy DN265. Search for straggler – found OK. Night landing. |
| 14.12.44 B3 | as above | Crocodile A/S patrol. Convoy SC162. Attacked suspicious black object with D/Cs alone. Weather filthy. |
| 21.12.44 NF193 B1 | Gifford/Self/LAC Peace | Test flight at Maydown. Force landed with dinghy wrapped round tailplane. |

## 'Lily'

As a follow-on to operating aircraft from small decks, mention should be made about plans for a floating aerodrome with the code-name 'Lily'. The idea was not new: *Boy's Own* comics of the 1930s had envisaged such platforms in their stories and the idea had been discussed before in military circles. The advantages were obvious: it could be easily assembled/disassembled by relatively unskilled personnel and located in areas near the action, in fact being able to follow a moving front by being towed short distances. No one had come up with a workable plan, the main problem being how to compensate for undulating tidal waters.

The Royal Navy sponsored a floating aerodrome idea by a Mr R. M. Hamilton, a professional inventor who had served in the early part of the war as a Petty Officer in the Royal Naval Patrol Service. He had caught their Lordships attention when he successfully designed a floating surface code-named 'Swiss Roll'. The idea was very basic and consisted of nothing more than a reinforced tarpaulin over some fencing strips which strengthened the surface tension of water. He had tested it himself by putting a section across a local stream and riding over it, first on a pedal cycle and then on a motorbike, including a passenger. It was used in conjunction with Mulberry Harbour sections following the D-Day landings on 6 June 1944.

Eventually, with the help of a mathematical friend, J. S. Herbert, a housemaster at Eton College, he devised a floating aerodrome. It was constructed of 1,100 hexagonal-topped steel buoyancy chambers, the top of each chamber being 6ft (1.8m) in diameter and 3ft (0.9m) deep. By means of lugs on each of the six sides of the hexagon, each chamber was bolted to its neighbour, making a continuous structure on the honeycomb principle. The bolts were a loose fit so that the whole structure was completely flexible, undulating with the surface of the water. To increase stability, at each end were chambers that were 12ft (3.7m) deep. The structure was assembled with a working distance of 540 × 75ft (165 × 23m) wide. The complete landing strip could be moored in such a way that it swung with tide and wind, so that aircraft could take-off, approach and land into wind.

The strip was assembled on the surface of Lamlash harbour in the Isle of Arran. It was thought a Swordfish would provide an ideal testing machine (along with the Auster light spotter aircraft) and Lt Ray Jeffs was selected to carry out the trials. Lt Jeffs had been flying Swordfish from MAC-ships, which gave him the right background for the job, and he recalls the trials:

> Before we started these trials, I went over to Lamlash Harbour to have a look at 'Lily' so that I'd have a fair idea of what was going to happen when I was flying from the strip. I was amazed to see how flexible the strip was – each little wave was accurately reproduced, and it didn't seem possible that an aircraft of 9,000lb could operate safely. From the air, the strip looked quite solid and its usable size, 520 × 60ft, was in fact up to 100ft longer than the flight deck on MAC-ships. I'd served in these ships on the Atlantic convoy route for just over 18 months.
>
> The strip, officials, observers and aircraft were all ready and I set off. I, for one, held my breath as I approached to land on. The main difference between landing on the strip and a carrier was that the approach was made so low over the water, the freeboard of the strip being only

***(Above)*** **'Lily' the floating aerodrome in Lamlash Harbour. A high-speed launch has just run down the port side to create a wave effect. The undulations can be clearly seen.**
IWM

***(Left)*** **The Swordfish flown by Lt Jeffs during the trials. Taking off with a full load, the aircraft picked up a wire on the tailwheel, seen here, and it was only by good flying, and perhaps a spot of luck, that Lt Jeffs managed to take off and keep airborne.**

17in high! The undulations could not be seen until the aircraft was quite close to the strip and even then they seem pretty small. In calm weather the landings and hooking of the arrestor wire were exactly the same as on a carrier, except of course, as the aircraft touched down there was a prolonged clanging from the cans. This could be heard above the engine noise. As the Swordfish came to rest its weight caused an indentation of about 10in.

Taking off was rather frightening at first – the effect of the groove caused by the aircraft's weight was like driving through deep sand when you are on the point of becoming bogged down. The Swordfish, which was fully loaded for its type, was fitted with rocket-assisted take-off gear and when this was fired the aircraft jumped forward and the groove got shallower as the aircraft speed picked up. The trials were most successful, with me landing on and flying off in winds down to 7kt. Here lies another advantage of the strip: on the carrier when we wanted to fly the skipper had to leave the convoy to steam into wind; with the strip buoyed it could swing so that you got the best wind down the runway.

Only on one occasion did we nearly meet with disaster, and that was actually the last take-off that day. I was sure that both the aircraft and I were in for a ducking. There I was (as they say in the RAF) with engine and rockets doing their utmost to get me airborne and the wire trying to hold me back. All was well, I managed to pull the aircraft up, although I wished I had a pair of sculls at the time.

One of the observers was Lt May and he says:

> The plane revved up and moved off, very slowly at first, pushing a wave in front of it with a smaller wave coming up astern, as with a motorboat. But I watched in horror as the Swordfish's tailwheel caught on a wire halfway along the runway, but the plane carried on and only just cleared the mooring buoy at the end of the strip. Then it skimmed the water, hanging on to its propeller, trying not to slip back, but it made it and climbed away.

CHAPTER NINE

# The Mediterranean, 1939–43

## Italy Enters the War

When Italy entered the war on 10 June 1940 her navy altered the whole situation in the Mediterranean. The Italian fleet included six battleships, around twenty-five cruisers, over 100 destroyers and large torpedo boats, and about the same number of submarines.

British bases in the Mediterranean included Gibraltar to the west, Malta in the middle and Alexandria to the east. The reason behind this commitment was to protect British ships moving oil supplies from the Middle East coming to Britain, and raw materials, food and service personnel going to and from India, East Africa and Far East locations such as Singapore, Australia and New Zealand, via the Suez Canal. It was the these lifelines that the Mediterranean Fleet was tasked to protect. Between September 1940 and February 1941 the only carrier available for the Mediterranean Fleet was *Glorious* with Nos 812, 823 and 825 Squadrons with twelve Swordfish each, and No. 802 with twelve Gloster Sea Gladiators.

In May 1940 *Eagle* sailed from her Singapore station to join the Mediterranean Fleet, bringing with her Nos 813 and 824 squadrons with nine Swordfish each. No. 813 had picked up three Sea Gladiators from the reserve aircraft storage depot at Dekheila for fighter protection. There were no fighter pilots aboard *Eagle*, but four Swordfish pilots with some fighter experience were tasked to fly them under *Eagle's* Commander Flying, Commander L. P. Keighley-Peach. They were to come in useful! On 11 June *Eagle* left Malta to seek units of the Italian Navy reported to be at sea, and move to Alexandria, the Royal Navy's wartime base. At the end of June the carrier escorted a convoy going from Malta to Port Said, and on 29 June her Swordfish attacked a submarine but were unsuccessful. Nine Swordfish from No. 813, operating from Sidi Barrani in the Western Desert while the carrier was in harbour, attacked enemy shipping in Tobruk harbour on 5 July. Seven Swordfish dropped torpedoes, hitting four ships: the 15,000-ton liner *Liguria* and destroyer *Zeffiro* were sunk and another freighter and destroyer damaged.

The first encounter with the Italian Fleet was made on 9 July when No. 824 Squadron was involved in two strikes. One was against a cruiser squadron sailing about 100 miles (160km) to the west of the Fleet and a second against enemy battleships discovered not far from *Eagle*. Unfortunately neither attack was successful due to the small numbers of aircraft available, some being allocated to anti-submarine patrols and others to reconnaissance duties. The following day the Fleet was alert to the possibility of another sortie by the Italians, but none were found. Therefore, No. 813 Squadron left *Eagle* at dusk with nine Swordfish and made a strike at Augusta Harbour in Sicily. There was no sign of the battleships or cruisers, and the squadron left after sinking the destroyer *Leone Pancaldo* and damaging a fleet oiler.

The British Fleet set sail for Alexandria on 11 July and found themselves under attack by the Regia Aeronautica, the Italian Air Force. They failed to score any hits and tried again on the 13 July, but at the end of the three days Keighley-Peach and Lt L. K. Keith, flying the Gladiators, shot down four Savoia-Marchetti SM.79 *Sparviero* (hawk) bombers and damaged three others for no loss.

With *Eagle* in Alexandria her squadrons flew ashore. No. 824 took her Swordfish to Sidi Barrani where, on 20 July, they sank the enemy destroyers *Nembo* and *Ostro* in a moonlight torpedo attack. After a report that a submarine depot ship was anchored in Bomba Bay, with a submarine approaching from seaward at dusk, a strike was planned. Captain Oliver Patch RM arrived from Dekheila the following morning to take charge of the three Swordfish left at the airstrip. A dawn reconnaissance revealed that the enemy ships were still in Bomba Bay.

The three Swordfish took off at 10.38am, armed with torpedoes. Captain Patch took them out to sea, flying at 50ft to avoid any fighters. They turned towards the shore at 12.30pm and, as they approached Bomba Bay, spread out fan-shaped and about 200yd (180m) apart. From 4 miles (6.4km) out they saw a large submarine dead ahead making about 2kt, probably recharging her batteries and the crew taking advantage of the situation by putting their washing out to dry. The Swordfish dropped to 30ft but the submarine had seen them and quickly opened fire. Captain Patch took avoiding action, swinging first to the right, then left, before lining up at only 300yd (280m) and releasing his torpedo, which struck the submarine just below the conning tower, causing her to blow up. After the smoke had cleared only a small part of her stern was visible, and Patch flew back out to sea.

The two remaining Swordfish were about a mile apart and heading into the Bay where the enemy were opening fire with pom-poms and multiple machine-guns. One Swordfish, flown by Lt J. W. G. Wellham, with PO A. H. Marsh as observer, dropped its torpedo on the starboard beam of the depot ship *Monte Gargarn* just below the bridge, as a result of which she started to blaze furiously. The other Swordfish, flown by Lt N. A. F. Cheesman with Sub-Lt F. Stovin-Bradford as observer, was just about to launch its torpedo when Stovin-Bradford said they were over shoal water, and if released the torpedo would stick in the mud. Lt Cheesman flew onwards to within 350yd (320m) of a submarine in deeper water before releasing his torpedo, which ran true and struck the submarine amidships. This exploded instantly and set fire to the adjacent destroyer. Swinging away, they heard a tremendous explosion behind them – the depot ship's magazine had exploded and all three ships disappeared in a cloud of smoke and steam.

The three Swordfish flew back to Sidi Barrani, landing at 3pm after flying a 336-mile (540km) round trip. The only damage was to Wellham's aircraft, which had taken a hit in the main spar extension, so rendering it unserviceable. The Operations Staff listened in disbelief to the story of three Swordfish dropping three torpedoes and sinking four ships! Reconnaissance brought confirmation of their success.

## Operations Against the Vichy French

*Ark Royal*, with the Swordfish of Nos 810, 818 and 820 Squadrons, No. 800 with Skuas and No. 808 with Fulmars embarked, had arrived at Gibraltar on 23 June 1940 after taking part in the Norwegian campaign. Admiral Somerville had been tasked with raising Force H to protect the areas in the western Mediterranean not covered by other units after the French fleet withdrew to North Africa following the fall of France. At that time the French fleet consisted of two new battlecruisers, the *Dunkerque* and *Strasbourg*, two battleships, a number of light cruisers, plus a few destroyers and submarines, all at moorings at Oran and Mers-el-Kebir, along the Moroccan coast. The Royal Navy was concerned as to their future use, as the French capitulated and split into Free French and Vichy forces just as the Italians entered the war. The French were invited to join the Allied navies or suffer any subsequent action, including internment, that might be required to see that the ships did not in any way support the Axis forces. The French declined to join the Allies and Force H was given the unpleasant task of immobilizing their fleet which, up until the outbreak of war, had taken part in exercises with the Royal Navy; many friendships had been forged between the two fleets.

Just before 6pm on 3 July 1940 Force H started a bombardment of French ships, fall of shot being recorded by Swordfish from *Ark Royal*. During the bombardment, the old battleship *Bretagne* blew up and the *Dunkerque* was beached after being damaged. The entrance to Mers-el-Kebir harbour was mined by five Swordfish, but the *Strasbourg* avoided being 'bottled up' and made off to the east with a destroyer escort. A dive-bombing attack by six Swordfish, under intensive anti-aircraft fire, straddled her but scored no hits, two Swordfish being lost. At 8pm another strike was made by six Swordfish armed with torpedoes, this being the first torpedo attack against a capital ship at sea by Swordfish from *Ark Royal*. However, lack of recent torpedo practice and poor tactics during the attack resulted in six misses.

***(Top)*** **An atmospheric picture of No. 820 Squadron Swordfish ashore at Dekheila in April 1940. The squadron was normally based on *Ark Royal*. Identifiable are P4137 '4K' and L9729 '4A'.** Cdr R. N. Everett

***(Above)*** **No. 820 Squadron ashore at Dekheila in April 1940.** Cdr R. N. Everett

The following day aerial reconnaissance of Oran harbour showed that the *Dunkerque*, although damaged and beached, was still capable of action, and if repaired would still present a threat. Consequently, Admiral Somerville decided to disable her totally and on 6 July six Swordfish from No. 820 Squadron attacked the ship with torpedoes. However, five missed and the one that did strike the ship failed to explode. As a consolation, one of the torpedos that missed the *Dunkerque* hit a lighter alongside, the explosion from this causing severe damage to the battleship. Two further strikes by Swordfish were made, with one hit on the ship, but with little outward sign of damage.

Missing from this action was the recently commissioned French battleship *Richelieu*, which had gone to ground at Dakar in French West Africa. However, the British being uncertain of her intentions, she had been shadowed by the carrier HMS *Hermes*, which carried No. 814 Squadron with nine Swordfish. At the outbreak of war No. 814 had been serving in *Ark Royal* with six Swordfish, but transferred to *Hermes*, ironically to join French ships operating out of West Africa in a search for the German pocket battleship *Graf Spee*. The plan was to put *Richelieu* out of action with a torpedo strike while she was still in Dakar: what followed was a classic Swordfish torpedo attack against a difficult target amid great adversity. Just after dawn on 8 July 1940 six Swordfish from No. 814 Squadron positioned themselves for the strike. A strong tide was running which could create difficulties for a good torpedo drop and run. Diving down, the Swordfish were subjected to intense anti-aircraft fire all the way through their run-in, which had to be made between two rows of merchant ships, so it was not surprising that they only achieved one hit. This one hit was enough, though: it struck near the stern causing considerable damage, twisting the propeller shafts, damaging the steering gear and causing extensive flooding in the aft section of the ship. With only limited repair facilities at Dakar she was out of action for over a year, although her armament was undamaged and could have been used for defence if necessary.

As the extent of the damage was now known, a further series of strikes were planned alongside Free French forces landing just south of Dakar. *Hermes* now sailed for the Indian Ocean and *Ark Royal* joined Operation *Menace*, the planned amphibious assault on Dakar on 23 September 1940. On the premise that Vichy Frenchmen would not fight against Free French forces, emissaries of the latter were flown ashore to the nearest airfield in Swordfish and two French Caudron Luciolle biplanes, which had been embarked for this purpose. The premise was wrong: the mission failed and offensive action initiated.

Aircraft from *Ark Royal* found themselves looking for targets in poor visibility and were surprised by the ferocity of the opposition. The Swordfish, escorted by Skuas, were unable to operate in the face of determined attacks by Vichy French fighters as the Skuas were hard put just to defend themselves. The flak was now more intense as three French light cruisers had joined *Richelieu* after the July strike. Against mounting odds several torpedo and dive-bombing attacks were made with little to show for it, except the loss during all operations of nine aircraft. In fact, the *Richelieu*'s gunnery had been first class, with hits on the battleship HMS *Barham* and other ships. This damage, bombing attacks by Vichy French Martin 167 bombers and a torpedo attack on *Resolution*, convinced the force commander, Vice-Admiral J. H. D. Cunningham, that little was to be gained by continuing, and the operation was abandoned on 26 September 1940.

## Force H

Meanwhile, Force H had been used to good effect escorting *Argus*, which was ferrying Hurricanes to Malta. On 2 August 1940, while *Argus* was flying off the Hurricanes with two escorting Skuas providing navigational assistance, *Ark Royal* took the opportunity to make a strike on enemy positions on Sardinia. Swordfish bombed Cagliari airfield where they destroyed four hangars and four parked aircraft, with three other Swordfish mining the harbour. There were no casualties and the escorting fighters shot down a number of shadowing enemy aircraft.

The latter part of August was spent in the Atlantic worrying about whether *Richelieu* would break out, the extent of her damage still not being fully realized. To cover the arrival of *Illustrious* in the Mediterranean, Swordfish from *Ark Royal* dive-bombed the airfield at Elmas on Sardinia on 1 September, after which she returned to the UK for a refit. She returned to action by early November, with her Skuas replaced by the new Fairey Fulmar eight-gun fighter. On 9 November Swordfish of Nos 810, 818 and 820 Squadrons from *Ark Royal* attacked Sardinian airfields, the beginning of a series of operations that culminated in the strike on Taranto, surely one of the most audacious raids in the history of air warfare, and described in detail on pages 129–35.

In the meantime, *Illustrious*, one of the new carriers, had worked up off Bermuda and joined the Mediterranean Fleet on 2 September 1940. Displacing 23,000 tons, she had an armoured flight deck 3in (75mm) thick that was 760ft (230m) long, and could steam at 32kt. She was equipped with radar, or RDF (Radio Direction Finding) as it was then known. Her aircraft complement consisted of three squadrons, No. 806 with Fulmars, plus Nos 815 and 819 Squadrons with nine Swordfish each. The latter two, of course, had been operating ashore with RAF Coastal Command, but were now back under the Royal Navy mantle.

***Ark Royal* under attack by Axis aircraft in the Mediterranean.**

Operating *Eagle* and *Illustrious* as part of the Mediterranean Fleet, Admiral Cunningham was to state that 'From that moment, whenever an armoured carrier was in company, we had command of the air over the Fleet.' This was only partly true, the Fulmar only had a top speed of around 240mph (390km/h), hardly better than the Sea Gladiators and certainly slower than monoplane single-engined fighters of the Italian and German air forces. Whatever the Fulmar lacked in performance was made up by the skill of the pilots that flew them, however. For the first five months that *Illustrious* was with the fleet no ships were lost or damaged, and the Fulmars accounted for more than a dozen Cant patrol aircraft and nine SM.79 bombers, for the loss of a single Fulmar.

Admiral Cunningham put his aircraft to good use, letting the enemy know he had superior air power. Operating together, Fulmars and Swordfish carried out a wide range of strikes against shipping in North African harbours and at sea, dive-bombed airfields, mined harbours and attacked lines of communications. Nine Swordfish of No. 813 Squadron took off at dusk on 10 July to attack the Italian naval base at Port Augusta. When they arrived they found that most of the heavy ships had already left and had to be content with sinking the destroyer *Leone Pancaldo* and damaging a fleet oiler, bringing back some unused torpedoes.

## Operations in the Eastern Mediterranean

At the other end of the Mediterranean a mixed force of Swordfish, made up from Nos 810 and 820 Squadrons, left *Ark Royal* on 2 August to attack the enemy airfield at Elmos on Sardinia. Led by Lt Cdr G. B. Hodgkinson, they destroyed at least four aircraft on the ground, wrecked four hangars and set fire to buildings. The Swordfish left the scene by flying low along a country road – waving to the locals as they flew by! On 1 September No. 810 went back to Elmos in a morning raid, repeating the dose the following morning. On 4 September three Swordfish from No. 815 and five from No. 819 took off in the dark and bombed the airfield at Calato on the island of Rhodes; 819's sixth Swordfish, flown by Sub-Lt Forde, with Lt Hunt as observer and NA Dodwell, hit the island structure on take-off and turned completely over on top of the forward pom-pom. No-one was hurt but it blocked the flight deck and other Swordfish intended to go on the raid could not take off. No. 815 dropped its 250lb bombs on the ammunition dumps and buildings on the western side of the airfield, while No. 819 bombed the airfield buildings.

On the way back to Alexandria, Cunningham took the opportunity to make a strike at Maritsa airfield on Rhodes using *Eagle*'s Nos 813 and 824 Squadrons, but there was a delay in launching and the strike was made in daylight. Dropping 250lb and 500lb bombs, the thirteen Swordfish destroyed at least three enemy aircraft and started fires, but the four Swordfish, 'E4C' (Lt Drummond/Mid Todd/LAC Derwent), 'E4H' (Lt Collins/PO Marsh/NA Wilson), 'E4K' (Lt Hook/Lt Bell/NA White) and 'E4M' (Lt Hain/Sub-Lt Smith/NA Taylor) from *Eagle*'s No. 813 Squadron were caught without an escort by Fiat CR.42s and shot down. Drummond, Bell, Todd and Derwent were killed and the rest made POW. Lt Wellham described the raid as follows:

> We found the sky full of CR.42s, at least we could see three or four of them. There was nothing we could do about it so we dive-bombed the hangars and dispersed aircraft, leaving them blazing very satisfactorily. My observer, Pat Humphreys, told me that there two CR.42s chasing us so I dived down on to the sea, flying at about 40ft above the water. The fighters followed us down, and the TAG was firing his Lewis gun while Pat was firing his Very pistol. This might seem rather pointless but was based on the fact that we knew that the Italians had heard some rumour about a 'Churchill Secret Weapon' and we thought that they might mistake this for it.
>
> While Pat was engaged with these antics he gave me a running commentary on the position of the fighter, and when it came into range I closed the throttle and made a vicious turn towards it. I don't think that any other aircraft but a Stringbag could do this without spinning into the sea. Anyway, our various efforts seemed to work, as one of them pulled out and went home while the other left it too late and flew into the sea. We didn't seem to have been hit by anything so set course for the fleet. We had just come in sight of it when my engine started to make expensive noises, which was no shame to it as I had flown with the boost override in for nearly half an hour when the maximum permissible is five minutes! However, with much banging and coughing it kept going until we landed safely on *Eagle*.

When ashore, Nos 813 and 824 Squadrons were put to good use in the Western Desert until such time as *Eagle* was ready to sail again.

*Illustrious* proceeded to sea for another offensive patrol on 15 September. The following night at 11pm Nos 815 and 819 Squadrons were launched, about 100 miles (160km) north of Benghazi. No. 815, with nine Swordfish, dive-bombed shipping in the harbour, and drew the flak, as No. 819 laid mines in the channel leading into Benghazi harbour. One ship, either a destroyer or an ammunition ship, received a direct hit and blew up. The following day Swordfish provided anti-submarine patrols as the cruiser *Kent*, damaged in action, made its way along the Libyan coast to safety. The next day they reached Alexandria and the two squadrons flew ashore to Dekheila, where replacement Swordfish were acquired from Abu Sueir.

In October *Eagle* was part of a convoy escort to Malta and on 12 October was the subject of a bombing attack. They all missed but her plates suffered shock damage, the full extent of which was not recognized at the time. The same day *Illustrious*, back at sea, launched three Swordfish of No. 815 Squadron who carried out a torpedo attack on two Italian destroyers. They were attacked in error by Fulmars, who thought they were going after British ships. All three were damaged before the Fulmar pilots realized their mistake, but managed to get back to the carrier. Six Swordfish of No. 815 and nine from No. 819 took off during the night of 13 October for a raid on the island of Leros. On a bright, moonlit night the Swordfish bombed seaplane hangars, barrack blocks, hangars, buildings and ships in the harbour at Portolargo Bay. It was the other way round when another strike was laid on for 26 November: nine Swordfish of No. 815 led off six of No. 819 and attacked the same target, and although the results were not as good as the first raid all but one returned safely.

*Eagle* covered the delivery of the first Commonwealth forces to go ashore on Crete later that month, her Swordfish making a dawn attack on 27 October, attacking the Maltezana seaplane station situated on the island of Stampalia. *Eagle*'s fuel system was then found to be damaged from the bombing on 12 October and she had to go in for repairs, so missing the attack on Taranto during the night of 11 November. However, she was represented by the transfer of five Swordfish from Nos 813 and 824 Squadrons to *Illustrious*, plus eight crews, and a selection of these were included in the raid.

On 6 November *Illustrious* left Alexandria with twenty-four Swordfish on board, though three aircraft from No. 819 had to ditch during anti-submarine patrols on 10 and 11 November. *Ark Royal*, sent to reinforce the Mediterranean Fleet and ferry troops to Malta, made odd diversionary raids to keep the enemy on their toes. On 9 November she launched nine Swordfish from Nos 810, 818 and 820 Squadrons to carry out a dive-bombing attack on Cagliari airfield on Sicily. Attacking from 3,000ft, they dived through light flak to get hits on hangars, damage seaplanes near the jetty, set fire to AA batteries and hit a factory. Nine Swordfish of No. 815 Squadron led six from No. 819 to Portolargo Bay in the early hours of 26 November to make a another bombing attack on Leros. Another dawn strike was made that day when Swordfish of Nos 813 and 824 Squadrons from *Eagle* attacked enemy shipping in Tripoli harbour using 250lb SAP (Semi-Armour Piercing), 250lb GP (General Purpose) and 500lb SAP bombs, scoring several direct hits when dive-bombing a large freighter. Eric Tyler, a TAG with No. 813 Squadron, remembers the raid:

> Dawn, 26 November. No. 813 Squadron took off in the dark to make an attack on the harbour and its installations at Tripoli. Arrived over the target at dawn without incident, and proceeded with the attack in the face of intense fire, both close-range and high altitude. My pilot, Sub-Lt Timbs, dived in and dropped his bombs across the mole and a large ship alongside. All bombs burst on the target, and at least two of them were hits on the ship. Then we turned away, pursued by fire from the ground defences, which they continued to do until we were well out of range – but seen clearly by viewers on *Eagle*, 90 miles away.

the enemy by sailing 1,000 miles (1,600km) in three days and attacking a convoy off Sfax on the coast of Tunisia. On 21 December 1940 six Swordfish made a night torpedo attack on two large Italian merchant ships, one of 6,000 tons and one of 3,000 tons, bound for Cyrenaica carrying vital military stores, and sank both for no loss. Tripoli was bombed again the following including domination of the Suez Canal. To stop the rot, advance parties of the new Afrika Korps were sent to Tripoli, supported by the Luftwaffe. *Fliegerkorps* (Flying Corps) X, one such Luftwaffe unit to arrive, had just completed intensive training in the anti-shipping role using Junkers Ju 87 and Ju 88 aircraft. Both sides viewed 1941 with some trepidation.

**Bombed-up Swordfish of Nos 813 and 824 Squadrons aboard *Eagle* prepare to take off to attack enemy shipping in Tripoli harbour on 26 November 1940.**

During the Battle of Cape Spartivento on 27 November the Italian Fleet, although enjoying a favourable tactical position, which included a strength of two battleships, seven cruisers and sixteen destroyers, was subjected to a torpedo attack by eleven Swordfish of No. 810 Squadron from *Ark Royal* which, although claiming hits, did no damage. This was followed up by another torpedo attack by nine Swordfish of Nos 810 and 820 Squadrons from *Ark Royal*, who fired at two cruisers and claimed a hit.

As 1940 drew to a close a series of strikes were laid on. In the early hours of 16 December five Swordfish of No. 819 Squadron from *Illustrious*, led by Lt Cdr Hale DSO, bombed the naval base at Stampalia in the Dodecanese islands. Two nights later No. 819 took five aircraft and, using 250lb bombs, dive-bombed the port of Stampalia again. They bombed Rhodes again on 17 December and then confused night by fifteen Swordfish of Nos 815 and 819 Squadrons, who dropped some fifty bombs in the face of intense flak.

The year's end saw a definite tactical advantage by having two carriers either escorting Allied convoys and/or attacking enemy ships and positions ashore. Admiral Cunningham's problem now was lack of suitable naval aircraft to carry the war right into the enemy's own backyard. Replacement aircraft were slow arriving and spares were always a problem. However, the overall tactical advantage was to be eroded just before the end of the year. The German High Command had been unhappy with the way things were going in the Mediterranean and lacked confidence in their Italian counterparts. They could see that unless something was done, the British forces' air superiority would allow them to cut off supplies being sent from Italy to North Africa, and so end any attempts against British interests there,

## Taranto

As early as 1935 the Royal Navy had realized that control of the Mediterranean could only be achieved if any hostile fleets were reduced to a state in which they no longer presented a threat to British operations in the area. The only significant threat would be from the Italian Navy, which, like Germany's, was re-arming with modern ships, so a number of plans were drawn up for attacks on Italian naval bases. By 1938 it was becoming obvious that war with Germany and Italy was almost inevitable. Admiral Sir Dudley Pound, Commander-in-Chief of the British Mediterranean Fleet, asked Capt A. L. St G. Lyster of *Glorious* to prepare plans to attack the main Italian fleet at Taranto in southern Italy.

Taranto, like many big ports, had well-defined outer and inner harbours. The outer harbour was roughly the shape of a half moon, running north to south. The inner harbour was joined to the outer harbour at the northern tip by a short, narrow channel. Lyster delegated the task of updating earlier plans for such a torpedo strike to Cdrs G. Willoughby and L. Mackintosh, respectively, *Glorious*'s senior FAA officer and Senior Observer. The ship's three TBR squadrons, Nos 812, 823 and 825, with twelve Swordfish each, were to spearhead the attack with crews specifically trained for such an mission. Reconnaissance flights kept track of the Italian fleet and Taranto.

However, when the war eventually came, *Glorious* was required to join the ill-fated Norwegian campaign and left on 10 April 1940. She was replaced in the Mediterranean by a new carrier, *Illustrious*, which had embarked Nos 815 and 819 Swordfish squadrons and No. 806 with Fulmars. Traditionalists to the end, the Navy's plan was to make the attack on the night of 21 October 1940 – Trafalgar Day. The ship would sail to within 200 miles (320km) of the harbour before launching her aircraft. To increase the number of aircraft to that approaching the original plan *Eagle*, with Nos 813 and 824 Swordfish squadrons, was to join *Illustrious* for the attack. Thirty Swordfish would attack in two waves of fifteen aircraft, nine of each formation with torpedoes and six with bombs.

*Eagle* unfortunately developed a leak in her fuel system and had to sail for Alexandria to effect repairs. Before she left six Swordfish, taken from both squadrons, were transferred to *Illustrious* with eight crews. It was decided to fit 60gal (273ltr) auxiliary fuel tanks in the rear cockpit of the Swordfish to enhance their range and allow for any contingencies: this meant that the TAGs would have to be left behind.

Another setback occurred when a rating, working on one of the Swordfish, dropped a screwdriver, which landed across two exposed terminals creating a short circuit and a spark. Working space in a carrier hangar is restricted at the best of times, and on this occasion the air was also saturated with petrol fumes. The spark created a flash, which in turn created an explosion and destroyed the tailplane of the aircraft he was working on. Although the flames spread rapidly, sprinklers and zealous crewmen soon had it under control. However, not one Swordfish was fit to fly! Two were complete write-offs and the rest had to be taken up on deck and thoroughly washed down. Engines, instruments, radios, and so on, were removed, cleaned, serviced, reassembled and put back in the aeroplanes. The planned date for the attack had to be scrubbed and a new one set for 30/31 October, but the weather was unsuitable that night so they did not go. The next suitable night, according to the Met officer, would be 11 November.

RAF reconnaissance showed the Italian fleet in Taranto, including what appeared to be five battleships, two of which were of the modern 'Littorio' class, and three were more conveniently moored behind anti-torpedo nets right in the middle of the best line of approach for attacking aircraft. The main worry for the British was the balloon barrage: these were shown to be about 300yd (270m) apart and spaced around the harbour, not only impeding the route in but possibly also getting in the way on the way out.

The raid was almost cancelled again on the morning of the 11 November when

**Taranto harbour reconnaissance photograph showing the positions of the major Italian ships.** IWM

cruisers in the outer harbour. During the day another battleship joined them, so that by that night the entire Italian fleet would be, as one officer said, 'obligingly just where we wanted them'. The Italian battleships lay in the outer harbour, close to the shore in the centre of the half moon, protected on the south by a long mole; further to the north lay the cruisers, which Lt Sammy Morford, out on an anti-submarine patrol, had to ditch in the sea when his engine failed. He thought it was caused by water in the fuel and a check on fuel stocks revealed this to be true. As Leading Air Fitter Ted Whitley said:

> There was no option but to drain and refill every aircraft on board, and we carried some from

*Eagle* as well as our own. The fuel tank drains were inside a panel over the torpedo rack, so this meant that all the 'fish [i.e. torpedoes] had to be removed. To ensure that all the fuel and, more importantly, any water, was drained, the aircraft had to be put in the flying position. This required the tails to be lifted – with the wings folded – so bombs and flares had to be removed. It was a case of all hands to the pump: whoever was available was called in to lift tails and move bombs, 'fish, flares, jacking equipment etc. The aircrew were there as well, hardly the sort of thing to do with a night operation ahead. Eventually, all the aircraft were finished, drained, filters checked, carbs drained, everything replaced and the aircraft all refuelled through chamois leathers. We made it just in time!

**Plan of the attack on Taranto.**

Shortly before sunset on the evening of 11 November, at 6pm, the C-in-C signalled *Illustrious* to the fly-off position with the signal: 'Proceed in execution of previous orders for Operation *Judgement*.' *Illustrious* was escorted by four cruisers and four destroyers. Due to the changes and accidents only twenty-one Swordfish were now available. These were to attack in two waves, one consisting of nine from *Illustrious* and three from *Eagle*, led by Lt Cdr Kenneth Williamson, CO of No. 815 Squadron, with Lt N. J. Scarlett as his observer. On this first strike six Swordfish would be armed with torpedoes, four with bombs and two with flares and bombs. Leading the second strike of nine aircraft, two of which came from *Eagle*, was Lt Cdr. J. W. Hale, CO of No. 819 Squadron, with observer Lt G. A. Carline. Of the nine, five Swordfish were to attack with torpedoes, two with bombs and two with flares and bombs.

The reason for the varied loads was the aerial reconnaissance, which had shown a formidable defence system consisting of at least twenty-one 4in anti-aircraft gun positions, some 200 automatic machine-guns, barrage balloons protecting the approaches, and nets across part of the harbour. All torpedo-carrying aircraft were to attack the battleships lying in the outer harbour, with diversions being laid on by flare-droppers and bomb attacks against the cruisers and destroyers in the inner harbour. The torpedo phosphor-bronze warheads had 'Duplex' pistols which would only be set off by a direct hit, or by a change of magnetic field as the torpedo passed beneath the target. A problem now arose: the actual details of where and to what depth the anti-torpedo nets were meant that the torpedoes had to be set to run deep in case they had to be dropped outside the known/existing nets. Taranto was known to be a shallow harbour and if this was the case and the torpedoes were set to run too deep to cause a direct hit, then the magnetic device would hopefully operate as it passed below the target, and not ground in the shallow water. It meant that the pilots would have to make a precision drop with very little room for error.

Unknown to the crews were two factors in their favour. Only twenty-seven balloons would be up due to recent storms; and Admiral Campioni of the Italian Navy had restricted the use of the anti-torpedo nets: his intelligence was that Admiral Cunningham may well be on his way back to Alexandria, and he planned to take the fleet out the next morning to bombard Suda Bay, so he did not want movements in and out of the harbour to be hampered by unwieldy lines of nets. Also, the anti-torpedo net defence was not as extensive or well sited as it might have been, due to a shortage of net materials.

### First Wave

Swordfish 'L4A' flown by Lt Cdr Williamson was the first to take off from *Illustrious*, at 8.35pm. He climbed away to 1,000ft and 8 miles (13km) from the ship, where he dropped a flame float and orbited with his wing-tip lights on so that those following could form up on him. After five minutes the flight deck was clear of Swordfish as they took off and set course for the rendezvous. Flying slowly, the aircraft formed themselves into four vics of three and set course for Taranto 170 miles (270km) away at 8.57. Lt Morford had to return early: his extra fuel tank on the torpedo rack had fallen off and the broken straps were flailing the side of the fuselage, making a terrific din.

To make flying in formation easier, dark blue formation lights had been fitted to the port and starboard interplane struts and on the tail. Despite this and the fine moonlit night, the pilots did not find keeping formation easy. At around 4,000ft they ran into scattered cumulus and as they climbed it got colder. The cloud layer increased and the already struggling formation found that to be safe they needed to widen the gap between aircraft. They broke into clear air at 7,500ft but Williamson could only count eight aircraft, the others having become separated in cloud. However, he wasn't worried: he could see his five torpedo-carrying aircraft and the flare/bombers were to attack independently. At 10.52 Williamson saw the sky ahead suddenly become a blaze of multi-colour fireworks as the defences opened up against the first flare droppers. The cone of light covered the harbour area up to several thousand feet.

Lt Swayne in 'L4M', with observer Lt Buscall, had become detached from the formation in cloud and set off on his own. Making better time, he had arrived some 30 minutes before the others and was orbiting over the Gulf of Taranto waiting for them. The flare-droppers, Kiggell in 'L4P' and Lamb in 'L5B', broke away towards Cape San Vito. Arriving over his first target Kiggell dropped a flare and then dropped eight more at half-mile (800m) intervals.

The flares did their job and with the flak the crews could see everything. Williamson swung 'L4A' at the southern half of the ellipse and pointed his nose at the Mar Grande, the outer harbour holding the battleships. The flak was now one continuous stream, almost like a volcano erupting. Williamson knew he had a run in of 3½ miles (5.5km) and needed to be as low as possible to avoid getting hit. He started his dive. Flattening out he sped on, just missing a balloon cable in the semi-dark. He lined up on a 'Cavour' class battleship and gritted his teeth as two Italian destroyers concentrated their fire at point-blank range on him. Releasing his torpedo, Williamson banked steeply to port, but the destroyers had their day – the Swordfish dropped into the sea. Fortunately Williamson and Scarlett were alright and later picked up by the Italians to become POWs.

Sub-Lt Sparke in 'L4C', with observer Sub-Lt Neale, followed Williamson down in his dive but broke off to make his own attack. At 700yd (640m) he released his torpedo at a battleship, pulled round hard on his wingtip to port, completed a 180-degree turn and headed out of the harbour as fast as he could. Looking back he saw a column of spray leap upwards from his target. Swordfish 'L4R' flown by Sub-Lt Macauley, with observer Sub-Lt Wray, was following Sparke and dropped his torpedo at 600yd (550m). Watching it run for a second, he turned seawards. He had a sudden panic as he thought of the balloons. He called Wray over the Gosport tube, 'Where's that bloody balloon barrage?' Tony Wray laconically said, 'We've been through it once and we're just going through it again!'

Lt Kemp in 'L4K', with observer Sub-Lt Bailey, leader of the second vic, had skirted the inferno to the west then came in at 4,000ft (1,200m) over the breakwater. Diving steeply, he could see flak coming at them from all directions; flying just above the surface, he noted smugly that the big guns on one cruiser were so depressed that their fire was hitting a merchant ship instead of him. He picked the most northerly of the battleships and when he judged he was closer than 1,000yd (900m) he released his torpedo, climbed steeply to starboard and fled southwards.

Swayne in 'L4M' followed Kemp down and was surprised that most of the gunfire was missing them. He wondered why they didn't use searchlights – the latter were part of the harbour defence, but for some reason the Italians never switched them on. Probably if they had, the Swordfish would have been shot down long before they got to the strike area. Releasing his torpedo at 400yd (370m), Swayne was unaware that Kemp had just dropped his as well, and was climbing away just above him. Swayne flew straight on, pulling up over the battleship but passing through the upper masts.

Last aircraft in that wave was 'E4F', one of *Eagle*'s Swordfish, flown by Lt Maund with Sub-Lt Bull as observer. Maund had dropped to 100ft, checked his position and dropped

**Bombs on the flight deck of *Illustrious* before the Swordfish were armed up for the attack on Taranto. The chalk message on the first one reads 'Next Stop Taranto'.**

even further until he was just above the surface. At around 1,300yd (1,200m) he released his torpedo and turned away to starboard. This brought him into the commercial basin and he spent the next few minutes jinking and weaving between packed merchant ships. Breathing a sigh of relief, he looked over the side – straight into the guns of a destroyer's pom-pom battery. Fortunately the gunners hesitated and Maund flew out to sea over San Pietro Island. Looking back at Taranto he could not believe that they had just flown through that inferno.

A Royal Marine pilot, Capt Patch, was flying *Eagle* Swordfish 'E5A' with observer Sub-Lt Goodwin; their task was to dive-bomb enemy cruisers and destroyers berthed at the south shore of the Mar Piccolo. Arriving over San Pietro Island at 8,500ft Patch looked down on the 'wonderful Brock's display', positioned his aircraft and started his dive. Banking steeply from the north-west he hesitated at 1,500ft to be sure of his target and then dropped to mast height, releasing his six bombs (and a pair of well-worn Marine marching boots!) across the ships. As he cleared the harbour he noted that the seaplane base to the east was blazing merrily. Staying low, he hedge-hopped across the Italian countryside at 50ft but was suddenly fired on by an isolated gun site. He jinked and took refuge behind some convenient hills until he crossed the coast.

The blazing seaplane base Patch had seen was due to Sub-Lt Sarra with Sub-Lt Bowker in Swordfish 'L4L'. Arriving over the harbour at 8,000ft he dived towards his target, the cruisers and destroyers on the south shore. In the maelstrom his target was difficult to pick out, and as he descended he saw the seaplane base and decided to go for that instead. His stick of bombs, released at 500ft, hit their target, at least one going through a hangar roof. Surrounded by tracers on all sides, he fled to the south-east and the coast.

The last Swordfish carrying bombs was 'L4H', flown by Sub-Lt Forde with observer Sub-Lt Mardel-Ferreira. They had become separated from the others, and arriving over the harbour had little difficulty identifying their target. Diving to 1,500ft, Forde dropped his bombs, but just to make sure he went round again, then fled north-west, crossing the coast a few minutes later. The flare-droppers, Kiggell and Janvrin in 'L4P', with Lamb and Grieve in 'L5B', cruised round the eastern

**After the Swordfish attack on the Italian Fleet in Taranto harbour on the night of 11 November 1940. The *Conte di Cavour*, sunk in shallow water.** Italian Navy

end of the Mar Grande watching the torpedo attackers going in. Their target was the oil storage depot behind Cape San Vito, which had a pipeline running to an oiling jetty located in the south-eastern corner of the harbour. They both dived to 1,500ft and dropped their bombs across the target area before turning southwards to clear the coast.

Despite the feeling that it had lasted a lifetime, the whole attack from beginning to end lasted 23 minutes! The first-wave leader, Lt Cdr Williamson recalled what happened to him:

> About 20 seconds after I dropped my torpedo at the *Cavour* I ran into a lot of flak from a nearby destroyer and crashed in the harbour. I eventually surfaced and swam to a floating dock, hotly pursued by armour-piercing and incendiary bullets. I climbed onto the dock and was immediately set upon by six Italians and I feel I enjoy the doubtful distinction of being the first British naval officer to be captured by enemy dockyard maties. These creatures proceeded to strip me naked, and for a moment I feared I was to suffer a 'fate worse than death', but I was spared that!
>
> After the raid was over I was taken to a destroyer, the *Fulmine*, which ship I joined in my birthday suit. The Italian officers were rather ashamed and gave me (and my observer Lt Scarlett, who was also captured on the dock) some clothes and a glass of brandy. The following morning we were allowed to see the local newspaper which stated that no damage had been sustained by the Italian fleet. This always seemed to me to be singularly stupid since, apart from any other damage, three battleships could be clearly seen sitting on the bottom and one cruiser had a heavy list to starboard.

### *Second Wave*

The nine Swordfish of the second wave started taking off at 9.23pm, led by Lt Cdr Hale in 'L5A' with Lt Carline as observer. As the eighth aircraft, 'L5F', one of the flare-droppers, taxied into position it struck the last machine and had to be struck down for repairs. Lt Goring, the observer, asked the Captain if they could still follow the strike force when repairs (some broken wing ribs and torn fabric) were complete, assuming they did not take too long. He was granted 10 minutes, but such was his determination to go that it was 24 minutes after the last Swordfish had taken off before the repaired 'L5F' set off on its own.

Hale, circling to form up, fretted as he waited for the ninth aircraft: every minute lost allowed the enemy time to prepare themselves for the possibility of another strike. A signal lamp told his observer that Goring had joined, and they set off at 9.45. Another setback occurred at 10.10 when 'L5Q', flown by Lt Morford and Sub-Lt Green, lost its auxiliary fuel tank when the retaining straps parted. The engine stopped and by some deft handling Lt Morford regained control, but he had to land back on *Illustrious*.

As the formation climbed they broke through the cloud base and at 11.10 they could see a glow in the sky ahead – Taranto, 60 miles (100km) away on the nose. Arriving to the north at 8,000ft, Hale despatched his flare-droppers/bombers – these were Lt Hamilton in 'L5B' with Sub-Lt Weekes, and Lt Skelton with Sub-Lt Perkins in 'L4F'. Hamilton circled the harbour at 5,000ft, dropping sixteen flares at 15-second intervals, with Skelton dropping another eight to the south-east. They then dive-bombed the oil storage depot from different directions, noting flames shooting up from a direct hit by Hamilton. Pulling away from their dives they made for the coast as fast as a Swordfish could go – which wasn't all that fast!

Hale ordered the five torpedo aircraft to go line astern and then approached from the western shore end of the Mar Grande. By now, with the flare-droppers/bombers clearing the area, the Italians were firing every gun they had virtually non-stop – it seemed every foot of sky was filled with gunfire. Hale later said that as he dived it appeared as if his Swordfish was sliding down a chute of multi-coloured fire. The aircraft rocked and bucked as shells burst nearby, but Hale kept resolutely on until he was only 30ft above the water. Lining up a battleship, he released his torpedo at 700yd (640m), broke sharply to starboard and set off for the harbour mouth, passing through some balloon cables as they passed the end of the Taranto mole.

The pilot of 'L5H', Lt Lea, with Sub-Lt Jones as observer, decided he would get lower before making his run and made a descending turn that ended less than 30ft above the water. He lined up a perfect beam shot at a battleship and released his torpedo at 800yd (730m). Banking steeply to starboard he just missed the masts of a fishing smack, but his new course took him between two cruisers, the blast of its guns lifting them out of their seats. Still at 30ft, Lea raced across the water towards the northern tip of San Pietro Island.

Following Lea over Cape Rondinella was Lt Torrens-Spence with his observer Sutton in 'L5K'. Diving steeply, he had picked out the most northerly of the battleships as his target and was trying to line up amid the flak when, horrified, he saw another Swordfish appear in front, weaving from side to side to avoid the gunfire. Torrens-Spence pushed the stick forward and as they passed beneath it there was a bright flash. What they had seen was the last moments of 'E4H'. Neither Bayly nor his observer, Slaughter, were seen alive again after this. 'L5K' came out of its plunge just above Italian cruisers anchored in the centre of the Mar Grande. Surrounded by masts, funnels and gun turrets Torrens-Spence kicked and shoved on the controls to regain full control and at the same time pick a new target – his original plan having been abandoned. He saw a battleship, lined up and pressed the button at 700yd (640m): the torpedo didn't drop. Horrified, he immediately thought he had a hang-up. He tried again as they watched the battleship loom up in front of them. This time it released and he hauled the Swordfish round in a steep right-hand turn. Straightening up, the aircraft suddenly gave a big jolt, just as a shell exploded behind them in the water. They thought they had been hit, but in fact Torrens-Spence had been flying so low in the semi-darkness that his undercarriage had hit the water, and even as they watched the wheels were skimming the surface! They cleared the harbour amid more flak from shore batteries and set course for the ship.

Lt Wellham in one of *Eagle*'s Swordfish, 'E5H', with Lt Humphreys as observer, had looked at the flak-filled sky and decided to approach over Mar Piccolo and the town of Taranto. Letting down for his run he jinked to avoid a balloon, but a moment later his aircraft was hit by gunfire. One bullet hit an outer aileron rod and he had a job to keep control. Weaving about at 30ft, he finally tried an angled torpedo shot at one of the ships, leaving the drop until he was only 500yd (460m) away. The torpedo appeared to run true and he broke away, but as they turning back across the harbour they were exposed yet again to intense anti-aircraft gunfire: one 40mm shell hit the port wing breaking some wing ribs and tearing fabric. It went quiet as the last aircraft cleared the outer harbour area.

However, Lt Clifford in the repaired 'L5F', with Lt Going, some 50 miles (80km) behind the rest of the second wave, now approached the target. Clifford circled the Mar Piccolo, sizing up the situation, and dived almost vertically, levelling out at 500ft and dropping his bombs across two cruisers. They were disappointed when there were no explosions, but they did not know at the time that the semi-armour piercing bombs had gone right through the Italian ships' thin plating without exploding.

It all went quiet again. The Italian shore batteries alone had expended 13,489 rounds at the intruders, but there were no statistics from the navy on how much ammunition their ships had used. 'L4C' was the first to land back on *Illustrious*, sometime after 1.20am, followed by ten others in rapid succession. The deck hands just had time to get the Swordfish stowed below when the second wave arrived. At 2.50, Clifford landed 'L5F', the last aircraft, safely back on *Illustrious*.

Amid the excitement of returning from what had been a traumatic experience was the underlying feeling that the raid had been a success – the loss of two aircraft and crews was considered light for what had been a major strike at the enemy fleet. Early reconnaissance showed the battleship *Littorio* with a heavy list and the fo'c'sle under water; the bows of the *Caio Duilio* were aground; and the *Conte di Cavour* was listing to port with her starboard upper deck and stern awash – she settled on the bottom the next morning. Two 'Trento' class cruisers were damaged, two fleet auxiliaries had their sterns under water and there was other lighter damage to the seaplane base and oil storage facilities. The small bombs carried by the Swordfish were not powerful enough to cause more damage.

**The *Littorio*, partly under water after two hits by torpedoes.** Italian Navy

Another strike was laid on for the following night to finish the job. The news was received with mixed feelings after the previous night: one of the tired pilots was overheard to remark 'Good God, they only asked the Light Brigade to do it once!' However, during the day the weather deteriorated and there was more than one sigh of relief when the strike was called off. After weighing up the night's attack and the resultant damage, the Italian Admiral Riccardi admitted that the British attack had been carried out with skill and daring. On *Illustrious* Captain Boyd remarked:

> It is impossible to praise too highly those who in these comparatively slow machines made studied and accurate attacks in the midst of intense anti-aircraft fire. It is hoped that this victory will be considered a suitable reward to those whose work and faith in the FAA has made it possible.

Initially decorations were only awarded to the two strike leaders, Williamson and Hale, who both got the DSO, with their observers, Scarlett and Carline, getting DSCs. Capt Patch and his observer, Goodwin, also received DSCs, but surprisingly none of the other crews were decorated. Admiral Lyster received a CB in the New Year's Honour List and Capts Boyd of the *Illustrious* and Bridge of the *Eagle* received the CBE. Six months later, however, a revised list was issued – DSOs for Bailey, Clifford, Going, Hamilton, Janvrin, Jones, Kemp, Kiggell, Lea, Macauley, Neale and Torrens-Spence. Weekes and Wray got a DSC, and Sparke added a bar to his DSC. Eighteen were Mentioned in Despatches. For many, however, these awards were too late – at least one third of those who took part in the attack on Taranto had since been killed in action.

## 1941 in the Western Mediterranean

On 2 February 1941 eight Swordfish from No. 810 Squadron were launched to carry out a torpedo attack against the dam at Tirso on Sardinia. One aircraft had to return after getting separated from the main force, two aircraft iced up and had to jettison their torpedoes to stay aloft, and Lt O'Sullivan was shot down approaching the target. The other four dropped their torpedoes at the dam, apparently with little damage. On another occasion fourteen Swordfish were tasked with bombing the oil refinery at Azienda, but again no positive result was seen. Four Swordfish from *Ark Royal* mined the entrance to Spezia harbour while three others spotted for the fleet as they bombarded Genoa from the sea.

Late in 1941 Swordfish of No. 812 Squadron were airborne from *Ark Royal* when she was torpedoed on 13 November, and flew to Gibraltar. New aircraft joined the survivors to re-form No. 812 to patrol the Straits of Gibraltar. Fitted with ASV, the squadron damaged five U-boats in three weeks and sunk U-451 on the night of 21/22 December, showing the importance of airborne radar in naval aircraft to locate enemy vessels.

## Greece

On the morning of 28 October 1940, the Italian Minister in Athens handed a note to the Prime Minister of Greece, General Metaxas, saying that his Government protested most strongly about alleged Greek assistance to the Allies and demanding the right for Italians to occupy strategic bases in Greece. Metaxas regarded this note as an ultimatum which he promptly refused, and a few hours later Greece was at war with Italy. The Greek forces were not prepared for war, unlike the Italians who had modern mechanized equipment. The Italians made their first attacks through the mountainous Albanian border area and overwhelmed the gallant Greek Army, fighting for every foothold.

The Greek Air Force, although small and outnumbered by the Italians, fought back with great bravery. Operationally, the Greek Air Force was controlled by the General Staff and was used almost entirely in support of their ground forces. Many of their pilots had attended courses in England, including at the Central Flying School. Their aircraft were old and of foreign origin, mainly French or Polish, and lacked spares. As a consequence they suffered severe casualties in the opening stages. Following an urgent appeal from the Greeks, the British Government decided to send a small expeditionary force from the Middle East Command, the RAF sending two medium bomber squadrons equipped with Bristol Blenheims and two fighter squadrons equipped with Gloster Gladiators.

No. 815 Squadron had been assembled from the remnants of Nos 815 and 819 Squadrons after the devastating attack on *Illustrious* had killed or injured many of the aircrews. Without a carrier, No. 815 was sent to a new airstrip at Maleme on Crete. Five of the six machines had been fitted with a long-range tank in the rear cockpit, so they could only be operated with two crew members. The sixth machine, flown by the CO, could still carry a crew of three. The tanks did, however, increase their range and endurance to 1,000 miles (1,600km) and nine hours, respectively. On 3 February 1941 Lt A. W. Burnaby Drayson with his observer, Lt J. A. Caldecott-Smith, ran out of fuel on an anti-submarine patrol and force-landed on Antikythera Island, the Swordfish being a write-off. Three Swordfish flew to Heraklion, also on Crete, on 10 February and that night attacked Stampalia using 250lb bombs, the target being lit by flares. They continued with these types of raid for six weeks. On 11 March six Swordfish of No. 813 Squadron arrived in Greece and proceeded to Paramythia, from where they operated against Valona and Durazzo harbours in Albania. The high ground surrounding Valona made a night approach very awkward, while it was almost impossible to get into the harbour undetected. At Durazzo the water was shallow and approaches therefore limited. The first raid on Valona was planned for 13 March after RAF reconnaissance showed a number of ships in the harbour. Charles Lamb said:

> We knew from a previous reconnaissance by one of the Wimpey [Vickers-Armstrongs Wellington] pilots who had flown over Valona that afternoon that the anchorage was ripe with fat pickings. There were at least half a dozen big ships lying at anchor in deep water and our torpedoes were fitted with Duplex pistols. A torpedo attack from the air was the last thing they were expecting, and with the lights of the town behind the ships, we couldn't miss.
>
> An hour later, at about 4am, I followed the leading Swordfish, with Jackie, Caldecott-Smith and Pat Beagley as TAG down through a gap, re-setting my altimeter to 1,300ft as we passed through. It wasn't possible to do accurately, because I had to concentrate on the blue formation light of Jackie's aircraft very close ahead, and the gap between the black shadows of the hills was not very wide. A few seconds later, when we were gliding across the inside of the harbour with the throttles almost closed, steadily losing height, the flaming onions streaked past us on either side and Jackie's light disappeared. One second he was there, the next he had gone. From that moment I was leading, and I thought I had plenty of height to reach the shipping at anchor right ahead, which was almost within range, when my wheels struck the water with a dreadful lurch. Instinctively I held the aircraft steady in case it somersaulted, and opened the throttle wide and pressed the release button, because the water would have activated the Duplex pistol on the nose of the torpedo and started the pistol's propeller. The sudden deceleration only lasted for about two seconds, when we were airborne again, but they were the longest two seconds I have ever known. Fortunately we were within 1,500yd of a big ship, right ahead, her hulk a black shape against a searchlight, wavering about from the town behind her, so my 'fish wasn't wasted. But ever after that experience I set my altimeter with very great care when coming through that gap.
>
> It says a great deal for the sturdy construction of the Swordfish undercarriage that it could be dipped in the sea at a speed of 90kt or more and held there for a few seconds, without being torn off; and for the power of the Bristol engine and the stability of the aircraft as a whole, that the ailerons and wings were sufficiently strong to keep it steady with such a sudden deceleration, and force it through the water into the air again without any damage whatsoever.

After the loss of Jago and Caldecott-Smith, Torrens-Spence took over as CO of No. 815 squadron with A. W. F. Sutton becoming Senior Observer. The squadron was split in half so that one half was in the mountains ready to carry out any strikes required, while the other half was in Athens re-arming. On the next raid into Valona harbour the Italians had positioned a small flak ship near the entrance and Lamb put a torpedo into it. A few days later, after a meeting in Athens, he was on his way back when the passenger he was giving a lift to shouted 'Fighters astern, on both sides!':

> At the time I was at 5,000ft over Corfu and a glance over my shoulder revealed two Fiat CR.42 biplane fighters. I jettisoned my torpedo immediately and hoped that I was over the sea. I later learned that it blew a hole in the south-west corner of Corfu. Then the routine I had learned in Bermuda came to the rescue, and as the Fiats opened fire I stood the Swordfish on its tail and their bullets missed ahead, and they spun over on to their backs and nearly collided. I hoped that the Sub-Lt in the rear was firmly strapped in, because I had to get down to sea-level in double-quick time, and then pull out of the dive in a violent manoeuvre which might toss him out of the aircraft; but there was no time to speak. I have never dived a Swordfish so close to the vertical before, nor pulled out so close to the sea. In the dive I kept the throttle almost fully open, and the engine screamed in protest. When I banged the throttle into the closed position and hauled the aircraft out of the dive, I was doing nearly 200kt, and would not have been surprised if the wings had folded or come off completely. I only just missed the sea and had to do a steep climbing turn to avoid it, which blacked out the observer completely for a few seconds.
>
> The Fiats then made a fatal error; they had recovered from their inverted spin and had

climbed to attack again, and they came in together, in unison, almost side by side. Had they attacked separately, one after the other, they would have shot me out of the sky as easy as snuffing out a candle. I had enough time to dive down to water-level again, to build up speed in order to climb vertically with the throttle closed, so that the aircraft stalled. This time I let it go slightly over the vertical, in a tightly stalled upward half of a loop, and then had to jam the throttle wide open and roll sideways into a completely stalled turn, and for once only just avoided an immediate spin; but the engine pulled her round, though for a split second I am sure that the whole weight of the Swordfish was hanging from the propeller. At the commencement of that turn I was just in time to see two big splashes as both Italians spun into the sea.

By 23 March 1941 No. 815 Squadron had sunk five ships but had lost a number of Swordfish, with engine problems mounting. Six replacement Swordfish were actually aboard *Formidable* but she was held up in the Suez Canal waiting for enemy mines to be cleared. The Swordfish were eventually delivered and flown to Paramythia on 9 April. They were involved in sinking another four ships before the end of the Greek campaign, and the squadron flew to Crete. With the replacement aircraft No. 815 now had eight Swordfish, of which only three were serviceable. One was required for patrols but the other two were being worked on to prepare them for the flight to Egypt. A visit to inspect the aircraft by Capt Jones, an engineering officer from Egypt, resulted in all eight Swordfish being grounded as unfit to fly, five at least needing new engines. The remaining men on the squadron rebuilt three Swordfish using parts from the others. On 22 April the three were all test-flown, but only one take-off, circuit and landing was allowed, the engines sounding very rough. All three managed to keep going over the 300 miles (500km) or so to Egypt, and survived to have replacement engines fitted, one disintegrating as it arrived over Dekheila airfield.

**An Albacore of No. 815 Squadron when on detachment to Cyprus in May 1941. They operated against Vichy French shipping, sinking one destroyer and damaging another.**
D. W. Phillips via Ray Sturtivant

**Looking as though it may have seen better days, Swordfish L7648 'X' of No. 815 Squadron at Heliopolis, near Cairo. It later went on to serve in No. 775 Squadron during 1944.** RAF Museum

## Battle of Matapan

A patrolling Sunderland from Malta spotted the Italian fleet heading towards Crete on 27 March 1941. The Mediterranean Fleet, including *Formidable*, left Alexandria and set off in pursuit. The following morning *Formidable* flew off her Albacore reconnaissance aircraft, one of which found the enemy fleet at 7.20am and continued shadowing it.

On board *Formidable* were Nos 826 and 829 Albacore squadrons, although the latter had a few Swordfish as well, due to a shortage of Albacores in the Middle East; fighter protection was afforded by Nos 803 and 806 Squadrons flying Fulmars. A strike force of Albacores was sent off, in conjunction with Swordfish of No. 815 Squadron from Maleme on Crete. The Italian flagship, *Vittorio Veneto*, was attacked through intense flak but all missed. During the afternoon another strike was laid on led by Lt Cdr J. Dalyell-Stead, which resulted in one torpedo hit but at a loss of the formation leader, who was shot down pressing home a close-range attack. The flagship was surrounded by the fleet as she made some repairs and the opportunity was taken to make another strike in an effort to slow her down until the British surface ships arrived.

Six Albacores and two Swordfish, led by Lt Cdr W. H. G. Saunt, took off at 5.35pm; shortly before this two Swordfish from No.

815 Squadron, flown by Lt Torrens-Spence and Lt Kiggell, had left Maleme to attack the Italian ships as well. The attacking aircraft circled the enemy fleet waiting for the sun to set, giving the Italians time to put up a smoke-screen. Torpedo-carrying aircraft then attacked independently between 7.30–7.45pm through a tremendous barrage of flak, risking collision in the mix of smoke-screen, searchlights and false cloud horizon. The *Pola*, an Italian 10,000-ton cruiser, was hit by a torpedo at 7.46pm, causing her to stop engines. Two other cruisers, the *Fiume* and *Zara*, came to the rescue but were caught by the British that evening and sunk in an exchange of gunfire. *Pola*'s crew were taken off by British destroyers, after which she was sunk by a torpedo. All but one of the aircraft taking part returned safely, the unlucky one running out of fuel and ditching in the Kithera Channel, the crew being picked up by the British destroyer *Juno*.

This action was later called the Battle of Matapan and convinced the doubters of the value of having aircraft carriers to carry out attacks on the enemy from beyond gunfire range. After the war Italian Admiral Iachino was to put on record his feelings about the battle:

> It was conducted with particular ability and bravery by aircraft of the Swordfish type. It was a concentrated bomb and torpedo attack. They kept formation at a low level, machine-gunning the bridge and upper works of the escort vessels so as to distract the anti-aircraft fire. The leading aircraft showed great skill and courage, and I saw him hit several times, and his machine seemed to stagger and dip violently across our trail some dozen metres from our bows, then fall into the sea, the bold pilot perishing without having the satisfaction of seeing the successful result of his shoot. It has to be recognized that the Swordfish performed a very useful service throughout the day, organizing the three most dangerous attacks on us. It is certain that the major success of the day was achieved by the aircraft carrier.

## Bizerta Lake

No. 813 Squadron took over the role played by No. 812 at Gibraltar for a time, with sub-flights stationed at Bone and another at Blida in Algeria. In what was probably the last Swordfish torpedo attack of the war, seven aircraft of No. 813 based at Bone took off during the night of 14/15 December 1942 and attacked two enemy vessels on Bizerta Lake in Tunisia. The vessels were detected anchored about 1½ miles (2.5km) off the North Mole.

The first wave of four Swordfish consisted of three carrying torpedoes armed with the Duplex pistol: '4A' (Lt Hankey, Lt Hutchinson and PO Hensman); '4B' (Sub-Lt Allison, Sub-Lt White and LAC Tidd); '4C' (Sub-Lt Hill, Sub-Lt Abel and LAC Parry); and '4F' (Sub-Lt Empson, Sub-Lt Pears and APO McBride), this aircraft carrying twenty-one flares and two 250lb bombs. The second wave consisted of three Swordfish, of which '4K' (Sub-Lt Heath, Lt Weatherall and PO Goddard) and '4L' (Sub-Lt Robinson, Sub-Lt Timberlake and LAC Smith) carried Duplex pistol torpedoes, and '4Q' (Sub-Lt Baring, Sub-Lt Legood and LAC Johnston) carried twenty-one flares and two 250lb bombs.

'4A' and '4B' arrived over the target at 2,000ft and, letting down to around 100ft and then 50ft, '4A' released his torpedo at a range of 700yd (640m), resulting in a flash. Swordfish '4B' held off until the first flares went down and then made his attacking run from about 30ft. Aircraft '4C' became detached in the dark and failed to locate the target. The flare-dropping Swordfish, '4F', had also become temporarily 'uncertain of position' and arrived late, dropped his flares and bombing what was thought to be a radio building. The leader of the second wave, '4K', made a classic torpedo strike using the light of the flares and was rewarded with a large explosion and smoke climbing to 2,000ft. Like a number of pilots '4L' got too low, dipped his wheels in the sea and released his torpedo to get out of his predicament, not noticing where the missile went. '4Q' bombed the dock area but saw no results. All aircraft arrived back at Bone safely.

**Swordfish of 'X' Flight, No. 813 Squadron, ashore at North Front, Gibraltar. Some of these machines took part in the last torpedo attack by Swordfish in World War Two, on 14 December 1942.**

## Malta

The Swordfish and Albacore were no strangers to Malta: after being introduced into FAA front-line squadrons and embarking on carriers, a cruise in the Mediterranean would mean an obligatory visit there. The island was only 17 × 9 (27 × 14km) miles and, lying between Libya and Sicily, was a key military point in the central Mediterranean. When the Suez Canal was opened, allowing access to the Indian Ocean without the need to go all the way round Africa, a British naval base

Operating from Bone in North Africa between December 1942 and March 1943, No. 813 suffered a few losses, as in this picture, the damage being extensive.

A Swordfish floatplane, K5931 '092' of No. 705 Flight, tacks across Valletta harbour in 1936. Some pilots said the take-off, flying and alighting speeds in a Swordfish floatplane were all the same!

with an anchorage in Grand Harbour was set up. A RNAS base was established at Kalafrana, on the most easterly point of the island, during World War One for anti-submarine patrols. Nearby, an airfield was established at Hal Far in 1929 followed by two others, Luqa, to the east of Hal Far, and Takali (also spelled Ta'Qali or Ta'kali) towards the middle of the island.

In 1939 an AMES (Air Ministry Experimental Station) Mk 1 Type 6 radar site was established at Fort Ta Salvatur; known as No. 241 Transportable Radio Unit (TRU), it was to become an essential piece of equipment in the conflict that followed. It had a range of 100 miles (160km) in all directions up to 8,000ft. A second TRU was in the process of being set up. Early in 1941 two other radar sets were delivered by sea. These were the COL (Chain Overseas Low Type 5) radars, one being established at Fort Maddalena on the north coast west of Valletta, and another at Ta Silch.

Before the outbreak of war No. 3 Anti-Aircraft Co-Operation Unit (AACU) moved in, flying Swordfish and towing drogues to support sea and land gun firing exercises. After Italy declared war against the Allies on 10 June 1940 the AACU also carried out coastal patrols around the island. The relatively easy conversion to floats meant the Swordfish could also be used in the air-sea rescue role. One such Swordfish, K8369 flown by Flt Lt Leslie, was despatched on 21 July to find a Savoia-Marchetti SM.79 that had been hit by anti-aircraft fire during a raid and ditched about 20 miles (32km) off the Sicilian coast near Cap Pessaro. Nothing was heard from the Swordfish but the pilot was picked up later by the Italians and became a POW. Three Swordfish were detached to Gibraltar so the unit could ill afford such incidents, but a few nights later Plt Off Sugden in K5935, refitted with its normal undercarriage, landed short of the flare path at Hal Far and damaged the aircraft.

The detached flight of three Swordfish that moved to Gibraltar came under Fg Off Hugh Garlick, although his operational tasks were set by the Rear Admiral, Gibraltar. Apart from anti-submarine patrols, escorting inbound and outbound convoys and the odd leaflet drop over Moroccan towns, they kept a running watch on German ships along the coast and in Spanish harbours. These three Swordfish, K8354, L2808 and L9770, remained at Gibraltar after No. 3 AACU was absorbed by No.

830 Squadron on Malta. On 27 October they became B Flight of No. 202 Squadron under Sqn Ldr T. Q. Horner, with the promoted Flt Lt Garlick as Flight Commander. Their duties remained much as before, but L2808 was badly damaged on 28 January 1941 when it hit the harbour boom defence; L9770 was badly damaged when a gale collapsed the hangar roof on 11 April and K8354 'TQ-D' was withdrawn on 9 June.

After the fall of France in 1940 the situation in the Mediterranean altered dramatically. The western end was in the hands of the French with harbours and a relatively strong fleet operating out of North Africa and the south of France. The British fleet dominated the eastern end from their base at Alexandria. However, the central area had been left to the Italians. There had been a gradual build-up of Italian naval forces since Mussolini had taken power in Italy in 1922. By 1940 Italy's young and powerful fleet had fast modern ships, from destroyers to battleships; a considerable fleet of submarines; and extensive modernized harbours and port installations, such as Taranto on the eastern heel of Italy and bases in Sicily. Theoretically, the Italians should have been able to control the central Mediterranean and subdue anyone threatening that control.

**The torpedo store for No. 830 Squadron on Malta. There was always a shortage of torpedoes on Malta, with some delivered by submarine and some by Sunderlands, which landed in Kalafrana Bay.** R. E. F. Kerrison

However, they had several Achilles heels: they did not have radar, which the British fleet did; they did not have any aircraft carriers; and most problematic of all, they did not have a reliable source of coal and fuel oil for their ships, having to depend on Germany and certain Balkan states. As the war progressed even these sources dried up and the Italian fleet was therefore very limited in its freedom of action. Also, the British Royal Navy was held in high esteem by many nations, including Italy, and this made the Italians reluctant to start a fight. There was never any doubt about their bravery, but this was constrained by the restrictions mentioned above.

## *Operations Begin*

Admiral Cunningham, Commander-in-Chief of the British Mediterranean Fleet, had never been in any doubt about the strategic importance of Malta, and when France capitulated on 24 June he laid his plans accordingly. When he discovered there were some dismantled Gloster Gladiator fighters on the island he ordered that four be assembled for use: these would constitute the sole fighter force on the island in those early days. To supplement these came Swordfish of No. 767 Squadron. To take advantage of the good weather usually associated with southern France this training squadron had arrived aboard *Argus*, the carrier used for deck landing training. From October 1939 the Swordfish were based at the French airfield at Hyeres, near Toulon. When Italy entered the war the CO of No. 767, Lt Cdr G. C. Dickens, led nine Swordfish, armed with 12in shells 'borrowed' from the French, and lashed to the aircraft with spun yarn that had to be fused before take-off, and then bombed Genoa. The Vichy French authorities took a dim view of this and No. 767 left in a hurry! Twelve Swordfish flew to Bone in North Africa. Here the squadron split up, one half returning to the UK and the other becoming a strike force under Lt Cdr F. D. Howie. Flying via Medjez-el-Bab the aircraft flew to Malta, but had difficulty landing, as the defenders had placed old transport vehicles across the airfield to stop any chance of an airborne invasion!

These Swordfish later merged with those of the Malta Communications Flight to become No. 830 Squadron. They immediately started to work up with their inexperienced crews, mindful that they represented the only air strike force on the island. Most of the aircraft, which had been used for training, were old 1936 standard aircraft with no 'blind-flying' panels. Without sensitive altimeters and artificial horizons they were difficult to fly, especially low and at night over the sea, which they would have to do if they were to make torpedo attacks.

However, on the night of 30 June/1 July 1940 No. 830 carried out its first operation when they dive-bombed the oil refinery and oil storage tanks at Augusta on the east coast of Sicily. On July 6 nine Swordfish attacked the airfield at Catania, destroying aircraft in a hangar and setting fire to other targets. As they flew back they gazed ruefully at enemy ships in Augusta harbour and wished they had torpedoes. One Swordfish, out on patrol 19 July, found a submarine on the surface and bombed it, without any observable results.

Nine Swordfish went out on the night of 13/14 August to attack shipping in

**Loading a torpedo onto an Albacore on Malta. The Swordfish and Albacores all had black under-surfaces for their nocturnal activities.** R. E. F. Kerrison

Augusta harbour. Arriving at 8,000ft, six dive-bombed the ships from above while three torpedo-carrying Swordfish attacked from seawards. Flak of different types was intense. The six dive-bombers returned safely but all three torpedo aircraft were lost, two in action and the third running out of fuel and ditching within sight of Hal Far. Six new Swordfish, straight from the factory, were delivered by pilots aboard *Illustrious*, which was escorting a convoy through to Egypt. These were to the latest standard with blind-flying instrument panels. A quantity of the latter were also delivered to Malta to be fitted to the earlier Swordfish that lacked them, but in fact were not fitted until eight or nine months later. Also delivered were a number of long-range fuel tanks that were fitted to Swordfish by RAF mechanics at Hal Far.

## *Anti-Shipping Operations*

Apart from aircraft carriers staging through with convoys, the Swordfish of No. 830 Squadron were the only anti-shipping strike force in the central Mediterranean. Tripoli harbour in North Africa became a regular target for the Swordfish as they sought out enemy ships, but there were many long, tiring and boring sea patrols. The Italian army in Libya advanced into Egypt on 13 September and extended its supply lines even further from Italy. At one time single Swordfish went out on long, deep patrols looking for enemy shipping and frequently approached the Sicilian coast where they could see Mount Etna. The squadron back at base was kept on alert in case a sighting was reported. These patrols by single aircraft were stopped after one Swordfish only escaped from two Italian fighter seaplanes by diving to sea level. Encounters with enemy aircraft were infrequent but rating pilot PO (later Lt Cdr) Charlie Wines recalls when he met one:

> It was 16 October 1940, my crew were Lt (O) Walford and NA Pickles and we were out on a recce when we came across a Cant 105 flying boat. I decided to engage it in a 'dogfight' as the Italian pilot probably thought he had a Gladiator to contend with. I got away most of my front gun ammo before the gun jammed, and Pickles swore at me for not giving him sufficient opportunities to use his Lewis gun. The Cant 105 got away at about 135kt, while the best I could do was 115kt! We did not receive any hits by return fire, if indeed he was armed.

In September three RAF Martin Marylands arrived to form No. 431 General Reconnaissance Flight and carry out long-range reconnaissance, a welcome addition that provided much-needed photographs of enemy positions such as airfields and harbours. Marylands kept up a constant surveillance of Taranto harbour where most of the Italian fleet appeared to be based. Around this time a plan was hatched for an attack by No. 830 Squadron on Taranto, but this was rendered unnecessary by the highly successful raid on 11 November by Swordfish from *Illustrious*.

On the night of 10 December eight Swordfish from No. 830 Squadron dive-bombed shipping in Tripoli harbour and claimed three hits. One aircraft, K8866, was lost in this raid with the crew, Sub-Lt R. H. Thompson and Sub-Lt A. E. Dyer, being killed. Nine Swordfish went back on the night of 21 December, with three attacking buildings with 250lb bombs while the others laid mines in the harbour. PO Charlie Wines also went on this one:

> My air gunner on 21 December was Cpl 'Peachey' Parker (later to achieve fame flying in Mosquitoes over Europe). Our orders were to bomb the seaplane hangars and slipways at Tripoli harbour. Whilst the AA fireworks were engaging the rest of the squadron aircraft I glided in with the engine throttled back from the desert side and spread three 500lb bombs and two sticks of incendiaries across the hangars, clearly seen in the moonlight. According to Parker the result was something worth seeing, but I was too busy making myself small in the cockpit as I dived for sea level amid flak turned on us as soon as they heard me gun the engine. Years later I walked over the target area and actually spoke to the night watchman who had been on duty during the attack. He said that nine assorted seaplanes and flying boats had gone up in my attack on the hangar, plus some MTBs and patrol craft on the slipway for repairs.

General Wavell's 8th Army counter-attacked from Egypt on 9 December and started to drive the Italians back along the Libyan coast. Attacking enemy shipping, harbours and stores provided much-appreciated support from Malta's defenders. On 10 January 1941 four flights of three Swordfish took off to attack enemy shipping reported in Palermo harbour. Armed with a mix of flares, bombs and torpedoes, the raid was of limited success with no aircraft lost.

## *Germany Enters the Fray*

The Luftwaffe had by now taken over the attacks on the island and on 19 January around eighty enemy aircraft, escorted by fighters, bombed Malta. *Illustrious*, damaged at sea by enemy air attacks, had limped into Grand Harbour badly in need of a respite to affect some repairs. During this period some of the deck hands from *Illustrious*' No. 819 Squadron were 'loaned' to No. 830, who were very short-handed. One of these was Leading Air Fitter (later Lt Cdr) Ted Whitley who had been responsible for setting all the torpedoes carried by Swordfish on the Taranto raid. On one occasion, after a particularly busy period on *Illustrious* he was so tired he fell asleep on a camp bed under the wing of a Swordfish loaded with 110lb anti-submarine bombs. When he awoke the aircraft had gone! He stayed on with No. 830 at Malta along with some torpedo ratings.

On 27 January 1941 a Sunderland flying boat of No. 288 Squadron, based at Kalafrana, sighted two enemy merchant ships, the *Ingo* and *Inza*, escorted by the 7,500-ton *Duisburg*. When the sighting signal was picked up at Malta seven Swordfish, all that was available, were armed, six with torpedoes and one with bombs. All the torpedo aircraft carried a 60gal (270ltr) extra fuel tank in the rear cockpit, which meant that only one other crew member could be taken. The CO however, always wanted a TAG in the rear cockpit and his Swordfish was fitted with an ex-Hurricane 69gal (314ltr) tank slung on the torpedo crutches. Their weapon was the 1,610lb (730kg) Mk XII 18in torpedo, fitted with a Duplex pistol and set to run at 20ft (6m), so it could be detonated by a ship's magnetism beneath the keel. In a cloudless blue sky the Swordfish arrived unseen at 10,000ft and attacked out of the sun, sinking one ship and damaging the other two. Rear-Admiral Clement Moody, Director of the Naval Air Division reported:

> This operation provides an example of perfect co-ordination and execution. Though on a small scale, it is in fact a classic, which achieved the success it deserved without any element of luck. Good reconnaissance and shadowing by the RAF Sunderland, combined with accurate navigation on the part of the striking force, enabled the convoy to be located and attacked at a distance of some 180 miles from Malta.

There had been an element of luck however: on a cloudless sunlit day there had been no enemy fighter opposition and only light flak. On 31 January a Maryland, fleeing a Fiat G.50, noted fourteen merchant ships and five destroyers in Tripoli harbour. That night four Swordfish armed with torpedoes roamed along the Libyan coast while RAF Wellingtons bombed the harbour. The almost daily attacks on Malta resulted in many British aircraft being written off, but most of the Swordfish somehow survived.

## *Enter Rommel*

In February 1941 General Erwin Rommel was appointed to command the new Afrika Korps, which was to join the Italian army and stop the British taking Tripoli. The first German supply ships left Naples on 8 February, these being the freighters *Ankara*, *Arcturus* and *Alicante*, escorted by the Italian destroyer *Turbine* and three MTBs. As a surprise reception No. 830 were tasked with mining the harbour, and ten Swordfish left that night. Three aircraft in the first wave of six were actually going to mine the harbour, armed with torpedoes attacked from the eastern flank through intense flak, dropping their torpedoes at only 600yd (550m). As they were unable to confirm any sinking, a second wave of four Swordfish left in the early hours of the following day but were unable to find the convoy.

That night two formations of four aircraft took off to sweep from Kuriat Island to just south of Kerkeneh Bank. Each leader had flares, the other three being armed with Duplex torpedoes set to run at a depth of 22ft (7m). The first wave found an enemy merchant ship of around 7,000 tons, subsequently found to be the Italian *Juventus*, some 17 miles (27km) south of the island and escorted by a small ship of around 200 tons. Flares were dropped to the east of the

**Three Albacores climbing out of Hal Far. Although they are carrying torpedoes, it is daylight and they are probably flying a training detail. All three torpedoes have been fitted with air tails.** IWM

the rest carried bombs and flares. Flak was intense and tracer passed through the fabric-covered aircraft though without doing too much damage. In the second wave of four, two laid mines and the others bombed the seaplane base and a quay. Flown by Sub-Lt C. C. Thornton and LAC F. W. Pickles, Swordfish L2849 crashed near Garzis, the crew being interned by the French.

Four Swordfish went out on an armed reconnaissance on 13 February and found the supply ships from Tripoli returning to Naples. The ships heard the approaching Swordfish and split up so that when the first flare ignited little could be seen, except against the backglow. Three Swordfish ships and at two-minute intervals the Swordfish carried out a torpedo strike. Releasing their torpedoes at 600–700yd (550–640m) range, one hit was obtained near the stern, the ship stopping and started to settle. The three torpedo aircraft left the scene to return to Hal Far while the leader stayed to watch developments. The second strike force saw his flares from 50 miles (80km) away but it was some time before they arrived. By now the visibility was poor and it was difficult to keep the ship in sight. After releasing more flares one Swordfish attacked with a torpedo which struck her amidships. Already down by the stern, she listed heavily to starboard and started to sink. While this had been going on the second supply convoy for the Afrika Korps slipped by in the dark.

Fliegerkorps X stepped up its campaign to get the convoys through and intensified the aerial attacks on Malta. Each day dive-bombing attacks were made on the airfields, with fighter sweeps across the island and bombing continuing through the night. Such attacks were bound to have effects and on 5 March three Swordfish were written off and the rest rendered unserviceable after a visit by sixty enemy bombers. Luqa and Hal Far were both unuseable and a number of enemy convoys got through to Tripoli: the German strategy was working. British submarines based at Malta did manage to sink a number of enemy ships but supplies were still getting through. The groundcrews on No. 830 Squadron patched up damaged Swordfish which ventured out on 'rat hunts' armed with torpedoes.

In a magnificent effort by the groundcrews, nine Swordfish were made airworthy for a raid on Tripoli on the night of 18/19 March. The leader carried ten flares and four 250lb bombs; three were loaded with six 250lb bombs each, with blast rods attached and screamers on the tail; and there were five minelayers. The bombers were to attack any enemy gun positions along the moles that might threaten the minelaying aircraft. Approaching from the north at 6,000ft, the Swordfish split up and started the attack. The mines were laid under a barrage of fast-firing pompoms and automatic gunfire. TAG 'Nat' Gold was flying with PO Charlie Wines that night:

> It normally took 2 hours 20 minutes to fly from Malta to Tripoli, plenty of time to reflect on things! I did not like those bombs underneath: why we had to dive-bomb I could not understand because RAF Wellingtons usually accompanied us and did their high-level bombing first, so stirring up the hornets' nest. Tripoli always put up a box barrage with plenty of searchlights so it was easy to see things. Consequently on arriving at the target Charlie yelled through the Gosports 'Look at that beautiful ship in the middle of the harbour – I'm going after it.'
>
> I yelled back 'You're mad, that's suicide', but as a passenger what could I do? I imagined it was no different to flying down the barrel of an anti-aircraft gun! We went over at 4,000ft and straight into a vertical dive. I clung on for dear life when something hit me in the stomach. It really hurt and I thought 'Oh God, I've been hit', but was too scared to touch the area. After a while I plucked up courage and felt – no blood! I then realized that a spare drum of ammunition, resting on the gun ring, had slipped off and hit me.
>
> I sighed with relief and hooked my arm over the side of the cockpit and heaved myself up. The sight before my eyes frightened the life out of me! It was like daylight, tracer coming up from all directions like flaming onions in different colours – swishing and crackling. The ship looked enormous and I thought Charlie had been hit. Then I felt that wonderful G pressure as we pulled out. We straddled the ship with our bombs – I heard all six go off as Charlie threw the old kite all over the sky to avoid the flak. He told me afterwards that he had pulled out at 800ft, but it seemed much lower.

On 2 April, in a disagreement at high level about the role of No. 830 Squadron on Malta, Admiral Cunningham stated:

> I do not concur that mining should be considered the primary function of No. 830 Squadron. The function of this squadron is primarily torpedo attack on enemy shipping, which form of attack, given adequate reconnaissance, is positive and deadly as compared with the 'lucky dip' character of mining operations. There is no objection to the use of the squadron for mining provided that offensive naval role of torpedo attack is not unduly interfered with.

On 12 April a Maryland sighted a convoy of five enemy merchantmen and three destroyers some 40 miles (64km) south-west of Pantellaria. Swordfish 'P' was sent out, crewed by Little, Walford and Sergeant Parker, to shadow the convoy. This they did, staying until the main force arrived and signalling their position by flares. Seven Swordfish made up the strike force, one with flares and bombs, five with torpedoes and one to act as a dive-bomber. Once the flares had been released the torpedo aircraft positioned themselves and attacked at two-minute intervals, releasing their torpedoes at 600–700yd (550–640m) against intense flak. Wines' aircraft was hit

**Many Swordfish and Albacores were lost on the ground to enemy action, such as this No. 830 Squadron Swordfish.** N. Gold

**Even in revetments aircraft were not safe from the constant bombing by the German and Italian air forces, as seen in this picture of a Swordfish.** R. E. F. Kerrison

continuously as he launched his weapon, the first and only petty officer in the Royal Navy to carry out a torpedo attack in anger. Hot oil coming back into the cockpit told him the engine had been hit and he subsequently force-landed his Swordfish L7689 'B' on the beach at Hammamet. He and his observer, LAC L. M. Edwards, were somewhat surprised, but delighted, when the French Vichy police took them to a large house owned by an expatriate American and his English wife, who gave them dinner before they were led off into captivity. The other torpedo aircraft made their attacks but results were indecisive due to the heavy flak and a smoke screen laid by the destroyer. Parr made two bombing attacks, one from 5,000ft and one from 2,500ft, but again no results were seen. The leader, in Swordfish 'A', stayed on the scene and continued to shadow the convoy. One other Swordfish, P4065 'F', had crash-landed and the crew, Sub-Lt H. P. Dawson and LAC A. Todd, were interned by the French.

Between 2–6 May five minelaying sorties were flown with only one loss – that of the Senior Pilot on the night of 6/7 May. Lt N. K. Campbell, Lt G. D. Nutt and PO W. G. T. Welsh in Swordfish P4232 'A' were hit by gunfire over Tripoli and had to ditch. In the high seas they were battered against the rockface; Nutt was thrown clear but Welsh died from his injuries the next day. Campbell could not get over the cliff and swam back to the Swordfish's tail, still sticking up out of the water, and sat on that until morning when the Italians rescued him.

### *Improvements*

Operations continued but the whole job was being done by eight pilots, seven observers and nine TAGs. All were getting extremely tired and most were overdue for a rest from operations. They flew every night when it was fine, often carrying out patrols of five to seven hours at night, quite often getting shot at and flying aircraft they knew had been patched up and should have been scrapped. During the day, normal activities took place and attacking German bombers meant air raid sirens and bombs crashing down with little opportunity to sleep. Something needed to be done: the authorities were concerned about the lack of success of No. 830 in sinking ships and reducing the supplies getting through to Rommel. In the first five months of 1941, fourteen operational missions had resulted in three ships sunk and four damaged, mines had been laid and bomb attacks made on Tripoli and Palermo. Another duty the squadron picked up was the delivery of spies to the mainland. Vice-Admiral Aircraft Carriers, Denis Boyd, with his HQ in Alexandria picked Lt Charles Lamb to 'sort it out'. Boyd had told him 'Go and find out what is wrong and put it right. Sink Rommel's shipping!'

Lamb had a reputation for getting things done with a personality to match. Boyd gave him written authority to get the job done but he had no special status, other than as another squadron pilot. On 9 May 1941 Lamb arrived at Hal Far in the middle of an air raid. Later, he inspected the Swordfish and quickly found that all the aircraft were of the early type with no blind-flying or sensitive height instruments. The more modern instruments that he had delivered eight months before were found still in their boxes in the stores. He was told there had been no time either to fit them or train crews under the circumstances. Lamb organized the fitting of the new instrument panels and made improvements that raised morale on the squadron. One primary problem he found was the lack of airborne ASV radar, which would allow patrolling aircraft to locate shipping much easier.

During the afternoon of 12 May a Maryland discovered a convoy 40 miles (64km) south of Lampedusa. This turned out to be a major convoy of seven merchantmen, seven destroyers and two cruisers. That evening five Swordfish left Malta, though one turned back when its cockpit lighting failed. The leading aircraft with flares was not required as it was a cloudless, moonlit night. The other three Swordfish, armed with torpedoes, attacked the three starboard merchant ships, but results were only seen from the leading ship which gave off a bright flash followed by white smoke. German convoys were getting through to Tripoli in increasing numbers despite daylight raids by RAF Blenheims some of which were lost to flak.

Crete fell on 30 May 1941 following the British withdrawal. It looked as if Malta would be next, but some forty-seven Hurricanes arrived flying from *Furious*, followed a few weeks later by another forty-three. HMS *Formidable* was damaged by Luftwaffe attacks on 23 May and had to go to the USA for repairs. Her air complement consisted of Nos 826 (Albacore) and 829 (Albacore/Swordfish) squadrons, and Nos 803 and 806 with Fulmars. No. 826 and the Fulmars were flown ashore to Dekheila. Six Swordfish from No. 829 Squadron were retained aboard *Formidable* to provide anti-submarine cover during the journey across the Atlantic. Four of the most experienced pilots and observers from No. 829 were transferred to No. 830 Squadron on Malta.

Limited numbers of ASV kits now arrived and the leader of each raid flew an ASV-equipped aircraft, increasing their chances of detecting shipping at night. The new crews carried out a torpedo attack against a French merchant ship and destroyer escort on the night of 6 June without any notable success. The following night they began the 'milk round' – regular trips to mine Tripoli harbour and attack local targets. Seven Swordfish went back on 8 June, setting fire to two merchant ships. On 10 June rainstorms and heavy cloud foiled an attempt by seven Swordfish to attack three merchant ships and escorting destroyers off Pantellaria. Six aircraft left on 12 June for Tripoli, and though two turned back with engine problems the other four dive-bombed ships in the harbour and buildings to the west of the town. The following day an enemy ship was discovered about 100 miles (160km) east of Malta and that evening four Swordfish went after it – only to discover it was an hospital ship – their torpedoes 'missed'. Shipping was to be the target in Lampedusa harbour on 16 June, but bad weather prevented a strike. Two days later a British advance against Rommel failed, due mainly to the fact that his convoys were getting through, and had delivered to him the whole 15th Panzer Division.

Germany invaded the Soviet Union on 22 June 1941 and Luftwaffe units normally over Malta were notable by their absence, as they were obviously required elsewhere. A Hurricane reported a convoy of four merchant ships with seven escorting destroyers south-east of Malta during the afternoon of 25 June. Seven Swordfish, six with torpedoes, arrived over the target at dusk. Independent attacks followed in the half-light and in the face of heavy flak. Two merchant ships were reported hit with the possibility of a third, but Sub-Lt D. A. R. Holmes and LAC J. R. Smith, flying in Swordfish P3996, were lost when they either miscalculated the distance in the evening light or were wounded and crashed into the side of their target. It was back to Tripoli the following night when five Swordfish joined four RAF Wellingtons in bombing ships and harbour installations.

Another fifty-six Hurricanes arrived on 30 June to replace losses and add to the build-up for the next Allied offensive planned in the Western Desert. Eight Swordfish went to Tripoli on 1 July, one attacking the flak ship, others scoring hits on ships in the inner harbour with one small ship being sunk. A strike against a convoy off the east coast of Tunisia by seven Swordfish on 3 July was thwarted by enemy night fighters. Similar strikes during the early part of July were unsuccessful due to bad weather. On 14 July the squadron went out to attack a convoy but failed to locate it. During the return journey dawn arrived and through the mist could be seen two merchant ships and a destroyer. This was not the convoy they had been sent to look for, but the commanding officer decided to have a go. Ironically, though all the torpedo-carrying aircraft dropped their weapons except one, which hung up, all missed, but the three ships had already been sunk by British destroyers and were sitting on a sandbank!

**A Swordfish caught in the open by Axis aircraft.** R. E. F. Kerrison

Three aircraft went out on 16 July, two carrying out dive-bombing attacks and Lt G. M. T. Osborne RN hitting with a torpedo dropped from only 250yd (230m) at the 6,000-ton tanker *Panuco*. Although it didn't sink, damage was caused to the point where none of the fuel could be transferred and the ship, after repairs, had to take it back to Italy. A convoy sighted 17 miles (27km) from Pantellaria consisted of four merchant ships and five destroyers. One merchant ship carrying ammunition blew up after a low-level strike by Blenheims. Another was damaged and taken in tow by one of the destroyers. Five Swordfish went out at dusk and Lt R. E. Bibby and Lt Osborne both scored torpedo hits on the 7,000-ton tanker *Brarena*, which drifted onto the Kerkeneh Bank and became a total loss. Sub-Lt D. B. A. Smith was believed to have hit the destroyer *Fuciliere* after a red flash was seen near the stern, but this was not confirmed.

Six Swordfish and crews arrived for No. 830 Squadron in late July, two of them carrying ASV, a welcome sight indeed! They were put to immediate use, leading a strike that night against four merchant ships and their escort south of Pantellaria. In poor visibility one torpedo hit a 6,000-ton freighter resulting in an explosion and fire, but not a sinking. On 5 August 1941 five Swordfish, each armed with eight incendiaries and two 500lb bombs, dive-bombed the U-boat base at Port Augusta in Sicily. A small ship was sunk, considerable damage done to the quay and numerous large fires started. The next night seven Swordfish, one with ASV and flares, and five with Duplex torpedoes set to run at 20ft, went after a convoy of six supply ships, five destroyers and an MTB, all heading for Tripoli. Two supply ships of 8,000 and 6,000 tons were sunk by torpedo attacks, the larger ship being attacked by Lt Lamb who released at 650yd (600m) and Williams who released at 800yd (730m). At least two other pilots attacked this ship, but Nottingham went for the 6,000-ton one, noting smoke pouring from it as he climbed away.

A large ship reported in the harbour at Syracuse was attacked during the night of 10 August. Four Swordfish made their way along the coast, avoiding the persistent flak. Little dropped his flares to light the target and the three Swordfish made classic torpedo attacks from the south-west, Osborn down to 60ft, Bibby only a little higher and Thorpe even lower at 35ft. All hit the target and reconnaissance photographs the next day revealed the ship down by the stern with a list to port and probably aground. It was found to be the Lloyd-Triestino passenger liner *California*, later salvaged and scrapped.

Charles Lamb took the squadron to Augusta again on 13 August to dive-bomb four submarines and a depot ship. They flew up the coast of Sicily at 6,000ft, avoiding the flak all the way. The Swordfish got separated in thickening cloud and with the warning from the flak batteries, the submarines were all on the bottom of the harbour. Those Swordfish that found the harbour dropped their bombs on buildings and other installations. The Director of Naval Operations was not pleased, saying:

> These operations seem more properly the function of RAF aircraft and must tend to reduce No. 830's striking power for torpedo attacks and minelaying, which is their job.

The following night, 14 August, the squadron did its job! A convoy 30 miles (50km) south of Lampion was detected, consisting of three 6,000-ton and two 3,000-ton merchantmen escorted by five destroyers. Nine Swordfish, six with torpedoes(three with contact heads and three with Duplex pistols), two with flares and an ASV shadower were briefed to attack the convoy. The ASV Swordfish, crewed by Garthwaite, Gillingham and Sgt Carter, took off from Hal Far at 6.30pm and located the convoy at 8.50. The first wave left Malta at 9.15pm, the second wave following ten minutes later.

At 11pm the first flares went down and Osborne flew a classic torpedo attack, not dropping until only 350yd (320m) away. He hit a 6,000-ton ship, followed by a big explosion, Campbell, following, made a similar

**An Albacore hit in an air raid.** R. E. F. Kerrison

attack on one of the 3,000-tonners and Whitworth had a go at a destroyer: this was seen by other crews to be stopped in the water with another destroyer alongside taking off members of the crew. Bibby launched his flares for the second wave, but two torpedoes missed, only Taylor scoring a hit, on a 3,000-tonner that took on a list to port. Reconnaissance photographs of Tripoli harbour the following day showed only three merchantmen. The success of the operation was mainly due to the ASV Swordfish keeping track of the convoy in poor visibility and informing the attacking aircraft.

The next target was a ship unloading supplies in Catania harbour. Five Swordfish each armed with two 500lb bombs and eight 25lb incendiaries started taking off at 10.30pm in staggered intervals. The aircraft were led by Cedric Coxon with Griffith as observer. The latter had his own 'bomb load' in the form of a crate of empty Maltese Blue Label beer bottles! Knowing the usual operating height of the Swordfish, the Italians put up a flak barrage between 4,000–6,000ft. The pilots managed to get up to 7,000ft and it was from this height that Coxon began his attack. Gliding down to 2,500ft, he proceeded to drop his bombs and incendiaries across the supplies on the quay while his observer unloaded the empty beer bottles, the open necks causing a screaming sound as they fell – the FAA answer to the *Stuka*, perhaps? The rest of the aircraft bombed the ship and quay, with the fires discernible over 70 miles (112km) away.

Six merchant ships and six destroyers were found on 17 August near Lampedusa. There were only five crews available for a strike, so two of the crews (Bibby and Thorpe) that had bombed Catania and only got back to Malta in the early hours were called out, making seven in total. By the time the squadron arrived at 6.25pm the convoy was only 8 miles (13km) from Lampedusa. Lt Whitworth fired his torpedo at a large ship from 400yd (370m) in intense and accurate flak. Whilst taking avoiding action his undercarriage hit the sea but he regained control and climbed away. Garthwaite, Osborne and Thorpe all claimed to have scored hits on other ships, confirmed the next day by a reconnaissance Maryland. Most of the Swordfish had flak damage and needed repairs. Another ship, the 5,000-ton *Maddalena Odero* had been beached and was later attacked by three Blenheims of No. 105 Squadron, resulting in fires that raged for three days and her total loss.

Intelligence informed Malta that a fast convoy was forming in Tripoli to run north to Italy for much-needed supplies during the night of 21 August. This was made up of four troopships, the *Esperia*, *Marco Polo*, *Neptunia* and *Oceania*, escorted by seven destroyers and one MTB. The 11,000-ton *Esperia* was sunk only 11 miles (18km) outside Tripoli harbour by the British submarine *Unique*. No. 830 were called into action and by a wonderful effort on the part of the groundcrews nine Swordfish were available by that night. Williams and Thorpe were to go out with two ASV-equipped Swordfish and locate the convoy. Once detected a third ASV Swordfish would lead six others carrying torpedoes set to run at a depth of 25ft. Unfortunately the weather turned bad, and with smokescreens laid by the destroyers the visibility was reduced to almost nil. Flares were quickly blown away and the ASV failed in the aircraft shadowing the convoy. Almost in desperation, two Swordfish dropped torpedoes at the escorting destroyers and the strike leader missed another with his bombs; four returned with their torpedoes.

During the night of 27/28 August six Swordfish attacked a convoy near Lampedusa, hitting a 6,000-ton merchant ship. However, one of the aircraft failed to get airborne, struck a dry stone wall and sheared the undercarriage off. Cloak and dagger activities continued – Lamb and Robertson in Swordfish V4292 delivered two agents to the mainland on the night of 29 August and brought two back. Going after a reported convoy on the night of 30/31 August five Swordfish could not find it and two torpedoed a 900-ton ship, the *Egadi*, which later sank.

On the night of 2/3 September nine Swordfish achieved complete surprise when they attacked a convoy of five cargo ships and seven escorting destroyers. One ship blew up after being hit by a torpedo, another was seen to be hit and two others damaged. The following night another convoy of five cargo ships with escort tried to get through. The *Andrea Gritti*, a 6,000-ton ammunition ship, was sunk and the freighter *Pietro Barbara* sank after arriving at Messina. That same night three Swordfish were sent out to attack a damaged tanker just outside Tripoli harbour. Unable to locate it, they fired their torpedoes at a destroyer resulting in a large explosion and reportedly the sinking of the destroyer; a supply ship of around 9,000 tons was hit by bombs but no results could be seen. More success came on 9 September when a convoy of three cargo ships and three destroyers were attacked 20 miles north of Pantellaria. Seven Swordfish went out with five scoring torpedo hits on two ships. The target on the night of 11 September was five cargo ships and seven destroyers 58 miles (93km) south of Lampion, two large ships being damaged. The same convoy was attacked the following night with six torpedoes being dropped and two ships damaged, both stopped in the water with one on fire.

RAF Wellingtons provided a diversionary raid on 16 September to allow seven Swordfish a chance to lay mines at the north mole of Tripoli harbour, one Swordfish failing to return. A convoy of five supply ships and four escorting destroyers heading south between Trapani and Martimo was attacked on the night of 17/18 September. Three torpedoes were dropped but only one claim of a hit was made due to dense smoke. Lt L. F. E Aldridge and his observer, LAC K. Pimlott, were killed when Swordfish L7660 'B' crashed while carrying out a strike against a convoy on 21/22 September. That night an 8,000-ton ship and a smaller vessel were attacked, with the larger ship being sunk and the other damaged. Six Swordfish laid mines off Tripoli harbour two nights later and on the 26 September they did the same at Palermo harbour.

More success followed: on 5 October seven Swordfish attacked a convoy moving south, and amid intense flak sank two vessels, one of 8,000–10,000 tons and one of 6,000 tons, with damage to another. On 8 October 830 Squadron attacked a convoy about 46 miles (74km) off Cap Bon, sinking a 6,000-ton ship with two torpedoes. Two more 6,000-ton ships were torpedoed on the 10th and an 8,000-ton ship 82 miles (132km) NNW of Tripoli was hit by two torpedoes the following night. The SS *Catarina* was sunk after being attacked by seven Swordfish on the night of 13/14 October, one of the escorting destroyers picking up survivors. On 17 October seven Swordfish were sent out after a convoy 15 miles (25km) from Pantellaria, two turning back with engine trouble. Two hits were recorded on two small vessels and another on a 4,000-tonner. Flying Swordfish 'O', Lt Nottingham and Sub-Lt Gillingham torpedoed a 5,000-ton merchantman but were severely shot up, the main petrol tank and port stub-plane catching fire; fighting the fire, they made it back to Malta safely.

### *No. 828 Squadron Arrives*

During October a welcome strengthening of the attacking force was made when No. 828 Squadron arrived from *Ark Royal*, equipped with Albacores. From now on operational flying would be shared by Nos 830 and 828 Squadrons and, if necessary, combined missions would be made to inflict the most damage on the enemy.

No. 830 had been struggling to keep its Swordfish serviceable and at one time was desperately short of crews to fly them. With this in mind the following mission could be ill-afforded. On the night of 11/12 November a force of seven Swordfish from No. 830 left to attack a convoy 10 miles (16km) west of Pantellaria. Three Swordfish had to turn back with engine problems and the other four, caught in a strengthening wind, never reached the convoy and ran out of fuel before they got back to Malta.

A large force of twelve destroyers, two cruisers and four supply ships were detected on 21 November and No. 830 was sent out to locate and attack it. They found the convoy 25 miles (40km) south-east of Cape Spartivento and attacked after flares had been dropped. One Swordfish, K5945 'M' flown by Lt P. E. O'Brien and Sub-Lt A. J. Griffith, was lost to flak, O'Brien being killed in the ditching but Griffith being picked up. On 22 November a combined force of Swordfish and Albacores attacked a southbound convoy of five cargo ships escorted by a cruiser and five destroyers. Lt R. E. F. Kerrison with Lt J. R. O. Stevenson were one of three Swordfish crews flying with torpedoes and hit the 10,000-ton cruiser *Duca degli Abruzzi*, leaving her wreathed in a cloud of smoke. Another crew claimed a hit on a 6,500-ton vessel.

A new CO now arrived for No. 830 Squadron, Lt Cdr Frank H. E. Hopkins, a battle-experienced observer. He quickly got into the swing of things and led a strike force on 12 December to find two blockade runners of the *Bande Nere* cruiser class carrying oil to Tripoli, but these had been sunk by British ships before the aircraft got there. An armed search for another tanker the following night resulted in nothing found. On 17 December four Swordfish attacked and probably sank a 4,000-ton tanker, thought to be the one from the previous night, 5 miles (8km) south of Lampedusa after a definite hit with a torpedo. Two nights later an armed search was sent out looking for a convoy of four merchant ships escorted by cruisers, destroyers and E-boats on their way to Tripoli, but there was no trace. During the nights of 24 and 25 December Swordfish laid mines in Tripoli harbour while Albacores created a diversionary bombing raid around the harbour.

### *1942*

As 1942 began the squadrons were, with the rest of the island, subjected to extensive raids by the Luftwaffe to reduce their effectiveness. Fliegerkorps II had arrived in Sicily after being pulled back from the Russian Front for the winter. This took its toll in aircraft destroyed or damaged on the ground and both squadrons were soon in need of urgent replacements. On 12 January four Swordfish attacked a convoy 85 miles (137km) south-west of Lampedusa with a tanker of 8,000 tons and a destroyer both hit by torpedoes. During the night of 15/16 January two Swordfish, all that were available, attacked a 4,000-ton vessel 50 miles (80km) east of Melita and left it wreathed in dense black smoke. This was a real effort: there was bad weather and gales, and Hal Far was bogged down so the Swordfish had to operate from Luqa. Nothing was found after another armed search on the 18 January.

Some outstanding flying was achieved on 23 January when Lt Cdr Hopkins led a torpedo strike in a north-easterly gale against the 20,000 ton SS *Victoria* and three other merchant ships, escorted by two battleships, five cruisers and twenty-seven destroyers. By the time the Swordfish had located the convoy they didn't have enough fuel to carry out an attack! Frank Hopkins flew all the way back to Malta, refuelled and set off again at 2.30am. The weather was now worse with heavy rain and low cloud. He relocated the convoy and torpedoed the *Victoria*, which sank. A vital supply convoy for Malta was sent out from Alexandria on 27 January with No. 830's Swordfish providing essential anti-submarine patrols. Another enemy tanker of 6,000 tons was left on fire on the night of 29 January when four Swordfish caught it 74 miles (119km) north-west of Tripoli – the airfield was being bombed as they took off. Unfortunately Swordfish K8351 'A' was shot down by flak, its crew of two being killed. Four Swordfish caught a convoy, consisting of an 8,000 ton vessel and destroyer escort, heading north about 70 miles (112km) out of Tripoli on the night of 30/31 January and left it damaged after hits by two torpedoes – the airfield was again bombed as the Swordfish took off. A gale and heavy rain stopped them going back the next night to finish the convoy off.

Another Swordfish, P4205 'J' was lost on 6/7 February when two aircraft carried out a torpedo attack on a 3,000 ton ship about 30 miles (54km) north-east of Cape Turgeunes. The ship was hit by a torpedo, followed by a large explosion and flames.

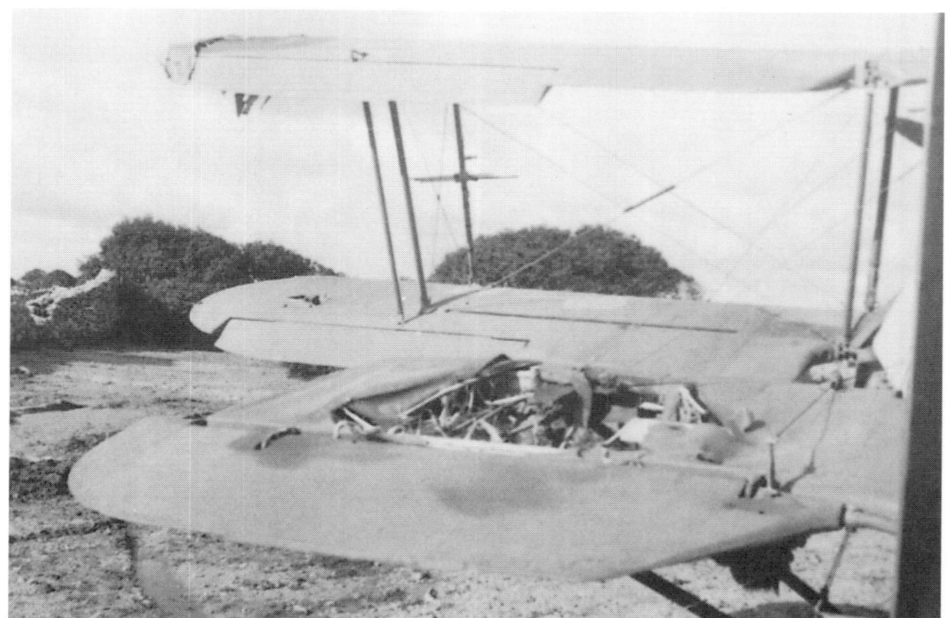

**Cannon damage to Swordfish V4587 after being caught by Bf 109s in the air over Malta.** C. Coxon

Another Swordfish was written off after a raid by the Luftwaffe, and when a force went to Tripoli on 16 February one Albacore and two Swordfish had to return early with technical problems. A torpedo strike failed to find the target on 21 February but on returning they crossed the coast in formation with a Ju 88 and were shot up by flak.

It was becoming increasingly difficult to keep these old biplanes flying – the rigging alone was a nightmare when aircraft continually returned shot up. Replacement machines had to be flown in and that, too, could be a problem. There was also a competition for the torpedoes between the submarine people and the air squadrons when fresh stocks arrived. They were delivered by submarine or Sunderland flying boats in small numbers and the question always was, who would cause the most damage in the most advantageous area to stop the enemy getting supplies to North Africa? In fact both aircraft and submarines did their bit to stop the enemy convoys getting through, but the numbers were too small.

There was a spell off operations due to bad weather and gales, but the Luftwaffe returned on 22/23 February destroying one Swordfish, damaging two badly and two more slightly – figures No. 830 Squadron could ill afford. Some Albacores were also damaged but despite this the groundcrews worked miracles and on the night of 23/24 February three Swordfish and three Albacores were available for operations. One Swordfish crashed on take-off and P4085 'A' was shot down in flames when the remainder went after shipping near Tripoli: the flak was so intense that the others sheared off.

**Another view of V4587, showing the damage to the port wings.** C. Coxon

On 2 March 1942 two Swordfish intended for No. 830 Squadron left El Adem: V4592, crewed by Mid J. A. K. Watson with Sub-Lt T. H. Greet, released by No. 821 Squadron; and V4590, crewed by Sub-Lts S. W. Chapman and P. F. C. Brown, released by No. 815 Squadron. Both failed to arrive. A 4,000-ton ship was the target for a torpedo strike laid on for 9 March with a hit confirmed later. Six Swordfish set off from El Adem on 10/11 March and set course for Malta. Each had an extra fuel tank in the rear cockpit but only V4369, crewed by Sub-Lts E. D. Dunkerley and N. C. Manley-Cooper, arrived safely. One aircraft was known to have exploded over Tobruk and another ended up over Sicily.

On 26 March 1942 the two squadrons, No. 830 with Swordfish and No. 828 with Albacores, were combined into a 'Naval Air Squadron' for operational purposes, but each retained its own identity for administrative purposes. When a convoy was found 25 miles (40km) off Linosa on 26 April three Albacores were loaded with torpedoes and made an attack, led by an ASV-equipped Swordfish, but with no discernible results. Due to the shortage of Swordfish the attacking role was mainly taken over by the Albacores. A couple of replacement Swordfish did turn up in May but another was destroyed in a bombing raid on 29 June. The last few Swordfish were now providing ASV and/or flare support to the Albacores. A report of 11 July said that the two squadrons had only a few operational aircraft, and as such RAF Wellingtons increasingly took over their roles. Despite these limitations the two squadrons still went out and did their bit, including collecting replacement aircraft from Egypt. Cdr C. R. J. Coxon, then a sub-lieutenant, recalls one such trip:

> The squadron needed replacement aircraft and they decided to send Acting Sub-Lt C. R. J. Coxon RN as one pilot, with observer Acting Sub-Lt Davies RN and one TAG to Fayid to collect two new Swordfish plus a replacement pilot. We duly took passage to Alexandria, together with some Luftwaffe aircrew POWs, in the MV *Breconshire*, which, after returning to Malta was sunk in Kalafrana Bay by a Ju 88. We also survived attacks by a Ju 88 on the way to Alexandria.
>
> After collecting the aircraft we moved along the coast to Benghazi where both Swordfish were fitted with 69gal long-range tanks attached to the torpedo rack.
>
> On nearing Malta the TAG announced our ETA by W/T and we were given clearance to enter Malta airspace. A few minutes later an air-raid alert was given – but not to us – and Hurricanes were scrambled as the German attack materialized. We dived to 'beat-up' the Officers Mess in traditional style and the Army, with no knowledge of our approach, thought the long-range tanks were bombs and promptly opened up on us! I had my wingman to starboard and the Bofors red tracer was cutting across my bow from port – at this point there was a yell over the Gosport tube

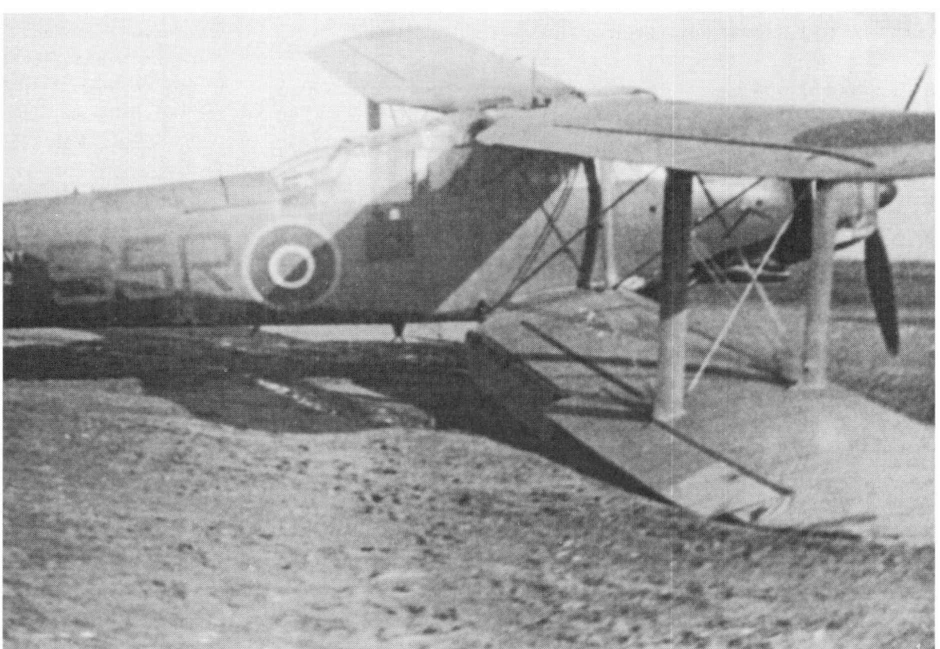

**Another squadron supporting Malta was No. 821, which moved in during November 1942 and stayed until June 1943 when it moved to Tunis. Albacore BF712 'S5R' suffered a landing mishap in December 1942.** I. G. Templer

from my observer and simultaneously the first burst of red tracer from an Me 109 passed my starboard side between the two aircraft. I immediately commenced a side-slip to starboard, waving away the other aircraft. This saved me from the next burst which hit the port wings. I went straight into a steep turn to starboard and the last squirt hit my tailplane.

Three 109s made the attack and I was told afterwards that the Bofors boys shot down the first as he overshot, and the other two were shot down by Hurricanes, although I have never been able to confirm that.

A night attack on 2/3 September by one Swordfish and two Albacores firing torpedoes at a 5,000-ton ship resulted in it being beached. A lone destroyer 20 miles (32km) east of Cape Spartivento was the target on 28/29 September when an ASV Swordfish led one other plus two Albacores, with a strike amidships. A convoy of four supply ships and seven escorting destroyers southbound for Tripoli were discovered on 18/19 October about 28 miles (44km) north-east of Pantellaria. Two Swordfish and an Albacore launched torpedoes, striking a 4,000-ton ship which started to go down by the stern and go round in circles. An 8,000-ton tanker was attacked 50 miles (80km) east of Sicily on the night of 19 October: an ASV Swordfish led one Swordfish and one Albacore carrying torpedoes, and two hours after the attack the ship was still stationary on the water. The same formation went out the following night and scored a hit on a 6,000-ton tanker 76 miles (122km) west of Tripoli. Swordfish 'Q' crewed by Sub-Lts G. Russell-Jones and G. P. Moon went out on the night of 23 November after a ship was reported, but their engine failed and they ditched in the sea, being rescued the following morning by a high-speed launch.

## *Victory in the Mediterranean*

By the end of 1942 the Afrika Korps was in full retreat towards the west and to help prevent any supplies getting through to them Nos 821 and 826 Squadrons, both with Albacores, moved to Malta to support the activities of the 'Naval Air Squadron'. Only half of No. 826 were released, the others being required at Dekheila. Swordfish of No. 830 made a few more raids but on 31 March 1942 it was absorbed into No. 828 Squadron. John Hone was one observer with No. 821 and had served in the Western Desert. He recalls:

My pilot most of the time was Lt Bramley and we arrived at Hal Far on the night of 27 November after a flight from Berka satellite of 4 hours 20 minutes. We were operational 1/2 December when we, as part of a larger formation, went out in Albacore BF713 'S5B' to look for an Axis convoy of four MVs [Motor Vessels] and five destroyers between Sicily and Cape Bon, Tunisia. The convoy was not located and we returned with our torpedoes after being airborne for over five hours. On 3 December we went after a tanker but only found hospital ships and brought our 'fish back again. We took Albacore BF710 'S5L' out at 10.36am on the morning of 11 December, looking for a missing No. 826 Squadron Albacore flying to Malta from Berka. In gradually deteriorating weather we found a dinghy, paddle and floating body but lost sight of them in extremely poor conditions. We returned but were told to search to end of endurance: we carried out oblong searches in very foul weather and heavy rain – nothing else seen after being out for over six hours. On 13/14 December we went out again in the same kite to make a torpedo strike on a 10,000-ton MV and other vessels west of Maratimo. Searched area – nil results. Found a 5,000-ton MV with two destroyers and three E-boats. Attacked down moon path with complete surprise but missed. MV was lit by flares and, hit by a torpedo, it exploded in two blazing halves. Out for nearly 5½ hours. We went out again that night and searched for an MV being towed between Ras Mahmur and Souse – no sighting but we attacked an MV beached 1½ miles north of Souse as ordered. We dropped beneath the flares but the 'fish hit a mud bank. One 'fish was seen to hit the ship. I did not fly for a few days but on Boxing Day we took BF673 'S5C' to find a small but supposedly important MV. That was the night the leaders 'ping' went u/s and we returned after half an hour – but I didn't hear anyone complain! Next day we were told to go and practise dive-bombing. Malta looked minute from 6,000ft as we bombed a rock close to Filfla and then got involved in a dogfight with three Spits. My logbook for 3 January 1943 shows that we took off in BF713 'S5B' just after midnight for a search in the Maratimo area. Much enemy night fighter activity, red-nosed jobs! Low flying and evasive action successful. No enemy shipping seen. On 10 January I was loaned to No. 828/830 Squadron while Lt Bromley was sick. I crewed with Sub-Lt Fraser in T9208 'G' and logbook states 'Formation broke up by red nosed fighters. Continued search in area but sighted nothing except many more fighters. Large explosion on water – learned on return that strike leader had not returned.' Whoops! It was fun and games again on 18 January when I went with Sub-Lt White in X9088 'A' to do a test flight. We did two vertical dives from 7,000ft to 500ft and then had a mock dogfight with two Beaufighters for about 10 min. On 18/19 January we were briefed to provide 'naval co-operation and nuisance raiding'. All this meant was another raid on Tripoli armed with flares and 250lb bombs. It was clear over the target with heavy flak but it wasn't very accurate. Very cold at 10,000ft but we went through some very grand cloud scenery. I went 'Gardening' [i.e. minelaying] in BF696 'Q' with Sub-Lt Simpson on the night of 25/26 January. I remember we laid the mine exactly where briefed with no opposition and returned low level over the sea in foul weather – we were gone nearly 5 hours. I was down to return to the UK and on 16 February I started off in a Wellington IA, transferred to a Wellington II and finally a Hudson III to Gibraltar, where a test flight in a Lancaster was a bonus. The next time I flew operationally was in 1952 when I flew Fireflies over Korea.

Also out on the night of 19 January 1943 were three torpedo Albacores of No. 821 and a 'ping' aircraft, looking for a convoy 5 miles (8km) off Cape Turguenes. There was a 5,000-tonner, one of 2,000 tons and three smaller supply ships: the bigger ship was left on its side and the other broke in half and sank. Crews of No. 821 attacked a 3,000-ton ship on 21 January, which turned over on fire and sank. Two Albacores were lost in two operations, and with illness No. 821 only had five crews instead of thirteen. However, the Afrika Korps finally pulled out of Tripoli on 23 January. This allowed Tripoli to be used as a leave centre and the Albacore crews could at last get a rest from the bombing on Malta, or so they thought: the first pair found themselves in the hotel cellar being bombed by the Germans!

With Tripoli now in the hands of the Allies, minelaying was set up at other Axis harbours. On 9 February four Albacores of No. 828 sowed 1,500lb magnetic mines at the entrance to Trapani. Sub-Lts Barr and Chalker in 'W' were picked up early by searchlights and light flak, and had to break away and make another run. They laid their mine from 100ft at 90kt (170km/h) but passed over an MTB at 150ft with rapid-firing guns causing damage to the upper port mainplane and shooting the pilot's side window away, fortunately without injuring Barr. On 21 March one special Albacore, 'M' carrying 250lb bombs with four others, 'B' 'H', 'R' and 'Q', were sent out to attack enemy shipping in the Maritimo area. An MV of 3,000 tons and a destroyer were sighted. Albacore 'Q' led the attack, releasing its torpedo at 50ft and 200yd (180m), and scored a hit near the stern. Albacore 'B' attacked from 60ft and 550yd (500m) but missed, as did the other two. 'M' dropped its bombs on the MV but due to smoke was unable to see whether they made a hit or not. Several small vessels came out of Trapani harbour to add their light flak to that already in use.

The following night No. 826 Squadron left for Bone in North Africa. On 12 March 1943 Albacores of No. 828 Squadron were sent out to search a bay east of Sicily for enemy shipping. This became the first formation of torpedo-carrying Albacores to cross Sicily since the start of hostilities. In the poor weather only one aircraft got through and found the convoy. The *Weekly Naval Notes* reported the raid in full:

On 12 March 1943, an enemy convoy consisting of a tanker and three medium-sized merchantmen escorted by at least four destroyers were reported to be off the north coast of Sicily. A force of Albacores of Naval Air Squadron No. 828 was sent from Malta to attack it, and for the first time these aircraft were routed across Sicily. The force started at 19.43 hours in overcast and showery weather; there was a half moon, but this was frequently obscured, as there was 3/10th cloud at 800ft and 10/10ths between 1,500 and 7,000ft. The leader, special Albacore X9160 'M' crewed by Lt (A) K. H. Appleton RN with Lt A. Gregory RN (acting CO) and LAC B. K. Forrest, in aiming to cross the south coast of Sicily at Cape Bianco went down after having passed Gozo to 50ft and switched off his formation lights, presumably relying on the moonlight to make him visible to his three consorts. This, however, was inadequate and at 20.02 hours two of the Albacores, 'R' and 'H', lost touch. They proceeded independently to the target area, but made no sightings through the cloud and returned, one across Sicily and the other round the west end of that island to reach Malta. At 01.00 hours Albacore 'B' crewed by Sub-Lt (A) T. Barr RNVR and Act. Sub-Lt (A) R. A. Chalker RNVR, managed to remain in formation on no more light than that provided by the leader's exhaust glow until 21.20 hours when, at about 25 miles south of Palermo and 5,000ft up touch was lost. While passing over Palermo the aircraft was hit by heavy flak before coming down to 800ft for the purpose of searching Castellamare Bay for the convoy. At 22.15 hours a convoy was dimly visible about 15 miles north of Tennasini, apparently heading westwards and at 22.20 hours ships about 7 miles west of Cape Gallo opened fire. The visibility was so poor that no estimate could be formed as to the composition or speed of this convoy. Albacore 'B' patiently circled over the area, hoping for an opportunity to attack, and was rewarded when at 22.43 hours a shaft of moonlight broke through the clouds to show an 8,000-ton tanker about 7 miles away to starboard, and a medium-sized merchantman escorted by two destroyers proceeding on course of 100 degrees at 14kt. Albacore 'B' seized the opportunity and immediately swept down and made a half-circle so as to attack the tanker

**Albacore N4378 of No. 826 Squadron returning from an abortive strike 6 March 1943.**
FAA Museum

from the south from a height of 40ft on a bearing of Green 090 degrees at a range of 500yd. Until the dropping of the torpedo the aircraft encountered no opposition, and while turning away had no difficulty in avoiding the wild AA fire from the tanker, which was hit amidships. A few minutes later the target was seen to have stopped with a destroyer alongside and the latter was again sighted proceeding very slowly eastwards. Albacore 'B' returned safely to Malta, but the leader, which had not been seen again after 21.20 hours, was reported missing.

With the loss of Lt Gregory, Sub-Lt Fraser took over as temporary CO but he was lost in action on 24 March during a 'Seaweed' operation over Sicily with his observer, Mid Barbour. An extensive search for them was undertaken involving Swordfish, Albacores, Spitfires and Baltimores, but nothing was found. Targets were obviously getting rarer but a No. 828 Squadron Albacore torpedoed and sank a tanker on 13 March and 'Q' was lost the following night off Marsala with its crew, Sub-Lts Richards and Dowell. Sub-Lt Russell-Jones then took over until Lt Britten arrived, but he was replaced by Lt Cdr Turner after only a month on the job.

Tommy Barr and Ralph Chalker had crewed up on 23 January to deliver Albacore X9160 to No. 828 Squadron and flew together until June 1943 when they both moved on. On 2 April Barr and Chalker took off on an air-sea rescue flight looking for two MTBs that were late on a trip between Malta and Benghazi. They sighted the boats just before 8.25am, one being down by the stern and being towed by the other. The crew of the damaged boat were taken off and Barr attacked it with his front gun to finish it off, the crews returning safely to Malta on the other boat. Minelaying at Trapani was the task on 4 April and Chalker recalls:

We set off in Albacore 'G' at 22.08 hours for the purpose of 'gardening' at Trapani. We arrived at Levanzo at 00.10 hours and circled waiting for the diversion to start at 00.30 hours. Searchlights and light flak started at 00.32 hours and we laid our American mine from 200ft at 90kt at 00.47 hours, 0.9 miles distant from the western end of the Mole. By this time upwards of fifteen searchlights and light ack-ack were going straight up, making it easy for us to lay the mine exactly and scram at 50ft.

My tenth operational flight from Malta was in Albacore 'R' when we went after enemy ships off Kirkenna Isles during the early hours of 11 April. Tommy and I were part of the strike force detailed to attack enemy ships reported north-east of Sfax. Our aircraft went u/s [unserviceable] with an oil leak and the strike force left without us at 01.30 hours. Shortly after the strike had departed one of the aircraft, 'R', belonging to an earlier strike, returned. We had it refuelled and a torpedo put on, and we eventually took off at 02.25 hours. Setting course, 248 magnetic from Filfla, we arrived in the area 10 minutes before the flares were dropped at 04.20 hours. We saw an MV of about 3,000 tons and two smaller ships of approximately 500 tons. The MV appeared to be well clear of the shoals around Kirkenna Isles so we attacked up the path of the flares, dropping our torpedo at 04.37 hours, range 400yd at a height of 30ft at 90kt. The MV was steering almost due north at about 6kt with smoke rising from her stern. Our torpedo had a 9ft contact pistol and was seen to run well, hitting the MV forward of the beam. The ship heeled over badly and when we returned to the scene shortly afterwards nothing could be seen. There was no enemy flak and we landed back at base at 06.30 hours. We were down to join three Albacores of No. 821 Squadron that night and, loaded with four 250lb bombs, we left in aircraft 'B' to search for enemy shipping between Marattimo and Cape Bon. We sighted seven-plus small MVs and positioned ourselves for an attack. Just then another aircraft dropped a flare right in front of us, blotting out the target. We circled and, diving from 5,000ft to 2,000ft, we dropped our bombs on an MV, noting that at least two bombs hit and exploded. The ship was seen to be sinking by the stern as we left. We were led to believe later that those particular ships were on their way to evacuate German troops in Tunisia. On 15 and 19 April we went on searches for enemy shipping but did not find any. A couple of times Bf 110s passed above us going about their business, probably after us! We narrowly missed a dangerous incident when returning from the second trip. We had just landed in the normal sense when an Albacore passed us landing the other way, i.e. downwind, and only the width of the flare path between us! Our constant speed unit broke on 23 April when we were 50ft over the water and 5 miles from land. By a piece of good piloting Tommy Barr somehow got us back to base. We were not so lucky on 3 May, however, we had quite a shock! We were testing Albacore BF676 'B' prior to going on ops that night and about 2 miles off Kalafrana at 1,200ft Tommy throttled back from climbing boost revs to normal boost revs and found the pointer on the boost gauge had dropped below –4lb. The throttle lever was extremely loose and although he moved it backwards and forwards to its full extent, no boost registered on the gauge. All switches seemed normal and he set the constant speed unit at 'fully fine', revs registering about 1,200. At 400ft and about 500yd off-shore in Kalafrana Bay he warned me there was no alternative to a ditching, other than a crash landing among wireless pylons, stone walls and gullies. I fired a two-star red Very cartridge, switched on my Worlitzer transmitter, clamped down the key and positioned the 'K'-type dinghy in the open gun hatch to make sure it would be thrown clear on impact. I then took up my ditching station, opening the hatch and, facing the stern with my arms, loosely braced against the side of the aircraft. In the meantime Tommy had tried to jettison his cockpit side panels but they failed to release. Having disconnected his Gosport tube and radio leads, he put the flaps down, turned into wind but parallel to the waves and we touched down tail first, wings level at about 55kt. Upon touching down in the water the nose went down so rapidly that I was flung out about 40yd away. Tommy had been flung forward against his harness and sustained superficial cuts to the face and legs. Going nose-down, he was trapped head-down in the submerged cockpit and swallowed a fair amount of water before releasing himself and popping up about 10yd from me. We climbed into the dinghy and 12 minutes after ditching we were in a high-speed launch on the way to shore! The Admiralty investigation included raising the Albacore and presumed that the failure was due to the throttle linkage, which was a bit worrying as Albacore X9262 of No. 821 Squadron had a similar failure the same month. There was always the threat that one of the groundcrew could leave things where they shouldn't due to being busy or tired. For instance, I went up on an air test in Swordfish 'P' of No. 830 on 9 April with pilot Lew McManus and the engine cut on take-off. Cotton waste was found in the fuel lead. Again, on 15 May I was crewed with Lt Britton in Albacore 'H' for an armed search in the Panellaria–Marsala area. The formation was cruising at 95kt, led by 'Ropey' Pope, but just north-east of Pantellaria we started having engine problems. Initially we had a job keeping up with the others and had to signal we were returning to base. Nursing the engine, we were still 20 minutes short of Malta when the engine grew seriously worse and I sent out an SOS. We finally landed safely but it was a near thing! Four of us went out on the 17th but found no shipping and bombed a power house from 4,000ft. On the 19th Tommy and I air tested a replacement Albacore, N4383, from Egypt and it became the new 'B'. It was totally destroyed two days later in an air raid, along with 'L'. I went up with Pope on 20th air-testing Albacore 'H' of No. 821 Squadron but the aircraft was absolutely non-airworthy and we nearly crashed in the bay. I went out with Lt Britton in 'K' with three others on 20 May and we found an MV of about 3–4,000 tons which we illuminated with flares. We caused some damage with our bombs but Chapman and Scotcher got four direct hits, setting it on fire from stem to stern. Jones and Bagnall bombed an F-boat but were chased off by a night fighter. We went out on a lone patrol on 25/26 May armed with a 'fish, but didn't see anything and brought it home. The previous night we had lost Sub-Lts Sinclair and Simpson off Catania in 'P'. The following day we were given a trials job which was in our line of business but experimental. With Lt Britton in Albacore 'R' we dropped four torpedoes in quick succession in Kalafrana Bay, landing after each drop and reloading. I recorded that the four drops were made at 25ft at 92kt, 20ft at 95kt, 15ft at 88kt and 15ft at 85kt. As you can appreciate, that is very low! No. 828 Squadron moved from Hal Far to Takali on 8 June 1943. First operational flight for me from here was on 15 May when we went out in 'G' on a lone rover patrol, covering from Cape Passaro to 15 miles south of Messina. It was a night of good visibility and a bright moon but we saw no shipping so attacked a block house near Passero with six 250lb bombs, scoring direct hits resulting in a violent explosion, yellow flashes and lots of sparks and dense clouds of white smoke. Our primary target on 19 May were two 1,000-ton ships in Syracuse and again I see we were on a rover patrol armed with six 250lb GP bombs. Visibility was fairly good, there being a full moon but slight mist up to 2,000ft. The wind, which was quite strong at the beginning, gradually decreased to about 10kt and the sea had a heavy swell. At 23.10 hours we were flying off Syracuse at 150ft. On sighting the ships in the harbour we turned north-west and climbed to 6,000ft. At 23.30 hours we commenced our run-in, but at this point a red beacon (or light) was seen dead astern and closing rapidly. Enemy night fighters were by this time playing a prominent part in the defence of the Sicilian coastal region – but they were easily evaded so long as they were seen (they usually carried a red light in their nose) before they attacked. One Albacore of No. 828 was lost to enemy night fighters – Sub-Lt Chapman and Mid Scotcher in 'R' on 4 June. We took violent evasive action, diving to 3,000ft and then to sea level, where we circled for about five minutes before starting to climb again. At 23.42 hours we were ready again, but the whole episode was repeated. A third attempt was made but by this time heavy flak started to come up when we were still 2 miles from the target. We decided to go out to sea and stooge around for a few minutes before having another shot at the target. Just after midnight we started our run again, but again we found an enemy fighter on our tail, ending up at sea level again. During this descent three E-boats were seen in line-ahead 2 or 3 miles from Syracuse. We made four attacks with our bombs, scoring a number of near misses, which did not seem enough, although two of the boats were going much slower and light flak started to come our way so we called it a night and went back to Malta. My last operational flight with No. 828 was on 22 June when we went out in 'G', loaded with a torpedo, but failed to find anything. Shortly after that I was posted out and later in the year Tommy Barr and I were most surprised when they gave us a DSC each!

Tommy Barr was later killed flying a Barracuda of No. 784 Squadron on 10 January 1944; Ralph Chalker went on to help pioneer naval night fighting in the FAA, training crews with No. 784 Squadron and then joining the first Firefly night-fighter squadron, No. 1790. After the war he joined No. 1840 RNVR squadron at Ford, flying Fireflies and Gannets, until the disbandment of the RNVR Air Branch on 10 March 1957. He shared his love of flying with a distinguished career in banking until his retirement.

During this period, through May and June, No. 821 had also been providing flare dropping and minelaying and joining No. 828 on strikes against shipping. Operation *Corkscrew*, the plan to capture Pantellaria, began on 31 May with No. 828's Albacores dropping flares and spotting for the cruiser *Orion*, which was bombarding the shore. This was repeated until 11 June when the island surrendered. Albacores were out during the night of 19/20 June when one sank an Italian naval tanker, the *Velino*, in Syracuse harbour. Others carried out searches along the eastern seaboard; another attacked Augusta harbour and another was attacked by a night fighter and jettisoned its bombs but returned safely. On 30 June No. 826 Squadron took over the three Albacores left in No. 828 Squadron and the latter ceased to exist. The first Allied forces stormed ashore on the southern coast of Sicily on 10 July and from there on, as the war moved further north and into Italy, the work of the naval squadrons in that area declined. Many of the young men who went out night after night in obsolescent biplanes, often in appalling weather, subject to long flights of between four and six hours, amid enemy flak and night fighters, should have had recognition such as was afforded the islanders, exemplified by the citation for the George Cross, which was awarded to the island on 15 April 1942:

> The Cross shall be awarded only for acts of the greatest heroism or the most conspicuous courage in circumstances of extreme danger.

**The bullet-ridden fuselage of Albacore X9256 on a dump in the Western Desert.**

## Western Desert

The Western Desert in North Africa seems an unlikely place for naval aeroplanes to fight a war, but Albacores in particular made a valuable contribution to the eventual victory over the Axis forces there. Swordfish also operated from bases around the edge of the desert when ashore from carriers, or when carrying out other odd duties.

It was during the Munich Crisis in 1938 that the first Swordfish arrived. Some eighteen to twenty of them, still in packing cases, were delivered to No. 102 MU at Abu Sueir. In April 1939 some airmen were given the job of removing them from the packing cases and assembling them for use. Tom Fagg was one of the fitters:

> We soon ran into a technical snag, as the normal practice to rig the wings was to adjust the bracing wires to what we knew as pin centre lengths. The wings were assembled on the hangar floor as port and starboard pairs – this was known as boxing the wings. They were then lifted into position and attached by the wing bolts at top and bottom rear spar root positions. They were then spread to flight condition and the front locking lever actuated. The snag was, we had forgotten to take with us the list of bracing wire lengths, so we had to rig the aircraft to set the correct dihedral and incidence of the wings using instruments. This done, we now attempted to fold the wings and found we could not withdraw the latches that locked them in the flight condition. The only answer was to adjust the various bracing wires until the latches were easy to operate, then measure the pin centres. This we did and the rest of the Swordfish were assembled quicker.

Nos 826 and 829 Squadrons, both equipped with Albacores, were part of the air group embarked in *Formidable* when she left for South Africa on 18 December 1940. When *Illustrious* was damaged in the Mediterranean *Formidable* was ordered to replace her. Sailing along the eastern coast of Africa towards the Red Sea, the opportunity was taken to attack the Italian port of Mogadishu. On 2 February 1941, five Albacores of No. 826 laid mines in the harbour while two others joined No. 829 in dive-bombing berths and other fixtures. Moving into the Red Sea/Suez Canal area, it was decided to strike at the U-boat and destroyer base at Massawa. Arriving just before dawn on the 13 and 21 February the Albacores of No. 826 made twelve dive-bombing attacks, No. 829 delivering eleven torpedoes. Flares were not used as it was thought the glare would blind the pilots. In the poor early light, however, enemy searchlights blinded them instead, and only superficial damage was done. Another strike was laid on for 1 March when No. 826 took five aircraft to Port Sudan and managed seventeen sorties over the next few days. The Albacores were refuelled at an emergency landing ground in Eritrea after each raid, with one aircraft being lost to enemy gunfire. The squadrons disembarked to Dekheila, near Alexandria, on the 9 March. *Formidable* went to sea two days later for training at sea, leaving six Albacores ashore. Three of these moved up to Benina airfield near Benghazi and on 18 March carried out a torpedo attack on enemy shipping off the Tripoli coast. Lt A. H. Blacow torpedoed and sank one ship and then sank two lighters, but an Albacore and crew were lost to gunfire.

Meantime, *Eagle*'s aircraft of Nos 813 and 824 squadrons disembarked to Dekheila. Although the groundcrews were re-embarked not long afterwards, ready to go to sea again, an order came through for a strike against shipping at Massawa. Eric Tyler went along:

> On 25 March seventeen of our Swordfish set off for Port Sudan. I flew with Lt Sedgewick and Mid Barringer in Swordfish L7657. On the first day we flew down the Nile and landed at Assuit to refuel, then again at Aswan, then at Wadi Halfa where we stayed the night. Total flying time that day was 6 hours 50 minutes. When the squadrons took off the next day I was left behind with Swordfish K4018, which had developed an engine fault. On 27 November we took off with an air mechanic as passenger for No. 6 Station landing strip along the Sudan railway, then at No. 10 Station where we picked up oil for our ailing engine. The engine was burning oil at a tremendous rate. At the stations we had to haul drums of oil from the depot's stores and refill the aircraft by hand. No easy job in such sweltering heat. The day ended with our arrival at Atbara, where accommodation was found for us with the small RAF contingent there. On the next day, after some tinkering with the engine by RAF mechanics, we left for Port Sudan, arriving after a three-hour flight. Squadron personnel were first accommodated at a former girls' school in the town, and we had to travel to the aerodrome daily to work on the aircraft, but later we were allocated a large Nissen hut on the aerodrome. Here we had to supply and cook our own food. Apparently there were six Italian destroyers still at Massawa and it was our job to destroy them. Operations were carried out daily with single Swordfish flying down to the area around Massawa to keep tabs on the enemy ships. I went down on 1 April with Mid Sergeant and Lt Lyle, landing first at Mersa Taclai for fuel and then down to Massawa. On this occasion we sighted an enemy destroyer just outside the port and shadowed it for some time, signalling reports back to base all the time. However, it being too late in the day for a striking force to intervene we watched the destroyer go into the harbour, then left for Mersa Taclai and Port Sudan. Early morning on 3 April we were all roused from our beds and had to bomb-up the aircraft for action. Apparently, four Italian destroyers had been detected at 05.45 hours about 20 miles from Port Sudan, steaming in towards the port. On completion of arming with 250lb bombs, both squadrons took off to attack. The enemy ships were sighted very soon after take-off and looked as if they were coming in to bombard the port. All aircraft immediately dived in to attack – one ship, hit by at least five bombs, just disintegrated, the pilot being Mid Sergeant. Another destroyer was hit, set on fire and later sunk. On returning to base I was detailed to go off again with Lt Welham and Sub-Lt Paine to shadow the remaining ships until our striking force had prepared for another attack. Our second strike succeeded in damaging two other ships and drove them ashore at Jedda. All the while the RAF had been put in the picture and they sent out aircraft to support our attacks. Sadly, they not once sighted the targets and lost a couple of aircraft into the bargain. A few days later Kingston visited the two stranded Italian destroyers and reported that the decks of both ships were strewn with dead sailors from our bombing and machine-gun attacks. Mid Sergeant was awarded the DSC and *Eagle* was presented with the ensign of one of the destroyers, *Pantera*, as a momento. On 7 April our aircraft was again on a recce around Massawa and we took the opportunity to have a look at the Dachlach Islands, some way from the port. In the lagoon we found about a dozen large ships anchored, some afloat, but a number of them scuttled and resting on the bottom. Then we sighted a naval launch going away from a sinking ship, apparently the scuttling party. We immediately went in to attack, the pilot firing with his front gun and, as we pulled out of the dive, I made use of my trusty Lewis gun. In all we made three attacks, and after the last one the launch had disappeared, probably sunk. We went back to Massawa later that day but the port had surrendered and the only ship afloat was a hospital ship flying the white flag. We returned to Port Sudan where *Eagle* arrived on 18 April to re-embark her squadrons.

Meantime, *Formidable*'s squadrons were in action again until 30 May when they disembarked to Dekheila. No. 826 was now 'loaned' to the RAF Middle East command for a time, which turned out to be some twenty months! Six Albacores were moved to Fuka, a satellite airfield east of Mersa Matruh, and then to Ma'aten

Bagush. Here they operated for three weeks, carrying out night bombing of supply dumps and airfields. They were then withdrawn to carry out a series of strikes against Vichy-French shipping, returning to Ma'aten Bagush by 1 August. The following night the squadron started night raids again – airfields, supply/ammunition dumps, motor transport, ports and so on. Over the next few months they made 337 night sorties, dropping more than 150 tons of high explosive and incendiary bombs.

The British 8th Army advanced into Libya during November 1941, No. 826 moving with them. On 25 November five Albacores landed at Landing Ground (LG) 75 – an advanced re-fuelling and re-arming strip – and proceeded to make eleven sorties against Afrika Korps armour near Sidi Omar, dropping 7½ tons of bombs. During January 1942 the squadron was withdrawn from night operations and did refresher torpedo training. On 23 January they were put back in the line, moving to Berka, near Benghazi, to get within striking distance of any enemy shipping moving between Tripoli and Italy. A convoy was detected on 23 January, 185 miles (300km) west of Benghazi. Five Albacores attacked with Lt Ellis sinking the liner *Vittoria*, Sub-Lt J. M. Brown damaged a destroyer but the CO, Lt Cdr J. W. S. Corbett DSO, was shot down and the crew taken prisoner. By 4 February the squadron had moved back to Ma'aten Bagush. Anti-submarine patrols were mixed in with, but separate to, the fifty-one flare 'pathfinding' and dive-bombing sorties. The main benefactors of the flare sorties were RAF Wellington bomber squadrons, and even No. 73 Squadron who carried out night strafing raids with Hurricanes in the light provided by the flares. On 5 March the new CO of No. 826, Lt C. W. B. Smith DSC, was ferrying four passengers in daylight when they were caught by the enemy and shot down. Two Albacores were picked on by a pair of Bf 109s four days later but managed to evade being shot down, but three crew members were wounded. After a brief spell on rest the squadron returned and continued its support to the campaign. By the end of May No. 826 was illuminating enemy targets for RAF Wellingtons and Hurricanes, and, a bit later, USAAF B-25 Mitchells. They laid mines in Derba harbour and bombed enemy vehicles, harbours and airfields.

The Axis armies were fought to a standstill just outside El Alamein in September 1942. Between May and September No. 826 had flown 414 sorties, including ninety-one during the bitter fighting for Ruweisat Ridge in July. Although four Albacores had been lost to night fighters and flak and another five on operations, the supply of spare aircraft from Egypt had improved and the squadron could quite often field twelve aircraft. Also, the pressure was off during May/June as No. 821 Squadron had arrived with their Albacores. This allowed No. 826 to withdraw for a short time in September to renew its skills as a torpedo unit. Operating from Dekheila, the squadron moved back to Palestine after a training flight of three Albacores were attacked by marauding Bf 109s. By now, of the original squadron only one pilot and one groundcrewman remained.

**No. 813 Squadron Swordfish V4615 '4A' flown by Sub-Lt Donohue on anti-submarine patrol near Gibraltar in 1942. The squadron was ashore when *Eagle* was sunk on 11 August 1942.**

Previously operating Swordfish, No. 821 Squadron re-equipped with Albacores on 1

March 1942, the CO being Major A. C. Newson RN. Their main task during April was convoy anti-submarine patrols but early in May the aircraft were fitted with internal long-range fuel tanks. On 30 May the squadron flew from Bagush Satellite to Gambut and that night made their first flare-dropping sorties for the bombers. They went out nearly every night over the next few days, illuminating Derna and Martuba for the bombers. Flak was usually intense and accurate with attacks pressed home and sortie times of 3–4 hours' duration. Sub-Lt Symonds was out over 4 hours in Albacore T9199 'G' on the night of 1 June when he illuminated his own target, dropped leaflets and noted many bombs being dropped on the target area. On 8 June he was briefed to take medical supplies in Albacore N4351 'H' to an Army garrison at Bir Hacheim. During the flight, which took 5 hours, the weather deteriorated with thick low cloud and they were unable to find the landing ground; the aircraft was damaged on landing back at base in high winds. On the night of 27 June he was out in Albacore 'F', dive-bombing various groups of enemy transports, but on landing back at base he crashed into a 'pranged' Hurricane and wrote the Albacore off. Out nearly every night again, the squadron bombed enemy transport and harbours, and illuminated for the bombers.

During their time in the desert the squadron were called on to undertake other duties. One of these happened on 9 July 1942 when nine Albacores of No. 826 flew 250 miles (400km) behind enemy lines, were refuelled at a secret rendezvous by Bristol Bombay transport aircraft, and then flew on to carry out a night attack on an enemy convoy off Tobruk. On the night of 18/19 July Sub-Lt Kemp in Albacore T9158 'M' carried out a glide approach to attack a ship in Mersa Matruh harbour. Although heavily engaged by light flak, he continued his approach and dropped his bombs from around 800ft and escaped into the darkness. The harbour was used by Axis light sea craft, such as E-boats, and the squadron was attacking these as well as road transport. On 24 August Symonds in Albacore X8972 'H' was illuminating transports for the bombers when he discovered ten enemy tanks. Circling overhead, he called in the Wellingtons and provided illumination for them to carry out a bombing attack. Enemy night fighters were active some nights but were mainly after the bombers.

During September/early October the squadron moved back and carried out training exercises, returning to the front line again on 9 October when they illuminated Fuka (LG.17) airfield for the medium bombers. On 20 October the squadron were briefed to illuminate LG.21 so that Douglas Bostons could bomb parked enemy aircraft. Lt Bramley in Albacore BF670 'L' made five attempts to reach LG.21, but each time was driven back by heavy flak. His aircraft sustained hits including one on the windscreen, fortunately not piercing it. LG.19 was not far away and on seeing that illuminated he went over and dropped his bombs there. For the next few nights they attacked the 21st Panzer Division and enemy transports. Although they found and illuminated numerous tanks, the number of Wellingtons available had little impact and after a raid on 4 November the squadron was withdrawn. They flew to Hal Far, Malta, on 30 November and the following night undertook a search, with torpedoes, for an Axis convoy, but failed to find it.

No. 826 Squadron, meanwhile, had been recalled to Dekheila on 19 October to support the pre-El Alamein offensive. By the end of the month they had flown eighty-nine illuminating and bombing sorties, continuing the same type of operations as No. 821. The Axis troops started their final retreat during the night of 1/2 November and the Albacores were kept busy illuminating and bombing the retreating forces. Thereafter, the targets were beyond the reach of the Albacores, and although they were moved up to Berka early in December there were few targets for them. Six Albacores were ferried to Malta for use by No. 828 Squadron and six others were moved up to the front line again, at Wadi Zem Zem, to resume bombing and illuminating operations. A number of aircraft were at Dekheila being fitted with ASV radar ready to undertake anti-submarine patrols. Following a spell of training and convoy escort duties the twelve Albacores of No. 826 flew to Algeria on 11 February 1943 for possible ship strikes. Two Albacores attacked a merchant vessel off the coast with torpedoes but later found it was already aground! During the night of 16/17 April four Albacores attacked a small convoy. In the following action Lt H. I. Shanahan and Sub-Lt D. A. Davies both scored hits on the 5,324-ton tanker *Monginevro* and sank it. In May, with the enemy in full retreat, the squadron returned to flare-dropping to investigate sightings. On 8 May 1943 the Axis forces in Tunisia surrendered and the squadron, operating out of Blida, flew 350 anti-submarine patrols over Allied convoys plying between Malta and Alexandria during the next five months. Nine Albacores found and attacked an Axis

**No. 821 Squadron operated out of Sidi Barrani during 1942 using Albacores, such as BF708 seen here.** RAF Museum

**Three Albacores of No. 821 Squadron, including X8953 and X8965, reforming near Fayid in April 1942, after a practice camera torpedo attack.** I. G. Templer

**Albacore 'B' of No. 821 Squadron flying over Egypt in January 1942. Albacores were used to support operations in the Western Desert including minelaying, bombing and flare dropping.** I. G. Templer

convoy off Cap Bon on 16 April, but conditions were not ideal and only one torpedo hit was claimed against a small merchant vessel. No. 826 Squadron moved to Hal Far, Malta, on 10 July to provide night anti-submarine patrols for Allied shipping during the invasion of Sicily. They would also be available as a back-up strike force to the Albacore squadrons embarked in *Formidable* and *Indomitable*. With the end of the fighting in Sicily No. 826 was disbanded. Over the previous forty-one months the squadron had made more than 1,000 bombing and illuminating sorties, dropping over 700 tons of bombs, mines, torpedoes and flares.

In November 1942 the Allies had invaded North Africa. Seven carriers were involved, the old *Argus*, *Furious*, *Formidable* and *Victorious* with three escort carriers, *Avenger*, *Biter* and *Dasher*. These had embarked 130 fighters and thirty TBR aircraft including Nos 817, 820, 822 and 832 Squadrons, all operating Albacores, most with an American star painted over the fuselage roundel. These were for easy identification purposes for Allied ship's gunners not familiar with the aircraft shape. The aim of Operation *Torch* was to land Allied troops ashore in Morocco and Algeria, Vichy-French territory. Then, when a beachhead had been established, they were to move eastwards and entrap Rommel, who was being driven back from El Alamein. This would give the Allies almost complete control of the North African coastline. Flying anti-submarine patrols, the Albacores also took part in bombing raids on shore targets such as naval forts. On 8 November Lt J. G. A. McI. Nares, CO of No. 822 Squadron, led an eight-Albacore strike force to bomb La Senia airfield, where they destroyed forty-seven aircraft and five of the six hangars. Vichy-French Dewoitine D.520 fighters attacked the force shooting down three Albacores and damaging others, and another was lost to flak. One D.520 was shot down by an Albacore TAG. No. 820 provided a smoke screen to protect ships from the batteries at Sidi Ferruch and dropped leaflets over Saouille. In a second attack they dive-bombed coastal batteries at Fort D'Estre, when six Albacores all dropped their bombs within 30 seconds of each other, over thirty hitting the target: the battery surrendered.

Aircraft from the carriers continued to give support until 10 November when some were required to escort convoys of ships that had been withdrawn. Albacores were in action again in July 1943 during Operation *Husky*, the invasion of Sicily. During the autumn of 1943 they were in support of Operation *Avalanche*, the Salerno landings. Two fleets were used, Force H, consisting of *Nelson*, *Rodney*, *Warspite* and *Valiant* plus *Illustrious* and *Formidable*,

**Loading six 250lb bombs under the wings of an Albacore of No. 820 Squadron embarked on *Formidable*. This was part of Operation *Torch*, the invasion of Vichy Morocco and Algiers by Allied forces. Just visible under the far bomb fin is the tip of the American star, which was applied to all participating aircraft for identification purposes.** IWM

providing air cover of fifty-five fighters, twelve Barracudas and eighteen Albacores, and Force V which included 100 Seafires embarked in *Attacker*, *Battler*, *Hunter*, *Stalker* and *Uniform*.

There was one incident involving an Albacore that had repercussions, both at the time and for many years afterwards. On 17 November a Walrus pilot, tasked with finding a disabled U-boat, spotted it stopped in the water and showing what appeared to be white flags. However, as he approached he was incensed when he saw Grumman Wildcats strafing it. He tried to stop this by flying across the line of fire with his observer shooting off red Very lights. Even as he watched, however, an Albacore from No. 822 Squadron, flown by Lt James Bridge, Sub-Lt Jock Cunningham and PO Shenner, put a torpedo into her side. Sub-Lt Roy Blatchley, the pilot of the Walrus, landed alongside to find the U-boat had sunk with thirty-two of her crew, but leaving sixteen including the captain, Hans-Dietrich von Tiesenhausen. Blatchley loaded all sixteen on board and taxied towards the destroyer *Wilton*, which lifted them on board. In 1988 Roy Blatchley met Hans von Tiesenhausen in Canada and the following year was Guest of Honour at a reunion of the survivors from U-331.

Other squadrons operating in the Western Desert included No. 815 whose twelve Albacores were based at Dekheila during February/March 1943 to spot for the heavy guns of ships bombarding enemy ports along the coast. At the same time detachments from the squadron were based at Nicosia, Cyprus and Haifa in Palestine, from where they made attacks on seventeen U-boats. No. 815 was moved into the Western Desert to supplement the other Albacore squadrons, carrying out similar types of operations. They took two ASV-equipped Swordfish to carry out night anti-submarine patrols from Fuka. More ASV Swordfish were acquired as gradual replacements for the Albacores, with more emphasis on anti-submarine patrols. It was Swordfish L4707 'L' of No. 815 that attacked and sank U-652 on 2 June, sharing it with a Blenheim from No. 203 Squadron. The squadron used three Albacores for bombardment spotting but was disbanded at Mersa Matruh on 24 July 1943, by which time the Albacore was being withdrawn from front-line squadrons.

# CHAPTER TEN

# Indian Ocean and Far East

HMS *Eagle* was the only aircraft carrier in the Far East when war broke out in September 1939. When the war between China and Japan started, some three years before, a British naval force had been despatched to protect British interests in the area. Aboard *Eagle* were Nos 813 and 824 Squadrons, each with nine Swordfish. In October 1939, hunter groups were set up to patrol and protect the busy shipping lanes that converged on the East Indies. Although Britain was not at war with Japan, *Eagle* moved nearer Singapore so that her Swordfish could patrol waters around the Malaya/Singapore peninsular.

To cover the area east of Suez and the approaches to the Red Sea near Aden, the carrier *Glorious* was detached from the Mediterranean Fleet. Her air complement consisted of Nos 812, 823 and 825 Squadrons, each with twelve Swordfish, with fighter protection supplied by six Gladiators of No. 802 Squadron. The Swordfish from the two ships, some 5,000 miles (8,000km) apart, carried out continuous air patrols and covered 2 million square miles (5 million square kilometres) of ocean. However, there was very little going on, and *Glorious* returned to the Mediterranean. In Aden itself, an important deep seaport, the resident No. 8 Squadron, equipped with Bristol Blenheims and Vickers Vincents, was struggling to cover its designated area. In August 1940 six ex-FAA Swordfish arrived to give some support and carried out patrols, but their contribution was limited and they were returned to Admiralty charge at Mombasa, East Africa, in January 1941.

*Eagle*, due for an extensive refit, was already in Singapore dockyard when the situation in Europe started to deteriorate and her refit was cancelled so that she could replace *Glorious*, who had since sailed to reinforce the Home Fleet. This meant that by August 1940 the only naval air element in the Indian Ocean was a flight of Supermarine Walrus flying boats aboard the heavy cruiser HMS *Kent*, and it would be February 1941 before a carrier could be spared to patrol the area. *Formidable*, with Nos 826 and 829 Squadrons with twelve and nine Albacores respectively, and No. 803 with twelve Fulmars, was en route to join the Mediterranean Fleet and, sailing along the East African coast, decided to attack the Italian base at Mogadishu. On 2 February Albacores laid mines in the harbour and bombed targets of opportunity, and, although little damage was inflicted on military targets, it demonstrated to the Italians that even in seemingly remote places the British could suddenly appear and strike.

A few days after *Formidable* left the area, *Hermes*, hosting No. 814 Squadron with twelve Swordfish, arrived and set up a blockade. Some sixteen Axis-manned merchant ships tried to break the blockade but most were found and sunk or captured before they got far. Swordfish of No. 814 detected six further ships out to sea, five of which responded to signals to formate on the cruiser *Hawkins*. The final one, manned by a German crew, elected to run for it but was bombed by the Swordfish and became a total loss. On 18 February the blockade was lifted and *Hermes* moved into the Indian Ocean to look for the German pocket battleship *Admiral Scheer*. Although the latter had been detected some 500 miles (800km) off Mombasa, she escaped in the haze and sailed back to Keil.

## Operations in the Persian Gulf

With the insurrection in Iraq of March–May 1941, *Hermes* moved further east and in early April escorted a troop convoy from Bombay to Basra. Lying offshore, her Swordfish remained available in support if required. This was soon called for and No. 814 dive-bombed rebel Iraqi forts and barracks around Shatt al Arab. The Swordfish operated from ashore as the ground forces

**A formation of Swordfish from No. 824 Squadron, flying over Happy Valley, Hong Kong, in August 1939. Left to right they are K8391 '952', K8386 '945', K8387 '948' and K8388 '950'. All have different fin markings with the squadron badge overlaid. The fuselage and fin bands were in black, with the leader's fin all black.**

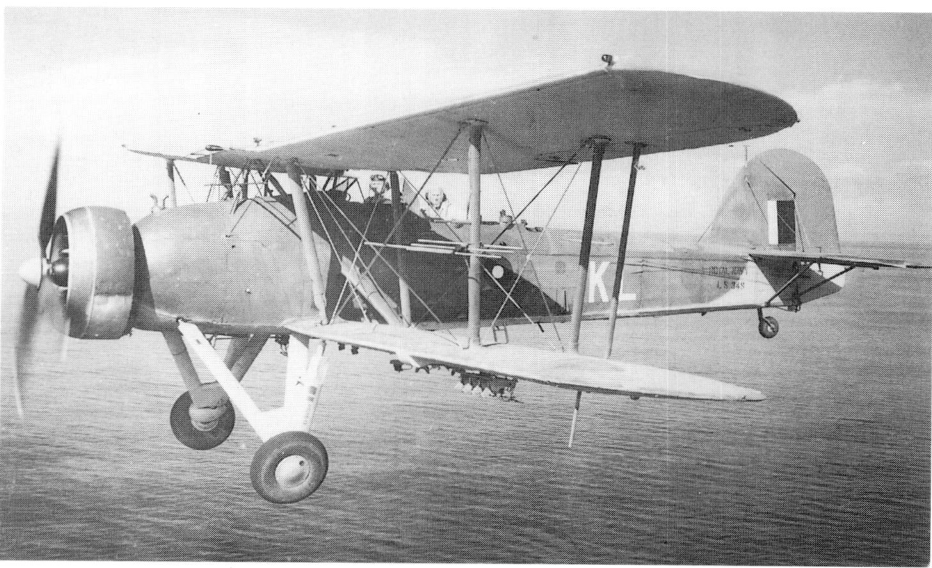

**Swordfish LS348 'KL' of No. 756 Squadron based at Katukurunda, Ceylon, during 1943–45. The squadron provided refresher training, deck-landing training and conversions from Swordfish/Albacores to monoplanes.** via Ray Sturtivant

moved up the Tigris–Euphrates valley, providing much needed and appreciated air support. The CO of No. 814 at that time was Lt Cdr N. Martin, who had this to say:

> I was CO of No. 814 Squadron from March 1941 until the old *Hermes* was sunk on 9 April 1942. We spent our time endlessly patrolling between the Seychelles and Colombo/Trincomalee. In June 1941 we were suddenly ordered into the Persian Gulf to operate our squadron in support of the Army who were trying to quell the invasion of Iraq by Raschid Ali. With temperatures of 100°F and 120°F, no wind and no catapult in Hermes, operating loaded Swordfish presented a problem. We had to operate from ashore as we would never have got off the deck with full petrol and bomb load. We were ordered to bomb and destroy a railway bridge at Samawa up the Euphrates. Operating out of Shaibah, an old RAF station, we duly took off but all twelve of us missed hitting the bridge. On the way back, Sub-Lt Pooley blew his engine and force-landed in the desert. Lt James Dundas, his flight leader, landed with great skill alongside him, picked up the crew and, with six people in the Swordfish, took off and returned to Shaibah. During the pick-up Dundas's TAG kept aggressive Iraqis at bay with his Lewis gun. Dundas was awarded a DSC for this unselfish act in saving his fellow squadron members.

By 31 May it was all over and *Hermes* returned to the Indian Ocean in July, where her Swordfish continued their vigil protecting Britain's trade routes. *Hermes*, due for a refit, sailed via the Seychelles to Ceylon (now Sri Lanka) where No. 814 flew ashore in September, and the ship proceeded to Simonstown, South Africa, for the refit. She was due to return mid-February 1942.

## The Advance of Japan

A number of squadrons were based in Malaya and Singapore. No. 36 Squadron had arrived at Seletar in December 1930 equipped with Hawker Horsley torpedo-bombers. They used these until April 1935 when they received the Vickers Vildebeest. They were still flying them when Japan attacked the Malayan Peninsular in December 1941. By then they shared the airfield with No. 100 Squadron, also equipped with the Vildebeest. In mid-December No. 36 Squadron received some additional aircraft in the form of five Albacores.

Supporting units in the area was the RAF's No. 4 AACU, based at Seletar under the command of Sqn Ldr T. S. Horry DFC, AFC. This unit had a variety of aircraft and in March 1941 formed a third flight with Swordfish transferred from the B Flight Spotter Unit at Seletar, which had been established in October 1939 with eight aircraft. It now consisted of eight Swordfish, six Sharks and two Queen Bee drones (a version of the Tiger Moth).

After Japan entered the war in December 1941, 4 AACU moved to Tengah as Japanese forces approached down Malaya. With aircraft in short supply, the unit's antiquated biplanes were pressed into operational service. Their first duty was reconnaissance flights in Sharks, the Swordfish having been loaned to the Army, who then refused to let them be used for any purpose other than their own! After Japanese bombers destroyed some of the aircraft during January the Swordfish were released, and on 2 February 1942 four of them, flown by RAF pilots Sqn Ldr Trevor Carter, Flt Lt Stuart Black, Fg Off Harry Leach and Flt Sgt Hunt, bombed Kluang airfield. On 9 February the Japanese attacked Tengah, destroying the four Swordfish.

The situation in Malaya was such that all the old biplanes were constantly in action. On 24 January 1942 three of the Albacores joined with No. 100 Squadron to bomb and destroy a bridge at Labis. A Lockheed Hudson out on reconnaissance discovered a Japanese convoy about 20 miles (32km) north of Endau. If the enemy forces landed ashore at that position they would cut off large numbers of Allied troops trying to get back to Singapore, but the only aircraft capable of making a strike were the Vildebeests of Nos 36 and 100 Squadrons. The crews were already very tired, having covered the withdrawal of an Australian battalion the previous night. Aircraft from both squadrons carried out classic torpedo attacks in broad daylight, hits being scored on three ships, but lost five Vildebeests in the process. A second strike was laid on for that afternoon with a force of nine Vildebeests and three Albacores, escorted by small numbers of Hurricanes and Brewster Buffalos. Making use of cloud, the formation made its way towards the convoy but were intercepted by Japanese Zero and Type 97 fighters, who shot down five more Vildebeests and the three Albacores. On 31 January 1942, the remaining flyable aircraft of Nos 36 and 100 Squadrons were loaded with torpedoes, and anything else they could carry, and flew to Kalidjati, Java. On a gradual withdrawal from base to base the squadron continued their attacks against Japanese shipping, but at night. The last two Vildebeests were lost in a failed effort to get to Burma.

The new carrier *Indomitable* was to join the Far East fleet, but had grounded off

Jamaica while working up. On board she had Nos 827 and 831 Squadrons, each with twelve Albacores, No. 800 with twelve Fulmars and No. 880 with nine Sea Hurricanes. A pre-fabricated bow section was fitted in ten days at the US Navy Yard at Norfolk, Virginia, but the carrier was only at Capetown when, on 10 December 1941, Japanese Navy aircraft attacked the British battleships *Prince of Wales* and *Repulse* off Malaya, sinking both. It is doubtful that *Indomitable*'s Hurricanes and Fulmars would have changed the course of the battle anyway, with Japanese Zero fighters escorting the attacking aircraft. To strengthen fighter cover in the Far East *Indomitable* was ordered to call at Aden, off-load her Fulmars and one squadron of Albacores, and embark fifty RAF Hurricanes. Over two days, 27/28 January 1942, the Hurricanes were flown ashore to Batavia in Java, but they had arrived too late to affect what was happening in the East Indies and most were lost on the ground to enemy bombing and strafing attacks within 48 hours. *Indomitable* ferried another fifty Hurricanes from Aden to Ceylon, providing a reasonably strong fighter force in what had been a virtually undefended area. She then returned to Aden to re-embark the Fulmars and Albacores, and joined Admiral Sir James Somerville's Eastern Fleet based at Addu Atoll in the Maldives.

The Eastern Fleet now consisted of three carriers: *Hermes*, with No. 814's Swordfish re-embarked; *Formidable* with twenty-one Albacores of No. 820 Squadron, one Swordfish acting as a target-tower and No. 888 Squadron's eighteen Wildcats; and *Indomitable*, with her air complement. There were also five battleships and various cruisers and destroyers. In addition to this force were Nos 803 and 806 Squadrons with Fulmars, which had been flown out from the Middle East and were based at Ratmalana. Also ashore were six Swordfish of No. 788 Squadron, which had formed up at China Bay on 16 February 1942 as a TBR pool. A bizarre incident happened with *Hermes* when the pilot of one No. 814 Squadron Swordfish was landing on after an anti-submarine patrol but went over the side. He still carried two depth charges and both exploded as the aircraft went under the sea: the blast actually blew the aircraft to the surface and the crew escaped into their dinghy without a scratch!

The Eastern Fleet was supported by a strong RAF element in the form of Hurricanes, Blenheims and Catalinas, to face Japanese Admiral Nagumo's strike force of no less than five carriers with over 300 modern fighters, bombers and strike aircraft, most of their crews with combat experience. Nagumo's objective was the total destruction of the Eastern Fleet and its base at Colombo – the Japanese needed the airfields on Ceylon to support their plans for East Africa and beyond. The only option open to Somerville, with his limited strike and fighter aircraft, was to detect the enemy fleet using long-range RAF Catalinas, and attack by night using torpedo-carrying Albacores. However, Nagumo's force remained undetected and the Eastern Fleet, less *Hermes*, which had gone to Trincomalee, and the cruisers *Cornwall* and *Dorsetshire* on other tasks, returned to Addu Atoll.

Just after dawn on 5 April 1942, Easter Sunday, the Japanese struck at Colombo, but only caused minor damage to small ships and port installations. The Zeros roamed across the island looking for enemy fighters and targets of opportunity. That morning the six Swordfish of No. 788 had taken off from Trincomalee to fly to Minneriya where they were to become the sole specialized land-based ship striking force: all six were shot down, but only two aircrew were killed, the rest ending up in hospital. The defences lost thirteen Hurricanes shot down. The enemy lost seven aircraft to all causes. *Cornwall* and *Dorsetshire*, caught without air cover, were sunk by Japanese dive-bombers, the crews being strafed in the water. *Indomitable*'s Albacores carried out extensive searches and around nightfall sighted one of the enemy carrier divisions. Contact was lost after dusk and an ASV search failed to relocate them, due to the fact that they had withdrawn south-east to replenish. The two fleets searched for each other, Somerville to the south of Ceylon, Nagumo to the north. When no contact had been made Nagumo struck at Trincomalee, but the defenders had been pre-warned by a patrolling Catalina and the harbour was empty. *Hermes*, with no aircraft embarked, had gone to sea to avoid the raid and was attacked by dive-bombers – suffering over forty hits in 10 minutes, she sank, along with four other vessels caught with her. However, the Japanese Fleet, like they had after Pearl Harbor, then failed to consolidate their position by further attacks, and sailed away to take part in the Battle for Midway in the Pacific.

## Madagascar

It was thought that the island of Madagascar, controlled by the Vichy French, would provide another stepping stone for the Japanese as they moved towards the important ports in South Africa. Operation *Ironclad* was the name given to the plan that would allow Allied forces to take

**Swordfish DK788 '2A' of Lt Everett after the attack on Diego Suarez. Shrapnel severed his fuel line during the raid and he had to ditch in the shallows.** Cdr R. N. Everett

the strategically placed harbour of Diego Suarez (Antsirane) at the north end of the island. Air cover for an amphibious assault could only be provided by carrier-based aircraft, so *Illustrious* sailed with Force F under Vice Admiral Syfret in April 1942. Arriving on station the fleet was joined by *Indomitable*, which had sailed from Bombay. *Illustrious* had Nos 810 and 829 Squadrons with eight and twelve Swordfish respectively, with Wildcats of Nos 881 and 882 providing fighter cover, and No. 806 had sent one Fulmar as a night-fighter. Her aircraft were to deal with any shipping and naval opposition. *Indomitable* with Nos 827 and 831, each with twelve Albacores, Nos 800 and 806 with Fulmars and No. 880 with Sea Hurricanes, was to support ground forces and neutralize any airfield activity.

**One of No. 810's Swordfish, HS164 '2F', patrolling along the East African coast after the strikes on Vichy French-held Madagascar.** Cdr R. N. Everett

Seaborne landings began on 5 May 1942, with eighteen Swordfish from *Illustrious* – six with torpedoes and six with depth charges from No. 829, and six from No. 810 with bombs – attacked Vichy French ships in the harbour. Some aircraft dropped leaflets over Antsirane and Orinjia, including an ultimatum to the Governor. When this was ignored an early strike was laid on. The sloop *D'Entrecasteaux* was attacked by the torpedo-carrying aircraft. Swordfish '3A' flown by Lt A. T. Darley was the first, but missed astern. The torpedo from '3F', flown by Lt Swayne, went under the ship without exploding. Lt Macauley in '3K' released his torpedo, which went under the stern of the armed merchant cruiser *Bougainville* and exploded, setting her on fire: she subsequently blew up. Still after the sloop, Sub-Lt H. H. Alexander in '3M' missed astern, but Sub-Lt A. J. B. Forde in '3P' missed ahead, the torpedo running ashore to explode on the beach. Sub-Lt B. W. Vigrass in Swordfish W5853 '3R' made a good aim, but the torpedo passed under her amidships.

The Swordfish with bombs arrived over their target area to be met by intense anti-aircraft fire from shore batteries and local ships. Leading was the CO of No. 810 Squadron, Lt R. N. Everett, in Swordfish DK788 '2A' with PO R. J. K. Groves in the rear cockpit. Everett carried out two dive-bombing attacks on a gun battery at Lazaret Point and two on the *D'Entrecasteaux*. On the last attack his engine received hits and he made a forced landing in the sea, the aircraft becoming inverted. Both men survived and were taken prisoner, but they were released a few days later when the area was taken by British forces. Next in was Sub-Lt G. H. Ervin flying V4698 '2B', who also dropped two sticks of bombs on the sloop but missed. Flying V4702 '2C' was Sub-Lt W. H. Newnham, who dropped two sticks of bombs but missed, and had to break off the attack due to the intensity of the flak. The flak battery at Lazaret Point was the target for Lt A. J. T. Temple-West, but he missed by 100yd and then aimed four bombs at the submarine *Beveziers*, all being near misses. Coming in behind was Sub-Lt R. B. Lunberg flying DK678 '2G' and he, too, dive-bombed the sloop with four bombs, but missed and had two bombs 'hanging up', these being jettisoned before landing back on the carrier. Last in but aiming short was Sub-Lt W. G. R. Beer piloting DK685 '2H'.

Albacores from *Indomitable* bombed Antsirane airfield, destroying many Vichy French aircraft in the hangers. Depth charge-carrying Swordfish of No. 829 also sank the *Beveziers*. First to attack was Sub-Lt R. T. Wolfe flying '3Q'; he dropped his depth charges from 50ft, one exploding near the starboard bow and other near the starboard beam in 30ft (10m) of water. The submarine, which had been getting underway, stopped and listed about 30 degrees to starboard. Sub-Lt A. G. McWilliam in '3G' then had a go, dropping one close to the port bow and the other astern, causing the submarine to cant over even further. Swordfish V4712 '3L' flown by Sub-Lt G. P. Bourke dropped two more on the port side: this time the submarine finally turned over and sank. Three other Swordfish carrying depth charges were not required and flew back to the ship. Aircraft '3L' had engine failure just short of *Illustrious* and ditched, the crew being picked up by the destroyer *Javelin*.

A second strike was laid on for six Swordfish armed with SAP bombs to bomb a ship in Diego Suarez harbour, which in fact turned out to be *D'Entrecasteaux*. Unfortunately, V4447 '2L', flown by Sub-Lt D. G. McQueen of No. 810 Squadron, caught the island structure with its wingtip and slewed round to hit Wildcat BJ559, blocking the flight deck and stopping the last two aircraft taking off. The first two, '3K' and '3Q', carried out their attacks and one bomb so damaged the sloop that it had to be beached. A third strike of nine aircraft was sent to finally finish off the sloop, these aircraft reporting the sloop out of action with no sign of a crew.

On the 6 May, to draw off enemy forces, three Swordfish dropped dummy parachutists to the south-west of Diego Suarez.

Twelve Swordfish from Nos 829 and 810 Squadrons were tasked to bomb targets south of Antsirane just before dawn. Flares were dropped to identify the target but Swordfish '3B' of No. 829 was shot down in flames, the crew of three, Sub-Lts Ervin and Micklejohn with LAC F. J. Haddrell No. 810 Squadron, all being killed. Lt Temple-West of No. 810, flying V4697 '2F', dropped his bombs on an armament depot which went up in a huge explosion. Swordfish also spotted for the fleet bombardment. Flying in support of Allied ground forces, Albacores attacked enemy positions with carrier fighters flying Combat Air Patrol (CAP).

In the early hours of 7 May two Swordfish from No. 810 and four from No. 829, all armed with Mk VII depth charges, were launched to carry out anti-submarine patrols. Three went to the entrance of Diego Suarez harbour and three to the invasion fleet anchorage at Coussier Bay. Sub-Lt Alexander in V4716 '3M' detected a submarine in the half-light and was then able to demonstrate the manoeuvrability of the Swordfish. On being detected the submarine started to dive: Alexander passed over her at 100ft, made a steep turn to port which brought him out on the same course as the submarine, flew slightly ahead and dropped his depth charges. They exploded each side of the submarine as she passed between them, and blew her back to the surface. The crew abandoned their damaged vessel and she sank 15 minutes later. That same day all Vichy resistance in the north of the island ceased. Some 309 operational sorties had been flown in what was the first successful amphibious assault undertaken at that time. Sub-Lt H. H. Alexander and R. T. Wolfe, both of No. 829, and PO R. J. K. Groves of No. 810 all received the DSC for their part in the action. The success of the whole operation was due to the carrier-based aircraft and participating aircrews. *Indomitable* later withdrew, leaving *Illustrious* the only Allied carrier in the Indian Ocean.

Four months later *Illustrious*' aircraft provided air cover for Operation *Stream*, the occupation of Antanarivo, the capital of Madagascar, and the southern part of the island. Ground forces landed around Majunga early on 10 September with nine Swordfish armed with bombs providing air support; in the event they were not required, and all returned safely to the ship. Although complete control of the island had passed to the Allies, there were one or two outposts that still refused to lay down their arms. On 18 September ten Swordfish of No. 829 Squadron, led by Lt Cdr F. M. Griffith, the CO, took off to participate in Operation *Jane*, a dive-bombing attack on the military installations in the town of Tamatave. Six Swordfish were armed with bombs and three with dummy parachutists to create a diversion if required. The military commander of the installations surrendered so the air strike was not in the event required.

*Illustrious* departed the area in January 1943, which left the Eastern Fleet without a carrier. In October 1943 the escort carrier *Battler* arrived in the area as part of a new anti-submarine escort carrier group. On board were twelve Swordfish and six Seafires of No. 834 Squadron. Based at Aden and on *Battler*, the Swordfish flew many anti-submarine patrols in the area, without results. The German and Japanese submarines based in the Indian Ocean operated from Penang and were supplied while on patrol by supply ships off the Seychelles. A Catalina sighted the *Charlotte Schliemann* which was sunk by the destroyer *Relentless*. On 12 March 1944 Swordfish spotted another supply ship, *Brake*, and guided in the destroyer *Rocket* to sink her. The loss of these essential supply ships curtailed the length of enemy submarine patrols, and sinkings of Allied shipping reduced.

The Seafires were then withdrawn and Wildcats joined the Swordfish of No. 834 Squadron. *Battler* continued to provide anti-submarine and trade protection duties until September, when No. 834 was withdrawn and the use of Swordfish ended in the Indian Ocean. By then most front-line squadrons operating Swordfish had converted to Barracudas or Avengers.

## RAAF Swordfish Operations

One little-known use of Swordfish in the Southern Hemisphere was when six Swordfish, V4688, V4689, V4692, V4693 and V4694, were loaned to the Royal Australian Air Force (RAAF). In March 1942 No. 25 Squadron, based at Pearce, near Perth, and equipped with CAC Wirraways and two De Havilland Moth Minors, had the doubtful distinction of being allocated them to provide patrols off the coast of Western Australia. The aircraft were assembled by 25's groundcrew, and after flight-testing three became available for operations; two others were thought to have joined 14 Squadron on communications duties.

The first patrol, in V4689, was made on 24 March by Flt Lt Ridgway with Plt Off Marr as navigator and Sgt Coulter as gunner. Four-hour patrols four times each day were carried out until 24 April, when the last sortie was flown. All the Swordfish were returned to RN charge the following month.

**A well-used Swordfish in South-East Asia markings shares a corner of the airfield with Corsairs and an elephant, presumably to tow the fuel bowser!** IWM

# Swordfish Production

## Built by Fairey at Hayes

| *Quantity* | *Mark* | *Serial range* | *Contract No.* |
|---|---|---|---|
| 1 | TSR. I | | |
| 1 | TSR. II | K4190 | |
| 3 | Mk I | K5660–K5662 | 402278/35 |
| 86 | Mk I | K5926–K6011 | 402278/35 |
| 104 | Mk I | K8346–K8449 | 466845/35 |
| 27 | Mk I | K8860–K8886 | 466845/35 |
| 150 | Mk I | L2717–L2866 | 534297/36 |
| 62 | Mk I | L7632–L7661 | 672134/37 |
| | | L7670–L7701 | |
| 60 | Mk I | L9714–L9743 | 743308/37 |
| | | L9756–L9785 | |
| 200 | Mk I | P3991–P4039 | 963679/38 |
| | | P4061–P4095 | |
| | | P4123–P4169 | |
| | | P4191–P4232 | |
| | | P4253–P4279 | |

692 built, plus the two TSRs

## Built by Blackburn at Brough/Sherburn

| *Quantity* | *Mark* | *Serial range* | *Contract No.* |
|---|---|---|---|
| 300 | Mk I | V4288–V4337 | B.31192/39 |
| | | V4360–V4399 | |
| | | V4411–V4455 | |
| | | V4481–V4525 | |
| | | V4551–V4600 | |
| | | V4621–V4655 | |
| | | V4685–V4719 | |
| 100 | Mk I | W5836–W5865 | B.31192/39 |
| | | W5886–W5925 | |
| | | W5966–W5995 | |
| 100 | Mk II | DK670–DK719 | B.31192/39 |
| | | DK743–DK792 | |
| 400 | Mk II | HS154–HS196 | B.31192/39 |
| | | HS208–HS231 | |
| | | HS254–HS299 | |
| | | HS312–HS346 | |
| | | HS361–HS410 | |
| | | HS424–HS471 | |
| | | HS484–HS519 | |
| | | HS533–HS561 | |
| | | HS579–HS625 | |
| | | HS637–HS678 | |
| 250 | Mk II | LS151–LS193 | B.31192/39 |
| | | LS214–LS248 | |

| *Quantity* | *Mark* | *Serial range* | *Contract No.* |
|---|---|---|---|
| | | LS261–LS299 | |
| | | LS315–LS358 | |
| | | LS362–LS403 | |
| | | LS415–LS461 | |
| 230 | Mk II | NE858–NE906 | B.31192/39 |
| | | NE920–NE957 | |
| | | NE970–NE999 | |
| | | NF113–NF161 | |
| | | NF175–NF217 | |
| | | NF230–NF250 | |

1,380 built: 400 Mk I/980 Mk II

## 400 Mk I/Mk II cancelled

RL435–RL480
RL492–RL535
RL548–RL590
RL605–RL646
RL659–RL699
RL714–RL758
RL771–RL816
RL829–RL873
RL886–RL993

## Built by Blackburn at Brough

| *Quantity* | *Mark* | *Serial range* | *Contract No.* |
|---|---|---|---|
| 120 | Mk III | NF251–NF274 | B.31192/39 |
| | | NF298–NF347 | |
| | | NF369–NF414 | |
| 200 | Mk III | NR857–NR898 | B.31192/39 |
| | | NR913–NR958 | |
| | | NR970–NR999 | |
| | | NS112–NS156 | |
| | | NS168–NS204 | |

320 Mk III built

## 200 Mk III cancelled (B.31192/39)

NS205–NS211
NS225–NS249
NS282–NS325
NS338–NS379
NS392–NS435
NS447–NS484

APPENDIX II

# Swordfish Operational Use

## Operational Swordfish during 1939–45

| *1939* | *1940* | *1941* | *1942* | *1943* | *1944* | *1945* |
|---|---|---|---|---|---|---|
| 140 | 139 | 129 | 112 | 118 | 179 | 198 |

## Swordfish Squadrons – First Line

Swordfish were operated within the dates quoted. It would be impracticable to list all the bases Swordfish squadrons operated from and those listed are examples in order of use.

| *Sqn* | *Dates* | *Shore bases* | *Sea time* |
|---|---|---|---|
| 810 | Sept 1937–Mar 1943 | Gosport, Evanton, Southampton, Old Sarum, Dekheila, Hatston, Tanga | *Courageous* 1937–38<br>*Ark Royal* 1939–40<br>*Illustrious* 1942–43<br>*Furious* Sept 1941 |
| 811 | Oct 1936–Dec 1944 | Gosport, Lee-on-Solent, Arbroath, Bircham Newton, Thorney Island | *Furious* 1936–38<br>*Courageous* 1939 until sunk on 17 Sept 1939<br>*Biter* 1943–44<br>*Vindex* 1944 |
| 812 | Dec 1936–Dec 1942 | Gosport, Hal Far Dekheila, Bircham Newton, North Coates, Thorney Island | *Glorious* 1939<br>*Furious* 1941<br>*Ark Royal* 1941 |
| 813 | Jan 1937–May 1945 | Gosport, Kai Tak, Seletar, Dekheila, Machrihanish | *Eagle* 1937–42<br>*Campania* 1944<br>*Vindex* 1945 |
| 814 | Dec 1938–Dec 1942 | Southampton, Worthy Down, Ceylon | *Ark Royal* 1939–40<br>*Hermes* 1939–42 |
| 815 | Oct 1939–Jul 1943 | Worthy Down, Bircham Newton, Aboukir, Dekheila, Mersa Matruh | *Illustrious* 1940–41 |
| 816 | Oct 1939–Aug 1944 | Hatston Thorney Island Machrihanish | *Furious* 1940–41<br>*Ark Royal* 1941<br>*Dasher* 1943, *Tracker* 1943/44<br>*Chaser* 1944 |
| 818 | Aug 1939–Oct 1944 | Evanton, Hatston, Thorney Island, Machrihanish | *Ark Royal* 1939–41<br>*Furious* 1939–40<br>*Formidable* 1942<br>*Unicorn* 1944 |
| 819 | Jan 1940–Mar 1945 | Ford, Dekheila, Thorney Island, Hatston, Abbotsinch, Manston, Belgium | *Illustrious* 1940<br>*Avenger* 1942<br>*Archer* 1943<br>*Activity* 1944 |
| 820 | Sept 1937–Jun 1941 | Southampton, Dekheila, Hatston | *Courageous* 1937–39<br>*Ark Royal* 1939–41 |

| *Sqn* | *Dates* | *Shore bases* | *Sea time* |
|---|---|---|---|
| 821 | Sept 1937–Mar 1942 | Southampton, Evanton, Hatston | *Courageous* 1937–38<br>*Ark Royal* 1939–40 |
| 822 | Aug 1937–Mar 1942 | Gosport, Manston, Donibristle, Hatston | *Furious* 1937–38<br>*Courageous* 1939 |
| 823 | Nov 1936–Apr 1942 | Hal Far, Dekheila, Hatston | *Glorious* 1937–40<br>*Furious* 1942 |
| 824 | Apr 1937–Oct 1944 | Kai Tak, Seletar, Dekheila, Lee-on-Solent, Machrihanish, Hatston | *Eagle* 1937–42<br>*Unicorn* 1943<br>*Striker* 1943–44 |
| 825 | Jul 1936–Apr 1945 | Hal Far, Dekheila, Hatston, Machrihanish | *Glorious* 1936–40<br>*Furious* 1940–43<br>*Victorious* 1941<br>*Ark Royal* 1941<br>*Avenger* 1942<br>*Vindex* 1943–44 |
| 826 | Jul 1940–Sept 1941 | Bircham Newton, St Merryn, Dekheila | *Formidable* 1940 |
| 828 | Oct 1941–Nov 1941 | Hal Far | *Ark Royal* 1941 |
| 829 | Jul 1940–Oct 1942 | Campbeltown, St Merryn, St Eval, Dekheila | *Formidable* 1940–41<br>*Illustrious* 1941–42 |
| 830 | Jul 1940–Mar 1943 | Hal Far | |
| 833 | Dec 1941–Sept 1944 | Lee-on-Solent, Crail, Thorney Island, Machrihanish, Dunino | *Biter* 1942<br>*Stalker* 1943<br>*Activity* 1944 |
| 834 | Dec 1941–Nov 1944 | Palisadoes Jamaica, Crail, Gibraltar, Ceylon | *Archer* 1942<br>*Hunter* 1943<br>*Battler* 1943–44 |
| 835 | Feb 1942–Mar 1945 | Palisadoes Jamaica, Lee-on-Solent, Hatston, Machrihanish | *Furious* 1942<br>*Battler* 1943<br>*Chaser* 1943<br>*Nairana* 1943 |
| 836 | Mar 1942–May 1945 | Maydown | 19 MAC-ships |
| 837 | May 1942–Jun 1943 | Palisadoes Jamaica, Lee-on-Solent, Hatston | *Dasher* 1942–43<br>*Argus* 1943 |
| 838 | May 1942–Feb 1945 | Dartmouth, Machrihanish, Inskip, Thorney Island | *Attacker* 1942–43<br>*Activity* 1943<br>*Nairana* 1943 |
| 841 | Jan 1943–Apr 1943 | Manston | |
| 842 | Feb 1943–Jan 1945 | Lee-on-Solent Machrihanish, Hatston, Thorney Island | *Fencer* 1943 |
| 860 | Jun 1943–Jun 1945 | Donibristle, Hatston, Machrihanish | *Nairana* 1945 |
| 886 | Jun 1943–Oct 1943 | Machrihanish, Gibraltar | *Attacker* 1943 |

## Swordfish Squadrons – Second Line

Swordfish were operated within the dates quoted. It would be impracticable to list all the bases Swordfish operated from, and those listed are examples in order of use.

| *Sqd* | *Dates* | *Base* |
|---|---|---|
| 700 | Jan 1940–May 1944 | Hatston, Twatt, *Fencer* 1943 |
| 701 | Sept 1936–Jan 1940 | Kalafrana, Malta |
| 702 | 1939–Jan 1940 | Lee-on-Solent |
| 703 | Oct 1942–Nov 1942 | Lee-on-Solent |
| 705 | Jul 1936–Jun 1940 | Kalafrana Malta |
| | Nov 1945–Jun 1945 | Ronaldsay I O M |
| 707 | Feb 1945–Sept 1945 | Burscough, Gosport |
| 710 | –Jun 1945 | Lee-on-Solent |
| 722 | May 1945–Oct 1945 | Tambaram |
| 726 | Aug 1943–Dec 1943 | Stamford Hill South Africa |
| | Sept 1944–Nov 1945 | |
| 727 | May 1943–Sept 1944 | Gibraltar, Ta'Kali |
| 728 | May 1943–Feb 1946 | Gibraltar |
| 730 | Jan 1945–Aug 1945 | Ayr |
| 731 | Dec 1943–Nov 1945 | Easthaven |
| 733 | Jan 1944– Nov 1945 | China Bay Ceylon |
| 735 | Aug 1943–Jun 1944 | Inskip, Burscough |
| 737 | Mar 1944–Jul 1945 | Inskip, Arbroath, Burscough |
| 739 | Dec 1942–Nov 1943 | Lee-on-Solent, Worthy Down |
| 740 | May 1943–Aug 1943 | Arbroath |
| 741 | Mar 1943–Mar 1945 | Arbroath |
| 742 | Dec 1943–Oct 1945 | Colombo Ceylon |
| 743 | Mar 1943–Mar 1945 | Yarmouth Nova Scotia |
| | Sept 1946–Nov 1948 | Dartmouth, Nova Scotia |
| 744 | Mar 1944–May 1945 | Yarmouth Nova Scotia, Maydown |
| 745 | Mar 1943–Feb 1944 | Yarmouth Nova Scotia |
| 747 | Mar 1943–Feb 1944 | Fearn, Inskip |
| 753 | Dec 1939–Jun 1945 | Lee-on-Solent, Arbroath, Rattray |
| 756 | Mar 1944–Feb 1945 | Katukurunda, Colombo |
| 759 | Nov 1939–May 1943 | Eastleigh, Yeovilton |
| 763 | Dec 1939–Jul 1940 | Worthy Down, |
| 764 | Apr 1940–Sept 1941 | Lee-on-Solent |
| 765 | May 1939–Jun 1941 | Lee-on-Solent, Sandbanks |
| 766 | Apr 1942–Nov 1944 | Machrihanish, Inskip |
| 767 | May 1939–May 1944 | Donibristle, Polyvestre S France |
| 768 | Jan 1941– Oct 1945 | Arbroath, Machrihanish |
| 769 | Nov 1941–Feb 1944 | Arbroath |
| 770 | Dec 1939–Apr 1940 | Lee–on–Solent, Polyvestre S France |
| 771 | May 1939–Apr 1945 | Portland, Lee-on-Solent, Evanton |
| 772 | Sept 1939–Aug 1945 | Lee-on-Solent, Campbeltown, Machrihanish, Ayr |
| 773 | Jun 1940–Apr 1944 | Bermuda |
| 774 | Nov 1939–Aug 1944 | Worthy Down, Aldergrove NI, St Merryn |
| 775 | May 1941–Jan 1945 | Dekheila, Gibraltar |
| 776 | Jun 1944–Dec 1944 | Millom |
| 777 | Aug 1941–Feb1944 | Hastings |
| 778 | Sept 1939–Feb 1945 | Lee-on-Solent, Arbroath, Crail |
| 779 | Oct 1941–Jan 1945 | Gibraltar |
| 780 | Jun 1940–1944 | Eastleigh, Lee-on-Solent |
| 781 | Sept 1940–Feb 1943 | Lee-on-Solent |
| 782 | Dec 1940–Mar 1941 | Donibristle |
| 783 | Jun 1942–Jul 1945 | Arbroath |
| 785 | Nov 1940–May 1944 | Crail |
| 786 | May 1941–1943 | Crail |

| *Sqd* | *Dates* | *Base* |
|---|---|---|
| 787 | Jan 1943 | Duxford, Wittering, Tangmere |
| 787Y | Jun 1944–Oct 1944 | Arbroath, Burscough |
| 787Z | Mar 1943–Jun 1944 | Lee-on-Solent, St Merryn, Inskip |
| 788 | Feb 1942–Jun 1944 | China Bay, Tanga, Mombasa, Eastleigh |
| 789 | Jul 1942–Nov 1945 | Wingfield, South Africa |
| 791 | Apr 1942–Dec 1944 | Arbroath |
| 794 | Aug 1940–Jun 1945 | Yeovilton, Angle, Dale, Henstridge, Charlton Horethorne |
| 796 | Jul 1942–Mar 1944 | Port Reitz, Tanga, Eastleigh |
| 797 | Nov 1943–Aug 1945 | Colombo Ceylon |

# Albacore Production

## All built by Fairey at Hayes

| *Quantity* | *Mark* | *Serial range* | *Contract No.* |
|---|---|---|---|
| 100 | Mk I | L7074–L7173 | 625954/37 |
| 200 | Mk I | N4152–N4200 | 625954/37 |
| | | N4219–N4268 | |
| | | N4281–N4330 | |
| | | N4347–N4386 | |
| | | N4387–N4391 | |
| | | N4420–N4425 | |
| 100 | Mk I | T9131–T9175 | 359/44/39 |
| | | T9191–9215 | |
| | | T9231–T9260 | |
| 250 | Mk I | X8940–X8984 | 359/44/39 |
| | | X9010–X9059 | |
| | | X9073–X9117 | |
| | | X9137–X9186 | |
| | | X9214–X9233 | |
| | | X9251–X9290 | |
| 150 | Mk I | BF584–BF618 | 359/44/39 |
| | | BF631–BF680 | |
| | | BF695–BF739 | |
| | | BF758–BF777 | |

**Albacores BF642 'D', BF643 'H', X9255 'C' and 'I' of No. 789 Squadron. This was a Fleet Requirements Unit based at Wingfield, South Africa, where it stayed from 1942 until November 1945.** K. Smy via Ray Sturtivant

# Albacore Operational Use

## Operational Albacores during 1939–45

| *1939* | *1940* | *1941* | *1942* | *1943* | *1944* | *1945* |
|---|---|---|---|---|---|---|
| nil | 12 | 63 | 84 | 94 | nil | nil |

## Albacore Squadrons – First Line

It would be impracticable to list all the bases Albacore squadrons operated from, and those listed are examples in order of use.

| *Sqn* | *Dates* | *Shore bases* | *Sea time* |
|---|---|---|---|
| 810 | Jan 1943–Jul 1943 | Tanga | *Illustrious* |
| 815 | Oct 1941–Aug 1943 | Dekheila, Haifa, Nicosia | |
| 817 | Mar 1941–Aug 1943 | Crail, Hatston | *Furious, Victorious, Indomitable* |
| 818 | Nov 1941–Jun 1942 | Hatston, Machrihanish, Ceylon | *Formidable* |
| 820 | Jul 1941–Nov 1943 | Hatston, Crail | *Victorious, Formidable* |
| 821 | Mar 1942–Oct 1943 | Dekheila, Nicosia, Western Desert, Hal Far, Castel Benito, Monastir | |
| 822 | Apr 1942–Aug 1943 | Crail, Donibristle, Machrihanish, Twatt, Gibraltar, Lee-on-Solent | |
| 823 | Apr 1942–May 1943 | Lee-on-Solent, Machrihanish, Hatston, Tangmere, Manston | *Furious* |
| 826 | Mar 1940–Aug 1943 | Ford, Bircham Newton, Jersey, Detling, St Merryn, Nicosia, Dekheila, Haifa, Benghazi, Blida, Hal Far | *Formidable* |
| 827 | Sept 1940–Jan 1943 | Yeovilton, Stornaway, Thorney Island, St Eval, Machrihanish, Hatston, Aden | *Victorious, Indomitable* |
| 828 | Sept 1940–Sept 1943 | Ford, St Merryn, Campbeltown, Hatston, Crail, Hal Far, Monastir | *Victorious, Argus, Ark Royal* |
| 829 | Jun 1940–Aug 1941 | Lee-on-Solent, St Eval, St Merryn, Dekheila, Lydda | *Formidable, Illustrious* |
| 830 | Sept 1940–Jul 1942 | Malta | |
| 831 | Apr 1941–Jun 1943 | Norfolk USA, Wingfield South Africa, Aden, Crail, Lee-on-Solent | *Indomitable* |
| 832 | Apr 1941–Dec 1942 | Lee-on-Solent, Campbeltown, Hatston, Crail | *Victorious* |

| Sqn | Dates | Shore bases | Sea time |
|---|---|---|---|
| 841 | Jul 1942–Nov 1943 | Lee-on-Solent, Machrihanish<br>Middle Wallop, Manston | |
| 119 (RAF)<br>415 (RCAF) | | | |

## Albacore Squadrons – Second Line

| Sqn | Dates | Base/Sea time |
|---|---|---|
| 700 | Jan 1946–Feb 1946 | Middle Wallop |
| 733 | 1944–45 | Minneriya, China Bay Ceylon |
| 747 | Mar 1943–Sept 1943 | St Merryn, Det. at Chivenor |
| 750 | Dec 1940–Apr 1945 | Piarco Savannah Trinidad |
| 753 | Aug 1941–Dec 1944 | Arbroath |
| 754 | Feb 1943–Dec 1943 | Arbroath |
| 756 | Oct 1943–Feb 1944 | Katukurunda Ceylon |
| 763 | Mar 1940–Jul 1940 | Jersey, Lee-on-Solent, Worthy Down |
| 766 | Apr 1942–Oct 1943 | Machrihanish, Inskip |
| 767 | Feb 1940–Dec 1943 | Polyvestre France, *Argus*, Hal Far (renumbered 830),<br>DLT on *Furious, Argus, Activity* |
| 768 | Jan 1943–Sept 1943 | Machrihanish with DLT on *Argus, Activity, Tracker* |
| 769 | Nov 1941–Feb 1944 | Arbroath, Easthaven with DLT on *Argus, Ravager* |
| 771 | Nov 1941– | Twatt |
| 774 | Sept 1940–Jun 1944 | St Merryn |
| 775 | Sept 1941–Nov 1943 | Dekheila |
| 778 | Feb 1940–Sept 1943 | Arbroath, Crail, Det. on *Pretoria Castle* |
| 781 | Jun 1942–Dec 1942 | Lee-on-Solent |
| 782 | Dec 1940–41 | Donibristle |
| 783 | Dec 1942–Feb 1943 | Drem, Det. Flights aboard *Campania, Nairana* and *Vindex* |
| 785 | Aug 1941–Nov 1943 | Crail |
| 786 | Nov 1940–Dec 1942 | Crail |
| 787 | May 1942–Mar 1943 | Duxford |
| 788 | Feb 1942–Mar 1944 | China Bay Ceylon, Tanga, Mombasa |
| 789 | Jul 1942–Sept 1944 | Wingfield South Africa |
| 791 | Mar 1941– | Arbroath |
| 793 | Nov 1943–Oct 1945 | Piarco Trinidad |
| 796 | Jul 1942–Jul 1943 | Port Reitz, Tanga East Africa |
| 797 | Jun 1943–Oct 1943 | Katukurunda Ceylon |
| 799 | Sept 1943–Jun 1944 | Wingfield South Africa |

*Station Flight*

| | |
|---|---|
| Eastleigh | Dec 1943–Aug 1944 |

*Communication Flights*

| | |
|---|---|
| Ceylon | Mar 1943–May 1943 |
| Coimbatore | Sept 1943–Dec 1943 |

# List of Abbreviations

| | |
|---|---|
| A&AEE | Aeroplane & Armament Experimental Establishment |
| AA | Anti-Aircraft |
| AACU | Anti-Aircraft Co-operation Unit |
| AAM | Air-to-Air Missile |
| AC2 | Aircraftsman Second Class |
| ADDL | Aerodrome Dummy Deck Landing |
| AFU | Advanced Flying Unit |
| AM | Air Mechanic |
| AMES | Air Ministry Experimental Station |
| APO | Acting Petty Officer |
| ASI | airspeed indicator |
| ASV | Air-to-Surface Vessel (radar) |
| BPF | British Pacific Fleet |
| CAP | Combat Air Patrol |
| CG | Centre of Gravity |
| COL | Chain Overseas Low |
| CPO | Chief Petty Officer |
| DAW | Director of Air Warfare |
| DAWFT | Director of Air Warfare and Flying Training |
| D/F | Direction Finding |
| DSC | Distinguished Service Cross |
| DSM | Distinguished Service Medal |
| DSO | Distinguished Service Order |
| EFTS | Elementary Flying Training School |
| ehp | equivalent horsepower |
| FAA | Fleet Air Arm |
| GP | General Purpose (bomb) |
| LAC | Leading Aircraftsman |
| LG | Landing Ground |
| MAEE | Marine Aircraft Experimental Establishment |
| Mid | Midshipman |
| MoS | Ministry of Supply |
| MTB | Motor Torpedo Boat |
| MU | Maintenance Unit |
| MV | Motor Vessel |
| NA | Naval Airman |
| NAGS | Naval Air Gunners School |
| NCO | Non-Commissioned Officer |
| Plt Off | Pilot Officer |
| PO | Petty Officer |
| POW | Prisoner of War |
| R/P | rocket projectile |
| R/T | radio telegraphy |
| RAE | Royal Aircraft Establishment |
| RAF | Royal Air Force |
| RATO | rocket-assisted take-off |
| RAuxAF | Royal Auxiliary Air Force |
| RCAF | Royal Canadian Air Force |
| RCN | Royal Canadian Navy |
| RDF | Radio Direction Finding i.e. radar |
| RFC | Royal Flying Corps |
| RN | Royal Navy |
| RNAS | (before 1 April 1918) Royal Naval Air Service); (1938 onwards) Royal Naval Air Station) |
| RNNAS | Royal Netherlands Naval Air Service |
| RNR | Royal Naval Reserve |
| RNVR | Royal Naval Volunteer Reserve |
| SAP | Semi-Armour Piercing |
| SFTS | Service Flying Training School |
| shp | shaft horsepower |
| STU | Service Trials Unit |
| TAG | Telegraphist Air Gunner |
| TBR | torpedo-bomber-reconnaissance |
| TRU | Transportable Radio Unit |
| TSR | Torpedo-Spotter-Reconnaissance |
| TTU | Torpedo Trials Unit |
| u/s | unserviceable |
| USN | United States Navy |
| W/T | Wireless Telegraphy |

# Index